Learning
Business Statistics
with
Microsoft® Excel
97

duke, had gotten married, and the ceremony was held in a castle that had the most famous gardens of the Blue Mountains, several days' journey away. He had just left his cousin and his new wife after escorting them to their new home halfway between the Blue Mountains and the Enchanted Mountains, and was still dressed in his wedding attire. The prince was young, although a bit older than Lynacia, and had a dignified presence.

Lynacia watched from a distance as he stopped to give his horse a drink from a stream that went through the center of her land. Although she had never seen a prince before, she knew from his clothes that he must be one. He immediately captivated her. She watched unnoticed from a side hill as he watered his horse and prepared a place to rest. He sat down and pulled out some maps and seemed to be talking to his horse because no one else was around. He began speaking of the distance they had come and the events of the wedding. He spoke of the garden where the ceremony had taken place. He described the garden full of multicolored flowers, huge trees with birds singing, and small animals everywhere. The event sounded more beautiful than anything Lynacia had ever imagined, and his voice sounded strangely familiar to her. Although it struck Lynacia as odd that he was speaking to his horse, she was drawn to his words and the tone of his voice. What was it that made her feel the voice was one so familiar?

Lynacia became so engrossed by his story that she approached the prince suddenly to ask him questions about the garden. Lynacia so loved flowers. The prince was quite surprised and, at first, speechless. Partly from realizing that someone had been listening to his conversation with his horse, but mostly from Lynacia's beauty. In her excitement, she rapidly and without pause, asked questions about the garden, the castle, and the dress that the bride had worn.

The prince just stood staring in awe of her, feeling like he was falling in love at that very moment. He replied to her by asking her name. She then realized that she must seem very rude. She apologized and told him that her name was Lynacia. He asked her to sit with him and said that he would tell her all about his travels and the wedding. However, unlike any of the other travelers Lynacia encountered before, he first wanted to know all about her. He introduced himself as Prince Louis. The conversation went on for hours. The prince was in total awe of Lynacia, and she was in awe of him and his stories. Lynacia did not mention that she was under a curse. When it was time for the prince to leave, as he had to return to his kingdom, he asked if he could return and visit her again, promising to tell her of other places he had traveled that were even more spectacular than the Blue Mountains. She enthusiastically agreed. This pleased the prince very much. Lynacia was delighted at the thought of more stories.

They met many times over the next few months, the prince telling his stories of adventure in different lands, while Lynacia taught him how to walk as one with nature. She was surprised that she had anything to share. She recognized that a deep friendship was developing, a relationship that neither had ever felt before or known could exist. Never had either met anyone quite like the other.

Lynacia's life was now an ongoing adventure. She lived through the prince's stories and he had become her best friend. Often the conversation would turn to the topic of how the friendship would be so much better if they didn't live in different lands. That if Lynacia could just leave the Enchanted Mountains. Then they could see each other more. However, this was yet to be.

So it was not a total surprise when, that following autumn, while sitting near the spot by the stream where they first met, the prince asked Lynacia to be his wife. He loved her and offered her a place beside him on his journeys.

It was then that Lynacia felt the acute pain of her fateful situation more than she did at any time before. Over the months, her new friendship had brought her so much happiness that she had almost forgotten about the curse. Through his stories, she felt so close to the freedom she desired. Now, painfully aware and burdened by the reality of her situation, Lynacia began to cry.

Should she risk telling the prince about the curse without knowing his reaction? Maybe she should have told him about her dragon in the beginning. After much sobbing and many tears, she decided she must explain her situation to the prince. She told him everything, starting with her mother's fears and ending with her current situation of confinement to these mountains. Lynacia told him that the dragon could not harm her but would stop her from leaving. However, she was not sure that anyone else attempting to rescue her would be free from harm.

With a strong sense of conviction, the prince quickly rose and told Lynacia that he would fight the dragon and free her! His battle gear was back at the castle, so he must go to prepare, but soon he would return, ready to destroy the dragon that imprisoned her.

Lynacia was overjoyed. At last she would be free to explore the marvelous world she had only dreamed of. She would be rescued by her handsome prince, for whom she would be eternally grateful. She dreamed of the Blue Mountains, castles and gardens, and adventures with Prince Louis.

However, deep inside, there was something that kept telling her that this would not happen. That is, *could* not happen! She tried to ignore this inner voice, but it concerned her greatly.

She asked herself, "If Prince Louis is not successful, what will become of me? Will I be forever trapped? He must succeed!"

The day came when the prince arrived back into the Enchanted Mountains. He was dressed for battle, looking ever so brave. He found Lynacia and put her on the back of his horse and began galloping off. His plan was to carry her off, and when the dragon came forward, he would slay it.

As they neared the border of the Enchanted Mountains, the voice that was loud inside Lynacia telling her she could not leave became so strong that she jumped off the horse. Initially, she fell quite hard and tumbled, but she soon was on her feet and running up the rocky part of the mountain. Lynacia was very skilled at running fast when she needed to get away from things. Prince Louis followed her as far as he could on horseback, but the horse could not maneuver the rocks of the mountains. He jumped off his horse and followed her on foot, yelling for her to come back. It was when he had lost sight of her that the dragon appeared.

The dragon was a mighty beast and came at Prince Louis. The prince had no choice but to try to outrun the dragon, as his battle equipment was left with his horse.

When he reached his horse, he prepared quickly for the fight. In the near distance, the dragon landed and started toward him, breathing fire. The prince was fearless as he raised his sword and charged the dragon, while his shield protected him from his opponent's fiery blaze.

The battle began! The prince was thrown many times by the dragon's tail. Each time, he regained his fighting position. Prince Louis was determined to rid Lynacia of this beast. He repeated to himself, "I must conquer this dragon. I must win!"

After hours of grueling combat, the prince, at last, had knocked the dragon down. It caused a loud thud, and the earth shook. However, the dragon was not defeated and was quick to regain its footing. The prince knew he had to make his move swiftly and make it count. He brought up his sword and aimed it at the dragon's throat. One good slash, and the dragon would no longer trap Lynacia. he thought.

It was then, for the first time, that he saw the dragon's eyes. They were strange eyes for a dragon, deep and full of secret longing. They seemed familiar to him. This recognition stunned him and caused him to hesitate. At that moment, the dragon returned to its feet and knocked Prince Louis's sword out of his hand.

Confused and defenseless, the prince retreated. He jumped on his horse and fled. He lost this battle, however, he was not going to lose Lynacia. He would return!

Back at his castle, while tending his many wounds, he called for the kingdom's wisest counselor. This was an elderly woman who held great knowledge. No one knew her age, as she seemed to have

Learning
Business Statistics
with
Microsoft® Excel
97

John L. Neufeld
University of North Carolina at Greensboro

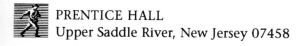

PRENTICE HALL
Upper Saddle River, New Jersey 07458

Acquisitions Editor: *Tom Tucker*
Associate Editor: *Audrey Reagan*
Editorial Assistant: *Melissa Back*
Editor-in-Chief: *James Boyd*
Marketing Manager: *Debbie Clare*
Production Editor: *Maureen Wilson*
Managing Editor: *Dee Josephson*
Manufacturing Buyer: *Diane Peirano*
Manufacturing Supervisor: *Arnold Vila*
Manufacturing Manager: *Vincent Scelta*
Copyeditor: *Marianne Riordan*

Microsoft and Windows are registered trademarks of the Microsoft Corporation in the U.S.A. and other countries. Screen shots and icons reprinted with permission from Microsoft Corporation. This book is not sponsored or endorsed by or affiliated with the Microsoft Corporation.

 Copyright © 1998 by Prentice-Hall, Inc.
A Simon & Schuster Company
Upper Saddle River, New Jersey 07458

Library of Congress Cataloging-in-Publication Data

Neufeld, John L.
  Learning business statistics with Microsoft Excel 97 / John L.
Neufeld.
     p.   cm.
  Includes index.
  ISBN 0-13-923442-X
  1. Commercial statistics--Methodology--Computer programs.
  2. Microsoft Excel for Windows.   I. Title.
  HF1017.N473 1998
  519.5'0285'5369--dc21   98-11985
                                                       CIP

Prentice-Hall International (UK) Limited, *London*
Prentice-Hall of Australia Pty. Limited, *Sydney*
Prentice-Hall Canada Inc., *Toronto*
Prentice-Hall Hispanoamericana, S.A., *Mexico*
Prentice-Hall of India Private Limited, *New Delhi*
Prentice-Hall of Japan, Inc., *Tokyo*
Simon and Schuster Asia Pte. Ltd., *Singapore*
Editora Prentice-Hall do Brasil, Ltda., *Rio de Janeiro*

Printed in the United States of America
10   9   8   7   6   5   4   3

always been there. She had been counsel to all generations before Prince Louis.

Prince Louis told her his story, and she listened intently. When he was finished, there was a tear in the wise woman's eyes. She looked at him sadly and told him that she was aware of the spell. She stated, "Lynacia only knows of the outward dragon. She does not know that the dragon, in reality, resides within her."

"It is her own self that imprisons her," said the wise woman. "Her mother had been hurt many times outside of the Enchanted Mountains and believed it was safer for Lynacia to stay within the land. She had forgotten the many wonderful things that could be experienced and, instead, chose to focus only the painful events. In her attempts to protect Lynacia from the possibility of pain, she deprived her of experiencing the fullness of life's adventures.

"She cast a spell, while on her deathbed, which confined the young Lynacia to the Enchanted Mountains. The dragon uses fear and lies to imprison Lynacia, and it is Lynacia's believing in the dragon that makes him real."

The wise woman believed that only Lynacia could destroy the dragon. However, it would require her to reach deep within to find the truth of her own strength and love, in order to free herself. With much caution, the wise woman then added, "It is unknown what would happen to Lynacia if someone else should kill the dragon."

The wise woman explained that most others who had been cursed like this had never tried to destroy their dragon but rather had accepted the situation. This surprised the prince, and he asked, "So there is no hope at all then?"

The wise woman then shared, "The others, very few, had the desire for freedom that Lynacia has. However, before she is able to experience the true freedom that she so desires, she must first travel within herself to conquer the one who confines her as only she can."

13

The prince was brokenhearted over hearing all this and concerned that he had almost killed the dragon. He wanted Lynacia to have the freedom she desired. He loved her so.

He eagerly returned to share with Lynacia the wise woman's words. As he approached her, she was overwhelmed with happiness and exclaimed, "You have returned!"

They embraced, and both cried with joy at seeing each other.

She admitted being sad and depressed knowing that her attempt to be free had created the fight with the dragon. She shared, "Why did I ever try? I thought you were scared away forever."

"No," replied the prince, "your dragon does not scare me."

The prince then told Lynacia that he could not destroy her dragon as it was within her. He told her of the dragon's eyes and that the only chance for her to escape was for her to destroy it from within.

This seemed to anger Lynacia. "I don't understand! The dragon that keeps me captive is within me, and only I can destroy it? I am but a young girl. You are a prince. I thought dragons could only be fought by princes. Why should I be cursed to deal with my own dragon?"

The prince was surprised at her reaction. He tried to calm her down and encourage her to try.

"You must! Only you can," replied Prince Louis.

Lynacia began to cry and, in her tears, told the prince that she would have to live out her life as her mother wanted. "We will just go back to the way it was. You can come visit me, and *your* stories will be my adventures."

Prince Louis, disappointed, replied, "No, I can't. Not knowing what I know now."

He stated that it would deeply sadden him to see her, as it would never be the same. He begged her *to try* to destroy the dragon so that they could live together. She cried harder and said, "I don't know how. I can't! How do you fight a battle within yourself and with what weapons—what is so strong and powerful?"

The prince pleaded, unsuccessfully, to have her try. Saddened by her decision, he left with the parting words, "I will always love you."

As she watched him leave, she grew even sadder at the thought of never seeing him again.

Many weeks went by, and Lynacia had never felt so lonely and frightened. She was confronted with the reality that only she could destroy the dragon within. Her restless thoughts always took her to the same response, *I can't. I don't know how.*

There was a time when she thought she was happy in her land, accepting that she could never leave and content living through other's stories, but that was before she knew she could free herself. However, maybe she was better off never having met the prince or dreaming for adventures. She resolved to accept her fate and be at peace as she did so love the hills, the animals, and the mountain.

It was the early part of the following summer when she was out for an evening stroll to see the rising of the full moon. This was something special to her as it meant new beginnings. She thought that it might be especially pretty to see it reflected in the water.

As circumstance or fate would have it, she sat by the stream where she first met Prince Louis. She started thinking about the places she had at once longed to see. It had been some time since she had these thoughts. She'd decided not to think about them anymore as it made her sad. She had already stopped listening to the tales of travelers through the land as it made her mournful. Lynacia became proud of how skilled she had become at being content in her situation. No more longing.

However, on this moonlit evening as she sat by the stream, she could not help but think of such things. Lynacia remembered that, when sharing with Prince Louis, she was happy and enthusiastic for life. She felt alive and believed that maybe she could experience adventure outside the only land she had ever known. But in the end, her prince could not slay her dragon.

These memories became yearnings and made her think about what the prince said, that the dragon was within and how only she could defeat it. She wondered how it could have survived all these years and why. Her mother had died so many years ago. How long could a spell last after the person who cast it was dead? What fed the dragon? Didn't it need to be fed? The wondering continued until she fell into a deep sleep. As she drifted to sleep, she was feeling emotions not felt in a long time, longing for what could be and wondering about what *was* meant for her life. Lynacia's curiosity and spirited energy seemed to awaken, even though she slept, perhaps stirred by the image in the stream.

She was asleep yet aware, having vivid dreams. In her dreams, there was a young girl, a child with the eyes she saw when she would look into the stream. The child was happily dancing and spinning. The child seemed to represent all of Lynacia's desires for freedom and adventure. Suddenly in Lynacia's dream, the dragon appeared and chased the child, who then hid. The child was doing the same thing she did when she tried to leave the Enchanted Mountains. The child was afraid. Lynacia realized that the dragon could not hurt her as it had never hurt Lynacia; it only caused fear.

She saw the child hiding and sensed that she was not just afraid but also angry that no one was coming to save her. But how could they? No one knew she was there. The child hid so well.

When Lynacia awoke, the sun was already up, and it was another beautiful day. The dream from the night before kept playing through her mind. It was then that she thought, *Was the child still within? Did my mother's spell put the dragon within to scare the child into hiding? Did my mother give breath to the dragon so that it had life, and because I believed in the dragon, it lived, like the prince had stated? Was it to prevent the child's adventurous desire from taking me out of the land that my mother considered safe? Was it the child's cries that stirred me so for wanting adventure, true freedom—no fear anymore?*

She wondered if perhaps *the child* could destroy the dragon and resume its rightful place within. Maybe then Lynacia would be free if she could reach the child within. The child was speaking from the heart; the dragon seemed to be in her head, but breathing fear into the heart—how was she to fight this?

Much more realistic than finding and fighting the dragon herself—the child was already within. Lynacia realized that she would need to help. She needed to reach the child and tell her to not be afraid of the dragon. As herself now, the gift the child had given her was the knowledge that the dragon was fear and fed on fear. This was the most important discovery: the dragon was fear. She was so grateful to the child for this realization. That is what her mother cursed Lynacia with—fear, fear that kept her trapped. She now realized she could leave at any time and that she always had the power to do so.

First, she felt she needed to forgive her mother for the spell as she did not mean it to be hurtful. She also needed to forgive herself for not listening to the child. Lynacia truly only saw the dragon. She was blinded to the child, the truth hidden by a curse. Oh, how many times now she remembered hearing and feeling the child, and not

To Karol, Paul, Adam, and Margot. Thanks again.

knowing that the longings were of the child trying to be freed. She screamed to the child, "Forgive me!"

Then, without thinking any longer, Lynacia stood up and started to laugh, dance, and spin as the child had done in her dream the night before. She acted as the child had before the dragon entered, as she sensed the child was showing her what to do to help her. She did not stop even when she was dizzy. The more she acted like the child, the more she felt the child within. She just kept dancing and dancing; laughing and laughing; and spinning, spinning, and spinning like she was never going to stop.

It was almost midday when she fell out of pure exhaustion. Even on the ground, she kept laughing and felt as though she were still spinning. She knew the dragon could not hurt her. She was no longer afraid of it. Lynacia felt the forgiveness and the happiness of being reconnected with the child.

When she finally felt stable enough to stand, she had no doubt that the dragon was subdued. She felt the child was once again strong within. She was also convinced that the child had always been with her and was the root of all her longings and dreams. Amazed and thankful by how strong this child must have been to persevere all this time.

Thrilled with this discovery and awakening, she was eager to experience a fuller life in which she had learned to forgive and live without fear controlling her. The dragon still lived, but it was controlled within by Lynacia by her focusing on the voice of the child instead. Lynacia controlled the dragon.

Although recognizing she was free to go, she was suddenly a bit sad about leaving what she had always and only known. She thought about Prince Louis and realized, perhaps for the first time, that she did truly love him. Understanding that love could not grow when there was fear and that, if the prince would have rescued her, the child may not have been freed. And that others cannot create your freedom to make you happy—it begins within. Her most important adventure was her first, and it was taken within herself, thanks to the child. Now, she was strong enough to have adventures outside; she had opened the door.

Lynacia then walked outside the borders of the Enchanted Mountains to pursue a life of adventure and love. She stopped as she heard the child inside say, "Lynacia, believe in the child within. Listen to *this*: the dragon was an illusion and only had power because you believed in it."

Lynacia smiled and started to dance along the path. She had learned which voices to listen to.

About the Author

L.M. Walsh grew up in Western N.Y. where her childhood wanderings among the hills and creek beds influenced her love of nature and independent spirit. She has written stories and poems as long as she can remember. Her greatest source of joy is her children and grandchildren. She also enjoys hiking, reading and traveling. She is an American and Irish citizen who currently lives in New Haven, CT.

Brief Contents

CPSIA information can be obtained
at www.ICGtesting.com
Printed in the USA
LVHW071127301221
707392LV00002B/28

Detailed Contents

Preface

▼ To the Student

This book is intended for the student learning business statistics who likes the idea of using Excel to help that learning. If you already know Excel, using that knowledge to help you learn statistics probably seems like a good idea. If you don't know Excel, or don't feel fully comfortable with it, using this book will enable you to learn it and become better at using it. No knowledge of Excel is assumed and the use of Excel is explained with clear and easy-to-follow steps.

There is a *synergy* between knowing computers and knowing statistics. Knowing how to use computers not only will help you solve practical statistical problems, *it can also help you understand statistical concepts*. The computer can empower you. Like any good tool, a computer enables you to do things you could not do without it. When you learn statistics, a computer will enable you to literally see statistical concepts which otherwise could only be imagined. Concepts which might otherwise seem abstract can be brought to life and thereby made easier to understand. Too many people approach statistics as a topic to memorize rather than to understand and therefore are never comfortable with the use of statistics. A good working knowledge of statistics doesn't require a rigorous mathematical approach, but it does require an *intuitive* understanding. Using computers to explore statistical concepts can make that intuition easier to acquire.

There are other good reasons why a knowledge of computers in general, and Excel in particular, is useful. Too often, people try to learn a program like Excel by itself without having a place to apply it. This is a very inefficient way to learn. For most people, computers are not so inherently interesting as to be an appropriate subject in themselves. You don't learn how to hammer by studying hammers. You learn how to hammer by needing to hit a nail. You learn computers by having a need the computer can help you fulfill. Do you need to learn business statistics? That's the nail. Using this book will enable you to learn Excel not for its own sake, but because it's going to help you learn business statistics.

If you already have a good working knowledge of Excel, you may feel that some of the steps in the beginning are too detailed. This feeling will not persist. My assumption is that by the end of the book, everyone will have learned Excel. As the book progresses, the Excel instructions become less detailed and less effort is made to explain its features. Excel is rich with features, and there are many alternative ways of accomplishing the same end. Even if you feel you know Excel well, you may learn some new tricks from this book that will help you use the computer more efficiently.

- This is not a book you just sit down and read at your desk (unless your desk has a computer). *This is a book you need to use with a computer.* Many of the paragraphs of this book have bullets (like this one). These paragraphs contain step-by-step instructions for you to carry out on your computer.

Using this book will help you learn business statistics, but it won't make the process automatic. Although the approach is often step-by-step, you must not follow the steps mindlessly. The objective of the steps is not to get the computer to display a particular number, it's to help you understand either a statistical concept or the process of solving a statistical problem. After you have completed a series of steps, reflect on what you have done. Read carefully the paragraphs which do not have bullets; they are designed to help you integrate your computer experiences with your growing understanding of statistical concepts and methods. Applying the methods you have learned in the text to a new problem can sometimes seem like a struggle, but it is in this struggle that learning occurs. You can test your understanding by doing the problems at the end of each chapter after the first. Getting through a chapter and yet being unable to do the problems indicates that you need to devote more thought to the ideas the chapters are leading you through. Answers to most of the questions are in an appendix and are provided to enable you to check your work and thus your level of understanding. Do the exercises at the end of each chapter *before* you look up the answers.

This book is primarily intended for use in an undergraduate or MBA introductory business or economics statistics course. You may find this book's approach helpful for such a course even if it is not required by the instructor. It also can be used by those who wish to learn the fundamentals of business statistics (and Excel) but who are not taking a formal course.

▼ To the Professor

I have had almost twenty years of experience as both a teacher and a user of statistics. During that time there has been tremendous advance in computing technology. This has brought about enormous change in the practice of statistics in business and by researchers. Sadly, it has had almost no effect on the pedagogy of statistics. As every college instructor knows, this is not owing to a lack of commercially available texts. You, like I, are probably inundated with textbooks and advertisements for textbooks, most of which are almost identical in their pedagogical approach. The problem is not that computers are ignored. Hardly a text today is published without an optional or accompanying data diskette. Most texts illustrate computer printouts in their pages. Many have supplements dealing with a particular software package—Minitab, SAS, and, increasingly, Excel. All of this, however, is very much of an add-on. The pedagogy of most texts has hardly changed over the past 20 years and doesn't really depend on computers at all.

Most statistical programs have really been developed with the researcher or statistical user, not the student, in mind. This is enormously valuable to those using statistics because it makes it easy to do complex statistical analysis on larger and larger sets of data. The intended users of these packages are expected already to understand the statistical concepts implemented in their code. It is, of course, important for students to gain some familiarity with these tools since that is how statistics is actually done. Unfortunately, these programs may hinder learning for the very reason that they are so easy to use. Why struggle with an understanding of regression when it can be done with a few mouse clicks? *Learning* statistics, which is done by hand or with a calculator, has become separated from *using* statistics, which is done with a computer. Even the widespread use of statistical tools has had remarkably little effect on pedagogy. How many textbooks continue to use the critical value approach as the primary method of teaching hypothesis testing even though the standard for computer programs is p values? Although both approaches are obviously equivalent, p values are more intuitive, but they are not as convenient to use with statistical tables. Statistical tables have more and more become used only by students. For most uses of statistics (certainly not all), they are an anachronism foisted upon students.

How is the approach used in this book different? Excel differs from most special purpose statistical packages in its versatility in handling all types of numeric manipulations, and it is easier for most computer novices to use than a statistical program. Consider the generation of a new variable. To do this in most statistical programs, you merely write an equation showing the new variable as a calculation of existing variables. Those of us who are used to using statistics have no difficulty visualizing this equation as operating on each of many observations generating a new value for each. Compare this to the approach with Excel. Each observation is seen as a row in a spreadsheet. A formula is entered into a new cell to calculate a new value using the values in existing cells. This value appears as soon as the formula is finished. That formula is then copied down the column, and the new value is immediately visible. This is an inherently more visual and more intuitive approach than that taken by most statistical packages. Although it may not be more convenient for the researcher, it is preferable for the student.

Excel contains procedures much like those in the standard packages that automatically do such analyses as regression. These are fully covered in this book. What sets the approach of this book apart, however, is the use of Excel to help students understand statistical concepts. Consider Chapter 8. Students explore the concepts of Type I and Type II error by performing 1,000 hypothesis tests in which the Null Hypothesis is either known to be correct or known to be wrong. A table showing the outcome of these tests is constructed, and the student actually sees the impact of significance level on incidence of Type I error and the impact of the difference between hypothesized and actual population parameter on the incidence of Type II error. Or consider Chapter 14 . If you, like many of us, think it is a good idea for students to have some experience estimating a simple regression by hand, you may like the approach taken there. Rather than immediately introducing the student to the use of the Regression Tool, the computer is first used to explore regression's concepts. Students experiment with trying to fit a line to data by guessing the regression coefficient. The regression coefficients are introduced by having the student construct the type of table which would be used in an estimation by hand. The relationship between the values in that table and the scatter plot is also shown. Is this better than simply calculating the coefficients by hand? Yes. First the arithmetical drudgery is eliminated, and it becomes a simple matter to change the data estimated. Students can see the difference in the calculations between data which are well-fit by a regression line and for which there is no clear relationship.

This book should be used by instructors who are interested in pedagogical innovation. It probably is best used as a supplemental text to a more conventional textbook. Its use requires a commitment to computers, and students will have to spend many hours working through the instructions. This is probably best done in a lab setting where all students are working together, but it can be done out of class. You will have to provide reinforcement in your lectures to the concepts students are working through. The careful step-by-step approach used in this book makes it possible for students to proceed on their own, but some will have a tendency to focus too much on the steps and may not fully grasp the concepts unless you reinforce them by referring to the process they go through on the computer.

The traditional approach to teaching statistics has been exhaustively worked out and is backed by enormous quantities of instructional material. Such a course is difficult for students to learn, but it is not a particularly difficult course to teach. This is probably a factor in the subject's pedagogical inertia. The approach used in this book is new. It will undoubtedly be improved. I believe that by using it you will provide greater value to your students. Your course may become more exciting and more effective, but it will not be easier for you. It is my fervent hope that the approach taken here will be taken up by others and that we will have a choice among high-quality material which makes effective use of computers in the pedagogy of statistics.

▼ What's New?

The release by Microsoft of Excel 97 required a thorough revision of this book, although almost no changes were made to Excel's statistical capability. In fact, the major change was to correct bugs in the Data Analysis Tools which had persisted through several previous versions of Excel. Excel 97 did, however, introduce some substantial changes in Excel's interface, particularly in the way formulas are constructed and in the area of graphics. Since this book uses a step-by-step approach, every chapter was carefully reviewed and revised to be sure that it accurately described the experience students would have with Excel 97.

In addition to the changes required by Excel 97, a number of other changes were made as well. An Excel Add-In has been included to provide simple tools for drawing multiple samples from a population and for making dynamic histograms—histograms that automatically reflect changes in the data. These tools replace complicated Excel formulas that were used in chapters designed to illustrate statistical concepts. My experience (and the experience of others) was that the complexity of the Excel in those chapters made it difficult for some students to easily grasp the statistical concepts those chapters were designed to demonstrate. In addition, I have removed some of the Excel steps that were primarily cosmetic.

I have also added a number of problems to the chapter ends and provided answers to those problems. As all successful students of statistics know, the only way to be sure you understand statistical concepts is to work problems using those concepts.

▼ The Data Diskette

A number of chapters require the use of files from a data diskette. This diskette can be downloaded from the Internet or can be obtained from Prentice-Hall college representatives. Please refer to Appendix A for detailed instructions on downloading the data diskette.

▼ Macintosh?

At the time this book was written, Excel 97 was available only for Windows 95. Microsoft has indicated, however, that it intends to produce current Office applications for the Macintosh. Excel 6.0 was the last Macintosh version; it was nearly identical in operation to Excel 6.0 for Windows. The differences were primarily due to differences in the keyboards and mice between PCs and Macs. With that in mind, I have tried to anticipate how Excel 97 would work on a Mac. Those interested in using this book with a version of Excel on a Mac should look at my web page for notes on differences. If you use Excel 97 (or 98) for the Mac, I would like to hear your comments and suggestions.

▼ Acknowledgments

Many people have helped me in developing this book by reading and working through chapters, making comments to me, and by talking with me about computers, statistics, and pedagogy. At my own institution I owe a particular debt to Andy Brod, Judy Tuttle, and Jim Watts as well as former colleagues Elizabeth Anthony, Mike Evans, and Terry Seaks. I am also grateful for the reviews and comments I have received from those at other institutions, including Kent S. Borowick at Baylor, Teresa Dalton at University of Denver, Paul J. Fields at the Naval Postgraduate School, Phillip C. Fry at Boise State University, Mehran Hojati at University of Saskatchewan, Steven Thorpe at the University of Northern Iowa, and David Tufte at the University of New Orleans. I have not been able to use every suggestion, and these people are certainly not responsible for weaknesses and errors that remain. I owe special thanks to Joseph Zaremba at SUNY Geneseo who class-tested the preliminary manuscript and provided me with much feedback.

I have also benefited from a large number of those who used my previous edition and were kind enough to send me email pointing out errors and offering suggestions. I cannot list them all, but many made major contributions, and I am grateful to all of them.

I am especially grateful to Karol Neufeld, whose love for me overcame her feelings about computers and statistics and who read every page of this edition. Her fifth-grade students have long benefited from her incredible knowledge of English grammar, punctuation, and syntax. Readers of this book will now share those benefits.

Thanks also to Tom Tucker, the Decision Sciences Editor at Prentice Hall, and to Melissa Back and Audrey Regan at Prentice Hall.

My greatest thanks go to the hundreds of students who have shared classrooms with me and from whom I have learned more than I have ever taught.

I wish I could promise that this book is without error. Despite all the help I have been given, errors will persist, and they are entirely my fault. I know from experience the frustration to student and professor alike of encountering errors in textbooks, especially statistics texts. It's only with this project that I have learned how truly difficult it is to eliminate all errors in a book of this sort. Before using this book, please check the errata list available at my World Wide Web site, whose address is given below. Please send me email if you discover an error not covered there.

If you have any comments, suggestions, or criticisms you would like to share with me, I will welcome them. I'm only a mouse click away.

John L. Neufeld
Department of Economics
University of North Carolina at Greensboro
Greensboro, NC 27412

email: **john_neufeld@uncg.edu**

WWW: **http://www.uncg.edu/bus_stat/**

Learning
Business Statistics
with
Microsoft® Excel
97

Chapter 1

▼

Introduction to Excel

Microsoft Excel is one of the most widely used computer programs. It belongs to the category of programs known as *spreadsheets*. Other well-known spreadsheet programs include Quattro Pro and Lotus 1-2-3. It's the versatility of spreadsheet programs that makes them so popular. When there is a need to analyze numerical data and prepare reports on that analysis, a spreadsheet program can often make the job easier. Spreadsheets are used by accountants, salespeople, managers, and nearly everyone working in business today. The ability to use a spreadsheet is a skill you will find useful in many different careers.

Spreadsheets traditionally have not been used for statistical analysis. Computers have long been used for statistical analysis, and computer programs to do that analysis existed long before the first spreadsheet program. As the use of computers became more widespread, statistics programs continued to develop even as the popularity of spreadsheets became firmly established for other types of quantitative analysis. Many excellent statistics packages, such as Minitab, SPSS, and SAS, are in wide use today. Spreadsheet programs also continued to develop, including the capability of doing statistical analysis. The current spreadsheet programs have considerable statistical capabilities—all you will need for the typical introductory college business statistics course.

Why use a spreadsheet program for statistics? There are two excellent reasons. First, spreadsheets are easier to learn and use than are traditional statistics programs. Although most statistics programs are constantly being improved, they continue to show their mainframe heritage in the way they require users to use cryptic commands much like a programming language. By contrast, spreadsheets use a newer interface, which, for most people, is more intuitive than the command language approach. In addition, the market for spreadsheet programs is huge, and the companies developing for that market can afford to devote enormous resources to develop any competitive advantage. Ease of use is one of the most important competitive advantages, and producers of spreadsheet programs are constantly working to improve their programs' ease of use.

1

The much smaller market for statistical programs makes it difficult for ease of use to receive as much attention. The other big advantage of using a spreadsheet for statistics is that, unless you become a professional statistician, you are far more likely to be using a spreadsheet in your career than a statistical package. For most business people, the need to do statistical analysis will be occasional. If you use a spreadsheet program for other purposes, statistical analysis will be easier (and will more likely be done) if you can use that same software.

Specialized statistical programs do have important advantages over spreadsheets. Most statistical programs provide a far greater variety of statistical procedures than does Excel. Even for those procedures which Excel does provide, statistical programs often provide additional or optional information not available with Excel. If your study of statistics goes much beyond the first course, you will need to learn to use a statistical program. If your career requires frequent statistical analysis or analysis near the "cutting edge" of statistical sophistication, you will need to learn and use a specialized statistical package. There is, however, every expectation that the statistical capabilities of spreadsheet programs like Excel will improve as new versions are released, and the role of spreadsheet programs in statistical analysis is likely to grow.

This chapter is designed to introduce you to Excel's basic features and operations. If you are familiar with any Windows or Macintosh program, some of the material here will be familiar to you, and you may be able to skim it. Some of the material is unique to Excel, and, unless you are already familiar with Excel, you should go over it more carefully.

▼ Using a Mouse

Although it is possible to use Excel without a mouse, it is not recommended. It takes most people a little practice to get used to using a mouse, so don't worry if you initially have difficulty controlling the mouse pointer. If you are using an IBM compatible PC, your mouse will have two buttons. Some PCs have a mouse with three buttons, but the middle button is not used with Excel. If you are using a Macintosh, your mouse will have only a single button. Many actions require that you position the mouse pointer at a particular location on the screen and click the mouse button. On a PC, most actions involve clicking the left button, but a few require clicking the right button. In this book, "clicking" a particular location on the screen will mean placing the mouse pointer on that location and then quickly pressing and releasing the *left* mouse button. If the right button is to be used, it will be clearly stated. Sometimes an action will require "double clicking." This means you position the mouse pointer and push the button quickly twice in a row. On a PC, double clicking is always done with the *left* mouse button. New users often find double clicking tricky at first, but it too will come with time.

▼ Starting Excel

- If you are using Windows 95, click the "Start" button on the lower left of your screen. A menu will open. Click "Programs." On the new menu, look for the Excel icon (shown on the left) and click it. If you don't find the Excel icon, look for an icon titled Microsoft Office in the shape of a folder and click it. The Excel icon will be in the window that opens.

(icon) Microsoft Excel

- If you are using a Macintosh, look for the icon in Finder and double click it.

When Excel starts, it will be in a *window*. That window may fill your machine's screen, or it may fill only a portion of the screen.

- If the window fills only a portion of your screen, make it fill the entire screen by clicking a special place on the upper right-hand corner of the window. In Windows 95, this is called the maximize button and looks like ☐. On a Macintosh, it is called a zoom box.

Once the Excel window fills the screen, it should look approximately like the picture on the next page. Don't worry if your window isn't exactly like that shown. Excel allows a user to change some aspects of its appearance. This may have been done with your Excel.

Pay attention to the names shown for various parts of the screen. You likely will want to refer back to this picture as those names are used later in this book.

- Practice moving the mouse pointer by moving your mouse. It's important that you be able to accurately place the mouse pointer on part of the screen. Notice that the shape of the mouse pointer changes as you move to various parts of the screen. The shape of the mouse pointer changes to indicate the kind of operation you can do with the mouse in that portion of the screen.

As long as you have the mouse pointer in the central part of the screen (the *cells*), it has the shape of a white plus sign ✛. This shape indicates that you can use the mouse pointer to *select cells* (which will be discussed later). Move the mouse pointer into the formula bar and it changes to this "I-beam" shape: I . When the mouse pointer has this shape, Excel will allow you to *enter numbers or letters* from the keyboard. Move the

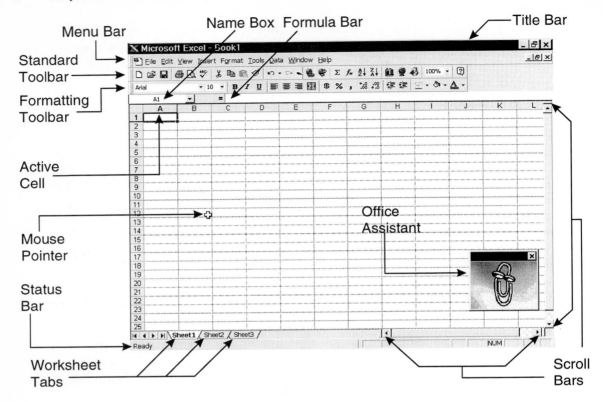

mouse pointer to the button bars, the Menu Bar, or the title bar, and the mouse pointer will have the shape of an arrow pointing to the upper left:

As you use Excel, you will discover that there are other shapes the mouse pointer can take. These shapes indicate the operation Excel expects you to perform. Sometimes, when you are having difficulty getting Excel to do what you want, the shape of the mouse pointer will clue you to what Excel thinks you should be doing.

Let's take a quick tour of the main Excel screen from top to bottom. The features mentioned here will be discussed in more detail later.

▼ The Title Bar

The *Title Bar* on top tells us what is in this window. As you use Excel, you will find that some operations open windows *within* the main Excel window. These "sub windows" will generally also have a Title Bar indicating the operation that window performs. For the main Excel window, this includes the name of the application (Microsoft Excel) and the name of the *workbook* (Book1). When you use Excel, you create a workbook that can be saved in a file. Another common name for what Excel calls a workbook is a *spreadsheet*.

Find the Close Box ✕ on the right side of the Title Bar. Most windows will have this box. Clicking it will generally close the window, and clicking the Close Box in the main Excel window will end the Excel session.

• Click the Close box. A window may open with a question of whether or not you wish to "save the changes in 'Book1'?" If you see this window (and you may not), place the mouse pointer directly on the word "No" and click the (left) mouse button. Your Excel session will end.

Many windows will have buttons or menu items that will close them, but using the Close Box or Control-Menu Box will work with virtually any window.

• Start Excel again by clicking or double clicking the Excel icon.

▼ The Menu Bar

Below the Title Bar is the Menu Bar.

• Place the mouse pointer over the word View . The outlines of a "button" will appear around the word. Click the left mouse button to "press" the button. If you are using a Macintosh, push and hold the mouse button.

The View menu will open as shown on the left. Notice the check marks beside "Formula Bar" and "Status Bar." These two features can be either *on* or *off*. The check marks indicate that both are currently *on*.

• Place the mouse pointer over the words "Formula Bar" and click the (left) mouse button (on a PC), or release the mouse button (on a Mac). The Formula Bar will disappear from your screen. (I bet you've forgotten where the formula bar should be. Look back at the picture on page 4.)

• Again open the View menu. Notice that the check mark beside "Formula Bar" is now gone (the feature is *off*). Choose "Formula Bar" as you did above (click on a PC, release button on a Mac).

The Formula Bar will reappear. If you lose the Formula Bar (or the Status Bar), this is the way you get them back. Be sure that they are showing whenever you use this book.

Some of the menu choices are followed by an ellipsis (…). This indicates that if you make that choice, there will be further choices to make. When you choose an item with an ellipsis, a *dialog window* will open. A dialog window will give you the opportunity to make further choices.

The "Toolbars" choice on the View menu has a small arrowhead pointing to the right ▶. This indicates that this choice has further choices made in a *submenu.*

- Open the View menu and place the mouse pointer over "Toolbars."

A submenu (like that shown on the left) will open, showing the names of all of Excel's toolbars (except the Menu Bar, which cannot be closed). When Excel is first started, the toolbars that are visible are the Standard and Formatting toolbars. These are the ones shown on the screen picture on page 4. (The Standard toolbar is on top in that picture, but may not be on your screen.) In the submenu shown, there are check marks in the boxes beside "Standard" and "Formatting."

✓	Standard
✓	Formatting
	Chart
	Control Toolbox
	Drawing
	External Data
	Forms
	Picture
	PivotTable
	Reviewing
	Visual Basic
	Web
	WordArt
	Customize...

- Even though it is already open, click "Toolbars" on the View menu. This will keep the Toolbars submenu open even if your mouse pointer moves off it.

A submenu will open whenever the mouse pointer rests on the main menu option referring to it so that you can see the choices in the submenu. Once you are sure you want to use the submenu, it is a good idea to click its name on the main menu.

- Place the mouse pointer on the word "Standard" and click the (left) mouse button. The menus will close and the Standard toolbar will also close (disappear). Reopen the menus and notice that there is now no check mark beside "Standard."

- Using the View menu, also make the "Formatting" menu disappear.

Both toolbars will be gone from your screen.

- Open the View menu again, and select "Toolbars" again. When the window opens, select "Standard." The Standard toolbar should reappear.

- Use the View menu to make the Formatting Toolbar reappear.

Your Excel screen should now have the same toolbars as the screen pictured on page 4. Whenever you are using this book, you should be sure that you start Excel with the Standard and Formatting toolbars showing (and no others). Use the procedures you have just practiced to make sure these toolbars are showing when you start an Excel session.

▼ Using the Toolbars

Each toolbar consists of a group of icons (little pictures) or "buttons" (also called "speed buttons"). When you place the mouse pointer over an icon, the outline of a button will appear as it did when you opened the View menu. You "press" a button by clicking (and then releasing) the (left) mouse button. When you do this, the button will appear to be pressed; it will seem recessed. When you move the mouse pointer away from a button, the color of the button will lighten, making it easier to tell which buttons are pressed. Most of the buttons perform operations that could also be performed by using the menus. The buttons are a convenience because they are faster to use than the menus, and they are always visible. The menus are designed to be organized logically by operation, while the buttons are meant to provide an easy way of accessing the most frequently used operations. Excel provides extensive facilities for the user to control what buttons are shown and even to define new buttons. If you are interested, consult a manual or the Help system (which is discussed below).

- Place the mouse pointer over one of the buttons, but don't click a mouse button.

Notice that the name of the button will appear directly below the button. Macintosh users can activate a similar feature by selecting "Show Balloons" from the Help icon menu near the right end of the Menu Bar. This useful feature can help you remember which button is which.

▼ Getting Help—The Office Assistant

Perhaps the most noticeable, and certainly the most entertaining, feature of the Excel screen is the Office Assistant. There are a total of nine different Office Assistants available in Excel 97, each presumably designed to appeal to a different personality or sense of humor. The one depicted here (to the left) is "Clippit," the Assistant that Excel initially comes with unless another one is chosen. They all work similarly, and Clippit will be the one depicted in this book.

If the Office Assistant does not appear on your screen, click the Office Assistant button— ? —on the Standard Toolbar.

You will notice as you work that Clippit is constantly in motion, rolling his eyes, taking notes, and changing shapes. If you enjoy watching him perform, he will gladly do so on command.

- Place the mouse pointer on Clippit and click the right mouse pointer. A menu will open. One of the menu choices is "Animate!" Place the mouse pointer on that choice and click the (left) mouse pointer.

Clippit has a repertory of motions. The next time you ask him to perform, he will do something different.

If you have a question about Excel, ask the Assistant. For example, let's suppose that you are working through this book, but have to leave the computer and want to save your workbook on a diskette. You can't remember how to do it. Here's how to ask the Assistant:

- Place the mouse pointer on the Assistant and click the (left) button.

A cartoon speech "balloon" will open in which Clippit asks "What would you like to do?" You may or may not see a list of possible actions. At the bottom will be a white field into which you can enter your own question.

- Enter "Save my workbook," as shown in the picture on the left. Place the mouse pointer over the word "Search" so the blue dot to the left lights up and click the left mouse button.

Clippit will search for the topics in its database that seem closest to your request. Clippit's "balloon" will close and reopen. When it reopens, it will show a new list of tasks. At the top, right below "What would you like to do?" will be "Save a workbook."

- Place your mouse pointer directly on the words "Save a workbook" or on the blue dot just to the left of the words. The blue dot should appear to "light." Click the (left) mouse button. A help window will open. Read what it has to say.

Within the Help system, Excel gives you the opportunity to get more information about certain topics through cross references and definitions. At various places you will see cross-reference buttons: ![»], which will provide you with more information on a topic. If you place the mouse pointer over one of these buttons (and sometimes over the text adjacent to the button), the pointer changes to a hand with a finger out, ready to press the button: 🖑 (done by clicking the (left) mouse button).

- Click the cross-reference button beside "Save a new, unnamed workbook." A new Help window will open. You can scroll the text in that window by using the up and down arrow keys on your keyboard. If this doesn't seem to work, click the mouse pointer in the Help window and try again.

- Scroll down to the "Tips" at the bottom so that you can see the entire first paragraph. Notice that it describes using the "Look in Favorites" icon (⊞). Place the mouse pointer directly over that icon in the help window and click the (left) mouse pointer. A small window opens, giving further explanation of that icon. Click the mouse button again and the window will close.

- In the same paragraph notice the word <u>shortcut</u>, which has a dashed underline and may be in a different color. Place the mouse pointer directly over that word until it changes to the hand ready to press a button. Click the left mouse button and notice that a definition for "shortcut" appears. Click the mouse button again and the definition window will close. Excel will define any word in a Help window with that dashed underline.

- At the top of the main Help window, just below the title bar, you will see a button labeled "Back." Click it and you will return to the previous Help window.

▼ Moving a Window

One problem with Help windows is that they cover up your work. This can be a problem with any type of window. One way of dealing with the problem is to move the window. Almost all windows have title bars, and you can always move a window with a title bar by following the instructions below.

- The only title on the Help window's title bar is "Microsoft Excel." Place the mouse pointer directly on the title bar. Press and hold the (left) mouse button.

- While pressing the left mouse button, move the mouse pointer. An outline of the window will move with the pointer. Try moving the window to the bottom of your screen so that only the title bar is visible and the rest of the Help window is below the screen. As long as the title bar is visible, you can move the window back.

This method of moving a window while you press and hold the mouse button is called *dragging*. The same technique will be used to move other objects in Excel.

- Click the close button on the Help window.

Although there is no title written on it, Clippit's window has a title bar.

- Use the method described above to move Clippit's window around on your screen.

▼ Getting Tips from the Office Assistant

Sometimes the Office Assistant will offer you help before you have even had a chance to ask for it. The Office Assistant pays attention to the steps you are doing with Excel, and if it thinks there is another, better way to accomplish what you are doing, it offers to give you a tip.

Generally, the Office Assistant only offers you a particular tip once. That way, every time it offers a tip, that tip is new, and you don't have to have it keep giving you the same tip over and over again. This does create a problem, however, if you are using a shared computer, such as one in a lab. If the person who used the computer before you has gotten a tip from the Office Assistant, you won't get that tip. One way to fix this problem is to reset the Office Assistant's tips. On a shared computer, you should do this each time you use Excel.

- Place the mouse pointer directly on the Office Assistant and click the *right* mouse button. A menu will open as shown on the left.

- Click "Options" on the menu. A dialog window will open as shown below. This window enables you to customize the way the Office Assistant works. Take a look at the features you can change.

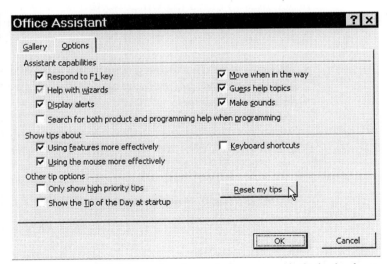

- With the "Options" folder tab selected, locate and click the button labeled "Reset my tips." Click that button. A message will appear in a balloon above the Office Assistant confirming the change. Click the "OK" button in the Options window.

One of Excel's clever features is its ability to automatically fill cells with a series of words or numbers once you have started the series. Excel, for example, knows the days of the week, and if you want to enter a series of days of the week, you can enter just the name of the first day and have Excel finish. We will explore this in more detail later. Here we will pretend we don't know about this so that Clippit will give us a tip.

- Place the mouse pointer in cell D1, in the top of row of cells just below the letter "D," and click the (left) mouse button. That cell will have a dark border around it, becoming the active cell.

- Type the letters "Mon" (without the quotation marks) and press the Enter or Return key. This three letter abbreviation for "Monday" will appear in the cell and the cell below it will become the active cell.

- Type the letters "Tue" (again, without quotes) and press the Enter or Return key.

Mon
Tue
Wed

- Type the letters "Wed" (no quotes) and again press the Enter or Return key. The three cells should look like the illustration on the left.

- Look at the Office Assistant. A light bulb should appear on the right side of the window. Place the mouse pointer directly on this bulb and click the (left) mouse button.

A balloon should appear with a light bulb on the left. Clippit's tip will begin with something like "This is quicker," or "A speedier way." Clippit has observed you entering three abbreviations for the names of the days of the weeks and wants you to know that there is quicker way than the way you are doing. Don't worry if you can't understand Clippit's explanation because this will be carefully explained below. Once you are really using Excel, pay attention when the Office Assistant offers a tip. Often (not always) they will be useful and will help you become a better Excel user.

- Click the "Close" button in the tip window.

If you feel Clippit is more of an annoyance than a help, click his Close Box, and he will gracefully depart until his button is clicked.

▼ The Active Cell

The heart of an Excel workbook is the *cells* in the central part of the window. Each of the cells has an address determined by the row and column in which the cell is located. At the top of each column is a *column head-ing* with a letter, and to the left of each row is a *row heading* with a number. A cell's address is the letter of its column followed by the number of its row. In the section of the worksheet shown below, the ac-tive cell is in column A and row 1. Its address is therefore A1. Notice that this address is shown in the Name Box. The Name Box shows the ad-dress of the active cell.

The active cell is the cell in which you can enter data. You can tell which cell is the active cell because it is surrounded by a special border, the ac-tive cell border: ⬚. In addition, the letter for the column heading (A) and the number for the row heading (1) will be darker than those of the other columns and rows and will appear slightly raised.

A cell is made active by placing the mouse pointer in the cell and clicking the (left) mouse button.

• Make cell C2 active.

If you have done this correctly, the Name Box will contain the address "C2." Notice the appearance of the headings of the "C" column and the "2" row. They should appear raised above the other row and column headings, helping you locate the active cell.

▼ Selecting Cells

The active cell is always a single cell. Some operations in Excel involve more than a single cell and require that you *select* a *range* of cells. A selec-tion of cells is usually a rectangular block of cells. Since it is rectangular, it can be referred to by the cell addresses of its corners. Excel requires these addresses be separated by a colon. For example, suppose we wanted to select the rectangular array of cells consisting of cells A1, B1, A2, B2, A3, and B3. The four corners of this array are A1, B1, B3, and A3. This book will use the convention of referring to the array by the ad-dresses of the upper left cell (A1 in this case), and the lower right cell (B3). This range would be referred to as A1:B3. Select this range of cells by doing the following:

- Place the mouse pointer on cell A1 and press and hold the (left) mouse button.

You will see cell A1 immediately become the active cell.

- While continuing to press the mouse button, drag the mouse pointer to cell B3 and release the mouse button (as illustrated below).

Start with the mouse pointer here (A1)

Then drag it to here (B3)

The selected region of cells will include the active cell (A1 in this case). When the active cell is in a selected region, it will be white while the other cells in the selected region are black.

- Press the Tab key repeatedly and notice how the active cell changes within the selected region. Press the Enter key repeatedly and notice the active cell also changes but in a different pattern.

When you select a region of cells, the headings for the rows and columns of all the cells in the region appear raised and their numbers or letters become darker.

▼ Entering Data

Data are entered into the active cell from the keyboard. There are three types of data that can be entered:

1. Numbers. When you use Excel for statistical or other quantitative analysis, numbers are the starting point of the analysis.

2. Text. Text should be used liberally in an Excel workbook to document the numbers and calculations to make it easy to remember what the numbers mean. Excel is capable of producing beautiful tables, which can be used in reports. Every table should have text defining the rows and columns.

3. Formulas. Much of the work done by Excel will be in formulas you enter, which tell Excel the calculations you want done.

▼ Numbers

To enter a number in the active cell, simply type the number on your keyboard. To complete the entry of a number, press the Enter key.

As you enter the number specified below, notice the following:

1. As you enter a number, the characters you type appear in the cell and in the Formula Bar.

2. As you enter a number, a vertical line called the *insertion point* shows where the next character you type will appear. As long as the insertion point is visible, you can correct typing errors with the Backspace key. Once you press the Enter key, the insertion point will disappear.

Insertion Point

- Click cell B1 (make it the active cell). This should also remove the black selected region.

- Enter the number "100.5" (don't enter the quotation marks). Observe the Formula Bar as you enter the number. Press the Enter key when you are finished.

▼ Editing a Cell

It is easy to edit a cell that already has an entry by placing the mouse pointer in the cell and double clicking. This will cause both that cell to become the active cell and the insertion point to appear within the cell. When you first were entering the number, the insertion point was always to the right of the last character you typed. When you edit a cell, you can move the insertion point by using the left or right cursor (arrow) keys or by positioning the mouse pointer exactly where you want the insertion point and clicking. This lets you add a character in the middle without re-typing the rest of the number. You can erase the character to the right of the insertion point by pressing the Delete key. The Backspace key deletes the character to the left of the insertion point.

- Double click cell B1. You should see the insertion point in the cell.

- Place the mouse pointer between the decimal point and the "5," and click the mouse button.

Notice that when a cell has been double clicked and is ready for editing, the mouse pointer changes shape when it is in that cell. The new shape (the "I-beam") makes it easier to point precisely where you want the insertion point to be. Clicking between the decimal point and the "5" will cause the insertion point to appear at that location.

- Type the character "4" (without the quotation marks) and press the Enter key.

The contents of cell B1 should now be 100.45.

It is also possible to edit the contents of a cell in the Formula Bar.

- Make cell B1 the active cell, but don't double click the cell.

- Move the mouse pointer to the Formula Bar. Place the mouse pointer to the right of the "5" and click.

An insertion point will appear at the end of the number.

- Type a "6" (without the quotation marks). Press the Enter key.

The number in cell B1 should now be 100.456.

▼ Entering Text

Entering text is as simple as entering numbers.

- Double click cell A1.

- Type the following text (without the quotation marks): "The First Number."

Notice that before you press the Enter key, the text that you enter goes beyond the right border of cell A1 and causes the contents of cell B1 to disappear.

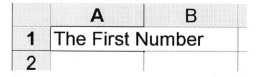

After the Enter key is pressed, the contents of B1 reappear, but part of the text is covered as shown at the top of the next page.

- Click cell A1 to again make it the active cell, but don't double click.

	A	B
1	The First N	100.456
2		

Notice the Formula Bar. The full text appears there. Even though cell A1 on the worksheet is not wide enough to show the entire text, *it is there.* Excel stores the entire text correctly. It displays what it can given the available space.

Excel behaves similarly with numbers. It keeps track of all decimal places even if the cell is too narrow to display them all and even though the value displayed in the cell may be rounded. The full number is stored and can be seen in the Formula Bar when the cell containing the number is made active.

- Click cell A2.

- Enter the following text (without the quotation marks): "The Second Number." As soon as you type the letter "T," Excel will immediately enter the last text you entered in a cell which started with "T" ("The First Number" in this case). Simply ignore this and continue typing "The Second Number."

- Press the Enter key. The cells should look like this:

	A	B
1	The First N	100.456
2	The Second Number	

Notice this time that the full text appears even after the Enter key is pressed. This is because cell B2 is empty. If something is later entered into that cell, part of the text in A2 would disappear just as you saw in the first row.

▼ Changing the Width of a Column

If you increase the width of column A, the full text of cell A1 can be viewed in the cell.

Carefully place the mouse pointer on the border between the heading for column A and the heading for column B. (Row and column headings are shown on page 12.) When you have it correct, the pointer will change to new shape: ╬. This is the *column width* mouse pointer.

The column headings and mouse pointer should look like the following picture:

A ⊹ B

- Once you see the column width mouse pointer, press and hold the (left) mouse button, and *drag* the headings boundary to the right. Move it to the right about half an inch (no need to be precise). Release the mouse button.

The width of column A will increase and shift the columns to the right further to the right.

- Again position the mouse pointer on the boundary between the heading for column A and that for column B. This time, *drag* the boundary to the left until it is just to the right of the word "First" in cell A1. Release the mouse button. This enables you to reduce the width of a column.

Although this method gives you complete control over column width, it is hard to know exactly how wide to make the column to display its contents without wasting space. Fortunately, there is a shortcut when you want simply to make a column wide enough to display the cell contents.

- Again position the mouse pointer on the boundary between the headings of columns A and B. Instead of dragging, double click without moving the mouse.

The width of column A will immediately adjust to display the text in the cells in that column. The cells should look like the picture below.

	A	B
1	The First Number	100.456
2	The Second Number	
3		

▼ Made an Error? Undo!

Excel remembers all the changes you make to the cells of a spreadsheet and allows you to "undo" any or all of them. This is a fantastic time saver if you discover you have made a mistake. (If you are the kind of person who never makes mistakes, you should be writing—instead of reading—this book.)

- Look for the Undo button on the Standard Toolbar: ↰ . Place the mouse pointer on the curved arrow and click the mouse button. Immediately you should see column A's width narrow until the right border is just to the right of the word "First" in A2. This is exactly where it was before you double clicked on the column boundary.

- Click the arrow on the Undo button again. Now you should see the column width become wide. This is the result of the first column width change you made.

- Click the Undo button again. Now column A has returned to its original width.

- Click the Undo button once again. The contents of cell A2 should have disappeared.

- Continue clicking the Undo button until the only thing remaining on an otherwise blank worksheet is "Mon" in cell D1. Click the Undo button one more time, and the worksheet should be completely blank.

Not only can you undo an operation, but you can also undo the undo (Excel calls this "redo").

- Click the Redo button on the Standard Toolbar: ![redo button]. The "Mon" should reappear in cell D2.

- Repeatedly click the Redo button. Each time you should see one of your earlier operations being replayed. Continue clicking the button until it no longer works. When this happens, the button will be "grayed." You'll be able to see the shape of the Redo button, but it will have lost its color.

- Click the small arrow on the right side of the Undo button. A list will open showing all of actions you have made that can be undone. By using the list, you can undo several changes in a single click. This, however, is usually not a good idea.

▼ An Editing Shortcut—Text Highlighting

Suppose that we wanted to change the word "First" in cell A1 to "1st," and the word "Second" to "2nd." One way of doing this would be to first erase the word "First" and then enter "1st." There will be many times when you will want to replace one thing with another, and there is a useful shortcut for this operation.

- Double click cell A1 so that you can edit it.

- Move the mouse pointer so that it is immediately to the left of the "F" in "First."

- Press and hold the (left) mouse button.

- Move the mouse pointer to the right (across the word "First") while continuing to press the mouse button.

As the mouse pointer moves across the letters, notice that the colors switch from black letters on a white background to white letters on a black background. This is called *highlighting* the letters.

- Continue moving the mouse until you have highlighted the word "First" and only the word "First." Release the mouse button.

Your screen should look like the picture below:

	A	B
1	The **First** Number	100.456
2	The Second Number	

- On your keyboard type "1st" (without the quotation marks).

As soon as you begin typing, the highlighted text ("First") is deleted and new text appears in its place. Your screen should look like the picture below:

	A	B
1	The 1st Number	100.456
2	The Second Number	

- Press the Enter key to complete the cell editing.

This "text highlighting" can be used anywhere in Excel (including dialog windows) when you want to edit text. "Text" in this sense means anything you could enter from the keyboard, including numbers and formulas.

- Practice the technique by changing the word "Second" in cell A2 to "2nd." Be sure to press the Enter key.

- Use the method described on page 17 to have Excel automatically adjust the width of column A to fit the data in the column. Although this was used above to expand the column's width, the same method can also reduce a column's width.

Your screen should look like the picture at the top of the next page.

	A	B
1	The 1st Number	100.456
2	The 2nd Number	

▼ Entering Formulas

- Make cell C1 the active cell.

- Enter (without the quotation marks): "=3+2" and press the Enter key.

- Again make cell C1 the active cell.

You indicate to Excel that you are entering a formula when you first enter an equal sign. Notice that cell C1 appears to have a "5" but that the Formula Bar shows the formula you entered. (As shown below.)

C1	▼		=	=3+2

	A	B	C
1	The 1st Number	100.456	5
2	The 2nd Number		

This formula, of course, directs Excel to add 3 and 2.

- Edit cell C1 and change the plus sign to a minus sign (-). Press Enter. Cell C1 should have a 1.

- Change the minus sign to a forward slash (/). This is the symbol for division, and the formula now directs Excel to divide 3 by 2. Press Enter and cell C1 should have 1.5.

- Change the forward slash to an asterisk (*). There is no real multiplication sign on a computer keyboard, and Excel uses the asterisk for that purpose. Press Enter, and cell C1 will have a 6, the product of 3 and 2.

- Change the asterisk to a carat (^). This is Excel's symbol for exponentiation, raising a number to a power. Press Enter, and cell C1 will have the value of 3^2 or 9.

▼ Order of Arithmetic Operations

When a long formula with several operations is entered, Excel uses the standard "order of precedence" to determine which operations to do first. This means that first exponentiation will be done. Multiplication and division will be done next. Addition and subtraction will be done last. You can control the order in which operations are done by using parentheses.

- Enter "=(3+2)*6" (without quotation marks) in cell C1 and press Enter.

The value will be 30. Excel first does the operation inside the parentheses by adding 3 and 2. The result of that operation, 5, is then multiplied by 6.

- Enter "=3+(2*6)" in cell C1 and press the Enter key.

This time the value is 15. Excel first multiplies 2 times 6 and then adds the result (12) to 3.

- Enter "=3+2*6" in C1 with no parentheses. Press the Enter key.

Again, the answer is 15 because the order of precedence causes Excel to do the multiplication before the addition. It's a good idea to freely use parentheses in any formula with more than one operation so that you will be sure that the calculations will be done in the order you want. Remember that you always have to explicitly use the asterisk to indicate multiplication, even if you use parentheses. In mathematics, notation like (2)(3) is often understood to mean that the two values should be multiplied. With Excel, however, the multiplication must always be explicitly shown by an asterisk.

In addition to the basic arithmetic operations, Excel has a large number of mathematical functions. These functions can be entered directly in a formula. For example, suppose we wanted to calculate the square root of 9.

- In cell C1 enter "=sqrt(9)" and press the Enter key.

Cell C1 should now show a "3." The square root function has the name "sqrt" in Excel. Notice that the "9" is in parentheses and immediately follows the "sqrt." The "9" is called an *argument* of the function; it's the value we want the function to work on. Some functions have more than one argument. A few functions have no arguments. Regardless of the number of arguments, they all appear within a single set of parentheses. If there is more than one argument, they are separated by commas. If there are no arguments, the function name is followed by empty parentheses "()."

- Make C1 the active cell. Notice the Formula Bar.

Excel converts the function name to uppercase. You can enter a function name either in uppercase or lowercase, but it will always appear in the Formula Bar as uppercase.

As you will learn later, Excel has a very clever feature that makes its built-in functions much easier to use. This feature is called the Formula Palette, and much use will be made of it in this book.

▼ Using Cell Addresses in Formulas

A particularly useful and powerful facility in Excel is the ability to create formulas that refer to a cell whose contents are used in the calculation.

- Enter the following formula in cell C2 (without the quotes): "=b1+10." Press the Enter key.

The value displayed in cell C2 should be 110.456, which is the number in cell B1 plus the number 10.

Use the up-arrow cursor key to make C2 the active cell again. Notice that in the Formula Bar, the contents of the cell are displayed as =B1+10. Just as in the case of the SQRT function, Excel changes a cell address to uppercase letters even if you enter it in lowercase.

- Click cell B1 to make it the active cell (but don't double click). Enter the number "50" (without the quotation marks). Press the Enter key.

Notice that entering something new in an active cell that already has something in it simply erases the old contents and replaces it with the new. What does cell C2 now show? It should have the value 60, the contents of cell B1 (now 50) plus 10.

- Change the value of cell B1 to -20. Press the Enter key.

No matter what value you enter in cell B1, the displayed value of cell C2 will be 10 more. In this case, 10 more than -20 is -10.

It is also possible to enter a cell address by pointing to it with the mouse pointer.

- Make cell C3 the active cell. Begin a formula by entering an equal sign (=). Move the mouse pointer over cell B1 and click the (left) mouse button once.

A "B1" should be entered into the formula in cell C3 immediately after the equal sign.

- Enter a plus sign (+). Move the mouse pointer directly over cell C1 and click the (left) mouse button once.

The formula in cell C3 should now be "=B1+C1."

- Press the Enter key.

The value of cell C3 should display as -17, assuming that B1 has the value -20 and C1 has the value 3. Remember that C1 contains a formula ("=sqrt(9)"), not a number. As long as a cell *displays* a number, its address can be used within a formula even though that number is the result of a formula.

- Change cell C1's value to 50. What now is the value of cell C3?

Cell C3 should now display 30. Whenever the value of a cell changes, the displayed value of any cell containing a formula that references that cell will also change. This very important feature makes it possible to set up a workbook to analyze a particular *type* of problem and easily use it to handle different data by simply changing the numbers in cells referenced by equations in other cells that do the real analysis.

▼ Scientific Notation

Sometimes the result of a calculation will be an extremely large or an extremely small number. When this happens, Excel uses a format that is similar to what is called *scientific notation*.

- Make C1 active and enter the formula "=55 ^ 13." Press the Enter key.

This formula directs Excel to calculate 55^{13}, which is a very large number. Cell C1 will have the value 4.2142E+22. (Your display might show other numbers between the "1" and the "E.") In scientific notation, this number would be:

$$4.2142 \times 10^{22}$$

where 10^{22} is twenty-two 10s all multiplied together. This number is a 1 followed by 22 zeros. The "E" in this notation is short for "exponent." In the scientific notation shown above, the "22" is called the *exponent* of 10. To represent this number in the notation we are most familiar with, the decimal place would have to be shifted 22 (the amount of the exponent) places to the right of where it is in 4.21. So this number is a bit larger than 4 followed by 22 zeros.

If you are not used to scientific notation, you probably don't feel comfortable with it. Excel can convert the number to the more familiar notation for you.

- Make cell C1 the active cell. Find the Comma Style speed button on the Formatting Toolbar: ﹐. Click it.

Excel automatically adjusts the column width to show the number in its new format. It may be easier for you to make sense of now, but it takes up a lot of space.

Very small numbers in this notation have negative exponents.

- Make cell D1 active and enter "=1/(55 ^ 13)." Press the Enter key.

This directs Excel to calculate 1 divided by the same huge number it just calculated. This, of course, will be very small. Excel will show it as 2.37293E-23. Notice that the exponent is *negative* (-23). To see this number in standard notation, we would have to shift the decimal place 23 positions to the *left* of where it is in 2.37293.

To get Excel to show you the number in more familiar notation, do the following.

- Make cell D1 active and click the Comma Style speed button.

You may be surprised that cell D1 appears to contain zero. This is because the Comma Style button sets the cell to display only two decimal places. Another speed button will increase the number of displayed decimal places.

- Click the Increase Decimal speed button: .00. You will have to click it many times before you see enough decimal places to display this number.

Here again, although this format is probably easier for you to read than Excel's scientific format, it takes up much more space. Numbers like this will occasionally be produced by some statistical procedures, and it is best (but not essential) to get used to Excel's standard representation of them.

▼ Error Codes

Some calculations cannot be done and result in an error. In these cases, Excel displays an *error value* in the cell. Let's see what they look like. The examples discussed below are going to involve making pretty obvious errors, ones you might be very unlikely to make. As your use of Excel becomes more sophisticated, however, errors become much more subtle and less obvious than these examples.

- In cell D1 enter the formula "=10/0" (without quotes). Press the Enter key.

This formula instructs Excel to divide the number 10 by zero, although division by zero is not defined. Instead of a value, cell D1 contains the error value "#DIV/0!" All Excel error values begin with "#." It's not hard to see that this error value warns of division by zero.

- Does Clippit want to give you a tip? Click its light bulb to read it.

- Make D1 the active cell. Look at the Formula Bar.

As in the case of a valid calculation, the Formula Bar shows us that Excel continues to store the formula in the cell and simply displays the answer as an error value.

- Edit the formula, changing the "0" to a "5." Press the Enter key.

A non-error value ("2") now appears in cell D1. Excel continues to display many digits to the right of the decimal point.

- Make cell D1 active and click the Comma Style button again. The display returns to showing only two values to the right of the decimal.

You are likely to encounter other error values as you work with Excel. The meaning of some of them may not be so obvious. Whenever Excel does something unexpected, a good first place to turn is the on-line help.

Suppose you wanted to use Excel to take the absolute value of a number and were unsure of the name Excel uses for the absolute value function. One reasonable approach to this problem is to guess.

- Enter in cell D1 the formula "=absval(-10)" without the quotation marks. Press the Enter key.

At this point you can probably guess what the error value, "#NAME?," means. Suppose, however, that you needed an explanation of the error message. This is an excellent opportunity to experiment with Excel's extensive on-line help system.

- Clippit is trying to show you a tip. Click the light bulb, and you should get a message explaining that the error message means Excel doesn't recognize a name that was used. Suppose we need more help.

- Click on Clippit so you can ask him a question. Simply enter the error code "#NAME?" (without quotes) and click the "Search" button.

- The first topic in Clippit's list should be, "What does the error #NAME? Mean?" Click on the dot just to the right of this topic and a Help window will open explaining possible causes of the error.

You will notice in the Help window that there are several possible causes for the error listed, including "Misspelling the name of a function." This is likely confirmation that we have misspelled the name of Excel's function to take the absolute value. How can we determine what the correct spelling is?

- Use Excel's help system to search for the name of the Excel formula that determines the absolute value. Do this by asking for help for "absolute value."

- The list of topics that first appear in Clippit's balloon are not helpful. Click "▼ See more…." From the new topics that appear, select "ABS." Read the Help window. This is the absolute value function, and ABS is the correct name.

- Close the Help window.

- Edit the formula in cell D1 to change "absval" to "abs." Press the Enter key. The error value should be replaced by 10—the absolute value of −10

▼ The Scroll Bars

Excel displays only a portion of a worksheet on your computer screen. It frequently will be necessary to view the other cells. Think of your screen as a small window on a very large worksheet. To view portions of the worksheet that are not currently visible, you need to move your screen's window on the worksheet until it is over the cells you want to see. One way of doing this is to use the scroll bars.

There are two scroll bars. The horizontal scroll bar moves the screen window horizontally, while the vertical bar moves the window vertically. The parts of the scroll bar are shown in the picture at the top of the next page. Note that the scroll bars on your screen will be longer than those shown on the next page, and your screen should include worksheet tabs.

Each scroll bar has a scroll box and two scroll arrows. The position of the scroll box within the scroll bar shows the relative position of the screen window on the worksheet. For example, in the picture on the next page the scroll box is at the top of the vertical scroll bar, indicating that the screen window is at the top of the worksheet. The first row of the worksheet is visible.

The scroll box in the horizontal scroll bar, on the other hand, is more or less in the middle of the scroll bar. The visible portion of the worksheet is to the right of the first column (column A). To move the screen window over the worksheet, you move the scroll box within its scroll bar.

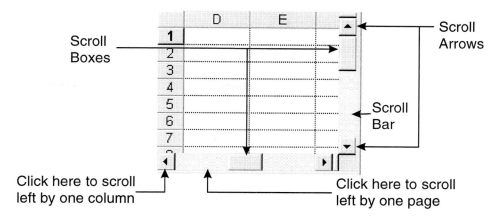

Scroll Boxes

Scroll Arrows

Scroll Bar

Click here to scroll left by one column

Click here to scroll left by one page

- On your worksheet, place the mouse pointer on the bottom scroll arrow of the vertical scroll bar on the right of your screen. Click the (left) mouse button once.

The screen window will move down one row. The top row visible on your screen should be row 2 and the bottom row should be one row below that which was originally visible.

- Click the top scroll arrow so that row 1 is again the top row visible on your screen.

- Place the mouse pointer on the vertical scroll bar so that it is below the scroll box and above the scroll arrow. Click the (left) mouse button once.

The screen window will scroll down by a "page" (the total number of rows displayed). All of the rows now visible are below what was the bottom row. Anytime you click the mouse pointer on any part of the scroll bar below the scroll box but above the scroll arrow, the screen window will move down a page. If you click the scroll bar above the scroll box, the screen window will move up a page.

- Place the mouse pointer directly on the scroll box. Press and hold the (left) mouse button. While holding the mouse button, slowly move the scroll box up. Notice the name box. Position the scroll box so that the name box contains "Row: 10." Release the mouse button.

Row 10 should now be the top row on your screen.

- Experiment with the horizontal scroll bar by clicking the scroll arrows, scroll bars, and moving the scroll box.

▼ Worksheets and Worksheet Tabs

An Excel worksheet, as you have seen, contains far more cells than can be seen on your screen at one time. In addition, an Excel *workbook* contains many *worksheets*. Tabs for some of these worksheets can be found at the bottom of the Excel window to the left of the horizontal scroll bar. The current worksheet is "Sheet1," and you will notice that the tab for that worksheet appears on top and is lighter than the other worksheet tabs.

- Click the "Sheet2" tab.

Notice that a blank worksheet appears with all the columns set to their original width. Notice also that the "Sheet2" tab now appears to be on top and is the lightest tab.

- Click the "Sheet1" tab.

The previous worksheet reappears.

Worksheets give you a way to help you organize the information in a workbook. In addition, some operations in Excel create new worksheets. As you will see, some worksheets will contain a graph rather than cells.

Initially, Excel starts with three worksheets. It is easy to add more.

- Click "Insert" on the Menu Bar to open the Insert menu. Click "Worksheet" on that menu.

A new worksheet, "Sheet4" will be created. It will not necessarily be placed after Sheet3. It is easy, however, to drag it to that location.

- Place the mouse pointer directly on the "Sheet4" tab. Click and hold the (left) mouse button. The mouse pointer will change shape to a white arrow with a sheet of paper under it: ▯. Move the mouse pointer to the right and notice the small dark marker that moves between sheet tabs. This indicator shows the position to which the worksheet will be moved once the mouse button is released.

- Move the mouse pointer until the marker is to the right of the "Sheet3" tab and release it. The worksheets should now be in order.

- Create enough new worksheets (six or more) so that not all the worksheet tabs will be visible at the same time on your screen.

When there are many worksheets, the tabs that are visible can be scrolled using the special scroll arrows immediately to the left of the worksheet tabs. The functions of those arrows are described in the picture on the next page.

Scroll to first sheet in workbook

Scroll to last sheet in workbook

Scroll 1 sheet to the left

Scroll 1 sheet to the right

- Click each of the worksheet tab scroll arrows and observe its operation.

In addition to entering data in cells, you can also put values in cells by filling, copying, and moving cells. "Filling" refers to the ability of Excel to automatically extend a sequence of values.

▼ Copying and Moving Cells

- Click the "Sheet2" worksheet tab so that you can work with a clean worksheet.

Excel provides a number of different methods to copy or move cells. It is common to want to copy the contents of a single cell to several adjacent cells, either in the same row or the same column. As will be discussed below, this is a particularly useful operation when the cell to be copied contains a formula, but the procedure will work when the cell contains text or numbers.

- Enter the number "1" (without quotes) in cell A1. Press the Enter key.

- Click cell A1 to again make it the active cell, but don't double click since you don't want to edit the cell.

Look carefully at the border around the active cell. In the lower right corner there is a small square called the *fill handle*. Carefully position the mouse pointer over the fill handle. When you have it correctly positioned, the pointer will change from a thick white cross to a thin black cross as shown in the picture below.

- Click and hold the (left) mouse button while it is in the shape of a black cross. Drag the mouse pointer down column A until the selection frame includes cell A10. Release the mouse button. Cell A1 will be white, and cells A2 through A10 will be black.

- Release the mouse button.

The "1" originally in cell A1 has been copied to all the cells in the range.

- Press the Delete or Del key on your keyboard. This will erase the contents of the selected range. (The Del key on the numeric keypad will only work if NumLock is *off*).

- Click cell A1 and enter the word "Total" (without quotes). Press the Enter key. Reselect cell A1.

- Position the mouse pointer over the lower right corner so that it changes into a black cross.

- Hold the mouse button and drag to the *right* until the selection boundary includes the cell at the top of row E. Release the mouse button.

The word "Total" will have been copied to all of the cells within the selected region A1 through E1.

- Erase the contents of cells A1 through E1 using the Delete key.

▼ Filling Cells

- Enter the number "1" in cell A1 and the number "2" in cell B1.

- Select the cell range A1:B1.

- Place the mouse pointer over the square in the lower right corner of the selection boundary until it becomes a black cross, as shown in the picture below.

- With the mouse pointer in the shape of a black cross, click and hold the (left) mouse button and drag the selection outline to the right along the first row until it includes cell G1. Release the mouse button.

Rather than copying the contents of cells A1 and B1 to the other cells, Excel continues the series begun in those cells, with cells A1 through G1 containing the numbers 1 through 7. A small indicator follows your mouse pointer and tells the value that will go in the last cell.

- Erase the contents of the cells in the first row.

- Put the number "5" (no quotes) in cell A1 and the number "10" in cell A2.

- Create a selected region containing cells A1 and A2 by placing the mouse pointer in the center of cell A1, pressing and holding the (left) mouse button, dragging the mouse pointer to the center of cell A2, and releasing the mouse pointer in cell A2.

- Place the mouse pointer over the small square in the lower right-hand corner, press the (left) mouse button, and drag the selection outline down to cell A10. Release the mouse button.

Since cells A1 and A2 had values that differed by 5, Excel extended the series by adding 5 to each number. Try repeating the process after putting "2" in A1 and "4" in A2. Try again with "1920" in A1 and "1930" in A2. Excel's ability to fill a range of cells is an excellent demonstration of intelligence in a computer program.

Excel's ability to fill with certain text values is even more remarkable.

- Follow the steps on page 30 to copy the word "Total" from cell A1 to E1, except use the word "Monday" instead of "Total" (without quotation marks).

Instead of copying, Excel fills the cells with the other names of the days of the week!

- Excel can also fill (and copy) several series at once. To see this, enter the values shown below in the first row of the worksheet. Excel recognizes the value in cell A1 as a date, but it, and all the others, should be entered in the same way as you enter text.

	A	B	C	D	E	F	G
1	2/25/96	Mon	Jan	january	Week 1	1st	1st Quarter

- Select the region from A1 to G1. Do this by placing the mouse pointer on A1, holding down the (left) mouse button, and dragging the selection boundary to the right until it includes G1. Your screen should look like the picture below:

	A	B	C	D	E	F	G
1	2/25/96	Mon	Jan	january	Week 1	1st	1st Quarter

- Notice that the selected region has a small square in the lower right corner, the same as that which you used earlier to copy and fill. Place the mouse pointer over that square until it becomes a black cross.

- When the mouse pointer is a black cross, press the (left) mouse button and drag the mouse pointer downward until the selection boundary includes row 15. Notice the small tag by the mouse pointer indicates what Excel will place in the last cell of the first column. Release the mouse button.

Excel has filled each column in the selected region. If you look carefully at each series, you will notice some remarkable examples of Excel's built-in intelligence.

Look at the dates in the first column. Notice that the date after 2/29/96 is 3/1/96. Not only does Excel know how many days are in each month, it also knows that 1996 was a leap year.

If a name begins with a lowercase letter (like "january" in cell D1), Excel will fill the series with names all beginning with lowercase letters.

Compare the series in columns F and G. Excel knows that there are only four "Quarters," and begins renumbering after the fourth.

▼ Moving and Copying Regions of Cells

Excel provides a method for moving and copying cells using the mouse. Let's use this method to move the information in columns E, F, and G one column to the right so that column E is cleared.

- Select the region of cells from E1 to G15. Do this by dragging the mouse pointer (with the mouse button pressed) from cell E1 to cell G15.

- Position the mouse pointer on a boundary (any of the four boundaries will work) of the Selected Region. When it is correctly positioned, its shape will change from a white cross to a white arrow: ▨.

- While the mouse pointer is in the shape of an arrow, press and hold the (left) mouse button.

- With the mouse button pressed, move the mouse pointer to the right. After you have moved at least one column, an outline of the selected region will appear which moves with the mouse pointer. A small marker will show the address the outline is currently on.

- Position the outline so that it is in columns F, G, and H, in the first 15 rows (F1:H15). Your worksheet should look like the picture on the next page.

- When the outline is correctly positioned, release the mouse button.

	A	B	C	D	E	F	G	H
1	2/25/96	Mon	Jan	january	Week 1	1st	1st Quarter	
2	2/26/96	Tue	Feb	february	Week 2	2nd	2nd Quarter	
3	2/27/96	Wed	Mar	march	Week 3	3rd	3rd Quarter	
4	2/28/96	Thu	Apr	april	Week 4	4th	4th Quarter	
5	2/29/96	Fri	May	may	Week 5	5th	1st Quarter	
6	3/1/96	Sat	Jun	june	Week 6	6th	2nd Quarter	
7	3/2/96	Sun	Jul	july	Week 7	7th	3rd Quarter	
8	3/3/96	Mon	Aug	august	Week 8	8th	4th Quarter	
9	3/4/96	Tue	Sep	september	Week 9	9th	1st Quarter	
10	3/5/96	Wed	Oct	october	Week 10	10th	2nd Quarter	
11	3/6/96	Thu	Nov	november	Week 11	11th	3rd Quarter	
12	3/7/96	Fri	Dec	december	Week 12	12th	4th Quarter	
13	3/8/96	Sat	Jan	january	Week 13	13th	1st Quarter	
14	3/9/96	Sun	Feb	february	Week 14	14th	2nd Quarter	
15	3/10/96	Mon	Mar	march	Week 15	15th	3rd Quarter	
16								F1:H15
17								

The selected region will move to the new area and column E will be empty. This method of moving a region of cells is called the *drag and drop* method. You drag a region of cells (holding the mouse button down) and drop it where you want it.

There is also a drag and drop method of copying a region of cells. Let's use it to copy the days of the week in column B to the now empty column E.

- Select the region of cells from B1 to B15.

- Place the mouse pointer over the border of the selected region so that its shape changes to a white arrow.

- With the mouse pointer in the shape of an arrow, press and hold the Ctrl key (PC) or OPTION key (Mac) on your keyboard. A small plus sign will appear beside the arrow.

- Continue to press the Ctrl or OPTION key and also press and hold the (left) mouse button. Drag the selected region outline until it is over column E (E1:E15).

- Release the mouse button first and then release the keyboard key.

The days of the week will be copied to column E and will also still be in column B.

▼ Copying and Moving Formulas—Relative Cell Addresses

Special attention has to be paid when formulas containing cell addresses are moved or copied. Let's examine the way Excel handles these situations.

- Click an unused sheet tab so that this exercise may be done on a blank worksheet.

- Enter the letters and numbers in cells A1 through B3 and C1 as shown below:

	A	B	C
1	1st Value	2nd Value	Sum
2	1	10	
3	2	20	
4			

Use Excel's fill capability to extend the series in columns A and B through row 10.

- Select the region A2:B3, then drag the small rectangle in the lower right corner down until the selection boundary includes row 10.

Column A should show the series of numbers from 1 through 9, while column B should shown 10, 20, 30, up to 90.

- Enter this formula in cell C2 (without quotation marks): "=a2+b2."

The value displayed in cell C2 should, of course, be "11."

- Move cell C2 to C3. A single cell can be moved exactly like a larger selected region. Click C2 to make it the active cell, place the mouse pointer on a boundary of the cell until the pointer turns into a white arrow, then hold the (left) mouse button and drag the cell boundary until it is in cell C3. Release the mouse button.

Moving the formula from C2 to C3 shouldn't change it. It still should display "11." The Formula Bar should show "=A2+B2" when C3 is active. *Moving* a cell with a formula doesn't change it. This may not surprise you since moving a number or text also doesn't change the value entered in a cell. *Copying* a formula, however, *may* change it in a way that can be quite useful.

- Move the formula from C3 back to C2.

- Now *copy* the formula from C2 to C3. Use the drag and drop method.

Instead of "11," cell C3 should display "22."

- Click on cell C3 to make it the active cell.

- Drag the rectangle in the lower right-hand corner down until the selection boundary includes cell C10.

- The displayed value of each cell will differ. Cell C4 shows "33," while cell C5 shows "44," and so on.

- Click on cell C6 to make it the active cell and observe the cell's contents in the Formula Bar.

Instead of "=A2+B2," the contents of C6 are "=A6+B6." When the formula was copied, the cell addresses were changed.

- Click on each of the cells in column C from C2 to C9 and observe the formula in each cell in the Formula Bar.

Each cell contains a formula adding the values in the two cells immediately to the left. Thus cell C2 adds the numbers in columns A and B, which are in the same row (2) as cell C2. The formula in cell C4 does the same, only since C4 is in row 4, the two cells whose values are added are also in row 4.

When you put the formula "=A2+B2" in cell C2, Excel interpreted the addresses "A2" and "B2" as *relative* cell addresses. Excel determined where those cells were *relative* to the cell containing the formula. Thus cell A2 is two cells to the left of cell C2, and B2 is one cell to the left of cell C2. When the formula in C2 is copied to another cell, those addresses are changed to the addresses of the cells that are in the same position *relative* to the copied formula's position. For example, the formula in cell C4 adds the value of the cell two cells to the left of C4 (which is A4) and the value of the cell that is one cell to the left of C4 (which is B4).

This ability of Excel to change cell addresses in this way is very useful. Many spreadsheet problems will require performing the same calculations on several rows or several columns of numbers. With relative cell addressing, you need only specify the calculation in a formula for one of the rows or columns, and then copy that formula to the other rows or columns.

Let's take a look at the use of relative cell addresses on operations involving columns. Suppose that we want the cells in row 11 to display the sum of the numbers in the column above. Thus cell A11 would show the sum of A2 through A10, B11 would show the sum of B2 through B10, and C11 would show the sum of C2 through C10.

Let's start by entering the formula in A11 to add the numbers in A2 through A10.

- Click cell A11 to make it the active cell.

Summing a row or column is such a common operation on a spreadsheet that Excel provides a speed button specifically for that operation.

- Find the AutoSum button on the Standard Toolbar Σ and click it.

Excel will insert the formula in cell A11 that it *thinks* you want. You should see the following in that cell: `=SUM(A2:A10)`. The most likely error Excel might make is to guess the wrong cell addresses you want added. To help you correct the cell addresses, Excel has already highlighted them in the formula. In this case, however, Excel has guessed correctly.

- Press the Enter key and the sum of the column, 45, will display in cell A11.

- Copy cell A11 to B11 and C11. B11 should display 450 and C11 should display 495.

▼ Absolute versus Relative Cell Addresses

Suppose that we would like column D to contain the percentage each value in column C is of the total for column C. The sum of the values in column C is 495, so we would like cell D2 to indicate what percentage of 495 is 11 (the value in C2). Cell D3 should indicate what percentage of 495 is 22, and so on.

- In cell D1 enter the text label "Percent" (without quotation marks).

- In cell D2, enter the following formula (without quotation marks): "=c2/c11." Press the Enter key.

The value 0.022222 should be displayed in D2. Note that this is a proportion rather than a percentage. To convert a proportion to a percentage, we must multiply by 100. Excel, however, has a special formatting that allows a proportion to *display* as a percentage.

- Make D2 the active cell. Click the Percent Style speed button **%** on the Formatting Toolbar.

The value 2% will be displayed.

- Click the Increase Decimal speed button on the Formatting Toolbar twice.

The value 2.22% should now be displayed. The Percent Style button formats the cell but doesn't change its value. If C2 were used in a mathematical formula, the value that would be used would be 0.022222, not 2.22.

- Copy the formula in D2 to D3.

Although our objective is for D3 to calculate C3 as a percentage of the total, this clearly did not happen. Instead, D3 shows an error (#DIV/0!). This error indicates an attempt to divide a number by 0.

- Make D3 the active cell and observe the formula in the Formula Bar.

The formula in D3 is =C3/C12. But this is not correct. C12 is blank. What we want is for the value in C3 to be divided by the value in C11, not C12. The problem is that when the formula in D2 (=C2/C11) was copied, the C2 was changed to C3 and the C11 was changed to C12. What we wanted, however, was for just the C2 to be changed. The way to do this is to make the C12 in the formula in D2 an *absolute* address, which won't change when it is copied.

- Double click cell D2 so that you can edit it. When you edit a formula with cell addresses, Excel uses color coding to show you the location of the cells in the formula.

- Highlight the C11 in the formula so that you can edit that portion of the formula.

- With the C11 appearing as white against a black background, press the F4 function key. The "C11" should change to "$C$11."

The dollar signs make the address absolute. Without the dollar signs, the address is relative. An absolute address will not change if it is copied to another cell, while a relative address will change. You can also make an address absolute by manually entering the "$" rather than using the function key.

- Press the Enter key to indicate that you have finished editing the cell.

- Copy cell D2 to cells D3 through D10.

Each of the cells should now display a correct value. Examine the formulas in several of the cells. Notice that in each of them the numerator is the cell address of the cell immediately to the left, while the divisor is always "$C$11."

Notice also that Excel has copied the formatting to the cells. Thus each cell appears as a percentage with two decimal points.

- Copy the formula in cell C11 (which sums column C) to cell D11 so that D11 will have the sum of the number in column D.

Are you surprised that the value is 1 instead of 100? Although the percentages add up to 100%, remember that the numbers in the cells in column D are *proportions*, not percentages. The Percent Style button causes them to be displayed as percentages, but the numbers that are added are all between 0 and 1. Of course, we could use the Percent Style on D11 to make it also display as a percentage.

Congratulations! You have now learned enough Excel to begin to use it to explore data and perform statistical analysis. You will be introduced to new features but this will always be done in the context of using Excel to explore statistics. Don't be surprised if you need to refer back to this chapter. As time goes on, you'll remember more and more about Excel, and you will find the discussions in this book will deal increasingly with statistics and decreasingly with Excel.

Chapter 2

Descriptive Statistics

Chances are that what you think of today as *statistics* is more precisely called *descriptive statistics*. There are many times when a business person will need to understand information provided by a collection of numbers—such as sales figures, labor turnover, expenditure records, and many more. We mortals do not have the ability to look at more than a handful of numbers and immediately have a sense of the information those numbers contain. To get a sense of the information contained in a huge collection of numbers, we have to summarize, or we have to convert the numbers into a chart or graph.

Vision is our keenest sense. You take advantage of that sense when you use graphics to represent the information in numbers. Before computers, graphical representations of data were difficult and time-consuming to do well. Computers, and programs like Excel, make it easy to prepare graphics, although it still takes some skill to know how to use graphics effectively.

Data summaries, or descriptive statistics, are also important. Most of your study of statistics will not be of descriptive statistics. It will be of *inferential statistics*. Inferential statistics provides us with a way to investigate the characteristics of a *population* when we only have data from a *sample*. A common example is a poll that provides information on the attitudes of an entire electorate by questioning only a tiny proportion of all the people in that electorate. The techniques of inferential statistics require calculating numerical summaries of the sample data and using them to develop information about the population.

▼ Using Graphics in Excel

Let's explore Excel's graphics capability through the use of an example using data on the size of the civilian work force in the United States, classified by gender.

Start Excel (if you have not already done so).

The data for this example are available in the Excel worksheet named labor.xls. To read that worksheet into Excel, do the following:

- Insert the data diskette in the A drive on your computer. If the files on that diskette have been copied to a hard drive or a network drive, skip this step. (See Appendix A to obtain the data diskette).

- Click the Open ☞ speed button on the standard toolbar. The Open dialog window will open.

At the top of the dialog window (shown below) you will see a field labeled "Look in:." In the picture below, that field refers to the folder "My Documents." To read from a diskette, you need to have that field refer to the diskette drive.

Click
Here

- Click the small downward-pointing arrowhead just to the right of the "Look in" field as shown in the picture. A list of locations will open (as shown below).

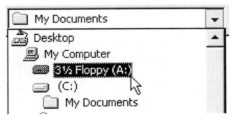

- Click the mouse pointer on "3½ Floppy (A:)." The dialog window should look like the picture on the top of the next page.

The data for each chapter is in a separate folder on the diskette. (Not all chapters have data).

- Since this is chapter 2, place the mouse pointer on the icon labeled "Chap_2" and double click. The "Look in:" field will now have "Chap_2."

- Two file names should appear in the large field, Ch2_data.xls and Labor.xls. Place the mouse pointer on "Labor.xls" and double click.

The Open dialog window will close and Excel will load the workbook shown in the second picture on the next page.

These data show the size of the civilian labor force by gender for several recent years. The numbers provide information on how the total labor force size has changed and how the proportion of the labor force consist-

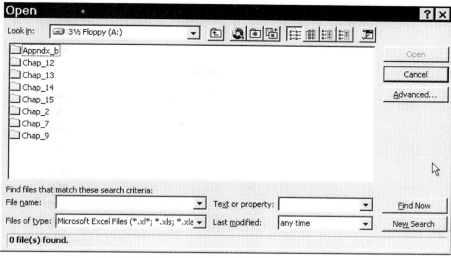

	A	B	C
1	**Civilian Labor Force (1,000)**		
2	Year	Males	Females
3	1960	46,388	23,240
4	1970	51,228	31,543
5	1975	56,299	37,475
6	1980	61,453	45,487
7	1983	63,047	48,503
8	1984	63,835	49,709
9	1985	64,411	51,050
10	1986	65,422	52,413
11	1987	66,207	53,658
12	1988	66,927	54,742
13	1989	67,840	56,030
14	1990	68,234	56,554
15	1991	68,411	56,893
16	1992	69,184	57,798
17	1993	69,633	58,407

ing of women has changed. This information would be much easier to understand, however, if it were shown in a chart. Let's use Excel to create such a chart.

You have the option in Excel to place a chart on the same worksheet as the data or to place it on a worksheet by itself. For this exercise, you will do the latter.

- Click the Chart Wizard button (📖) on the Standard Toolbar.

Excel will start the Chart Wizard, which provides a sequence of dialog windows for you to specify details about the type of chart you want. In the first step you tell Excel what type of chart you want. We'll create what Excels calls a *stacked column chart. A* column chart is a bar chart in which the bars are vertical. A stacked column chart divides each bar into two parts so that each bar graphically shows two numbers rather than one.

- In the left field ("Chart type") select *Column.* Notice that the sample pictures in the right field change as the selected chart type changes.

- In the right field ("Chart sub-type"), select stacked column. This is the second choice in the top row. Notice that beneath the sample pictures is an explanation of the chart sub type you have chosen. The dialog window should look like the picture below:

- Click the "Next>" button.

In the next dialog window (which has "Chart Source" in the Title Bar) we can tell Excel exactly which data we want charted. Excel makes a guess, and the small chart shown in the dialog window depicts the chart that would display if Excel's guess were accepted. Although Excel's guesses are pretty good, this guess is wrong.

The type of chart we want is one in which there is a separate bar for each year, and each bar is subdivided into two parts: one representing the number of males and the other representing the number of females in the civilian labor force.

There are two problems with Excel's guess. Look at the small chart in the dialog window showing the chart the guess would produce. Notice that Excel has numbered each bar. Instead, we want each bar labeled with the year. Instead of using the data in column A to label the bars, Excel has divided each bar into three parts and treated the year as data just like the numbers in columns B and C.

We can see this problem by looking at the legend in the window's proposed chart (shown on the left). The legend gives the colors Excel uses to label each part of the bar. Notice that the third item is year, and it is colored blue on your computer. If you look carefully at the bottom of each bar you can see a small blue segment. The segment is small because the value of year is less than 2,000, while the other values (number of males and number of females) are in the tens of thousands.

Another problem is that the legend is too wordy. It would be better to identify the data as "Males" and "Females" without the "Civilian Labor Force (1,000)." We can do this by telling Excel not to look at row 1 where those words appear.

In the dialog window is a field titled "Data range" with Excel's guess "='Civilian Labor Force'!$A$1:$C$17" already entered and highlighted. This is a slightly different form of cell address than we have seen before in that it contains the *worksheet name*, "Civilian Labor Force." The cell range on that sheet is $A$1:$C$17; Excel uses absolute cell addresses. Notice that these cells are surrounded on the worksheet by a border of dashed lines that move around the cell range like lights around the title signs at some movie theaters.

Since the current address is highlighted, it will automatically be erased when a new address is entered. We'll use the mouse to point to the cells we want rather than manually entering a range address (though that would work also). Remember that our object is to remove row 1.

- Place the mouse pointer in cell A2 (containing the label "Year"). Click and hold the (left) mouse button and begin to drag the pointer to cell C17. Don't release the mouse button until you have read the next paragraph.

As soon as you begin to point to a new range address, Excel removes all of the dialog window except for the field into which the new address will go. Excel is making it easier for you to include cells that would have been under the dialog window (although you probably won't need to). As you drag the mouse pointer, a small box follows showing how many rows and columns you are including. When you get to cell C17, you will have included 16 rows and 3 columns.

- With the mouse pointer in cell C17, release the mouse button.

The dialog window will return and the Data range field will contain "='Civilian Labor Force'!$A$2:$C$17." The moving border around the data will not include row 1, and the legend on the proposed graph will simply have "Females," "Males," and "Year." The next step is to make the year a label for the bars rather than data to be shown on the chart.

- At the top of the dialog window are two "file tabs." One has "Data Range" written on it and the other has "Series." Click "Series." This changes the fields in the dialog window.

On the left of the dialog window is the "Series" field, which shows all of the data values being charted.

- Remove "Year" from the list of series being charted by clicking the "Remove" button while "Year" is highlighted. Immediately the word "Year" should disappear from the field. How does the chart change?

"Year" has been removed as one of the data items to be charted. This is shown by the new legend, which now has just "Females" and "Males." The next step is to have Excel use "Year" to label the bars.

- The "Category (X) axis labels:" field (at the bottom of the window) is where we put the cell addresses of the bar labels. Click the mouse pointer in that field so that an insertion point appears there. Then place the mouse pointer on cell A3, press and hold the (left) mouse button, and drag the pointer to cell A17.

Once again all of the dialog window except for the field you are working on disappears until you have selected the 15 rows and 1 column. When you release the mouse button, the window will reappear and the chart in the window should have each bar labeled with the year as shown in the picture at the top of the next page.

- Click the "Next>" button. The "Step 3 (Chart Options)" dialog window will open.

This dialog window presents you with a number of options on how your chart will look. The "file tabs" at the top of the window give you access to the window's various features. It is easy to "try on" different options because they will immediately be shown in the small chart in the window.

- Click the "Titles" file tab. In the "Chart title" field enter "Civilian Labor Force." In the "Category (X) axis" field enter "Year." In the "Value (Y) axis field" enter "1,000's."

- Click the "Legend" file tab. Under "Placement" click the "Bottom" radio button. The window should look like the second picture on the next page.

Click the "Next>" button.

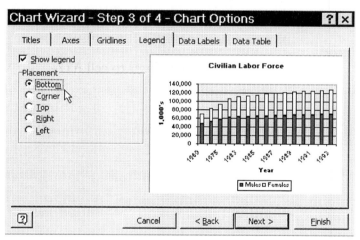

The last step lets you determine whether you want the chart on a new worksheet by itself or whether you want it to share a worksheet, perhaps so the chart and its data will be together. This decision will affect the way the chart will appear on your screen, and it also will affect the way it will appear if it is printed. With each choice there is a field in which you can enter a worksheet name. If you choose to put the chart on a separate worksheet, you can give that worksheet a name here (or Excel will give it the name already in the field, "Chart1"). If you choose to put the chart in an existing worksheet, and you have more than one worksheet, you can put the name of the existing worksheet here. Since there is only one worksheet in this workbook ("Civilian Labor Force"), Excel puts that name in the field.

- Have Excel put the chart on its own worksheet named "CLF Chart." The dialog window should look like the picture below.

- Click the "Finish" button. The Chart Wizard will close the last dialog window and you will see the completed chart on its own worksheet. Notice the name of the worksheet by looking at the worksheet tabs near the bottom left of your screen

- Save the work you have done up to this point by clicking the Save speed button 🖫 on the standard toolbar. Get in the habit of frequently clicking the button to ensure that a computer problem will not result in losing your work.

Let's examine some ways in which this chart might be changed. Suppose we wanted to make the following changes:

1. Convert the chart to a type of side-by-side bar chart with a three dimensional look to the bars.

2. Change the title to "Civilian Labor Force by Gender."

3. Change the bars from colors to gray-scale patterns that will show on a non color printer.

4. Print the chart.

Many other changes are possible, but these will demonstrate how you can change an existing chart.

▼ Changing the Chart Type

- Open the "Chart" menu on the Menu Bar. Select "Chart Type." The "Chart Type" dialog window will open. You should recognize this as the same dialog window first used by the Chart Wizard (and shown on page 42).

- At the top of the window are two folder tabs. The current one is labeled "Standard Types." Click on the "Custom Types" tab.

- Click several of the choices and observe the effect on the small chart in the window. Select, finally, "Columns with Depth" (as shown below). Click the "OK" button.

The display will return to the worksheet with the chart. As you see, the bars now appear three dimensional, and the data for males and females are represented by bars that are side by side.

Unfortunately, changing the chart type also changed a number of other things that we did not want changed. The legend, which was at the bottom of the chart, is now on the right side. The titles and the labels on both axes are now gone. These things can all be easily corrected.

- Open the "Chart" menu on the Menu Bar. Select "Chart Options...."

This is the same dialog window used by Step 3 of the Chart Wizard when you were first creating the chart (p. 45).

- Using the Chart Options dialog window, move the chart legend to the bottom, give the chart the title "Civilian Labor Force by Gender," label the X axis "Year," and label the Z axis "1,000's."

The next step is to change the colors used in the bars to gray-scale patterns, which print better on black and white printers.

▼ Changing the Chart Colors

You can change the color of every element in the chart. There are several ways of doing this, but each way starts the same: you have to select the element you want to change. Color can effectively add interest to a chart. Sometimes when we want to print a chart, however, we have to use a black and white printer. We will change the colors of the data series, that is, the bars, so that they will be black and white. In doing this you will learn how to make any color change and even how to add interesting patterns to any element of a chart.

- Place the mouse pointer directly over one of the bars in front representing a data value for females. Let it sit in one spot for a second. A small window will open identifying exactly which data series the pointer is on. If the window does not say "Series 'Females,'" move the pointer slightly to the right or left and wait a second until the window reappears. Do this until the window verifies that it is on a "Female" bar.

- Click the (left) mouse button once. Small squares should appear at four corners of several (but not all) of the bars representing data on females. If these squares do not appear or appear only on one bar, place the mouse pointer off the chart, click, and retry this step.

- To the right of the Fill Color button (⬛▾) on the Formatting Toolbar is a small downward pointing arrow. Click the arrow. A dialog window offering a choice of colors will open below the toolbar.

- Place the mouse pointer on one of the colored squares. After a second you will see a small window with that color's name. Place the mouse pointer on the white colored square and click the mouse button once.

The Fill Color dialog window will close and the bars representing females will all be white. Let's add a pattern. Excel will let you use very elaborate patterns (and even pictures) to color a chart element. These should be done carefully, however, lest a complex pattern detract from the information the chart is meant to convey.

- Make sure the bars representing females are still selected. If so, once again click the small arrow beside the Fill Color button. Once the dialog window appears, click the "Fill Effects..." button at the bottom of the window.

- The Fill Effects dialog window has several folder tabs at the top, labeled "Gradient," "Pattern," "Texture," and "Picture." Look at each of them except "Picture," try different selections, and observe the effect each has in the "Sample" area in the bottom right portion of the dialog window. You can choose only one fill effect. You cannot, for example, combine a pattern and a gradient; you have to choose between them.

- Switch to "Pattern," and choose the pattern that looks like this (don't worry if the dots are colored): ▦. Click the "OK" button. The window will close and all the bars representing females in the work force will have a polka dot pattern.

- Using the method just used, select the bars representing males and change their color to a light gray with no pattern.

▼ Changing the Chart Title Font

It is easy to make changes to the chart title or to either of the axis titles. These changes include moving the titles, changing the fonts, adding colors, and more. In this example you will increase the font size of the title so that it appears larger.

- Place the mouse button on the chart title ("Civilian Labor Force by Gender") and click the mouse button once. A border will appear around the title indicating that the title is "active": ▨.

- Find the Font Size button on the Formatting Toolbar (12 ▾). Click the arrow on the right side. A drop-down list of numbers will appear. Click the number "20."

The title will become larger. Once a title is active, you also can change its font with the Font button (Arial ▾).

- Note the font currently shown by the Font button ("Arial" in the illustration above.) If it is not Arial, write its name in the margin to the left. Click the arrow on the right side. A drop down list of fonts available on your computer will open. Experiment with different fonts by clicking another font name and observe the change in the title. Try this for several different fonts and leave the title with the font you think looks best.

Some of the fonts on your computer may be symbol fonts, which do not include the letters of the alphabet. Selecting one of these fonts will make your title unreadable. As will be explained later, you can change the font of a single letter. The symbol fonts have special characters not available on the ordinary alphabetic characters, and, by changing the font of a single letter you can include one of these special characters in your text.

- Change the title to a readable alphabetic font.

- With the title still active, place the mouse pointer directly on the title. Notice that the pointer changes to the "I beam" shape. This lets you directly edit a title by entering and deleting and by highlighting portions of the text. If you highlight one or more letters in the title, the buttons on the Formatting Toolbar will affect only the highlighted letters.

- Use the Italic button (*I*) to change the word "Gender" to italics.

This method of direct editing can be used to change any text not based on worksheet values. This includes all labels and notes.

▼ Adding Notes to a Chart

Excel makes it easy to add text to a chart. Notice in the chart you have produced that the bars are not evenly spaced; there is a ten-year gap between the two leftmost set of bars, a five-year gap between the next two sets, and a one-year gap for the sets of bars on the right. This makes the growth of the labor market appear deceptively rapid in the early years compared to the later years. Let's put a note in the chart warning the reader.

- Click the mouse pointer in the Formula Bar. (Forgot where the Formula Bar is? See page 4.)

- Enter the following text in the Formula Bar (without quotation marks): "Note: Years are not evenly spaced." Press the Enter or Return key on your keyboard.

The text you entered in the Formula Bar will appear in a "Text Box" in the center of your chart. It will be surrounded by a special "active object" border made up of dots: ▫▫▫▫▫. It may be a little hard to see clearly because of the bars behind it.

- Place the mouse pointer directly on the border around the Text Box. When it is correctly positioned, it will change to a white arrow with four small black arrows pointing in different directions: ⬚

- Press and hold the (left) mouse pointer. Drag the text window to a position below the labels on the horizontal axis so that the left side on the "N" in "Note" lines up with the "1" in "1960" (as shown below). Move the mouse pointer to a position off the chart and click the mouse pointer to deselect the text box.

0 ⌐ ▭▭▭◢ ▭▭▭◢ ▭▭▭◢ ▭▭▭◢ ▭▭◢

   1960   1970   1975   1980   198?

Note: Years are not evenly spaced.

With the text box selected, you can change the font or font size as you did with the chart title, and you can edit the text by placing the mouse pointer on the text and clicking once so that it changes to the "I-beam" shape.

The connection between a chart in an Excel workbook and the data on which that chart is made is dynamic. That is, if the data change, those changes will be immediately reflected in the chart. To see this, do the following:

- Click the worksheet tab titled "Civilian Labor Force."

- Change the word in cell B2 from "Males" to "Men," and change the word in cell C2 from "Females" to "Women."

- Return to the chart by clicking the "Chart1" worksheet tab. Notice how the chart legend has changed.

In this example, a change of labels in the data changed the legend in the chart. If, however, the numbers in any of the cells containing data were changed, the height of the bars in the chart would also change.

▼ Previewing a Printout

Although there is a Print speed button, you can often save time and paper by previewing a printout before it is actually printed.

- With the chart displayed on your screen, click the Print Preview button on the Standard Toolbar: ▣.

The Print Preview screen opens. The Print Preview screen gives you the best representation of how the chart will look when it is printed.

- Place the mouse pointer on the part of the screen showing the chart. Notice the pointer is shaped like a small magnifying glass: ◿.

- Place the mouse pointer over the chart legend. Click the (left) mouse button. An enlarged view of the area around the mouse pointer will enable you to examine details more closely.

- Notice the mouse pointer has returned to being an arrow. Click the mouse button again, and the view will return to its original magnification.

The print preview screen also allows you to change some of the characteristics of the printout. You can, for example, add text to very top of the page (in the "header") and the very bottom of the page (the "footer"). You also can control exactly how large the chart is on the printed page, whether it is centered, the width of the margins, and other things. For this chart, it is best to leave these things alone, but there will be times when you will want to make these changes. Let's modify the printout by adding your name to the right side of the header.

- The upper part of the screen has a row of buttons. Click the <u>Setup...</u> button. This will open the Page Setup dialog window, which will have several file folder tabs at the top. Each allows you to control different aspects of how the printout will appear.

▼ Adding Headers and Footers to a Printout

- Click the Header/Footer tab. The dialog window should look like that shown below.

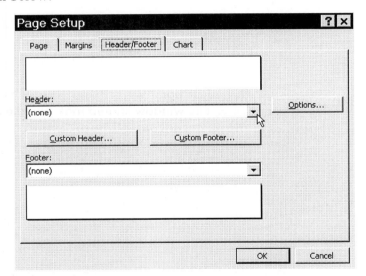

There are two ways of changing the headers and the footers that appear on the printed page. Excel has a number of preset headers and footers, which show such things as today's date and the name of the owner of the Excel software (which was entered when the program was installed). In addition, you can enter a "custom" header or footer, which will allow you to use anything for a header or footer. If, for example, you were submitting a printout from Excel in response to a homework assignment, you might want to have the course name and your name appear in the header.

You can use a preset header by clicking the small arrow to the left of the "Header:" field in the dialog window. (The illustration above shows the mouse pointer on this arrow.)

- Click the arrow allowing you to use a preset header. Scroll down through the list that opens. Click one of the preset headers. Then click the "OK" button at the bottom of the dialog window.

You should see your choice at the top of the page. The preset headers give you an easy way of selecting one of several useful headers, but sometimes you don't want that restriction. Let's make a header that has only your name on the right side.

- Click the Setup button and return to the Header/Footer part of the Setup dialog window.

- Click the ⟨Custom Header...⟩ button on the dialog window. The Header dialog window will open. The window has three fields for you to enter headers for the left, center, and right-hand portions of the header. One or more of these fields will contain text from the preset header you tried above.

- Erase the contents of all non-blank fields by clicking the mouse pointer in each field, highlighting all the text in the field, and then pressing the Delete key.

- Click the mouse pointer in the window for the right section and enter your name. The window should look like the picture below (except with your name, of course).

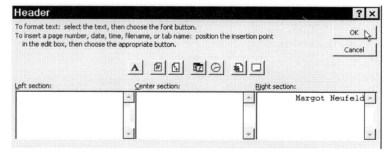

- Click the "OK" button to return to the Page Setup dialog window. Check the two preview windows to be certain the header is correct. If it is, click the "OK" button. This will return you to the Print Preview screen, with the new header displayed.

- Click the ⟨Print...⟩ button. One or more dialog windows will open concerning the print. If Windows has been properly set up, just click "OK" in each of these dialog windows, and your chart will be printed.

- Be sure to save the worksheet in its final form by clicking the Save button.

▼ Numerical Summaries

We will look further at graphical data presentations, but first let's consider the issues of numerical summaries, the core of descriptive statistics. There are a couple of approaches to descriptive statistics, the mean-variance approach and the quantile approach. Both approaches are frequently used, but the former is much more important in inferential statistics. One method starts with the *mean,* the other with the *median.*

When a set of numbers is reduced to a single descriptive statistic, that statistic should give the maximum information about the set of numbers. The mean (or arithmetic mean) is commonly known as the average, by far the most widely used descriptive statistic. The other commonly used measure of central location is the *median,* which, in a sense, lies in the middle of a set of numbers. Let's use Excel to examine the differences between these two measures. We can use Excel's built-in *functions,* which saves us from having to specify exactly how the statistic is calculated.

- Open the "File" menu from the Menu Bar and click "New." A dialog window entitled "New" will open. Simply click the "OK" button. A new workbook will open.

- Double click the worksheet tab "Sheet1." The name "Sheet1" will be highlighted, and you will be able to change that name. Change it to "Num Smry."

- Drop the "File" menu again and click "Save As...." A window will open similar in appearance to the "Open File" dialog window discussed earlier (page 5). Pay attention to the location where you want the file saved! Look opposite the words "Save in:." If you see ☐ My Documents ▾ , Excel will save the workbook in the folder named "My Documents," on the hard drive of the computer you are working on. If you are using your own computer, that's probably a pretty good place. If you are using a lab computer, or any computer you don't necessarily expect to use with this book next time, it would be better to store the file on a diskette. Click the arrow on the right side of the field and look for "3½ Floppy (A:)." Select that and be sure you have a diskette in the A drive. If you plan to save the workbook on the same diskette that has the data for this book, save it in the "Chap_2" folder by double clicking on that folder's icon in the large field in the dialog window. After doing that, the field should contain the names of the other workbooks in that folder (Ch2_data.xls and Labor.xls).

- Enter the name "Chap2.xls" in the "File Name:" field which is second from the bottom in the dialog window. The name you enter should replace a name like "Book2.xls." Press the Enter or Return key or click the "Save" button.

- In the first column (cells A1:A5), enter the numbers 10, 20, 30, 40, 50.

- In cell A7, enter the label "Mean" (without quotes).

- In cell A8, enter the label "Median" (without quotes).

- Click on cell B7 to make it active.

▼ Using the Formula Palette

In the previous chapter you learned how to directly enter an Excel formula into a worksheet cell. When you need to enter a formula containing one or more functions, Excel's Formula Palette makes the task much easier.

- With cell B7 active, click the Edit Formula button (=) located on the left side of the Formula Bar (p. 4). This will open the Formula Palette (shown below).

Most recently
used function

On the left side of the Formula Palette you will see a button with the name of the most recently used function on it ("SQRT" in the picture). If you want to use that function, simply click the button. To use another function, click the small arrow to the right of that name.

- Click the small arrow to the right of the name of the most recently used function. A list will drop down. This list contains the names of other functions of other recently used functions.

- Click the last choice on the list ("More Functions…"). The Paste Function dialog window will open.

The Paste Function dialog window gives you access to all of Excel's built-in functions. The window contains two lists. The one on the left is labeled "Function Category" and the one on the right is labeled "Function Name." Both lists have scroll bars that can be used to see choices not immediately visible. When you highlight a function, a description of that function appears in the window. This is very useful when you know what you want done but don't know the name of the Excel function that will do it.

- From the "Function Category" list, choose "Statistical" by placing the mouse pointer on that word and clicking the mouse button once. The word will then appear in white letters with a black background, and the choices in the "Function Name" list will change.

- In the "Function Name" list, choose "AVERAGE." The dialog window should look like the picture below. Notice the brief description of the function whose name has been chosen.

Description of Selected Function

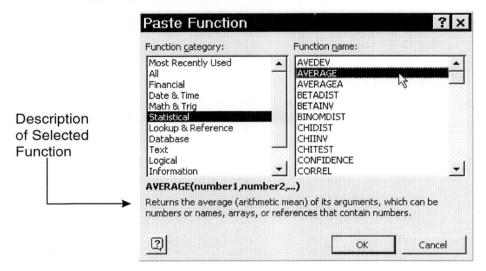

- Click the "OK" button. The Formula Palette will expand to include a dialog window for the AVERAGE function. Although different functions will have different dialog windows, all have certain features in common, as shown in the picture below:

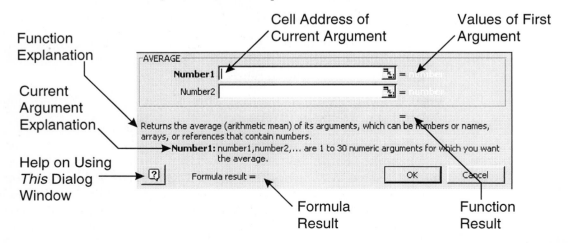

A function will have an *argument* or *arguments* from which it will derive a *result.* (Arguments are also often called *parameters.*) In the case of the AVERAGE function, the numbers to be averaged are the arguments and the value of the average is the result.

The dialog window provides quite a bit of information to help you use the function. Two fields are provided for you to tell Excel the cell addresses (or values) of the arguments. The first one is labeled **Number1** (in bold). The bold indicates that Excel requires you to provide information in this field. The second field, Number2, is not bold. You may use this field, but you don't have to. Usually it won't be used.

The dialog window explains what the function does and also explains the arguments. The argument with the insertion point is the *current* argument; that is the one explained. If you click the mouse pointer in another argument field, the explanation changes to that argument. In the case of AVERAGE, however, both arguments are the same.

Once you have entered values or cell addresses in an argument field, the values Excel will use in the calculations (usually the cell contents) appear to the right of the field. Excel also provides the function result and the formula result. When a formula consists solely of a single function (as in this case), the two will always be the same.

- The cell addresses that we want Excel to average are A1:A5. Unfortunately, the dialog window completely covers them. Move the dialog window by placing the mouse pointer anywhere in the window except a button or argument field, press the (left) mouse button, and drag the window down and to the right so that you can see columns A and B.

- Place the mouse pointer in the "Number1" field and click. An insertion point will become visible in the field.

- Although you could enter the cell addresses directly with the keyboard, use your mouse to perform the operation to "select" cells A1 through A5. When you finish, these cells will have a moving border surrounding them.

- Immediately to the right of the field where you have entered the addresses is a field in which Excel shows the *values* in those cells (10, 20, 30, 40, and 50). Checking this field helps you be sure you have given Excel the correct cell addresses.

- Look at the Function Result. You should see the value "30," which is the average of 10 through 50. Since the formula in cell B7 only has the AVERAGE function, you should also see "30" displayed as the Formula Result.

- Click the "OK" button at the bottom of the dialog window.

The dialog window will close and cell B7 should show "30." Look at the Formula Bar. It should contain "=AVERAGE(A1:A5)." This is what the Formula Palette has entered into the cell. You could achieve the same result by entering this yourself, but it is usually wise to use the Formula Palette unless you are very familiar with a particular Excel function.

- Use the Formula Palette to have Excel calculate the median of the numbers in cells A1:A5 and place the result in cell B8. The median function is in the same category as the mean function ("Statistical") and has the name MEDIAN. Be sure to check the Formula Bar that an Excel function has been entered. When you finish, your worksheet should look like the picture below:

	A	B
1	10	
2	20	
3	30	
4	40	
5	50	
6		
7	Mean	30
8	Median	30

▼ Exploring the Difference Between the Mean and the Median

For the data originally entered, the mean and median are the same, 30. To understand differences and the advantages and disadvantages of each of these measures, let's experiment with the types of changes that can cause these two statistics to differ.

- Change the value of the number in cell A5 from 50 to 523. The value of the mean changes to 124.6, but the value of the median does not change.

In a list of five numbers sorted in order, the median will always be the third number. The median divides the list into two equal-sized groups: those that are smaller than the third number (the first two numbers) and those that are greater (the fourth and fifth).

- Change the value of the number in cell A1 from 10 to -100. The mean will fall to 102.6, but the median remains unchanged. The list of numbers is still in order, and 30 is still the third number. There are still two numbers in the list greater than 30 and two numbers smaller than 30.

- Change the value of the number in cell A1 from -100 to 55. In addition to the mean changing, the median also changes—to 40. 30 is still the third number in the list, why has the median changed to 40? With 55 as the first number, the list is no longer in order. Let's resort the list.

▼ Using the Sort Buttons

- Select the cell region A1:A5.

- Click the Sort Ascending button ⬆↓. The list is put in order, and 40 is now the third number.

If the number of numbers in the list is odd (like five), and the list is put in order, the median will always be the middle number. What if the number of numbers in the list is even?

- Double click cell B7. Change the "A5" in the formula "=AVERAGE(A1:A5)" to "A6."

- Change the "A5" in the formula in cell B8 to "A6."

- Enter the number 610 in cell A6.

The mean showing in cell B7 should now be 213, and the median showing in cell B8 should now be 47.5. The number of numbers in the list is now six. There is no single middle number. Instead, the numbers in positions 3 and 4 are in the middle. In a sense, we can think of the middle as lying halfway between position 3 and position 4. There is, of course, no number, between the 40 in position 3 and the 55 in position 4. Instead, the median is defined as the number *halfway between* the two values 40 and 55. This is the same as the average of 40 and 55:

$$\frac{40+55}{2} = \frac{95}{2} = 47.5$$

- Change the number in cell A6 from 610 to 40. What is the median now?

Remember that the median will be halfway between the number in position 3 and the number in position 4 only if the list is sorted. Putting the value 40 at the end of the list makes the list out of order.

- Resort cells A1:A6 using the method described on page 59 (be sure to include A6 in the selected region). Is the median now halfway between the number in position 3 and the number in position 4? If you have done this correctly, both A3 and A4 should have the value 40.

- Change the number in position 4 (cell A4) from 40 to 42. The median is now 41, the number halfway between 40 and 42.

- Change the number in cell A6 from 523 to 521. The median should still be 41, and the mean should change to 118.

These examples only looked at sets of five and six numbers, but the definition of the median can be applied to any size set. If the set of numbers is ordered from highest to lowest, the median will either be the value of the middle number (if the set has an odd number of numbers) or halfway between the values of the two middle numbers (if the set has an even number of numbers).

▼ Measures of Dispersion

If the first and most important descriptive statistic is a measure of location, what is the second most important? For the mean-variance approach, it is the *variance* or *standard deviation* of the data. These are both closely related measures of dispersion—they indicate how far the individual data items are likely to be from the mean. Although Excel has built-in functions to calculate the variance and standard deviation, we will first use Excel to calculate these "by hand" to better see exactly what they measure.

The formulas for the sample variance and standard deviation are:

$$\text{variance} = s^2 = \frac{\sum (x - \bar{x})^2}{n - 1}$$

$$\text{standard deviation} = s = \sqrt{s^2}$$

The instructions below will direct you in the construction of a worksheet to calculate these formulas.

- Place the mouse pointer on the heading for row 1 and click the mouse button to select the entire first row. (See page 12 for the location of the row heading).

- Open the "Insert" menu on the Menu Bar and choose "Rows." This will insert a new row above the numbers on the worksheet, moving down the rows already there.

- In cell A1 enter the label "x" (without the quotes).

- Skip cell B1 and enter in cell C1 the label "x bar."

- Enter in cell D1 the label "x-x bar."

- Enter in cell E1 the label "(x-x bar)2."

- Select C2 to make it the active cell and begin entering a formula by typing an equal sign ("=").

- Place the mouse pointer on cell B8 (where the mean is now displayed) and press the mouse button. Look at the Formula Bar. You should see "=B8."

- Before pressing the Enter key, press the F4 (on a PC) or the COMMAND and T key (on a Mac) to make the address absolute. The Formula Bar should show "=$B$8."

- Press the Enter key, and the mean, 118, should be displayed in cell C2. (Note: It is important to follow the instructions in entering a *formula* and not just the *number* result.)

- Copy the formula in cell C2 to cells C3 through C7. The absolute address in cell C2 should copy unchanged, and all the cells in column C should display the same value (118).

Column D will be used to calculate the difference between each of the x values in column A and the mean of all of the x's in column C. Enter the formula in cell D2 to calculate the difference between the value of x in row 2 (the number in cell A2, which is 20) and the mean of the x's in cell C2.

- Make D2 the active cell, and enter "=" to start a formula. Place the mouse pointer on cell A2 and click the mouse button. Enter a minus sign "-." Place the mouse pointer on cell C2 and click the mouse button. The formula in the cell and on the Formula Bar should be "=A2-C2." Notice that relative addresses are used in this formula.

- Press the Enter key, and cell D2 should show -98.

- Copy the formula in cell D2 to cells D3 through D7.

Since relative addressing was used in D2, the address will change as it is copied to each cell. In each case, the number will be the difference between the value of x (column A) for that row and the mean of all of the x's (118), which appears in column C of each row. Cell D7, for example, should display 403.

Column E will be used to square the difference between each x value and the mean of the x's.

- Click cell E2. Enter an equal sign to begin a formula. Click cell D2. Enter Excel's symbol to square a value ("^2"). The formula in E2 should be "=D2^2." Press the Enter key and the value 9604 should be displayed.

- Copy the formula in cell E2 to cells E3 through E7.

- Have you remembered to save this worksheet as you work on it? If not, do it now and do it periodically as you continue to change it.

Because relative addressing was used in E2, the displayed values in E3 through E7 should differ, each being the square of the value displayed in the corresponding cell of column D. Cell E7 should display 162409.

The next step is to sum the values in column E. Although not required by the calculations, the values in column D will also be summed.

- In cell C8 enter the label "Sum."

- In cell D9 enter the label "Variance," and in cell D10 enter the label "Standard Deviation," and adjust column D's width.

- Make D8 the active cell. Use the AutoSum button, Σ, to put the sum of cells D2 through D7 in D8. You must press the Enter key for the result to be displayed. The displayed value in D8 should be 0.

- Make E8 the active cell and use the AutoSum button to put there the sum of cells E2 through E7. The displayed value should be 195586.

Cell E8 evaluates $\sum (x - \bar{x})^2$, the numerator of the formula for the variance (page 60). The next step is to divide this by the denominator, $n - 1$. The number of data values (n) in this table is 6, and $n - 1$ therefore is 5.

- Enter the formula in cell E9 that will divide the value in cell E8 by 5. The value displayed in E9 should be 39117.2.

- Enter the formula in cell E10 that will calculate the square root of the value in cell E9. This requires using the built-in square root function. One way of doing this is to use the Formula Palette. The Function Category is "Math & Trig," and the Function Name is SQRT. The value displayed in cell E10 should be 197.7807.

Check the appearance of your worksheet with the illustration on the next page. If you spot a difference, do not simply change cells in your worksheet so they contain the numbers displayed by the corresponding cells in the illustration. The x values in the A column are going to be changed. Many of the cells contain formulas, and if you do not enter the correct formulas, the effects of changing the x values will not be correctly calculated.

Notice that the sum of the x-x bar (D) column is 0. Some of the numbers in the column are negative and one is positive. Could this be a coincidence of the particular x values used in this example?

The numbers in column E2:E7 are the squares of those in D2:D7. Squaring a number always produces a positive result, and the numbers in

	A	B	C	D	E
1	x		x bar	x-x bar	(x-x bar)2
2	20		118	-98	9604
3	30		118	-88	7744
4	40		118	-78	6084
5	42		118	-76	5776
6	55		118	-63	3969
7	521		118	403	162409
8	Mean	118		0	195586
9	Median	41		Variance	39117.2
10				Standard Deviation	197.7807

E2:E7 are all positive. As long as any of the numbers in D2:D7 are nonzero, the sum in cell E8 must be a positive number.

If most of the numbers in a set of numbers are close to the mean, the differences between each number and the mean will be relatively small, the square of those differences will also be relatively small, and the variance and standard deviation will also be relatively small. Two different sets of numbers could have the same mean and yet differ in how far the individual numbers tended to be from that mean. Let's consider some examples.

- Enter the following numbers in cells A2:A7:
        80, 85, 90, 100, 110, 135.
  As you enter each number, notice that the worksheet immediately changes the calculated values, including the mean shown in column C. Once all six numbers have been entered, the displayed mean should be 100 and the displayed standard deviation should be 20.24846. Observe the values in column D, which show the difference between each x value and the overall mean.

- Copy the contents of cells A2:E10 to A12:E20. If you have forgotten how to copy a set of cells, review the method given on page 33. You now have two tables to calculate variances and standard deviations. (The formulas in C12:C17 still equal B8 instead of B18 since the copied references were absolute. As long as B8 equals B18, this will not cause a problem.)

- Now enter the following set of numbers in A2:A7:
        20, 40, 60, 80, 195, 205.
  These numbers have the same mean, 100, but a higher standard deviation, 80.06248. Again observe the values in column D.

- Compare the two sets of numbers in column A in the two tables on your worksheet. Compare the differences in column D between the numbers in each set and the mean.

Both sets of numbers have the same mean, but the top set has greater *dispersion*. All of the numbers in column D in the top set are greater in absolute value than the corresponding numbers in the bottom set. The individual values in the top set tend to be further from the mean than those in the bottom set, and this difference between the two sets is dispersion. The measures of dispersion—variance and standard deviation—are thus larger for the top set than the bottom set.

- Save the worksheet.

▼ Copying a Range of Cells to a New Worksheet

In the previous chapter you learned a method for using the mouse to copy or move a range of cells. Although convenient, this method is difficult to use if the range is very large or if there is a need for the move or copy to occur between worksheets. Another procedure is preferable for these situations. This procedure involves use of the *Windows clipboard*, a kind of holding area. You *copy* a selected range of cells to the clipboard and then *paste* the range from the clipboard to a new location. Let's do this in preparation for the use of the Descriptive Statistics Analysis Tool:

- Select cells A1:A7.

- Click the Copy speed button 🖺. This will copy the contents of the selected cell to the clipboard. Notice that a moving border appears around the selected range.

- Click the worksheet tab "Sheet2."

- Select cell A1 to make it the active cell.

- Click the Paste button 🖺. Cells A1:A7 on this worksheet will now be a copy of those on worksheet "Num Smry."

The procedure to move a range of cells is much the same. Instead of clicking the Copy button after the range of cells is selected, the Cut button ✂ would be clicked. Like the Copy button, the Cut button copies the selected range to the clipboard. The Cut button also erases the selected range of cells after the Paste button is clicked.

- Rename "Sheet2" to "Desc Stats Tool" (p. 54).

▼ Using the Descriptive Statistics Tool

In addition to the built-in functions, Excel contains a very useful set of analysis tools, which includes tools for statistical analyses. The analysis tools generally perform more complex calculations than does any single function. The results provided by an analysis tool are written to more than a single cell. For some of the procedures, the results will fill many cells.

An important difference between the Data Analysis Tools and the built-in functions is that there is not a link between the cells containing the input and the output of an analysis tool as there is between the cells containing the arguments of a function and the displayed value of the cell with the equation containing the function. If you change the value of the argument cells in a function, the value of the function immediately changes. The output of an analysis tool is numbers; these numbers will not change when the values of the analyzed cells change unless the analysis tool is re-run and the new results overwrite the old.

The Analysis Tools are provided by Excel's Analysis ToolPak. Although the Analysis ToolPak is a standard part of Excel, it must be specifically installed. Excel is often set up without the Analysis ToolPak; fortunately, it is easy to add after installation (see Appendix B).

- Open the "Tools" menu on the Menu Bar. It should appear similar to the picture at the left. If "Data Analysis…" is not on your Tools menu, follow the instructions given in Appendix B.

- Click "Data Analysis.…" The Data Analysis dialog window will open.

- Choose "Descriptive Statistics" by double clicking it or by clicking it once and then clicking the "OK" button. The Descriptive Statistics dialog window will open.

- The first field in the dialog window is labeled "Input Range," and the window opens with an insertion point in it. Use the same mouse operation you would use to select the cell range A1:A7. A moving border will appear around that range of cells, and the address "$A$1:$A$7" will appear in the field. As an alternative to using the mouse, the cell address A1:A7 could be entered directly into the field.

- Click the mouse pointer in the box beside "Labels in First Row." A check mark should appear in the box.

This box needs to be clicked because the cell in the first row (A1) contains a label rather than data. If the first field were given the cell range A2:A7, then the box beside "Labels in First Row" should *not* be checked because the first row (cell A2 in this case) contains data, *not* a label. When an Analysis Tool is "told" the first row contains a label, that label will be used in the Tool's output.

At the bottom of the dialog window is a section called "Output Options." Three radio buttons enable you to specify where you want the output placed. "Output Range" results in the output being placed on this worksheet. "New Worksheet Ply" causes Excel to create a new worksheet with the results, and "New Workbook" creates a new workbook with the results.

- Click the "Output Range" radio button.

- Immediately to the right of the words "Output Range" is an input field. Click the mouse pointer in this field so an insertion point will appear.

- Click cell B1. The address "$B$1" will appear in the "Output Range" field. This establishes the upper left-hand corner of the section of the worksheet where the Tool will place the results.

The four options below the radio buttons let you specify the output you want the tool to produce. At least one of these options must be chosen.

- Click the box beside "Summary Statistics" at the bottom of the dialog window. This option will cause the tool to produce what we generally think of as descriptive statistics.

When you have finished with the dialog window, it should look like the illustration at the top of the next page.

- Click the "OK" button.

The results of the Descriptive Statistics Tool will be in columns B and C and in rows 1 through 16.

When an Excel Analysis Tool finishes, the region where the results are placed will be selected. The Analysis Tool does not adjust the width of the columns so that you can see all of the labels.

- Make sure the region containing the output is still selected.

- Open the "Format" menu on the Menu Bar.

- On the drop-down menu, click "Column." A cascading menu will appear.

- Click "AutoFit Selection" as shown in the second picture on the next page. The widths of columns B and C will automatically adjust.

Descriptive Statistics   ? ✕

Input

Input Range: `$A$1:$A$7`

Grouped By: ⊙ Columns
               ○ Rows

☑ Labels in First Row

Output options

⊙ Output Range: `$B$1`

○ New Worksheet Ply:

○ New Workbook

☑ Summary statistics
☐ Confidence Level for Mean: 95   %
☐ Kth Largest: 1
☐ Kth Smallest: 1

OK   Cancel   Help

Format Tools Data Window Help

🖾 Cells...   Ctrl+1
  Row   ▶
  Column   ▶   ↔ Width...
  Sheet   ▶   AutoFit Selection
                                     Hide
  AutoFormat...   Unhide
  Conditional Formatting...   Standard Width...
  Style...

An alternative to using "AutoFit Selection" on the menu bar would be to double click the border between columns B and C in the column headers. Adjusting the columns is always needed after using an Analysis Tool, and sometimes more than one column will need to be adjusted. In those cases, using AutoFit Selection will adjust all the columns at once.

- Click any visible cell on the worksheet to deselect the region with the results.

As you can see, the Descriptive Analysis Tool automatically provides a number of descriptive statistics.

- Compare the mean, variance (called "Sample Variance"), and standard deviation with those on the "Num Smry" worksheet. Do they agree? (They should.)

- Click the "Desc Stats Tool" worksheet tab to make that the active worksheet.

- Change the "205" in cell A7 to "305." Do any of the descriptive statistics provided by the Analysis Tool change?

As discussed earlier, no link is maintained between the input of an Analysis Tool and its output. Thus when one of the data items changes, the Analysis Tool output is not automatically updated. To update the output of the Analysis Tool, it would have to be rerun.

Let's try the Descriptive Statistics Tool on another set of data.

- Open the workbook "Ch2_data.xls," which is located on the data diskette in the Chap_2 folder.

This workbook contains several worksheets. The first provides data by state on the median value of owner-occupied houses. (Data are from U.S. Bureau of the Census, *Statistical Abstract of the United States: 1994* (114th edition.), p. 736.

- Select the Housing worksheet.

- Use the Descriptive Statistics Tool to summarize the data on the median value of owner-occupied homes (in column B). Have Excel put the results in the region beginning with cell C1. Don't forget to use Format...Column...AutoFit Selection to adjust the column widths.

- If you have done this correctly, the mean should be 84209.80392, while the median is 68900.

Why is the median so much less than the mean in this case? The average value for the state medians is over $84,000, but only half the values exceed $68,900. Consider what must be true about the set of numbers for such a difference to exist. Answering this question requires understanding more about the distribution of data than location and dispersion. A graphical approach can provide insight.

▼ Histograms

One of the best ways to graphically describe a set of data is with a histogram chart. Many statistics texts describe a number of graphical techniques for describing data, but many of them, including stem-and-leaf charts and frequency polygons, are simply variations of histograms.

A histogram groups data into a relatively small number of intervals. A vertical bar chart shows the number of observations in each interval. Let's use Excel to produce a histogram chart of the data on median house value by state. We first must determine the intervals. Although Excel can automatically determine the intervals into which the data are grouped, doing that step manually may produce a better histogram.

From the descriptive statistics, we can tell that the minimum value in the data is 45200 and the maximum is 245300. The range is 245,300 − 45,200 = 200,100. The intervals should be equally sized, but Excel's histogram tool always makes the first and last intervals open ended (no minimum for the first, no maximum for the last). If eight intervals were used, each would be slightly over 25,000 ($\frac{200,100}{8}$). The intervals would be those shown in the table below.

Interval	More than...	But not more than ...
1	45,000	70,000
2	70,000	95,000
3	95,000	120,000
4	120,000	145,000
5	145,000	170,000
6	170,000	195,000
7	195,000	220,000
8	220,000	245,000

Since the largest value in this set of data is 245,300, it lies just above the upper bound of the largest interval. Since the difference is slight, including this value in the largest interval will bend the rules only slightly. Since Excel makes the last interval open, we will simply make that interval contain all data values greater than or equal to 220,000.

For the Histogram Tool to use the intervals (Excel calls them *bins*) that we have selected, the upper bounds of each interval, except the last, must be entered into a section of cells somewhere on the worksheet. Let's use the vertical section beginning with cell C18.

• Enter the label "Interval Upper Bound" in cell C18. Enter the values 70000 in cell C19 and 95000 in cell C20.

These are the upper bounds of the first two intervals.

• Use Excel's "fill" capabilities (see page 30) to complete the rest of the series (95000, 120000, 145000, 170000, 195000, 220000) in cells C20:C25. These values correspond to the values in the right-most column of the table above except that the last one is omitted.

Now you are ready to use the Histogram Tool.

- Open the "Tools" menu on the Menu Bar and select "Data Analysis...."

- When the Data Analysis dialog window opens, select "Histogram." The Histogram dialog window will open.

- The first field of the dialog window is "Input Range," and an insertion point should already be in that field. You need to enter here the cell addresses that contain the state median housing values. Because of the length of the list (greater than can be shown on the screen without scrolling), you may find it awkward to use the normal mouse actions. Let's look at an alternative method for selecting a large number of cells.

▼ Selecting a Range of Cells with the Keyboard

It is possible to use the normal technique of selecting a range of cells by placing the mouse cursor on the first one, pressing and holding the mouse button, and dragging down the column. If you move the pointer below the last visible cell in the column, the worksheet will begin to scroll up. If you move the pointer back up into the cell area, the scrolling will stop. This scrolling can be hard to control, however.

When selecting large regions, it is often easier to use the keyboard than the mouse. Once a cell is selected (by any means) the selected region can be expanded by pressing a Shift key while using the cursor (arrow) keys. Here are step-by-step instructions for this case:

- Select *any* cell in column B. That cell's address will appear (as an absolute address) in the dialog window's Input Range field.

- Press the End key on your keyboard. Release the End key and press the up arrow cursor key. The worksheet will scroll up, cell B1 will have a moving border, and $B$1 will appear in the Input Range field.

- Press and hold a Shift key on your keyboard. Press and release the End key on your keyboard. While holding a Shift key, also press the down-arrow key. The selected region will immediately move down to include all cells until an empty cell is reached. The cell addresses $B$1:$B$52 should appear in the dialog window's Input Range field.

The region is now selected, and we can turn our attention to the rest of the dialog window.

- The next field in the dialog window is "Bin Range." Click the mouse pointer in this field so that it will have an insertion point. The cell addresses that should go in the field are those containing the interval boundaries: C18:C25.

- Click "Labels" so a check appears in the small box.

Notice that when "Labels" is checked, Excel expects to find labels in both the Input Range and the Bin Range. If labels are not included, the first value in the range is interpreted by Excel as a label rather than as data. It is not included in the determination of the histogram.

- Click the mouse pointer in the "Output Range" radio button and then click the mouse pointer in the Output Range field. Click the mouse pointer in cell C27 or enter that address directly in the field.

- Select "Chart Output" at the bottom of the dialog window by clicking the square just to the left of those words so that a check appears.

The histogram dialog window should look like that which appears below. If you have entered any cell addresses directly, it is OK if they appear as relative rather than absolute addresses.

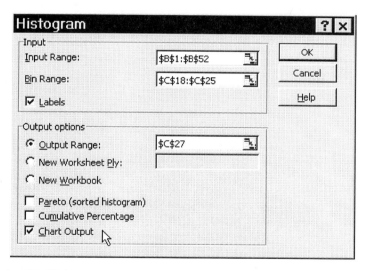

- Click the "OK" button.

You may need to scroll your worksheet in order to completely view the output. Two types of output will appear: a table and a chart. Both provide the same information; the chart is simply a graphic representation of the table. It's hard to clearly see the bars in the histogram because Excel has made the chart too short. Let's make it taller.

- Select the chart by placing the mouse pointer inside the chart on the white border away from any objects and click the (left) mouse button *once*. Small squares (called "handles") should appear at each of the four corners and in the middle of each of four sides. The one at the top of the chart should look like this ▬▪▬. These handles confirm that the chart is selected and enable you to change its size.

- Place the mouse pointer directly over the handle on the middle of the top border of the chart. When it is in the correct position, the mouse pointer will change shape to an arrow with two heads pointing up and down ⇕ .

- With the mouse pointer in the double-arrow shape, press the (left) mouse button and drag the mouse pointer up by four or five cell heights. You should see the boundary around the chart move with the mouse pointer.

- Release the mouse pointer. You have resized the chart to make it taller. It should look like the picture below.

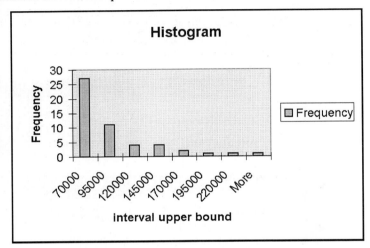

Handles on the side of an object allow you to increase the object's size in only one direction. If you drag a corner handle, however, you can simultaneously make an object (like this chart) both taller and wider.

This histogram shows data that are *right-* or *positively skewed*. Most of the data are close to the lower bound, but there are a number of extremely high values. From the output of the Descriptive Statistics Tool, we know that the median for the data is $68,900. Since this value lies within the interval represented by the first bar, that interval must contain more than half of all state median housing values.

▼ Printing the Worksheet

The process of printing a worksheet is very similar to that of printing a chart. If the amount of information on a worksheet is not too great, it is often useful to have Excel print the entire worksheet on a single sheet of paper. Excel will then reduce the size of charts and print so it will fit on a page. To avoid having Excel reduce things until they are too small, it is useful to have the information on the worksheet in as compact a rectangular area as possible.

To better examine the layout of the worksheet, you can have Excel reduce the size at which things on the worksheet are displayed on your monitor.

- If the chart is still selected (has handles), click the mouse pointer on any worksheet cell of the chart to deselect it.

- On the standard toolbar, click the down arrow to the right of the zoom control 100% ▾ . A list of zoom factors will open.

- Click on 75%. If you cannot see the entire list of states, change the zoom factor to 50% or 25%. Do not worry if the words or numbers become unreadable.

In order to make the information on the worksheet more compact, you should move the histogram chart down and to the left. First "select" the chart.

- Place the mouse pointer approximately in the border of the histogram chart (not on a chart object) and click the mouse button once so that the handles appear in the chart's border.

- With the mouse pointer in the approximate center of the chart, press and hold the (left) mouse button. You can now drag an outline of the chart to a new location. When you release the mouse button, the chart will move to the new position.

- Move the chart down and to the left as shown in the illustration on the next page.

- Deselect the chart by clicking any worksheet cell.

- Open the File menu on the Menu Bar. Select "Page Setup."

- When the Print Preview dialog window opens, click the "Page" folder tab.

- You have a choice between two orientations: *Portrait* and *Landscape*. You should choose Portrait whenever the material you want printed will better fit the page in a vertical orientation than a horizontal orientation. That's the case here, so click the Portrait radio button.

- In the "Scaling" section, click the radio button to the left of "Fit to," and be sure the numbers in the following fields are both 1 (for pages wide and tall). This tells Excel to reduce the print so that everything

Move the Chart from here…

… to here.

will fit on one sheet. The dialog window should look like the picture below:

- Click the "Header/Footer" folder tab, put your name in the header and eliminate the footer. Click the "OK" button.

- Click the Print Preview button to check what the printout will look like. You should see all of the state names (although they may be unreadably small on your screen) and the output of both Analysis Tools (including the histogram chart) on a single page.

- If the print preview checks out, click the "Print" button at the top of the Print Preview screen.

- When your screen returns to the worksheet, change the zoom factor back to 100%.

Look at the table produced by the Histogram Tool in your printout (cells C27:D35 of your worksheet). This table shows the number of observations in each interval. The first interval contains 27 observations, confirming that over half are in this interval. The extremely large values increase the value of the mean but not the median. Finding that the mean is larger than the median (as in these data) is an indication of positive skew. Notice that the output of the Descriptive Statistics Tool includes a measure for skewness (1.84961606). For positively skewed data like these, the skewness measure will be positive.

▼ Sorting the Data

The construction of the histogram will be clearer if you examine the state median housing data sorted by value. This is easy for Excel. Recall that we used the Sort button earlier. Now we look at another method of sorting which gives us a little more control than the Sort button.

- Select the range of cells including both the state names and the median housing values. Because of the amount of data, this is best done by using the keyboard method, the same as was done on page 70 but for a slightly different range. First select cell A1 by clicking the mouse pointer on that cell. Next, hold down a Shift key and press the right arrow key once. This will extend the selected region one cell to the right to include cell B1. Continue pressing a Shift key and press in sequence the End key and the down-arrow key. The selected region will include all the cells in columns A and B down to the bottom of the list, row 52.

- With the region A1:B52 selected, open the Data menu on the menu toolbar and choose "Sort" (see illustration to the left). The Sort dialog window will open.

The Sort dialog window enables you to specify multiple sort keys. In this case only one is needed. Excel will sort the entire selected region. The purpose of the dialog window is to tell Excel which column to sort the region by. The first column contains the state names and the second contains the median housing value. Sorting the region by the first column would alphabetize by state name (which is how it is currently ordered). Instead, we want it sorted by the second column.

At the bottom of the dialog window you will find two radio buttons allowing you to choose either "Header Row" or "No Header Row." This determines whether the dialog window refers to the column by the column's letter (A or B) or the column label in the first row ("State" or "Median Value Owner Occupied").

- Select the "Header Row" radio button.

- Click the small down arrow to the right of the top "Sort By" field. In the list that opens, choose the column containing the median state housing value. Your dialog window should look like the picture below:

- Click the "OK" button. Excel will sort the data. Scroll your worksheet so that you can examine the top of the list (cells A2 and B2 at the top of your screen).

Scroll down until you find a state whose median housing value exceeds $70,000. You have to go pretty far down in the list until you reach New Mexico, which has a median of $70,100. Continue scrolling down until you reach a state with a median value over $95,000. You need only look down a few states before reaching Vermont, whose median value is $95,500. Notice how few states you need to go down before reaching the next interval boundary, $120,000. Each $25,000 increase in median housing value requires moving down fewer states in the list. This confirms what the histogram tells us: although the range of median housing values is quite large, most of them are concentrated near the bottom, below $70,000.

▼ Let Excel Choose the Intervals

It's much quicker and easier to let Excel choose the interval widths than to determine them yourself, but Excel's choices are often not ideal. Let's look at this with a different set of data.

- Click the "Deterg" worksheet tab to bring it to the front and make it active. This worksheet contains information on the cost per load of a number of different liquid and powder laundry detergents available for sale at a single supermarket.

- Sort the data on the worksheet (A1:C33) so that the detergent with the lowest cost per load is at the top and the one with the highest cost per load is at the bottom. First use the keyboard method to select the region. Once selected, sort it by choosing "Data...Sort..." on the Menu bar.

- Choose the Data Analysis from the Tools menu on the Menu Bar and select Histogram.

- When the Histogram dialog window opens, enter the locations of the Cost/Load data in the input range, click the "Labels" and "Chart Output" boxes, and specify that the output should be placed beginning in cell D2. Clear the "Bin Range" field so that it is blank. The dialog window should look like the picture below:

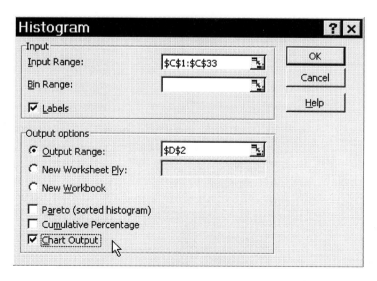

- Click the "OK" button. The results should look like those shown at the top of the next page.

- Compare this histogram with that for the housing data.

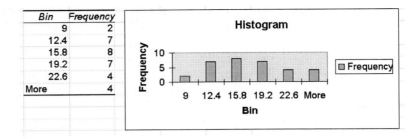

Bin	Frequency
9	2
12.4	7
15.8	8
19.2	7
22.6	4
More	4

In this chart, most of the observations are in the middle rather than close to lowest or highest values. This is reflected in the chart by the fact that the tallest bars are in the center rather than on one side. This distribution is less skewed, or more *symmetric*, than that of the housing data. If a distribution were perfectly symmetric, and you were to draw a vertical line in the center of the histogram chart, the portion of the chart to the left of the line would be a mirror image of that to the right. In such a case, the mean and the median would be the same value.

- Use the Descriptive Statistics Tool to calculate descriptive statistics for the detergent cost/load data. Have the output placed in the region beginning with D10. Adjust the column widths so the output is fully visible.

How do the mean and median compare? The median for these data is 15 while the mean is a bit more than 16.2. These are much closer together, although the fact that the mean is still greater than the median indicates some positive skew. This is confirmed by the positive coefficient of skewness, which is slightly over .50. Although positive, this is less than that of the housing data, which was just under 1.85. Perfectly symmetric data would have a skewness coefficient of zero, and negatively skewed data would have a negative coefficient of skewness.

When the Histogram Tool chooses its own intervals, it forms six intervals, which is a reasonable number, but may not be the most logical grouping for the problem at hand. Unfortunately, the first interval usually consists only of those observations with the minimum value in the data set. For continuous data only one observation may have the minimum value. Excel's self-chosen first interval will thus often have only one observation, although there were two observations for these data.

▼ Embellishing the Histogram Charts

You have already learned how to increase the height of the chart. There are many other changes you can make to the appearance of the chart. To change a chart element, you must first "activate" that element by clicking on it with the mouse pointer. When an element has been activated, it will be surrounded by an active mode boundary: ▓▓▓.

- Place the mouse pointer on the title of the chart ("Histogram") and click the (left) mouse button once. An active mode boundary will surround it. When you move the mouse pointer into that boundary, it will change to an insertion point, allowing you to change the title.

- Change the title of the histogram chart to "Distribution of Detergent Costs per Load" (without the quotation marks).

- Change the horizontal axis label from "Bin" to "Cost per Load."

Clicking on other parts of the chart will enable you to make changes to those parts. Double clicking will typically cause a menu to appear, permitting you to change such characteristics as color.

If you print from Excel while a chart is selected (or an object on it is activated), only the chart will print, and it will fill the output page just as it did when the chart was placed on its own worksheet. This does not necessarily mean that the printed chart will be formatted exactly the same as it would have been had it been on its own worksheet. Printing a small chart that shares a worksheet, for example, often results in large letters in axis labels and titles.

When a chart has been selected, or an object on the chart has been activated, the Menu Bar items change. They become the same as they did when a chart was on a separate worksheet.

- With the histogram chart selected, open the "Chart" menu on the menu toolbar. Choose "Chart Type...." The Chart Type dialog window will open. Click the "Standard Types" folder tab. In the "Chart type" field choose "Line." In the "Chart sub-type" field, select the option in the upper left-hand corner. Click "OK."

- Make the chart taller.

- Eliminate the legend by clicking on it (selecting it) and then pressing the Delete key.

- Make the chart wide enough so that the title is on a single line

- Add the note "Frequency Polygon Chart" to the top of the chart below the title (like a subtitle). Your chart should look like the picture on the top of the next page.

- Print the frequency polygon with your name on the right side of the header and nothing in the footer.

Your histogram chart has become a frequency polygon chart. It displays the same information as a histogram chart but in the form of a line chart rather than a bar chart. Some statisticians prefer a frequency polygon chart because it is more like the density function charts used to display distributions. We will examine these types of charts in later chapters.

▼ Run Charts

The last descriptive statistic we will consider in this chapter is the run chart, which has important application to quality control. Although a run chart is a simple plot of a set of data, it incorporates additional information: order or time. Let's look at an example.

- Click the "Wait" worksheet tab to bring it into view.

This worksheet shows the waiting time spent by each of 36 patients in a physician's office on a single day. The data are ordered so that the first number represents the waiting time of the first patient. The second number is that of the second patient, and so on.

Suppose that we want to determine whether or not there appears to be a problem with the process that this physician uses to schedule his patients. Let's first use the tools already discussed to examine this issue.

- Use the Descriptive Statistics Tool to produce descriptive statistics on patient waiting time.

The mean waiting time for patients in this office is a little over 24.5 minutes, which may indicate a problem. The slightly lower median (23 minutes) suggests a slight positive skew, which is confirmed by the skewness coefficient. A histogram would show that waiting time was approximately symmetric, as might be expected. None of this establishes clearly whether or not there is a problem. Let's see what can be learned from a run chart.

- From the Menu Bar, open the Insert menu. Choose "Chart...." Note that this has exactly the same effect as clicking the Chart Wizard button on the Standard Toolbar.

- In the dialog menu for the first step of the Chart Wizard, choose "XY (Scatter)" as the "Chart Type." Under "Chart sub-type," select the one that marks each point with a dot and connects them with a line (as shown below). Notice that the sample plots show plots with two data series. For the run chart discussed here, only one data series (patient waiting time) will be shown. Click the "Next" button.

- The second-step dialog window is where you give Excel the location of the data to be plotted. Using either the keyboard or mouse method, enter the range address for the data in columns A and B. Be sure to include the labels in row 1. (The keyboard method was explained starting on page 70.)

- Indicate to Excel whether the data are in columns or rows. If you are not sure, try one and look at the sample chart. The correct run chart should have only one plot on the chart. Click the "Next>" button.

Step 3 allows you to set certain options. We will change the titles, add axis labels, and remove the legend. A legend is useful only if a chart has more than one data series and more than one line. In such a case, a legend would tell which line went with which data series. Since only one data series is used in this case, the legend should be eliminated.

- Select the "Titles" folder tab. Change the chart title to "Patient Run Chart" (without the quotation marks). Label the horizontal axis "Patient Number" and the vertical axis "Waiting Time."

- Select the "Legend" folder tab. Set it so that no legend is showing. Click "Next>."

- In the last dialog window, have the chart placed by itself on a new worksheet titled "Run Chart." Click the "Finish" button. Your chart should look like the one below.

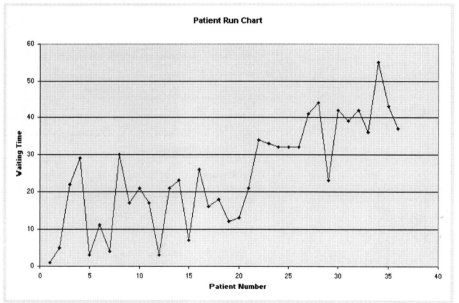

What does the run chart tell us that was not apparent from simply looking at the data? The large up and down movements of the graph suggest the physician often spends an amount of time with a patient that differs substantially from the amount of time scheduled for that patient. In addition, there is an overall pattern to the graph—as the graph moves to the right it had a tendency to move up. This indicates that the average wait for patients seen later in the day is greater than the average wait for patients seen earlier in the day. This suggests that the physician tends to spend a longer time with a patient than the scheduled time. Perhaps too many patients are being scheduled each day.

Univariate (one-variable) descriptive statistics do not reveal the problems with patient waiting time that are clear from the run chart. This is because a run chart shows a relationship between time or sequence (first, second, etc.) and the value of the variable to be analyzed while ordinary descriptive statistics cannot show this relationship. Run charts are used as an aid to understanding a repeated *process*. The manufacturing of a product is such a process, and run charts can be an important tool in quality control for identifying and diagnosing problems. A problem should be suspected whenever the run chart shows a clear pattern, such as a tendency to trend upwards (or downwards). Excessive variation can also be evidence of a problem.

▼ Exercises

1. Use Excel to produce a frequency polygon chart of patient waiting time. Does the picture of the distribution appear symmetrical? Print the polygon chart with your name on the page header.

2. The worksheet named "GDP per cap" provides an international comparison of per capita GDP valued by purchasing power parity for OECD countries in 1991. This measures the value of economic production per person in each country adjusted for differences in prices by country and is an indicator of average economic well-being by country.

   • Sort the data by per capita GDP from lowest to highest so you can easily tell which countries are at the top and which are at the bottom.

   • Produce a histogram chart showing the number of countries with per capita GDP between $0 and $4,000, between $4,001 and $8000, between $8,001 and $12,000, and so on. Do the data appear skewed? If so, in which direction is the skew?

   • Calculate descriptive statistics for these data. Which statistics, if any, confirm the judgment you made above about direction of skew?

   • Print the worksheet on a single sheet of paper showing the list of countries and GDP per capita sorted by GDP per capita, the descriptive statistics, and the histogram chart. Put your name in the header at the top of the page.

3. Amalgamated Hardware is a producer of specialty bolts for the automotive and aircraft industries. One of its products is a 20-centimeter high-strength bolt. The process used to manufacture that bolt is designed to produce bolts whose average length is 20 centimeters. The length of the bolts is carefully controlled, but some process variation is impossible to remove. When the process is operating normally, this

variation is completely random. Amalgamated calculates the average length of a sample of the bolts produced each day. The worksheet "Bolt Length" contains the data for 100 consecutive samples. The average of these 100 numbers is 20.0063, which seems high to management.

• Investigate the source of any possible problem by producing a run chart of the sample lengths. Do you see any pattern in the run chart that might indicate an equipment problem or other problem? If so, what is it?

Chapter 3

▼

Discrete Random Variables and Probability Distributions

Random variables and their probability distributions are the basis of inferential statistics. In this chapter you will explore the relationship between the distribution of a random variable and the distribution of data. You will start with one kind of random variable—discrete—and one way of representing a probability distribution—a table. In later chapters you will learn how to work with discrete probability distributions represented as mathematical formulas or Excel formulas and how to work with continuous random variables. Understanding random variables and probability distributions will help you make sense of sampling distributions.

▼ Probability Distributions

The value of a random variable can never be known in advance of its selection. If you toss a die, for example, you can't be certain before the toss what number will come up (assuming the die is not loaded!). You do, however, know the *set of possible values*. The toss of a die must result in an integer value between 1 and 6. The probability distribution of a random variable gives you this information and also provides you with the probability associated with each possible value.

Sometimes random variables have outcomes that are not quantitative. The outcome of a coin toss, for example, is heads or tails, not a number. The gender of a newborn child is also not a number. These nonquantitative outcomes must be represented as numbers to be usable in Excel. Usually, any integers will suffice, such as 0 for tails and 1 for heads.

Suppose your statistics professor assigns grades purely by chance. You have no idea what your grade will be, but you do know the probability distribution that is shown in the table on the next page:

Grade	Probability
4	.10
3	.20
2	.35
1	.25
0	.10

Remember that Excel's operations require the values of random variables to be numeric. Thus rather than represent the grades as A, B, C, D, and F, they are represented by integers with 4 for A, 3 for B, and so on.

- Start Excel with a new blank workbook.

- Enter this table into an Excel worksheet using Columns C and D and rows 1 through 6. Put the labels "Grade" and "Probability" in cells C1 and D1, respectively. Your worksheet should look like the picture below.

	A	B	C	D
1			Grade	Probability
2			4	0.1
3			3	0.2
4			2	0.35
5			1	0.25
6			0	0.1

- Open the File menu on the Menu Bar and choose "Save As...." If you plan to use the data diskette for this book, first select "3½ Floppy (A:)." When the dialog window shows the folders for each chapter, create a new folder by clicking the "Create New Folder" button at the top of the dialog window: ⌻. This will open the New Folder dialog window. Give the new folder the name "Chap_3" and click "OK." Double-click the icon for the new folder so the workbook will be saved in it. Give the new file the name "CHAP3.XLS."

- An important property of a probability distribution is that the probabilities must all sum to 1.0. Check that this is true in your worksheet by selecting cell D7 and clicking the AutoSum button Σ. Excel should respond by showing a formula to sum cells D2 through D6.

- Press the Enter key and the number 1 should appear in cell D7, confirming that the sum of the probabilities is 1.

▼ Mean and Variance of a Probability Distribution

Let's have Excel calculate the mean and variance of this distribution. We will then explore the *meaning* of the mean and variance of a probability distribution. The formula for the expected value or mean of a probability distribution is

$$E(x) = \mu = \sum (x \cdot P(x))$$

Where $P(x)$ is the probability of the random variable having the value x.

When calculating a formula like this, it is often best to have Excel perform the calculations on the expression within the summation $(x \cdot P(x))$ for each x value and then sum the result of these calculations across all x values. This is the procedure used to calculate the variance and standard deviation of a sample in Chapter 2. This will be done by having cell E2 contain the product of the value of x in cell C2 and the value of $P(x)$ in cell D2. Cells E3 through E6 will have the corresponding products for the values in those rows. The sum of these products will be the expected value.

- To document what you will be doing, enter the label "Mean" in cell E1 and the word "Variance" in cell F1.

The mean or expected value will be calculated in column E and the variance in column F.

- Select cell E2.

- Type an equal sign (=) to let Excel know that you are entering a formula.

- Move the mouse cursor to cell C2 and click the left mouse button. That cell address (C2) should appear after the equal sign in the formula in cell E2. Notice that this is a *relative* address, not an *absolute* address, since there are no $ signs in the address.

- Enter the Excel multiplication symbol (*), and then point to cell D2 and click the left mouse button. The formula appearing in cell E2 should be =C2*D2.

- Press the Enter key or click the check mark in the Formula Bar, and the formula should be replaced by its value, 0.4.

The next step is to copy this formula to the other cells in column E.

- Use the mouse cursor to select cell E2.

- Position the mouse cursor on the fill handle and drag the fill handle downward (while pressing the left mouse button) until the selection border surrounds cells E2 through E6.

- Release the mouse button.

Each cell in the selected region of column E should contain the product of the numbers in columns C and D for that row. Check this by selecting cell E5 and checking the Formula Bar. The formula that appears should be =C5*D5.

The last step is to calculate the sum of the values in cells E2 through E6.

- Select cell E7 and use the AutoSum ∑ button to have Excel automatically enter the formula summing cells E2 through E6. Press the Enter key, and the expected value of the probability distribution (1.95) should appear in cell E7.

We will explore the meaning of a probability distribution's expected value below. First, let's use Excel to calculate the variance of this probability distribution.

The formula for the variance of a probability distribution is given by the following formula:

$$\text{VAR}(x) = \sigma^2 = \sum (x - \mu)^2 \, P(x)$$

The structure of this formula is similar to that of the expected value—a summation of separate terms for each value of x. We will use the same strategy to calculate the formula as we used in that case. In cells F2 through F6 Excel will calculate the value of the expression within the summation (Σ) for the value of x for that row. In F2 we will put the formula to calculate this expression for $x=4$. That formula will then be copied to cells F3 through F6 and cell F7 will sum these values.

- Select cell F2 and type an equal sign followed by a left parenthesis.

- Click the mouse pointer on cell C2 (the value of x for that row), and "C2" should appear after the left parenthesis in the formula in cell F2.

- Type a minus sign and click cell E7. Cell E7 contains the expected value, the "μ" in the formula. Since we will want to copy the formula in this cell to the cells below E2, this address must be made an absolute rather than a relative address. Do this by pressing the F4 function key once. This should change the E7 in the formula to $E$7.

- Type a right parenthesis.

The expression within the parenthesis, "=(C2-$E$7)," corresponds to the "$(x - \mu)$" in the formula for the variance.

- To square the quantity in parentheses, enter "^2" after the right parenthesis.

The formula now corresponds to the expression $(x - \mu)^2$ in the formula for the variance. All that remains is to multiply this by the probability of x, $P(x)$.

- Enter the multiplication symbol, *, and click cell D2. The formula in cell F2 should be "=(C2-$E$7)^2*D2." Press Enter or click the check mark in the Formula Bar and the value 0.42025 will appear in the cell.

- Copy the formula in cell F2 to cells F3 through F6.

- Check to be sure that the copying is correct by examining the value of cell F5. It should be 0.225625. If this is not the value, check the Formula Bar or double click cell F2 to see the formula in the cell. It should be =(C5-$E$7)^2*D5.

If this is not the formula in cell F5, you probably entered the wrong formula in cell F2. Go back to cell F2 and be sure the formula there is =(C2-$E$7)^2*D2, then recopy it to cells F3 through F6.

- Use the AutoSum button to place the sum of the values of cells F2 through F6 in cell F7. This is the variance of the distribution.

If you have done everything correctly, your spreadsheet should look like the picture below:

	A	B	C	D	E	F
1			Grade	Probability	Mean	Variance
2			4	0.1	0.4	0.42025
3			3	0.2	0.6	0.2205
4			2	0.35	0.7	0.000875
5			1	0.25	0.25	0.225625
6			0	0.1	0	0.38025
7					1.95	1.2475

Thus the mean of the probability distribution is 1.95 and the variance is 1.2475. But what is the connection between the mean and variance of a probability distribution and the mean and variance of a set of data? Let's examine that relationship.

▼ Probability Distributions and Data

If we choose one student at random from the class whose grades are described by the probability distribution, there is no way we can know for certain what grade that student will receive. If, however, many students are chosen, the distribution of those grades should be similar to that given by the probability distribution. We can see this by taking advantage of Excel's ability to choose random variables from a probability distribution, a capability provided by Excel's Analysis ToolPack.

- Select the Tools menu from the Menu Bar. Choose "Data Analysis…" from the menu that opens.

- Choose "Random Number Generation" from the list in the Data Analysis dialog window. You may need to scroll the list down before you see this choice. The random number generation dialog window will open.

Let's start by having Excel draw one random number from the probability distribution on our worksheet.

The first two fields in the dialog window for which we must provide information are labeled "Number of Variables" and "Number of Random Numbers." You must enter a number in each field. The labeling of many of these fields is confusing. Despite the way the fields are labeled, the total number of random numbers Excel will draw is the *product* of the numbers you enter in these two fields. Excel will put the random numbers in a rectangular array on your worksheet. The value you put in the "Number of Variables" field determines how many columns Excel will use for the random numbers. The value you put in the "Number of Random Numbers" field determines the number of rows Excel will use. The names Excel uses are consistent with standard statistical practice, where data are usually arranged in rectangular arrays with each observation in a separate row and each variable in a separate column.

- Since our first use of the random number generator will be to generate only one random number, enter the number 1 in both the "Number of Variables" field and the "Number of Random Numbers" field.

The third field in the dialog window is labeled "Distribution." It is here that you tell Excel what kind of random number you wish generated.

- Click on the small downward-pointing arrow ▾ beside the Distribution field.

This will open a list of distributions.

- Choose the "Discrete" distribution.

The distribution you choose determines which fields appear in the dialog window. When Discrete is chosen, the fourth field in the dialog window is labeled "Value and Probability Input Range." In this field you must put the cell addresses of the probability distribution table showing each possible value for the random variable and the probability of that value.

- Click the mouse pointer in the field labeled "Value and Probability Input Range." An insertion point should appear in the field.

- Use the mouse or the keyboard to enter the cell addresses for columns C and D, rows 2 through 6. Note that you do not include the column labels in the first row. If you use the mouse, the cell addresses will appear as an absolute address, but you may enter a relative address with the keyboard.

- Click the radio button beside "Output Range:" and then click the mouse pointer in the adjacent field so that an insertion point will appear. Click the mouse button in cell A1. The absolute address $A$1 will appear in the field. An alternative to pointing at the cell is to type A1 directly into the field. When you have finished, the dialog window should look like the picture below:

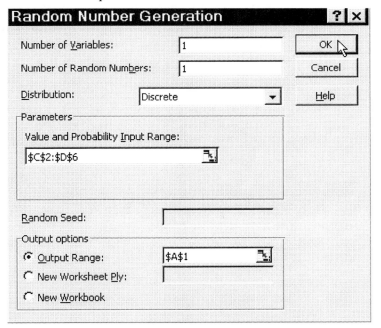

- Click the "OK" button. The dialog window will disappear and cell A1 will contain one of the integers 0 through 4. Since this is a random number, it is impossible to predict in advance what that number will be. Make a mental note of what the number is so that when you repeat this process you can observe how the value changes.

- Open the Tools menu again and again choose Data Analysis.

- When the Data Analysis dialog window opens, notice that Random Number Generation is already chosen. Click the "OK" button. The Random Number Generation dialog window will open.

- Notice that the fields you previously filled out in the Random Number Generation dialog window retain those values. Again, simply click the "OK" button. A warning window will open.

The warning window appears because you have asked the Random Number Generation tool to put a random number in cell A1, but cell A1 already has a value. Putting a new value there will destroy, or *overwrite*, the value already there. Excel is concerned that this may be a mistake. In this case it is not.

- Simply click the "OK" button on the warning window. A new value will be written to cell A1.

Is the new value the same as the old?

- Select a dozen different new random numbers by repeating this sequence: open the Tools menu, select Data Analysis, and click the "OK" button in the next three windows that open. Try to predict which value will come up next. Tally the number of times each comes up in the table below by placing a mark in the "Tally" column each time that value appears.

Value	Tally	Count
4	_____	_____
3	_____	_____
2	_____	_____
1	_____	_____
0	_____	_____
	Sum	

- After you have chosen and tallied all 12 random numbers, enter the total number of times each value occurred. Check your answer by summing these numbers. They should sum to 12.

Let's use Excel to automate the process of drawing many random numbers and tallying how many times each different value occurs.

- Recall the Random Number Generation dialog window (Tools, Data Analysis, "OK").

- Change the value in the Number of Random Numbers field from 1 to 1000. Click "OK" in this window and in the warning window.

Excel will generate 1,000 different random values and place them in column A (A1:A1000). This will, of course, take a bit longer than generating a single random number. While Excel is generating the numbers, you will be able to move the mouse pointer around, but you won't be able to do anything else. You can tell Excel is still busy if the mouse pointer is in the shape of an hourglass.

The next step will be to look at the distribution of these random numbers. We will tally the number of 4's, 3's, 2's, 1's, and 0's and also determine the proportion of the total made up of each of these values. In addition, we will calculate the mean and standard deviations of this group of numbers and compare all this to the probability distribution. We will also look at how these proportions change as the number of random numbers increases.

The thousand values in A1:A1000 are, of course, a sample of 1,000 random numbers. Rather than generating more samples, we will take the ten numbers in A1:A10 as a sample of ten random numbers and the 100 numbers in A1:A100 as a sample of 100 random numbers.

Use columns G, H, and I in the same rows as the probability distribution, which will be used to count the number of times each value of the random variable occurs in each of the three samples we will look at.

- Label cell G1, H1, and I1 as shown below:

	G	H	I
1	10 values	100 values	1000 values

In cell G2 we will have Excel put a count of the number of times the value "4" occurs in cells A1:A10. In cell H2 we will put a count of the number of times the value "4" appears in cells A1:A100, and in cell I2 we will put a count of the number of times the value "4" appears in A1:A1000. In cells G3, H3, and I3 we will put a count of the number of times the value "3" appears in each of the same ranges. Rows 4, 5, and 6 will contain similar counts for values "2," "1," and "0." Excel has a useful function named COUNTIF for just this purpose.

- Select cell G2. Click the Edit Formula button ▣. Open the list of recently used functions in the Formula Palette and choose "More functions...."

- In the Paste Function dialog window choose "Statistical" for function category and "COUNTIF" for function name. Click the "OK" button.

The COUNTIF function has two arguments: *Range* and *Criteria*. The *Range* argument is the cell addresses where you want Excel to determine the count for a specific value, and *Criteria* is the value you want counted.

We will first have Excel count the number of times the value "4" appears in the first ten numbers. We will then extend this to have Excel count the other possible values the random variable can have (3, 2, 1, and 0) and do this count for the first 100 numbers and all 1,000 numbers as well as for the first ten.

- Move the dialog window for COUNTIF to the lower right of the screen so you can see all the data on the worksheet.

- Click the "Range" field and use the mouse to select the first 10 random numbers in column A. Press the F4 function key once to make the address absolute ($A$1:$A$10). The contents of this cell can then be copied without this address changing. This address is where COUNTIF will look for the value we want it to count.

- Click the mouse pointer in the criteria field and then click cell C2. The cell address, C2, will go in the field. C2 contains the value "4," which is the number we want counted.

- Press the F4 function key three times. The "C2" in cell G2 should become "$C2." This is a "mixed" address; the column is absolute but the row is not. If the cell containing this address is copied, the row part of this address will change to be the same as the cell to which the address is copied, but the column will always refer to C.

- Click the "OK" button. Check to be sure the value in cell G2 really is the number of 4's in cells A1:A10.

The next step will be to copy the formula in cell G2 to cells G3 through G6. The copied formula in each cell will be slightly different. The Range will always be $A$1:$A$10 (because it is absolute), but the Criteria will change to $C3, $C4, etc., because the row portion of the cell address is relative.

- Copy the contents of cell G2 to cells G3:G6. Check by clicking on cell G6 and verifying that the formula there is "=COUNTIF($A$1:$A$10,$C6)."

- Further check your results by using the AutoSum button in cell G7 to calculate the sum of the values in cells G2:G6. Since G2:G6 contains the counts of all possible values in the ten cells, the sum of those values should be 10.

The formulas in cells H2:H6 should be just like those in G2:G6 except the range should be A1:A100 instead of A1:A10.

- Copy the formula in cell G2 to H2.

- Select cell H2. Click the Edit Formula button (▣). The Formula Palette will open with the COUNTIF dialog fields containing the values currently in cell H2.

- Change the cell address in the range from $A$1:$A$10 to $A$1:$A$100. This will cause COUNTIF to count the number of times each value in the Criteria occurs in the first 100 cells rather than just the first 10.

Notice that the cell address in the criteria field is $C2, the same value you originally entered in cell G2. Copying from G2 to H2 didn't change this address because although G2 and H2 are in different columns, the "$" in front of the "C" in $C2 made the column part of the address fixed. Since G2 and H2 are in the same row, the row part of the address didn't change even though it is relative.

- Click "OK." Cell H2 contains the number of times the value "4" appears in the first 100 random values.

- Copy cell H2 to H3:H6. Look at cell H6. What is the cell address of the Criteria of COUNTIF? As in the case of row G, copying the $C2 from cell H2 caused the row part of the address to change from 2 to 6 ($C6). What is in cell C6? The number 0. Cell H6 thus contains the number of times the value "0" appears in the first 100 random values.

- Use the AutoSum button in H7 to determine the sum of the values in H2:H6. If done correctly, the sum should be 100.

- Follow a similar procedure to put formulas in cells I2:I6. The formulas in column I should refer to A1:A1000 for their range.

- Check your work in column I by using I7 to sum the values of I2:I6. The sum should be 1000.

You now have a table counting the number of times each value appears in the sample. There should be a relationship between the number of times each value occurs in a set of random numbers and the probability of that value occurring. The relationship will be clearer if we convert the number of occurrences to a proportion. That will be done next.

Let's make a comparison table in the region C9:G17.

- Copy the contents of cells C1:C6 to C9:C14. This will provide the first column of the new table giving the possible grade values. The easiest way of copying a small number of cells is to first select the cells to be copied, place the mouse pointer on the cell boundary, and, while pressing the Ctrl key (PC) or OPTION key (MAC), drag the selection outline to the location where you want the copy.

- Copy the contents of cells G1:I1 to D9:F9. This will give a row of labels across the top of the table.

- Enter the label "Distribution" (without quotes) in cell G9.

- Copy the contents of cells D2:D6 to G10:G14. These are the probabilities of each value occurring.

- Enter the labels "Mean" in cell C15 and "Variance" in cell C16.

Cells G15 and G16 should contain the mean and variance of the distribution that are calculated in cells E7 and F7.

- Select cell G15 and enter the formula "=E7." Select cell G16 and enter the formula "=F7."

This section of your worksheet should look like the picture below. This provides the distribution probabilities for comparison with the sample proportions that still need to be calculated.

	C	D	E	F	G
1	Grade	10 values	100 values	1000 values	Distribution
2	4				0.1
3	3				0.2
4	2				0.35
5	1				0.25
6	0				0.1
7	Mean				1.95
8	Variance				1.2475

Next we will put formulas in cells D10:F14 that will calculate the proportion of each sized sample that is equal to the value given in the appropriate row of column C. For example, we want cell D3 to show the proportion of the first ten random values that have the value "4." This would be calculated by taking the number of times the value "4" appears in the first ten numbers (which is given in cell G2) and dividing it by the number of random numbers (ten in this case.)

The instructions below will demonstrate another use of a cell address that is "mixed." In this case the column portion will be relative and the line portion will be fixed.

- Select cell D10. Enter an equal sign to start the formula.

- Click cell G2. "G2" (which contains the number of "4"s in the first ten random values) will be written in the formula. Enter the division symbol ("/" without the quotes). Click cell G7, the number of values being counted, and press the F4 function key twice, which should change the "G7" to "G$7." Check the Formula Bar to be sure the cell contains "=G2/G$7." Press the Enter or Return key.

Cell D10 converts the number of "4"s in G2 to a proportion by dividing it by 10. The next step is to similarly convert all of the other cells in the G2:H6 to proportions.

- Copy the formula in D10 to D11:D14.

The "G2" in the formula in D10 will change to "G3," "G4," "G5," and "G6" as it is copied down because it is a relative address. The "G$7" divisor in G2 will not change because the cells you are copying to are in the same column as D10—which means the "G" part of the "G$7" won't change, and the "$7" part is an absolute address and thus can't change.

- Check the copying by clicking D13 and checking the Formula Bar. The formula should be "=G5/G$7." This converts the number of "1"s in G5 to a proportion.

- Be sure the region D10:D14 is still selected. Copy this region to E10:F14 by placing the mouse pointer on the Fill Handle and dragging it two columns to the right.

Copying the vertical region D10:D14 to the right has the same effect as if we first copied D10 to E10:F10 then copied D11 to E11:F11, D12 to E12:F12, and so on. Let's consider exactly what this does by looking at row 13 as an example.

- Compare the formulas in D13 and E13. Write them both down in the margin at the left.

Recall that D13 converts the number of "1"s in the first 10 values to a proportion. The formula in E13 is "=H5/H$7." The "G5" in D13 has changed to "H5." The numerator in E13 is the cell counting the number of "1"s in the first 100 values. The change from "G5" to "H5" increases the column part of the formula by one because, in copying from D13 to E13, we have moved one column to the right. There is no change in the row part of the formula because D13 and E13 are in the same row.

The "G$7" in cell D13 changes to "H$7" in E13. The denominator thus changes from "10" (in G7) to "100" (in H7). Since the column part of G$7 is relative, the copying changed it as it changed the numerator. Since the row part is fixed, it will remain "7" for all the values in the table.

The result is that E13 now contains the proportion of the first 100 random values that equal "1." Similarly, E14 will calculate the proportion of the 1,000 random values that equal "1." Were we to sum the values in each column (D10:D14, E10:E14, and F10:F14), we would get the value 1.0 in each case.

Each of the cells in D10:F14 should display a number between 0 and 1. The five proportions in each column will sum to 1.0.

Next, put formulas in rows 15 and 16 to calculate the mean and variance of each set of numbers.

- Use Excel's built-in function (by using the Formula Palette) in cell D15 to calculate the average of cells A1:A10. Similarly, in cell E15 calculate the average of cells A1:A100 and in cell F15 calculate the average of A1:A1000. (Note: the Formula Palette initially assumes you want the average of the values above the cell where the average goes. This is *not* what you want, and you will have to change the "Number1" argument field in each case.)

- In cells D16, E16, and F16, use Excel's built-in function to calculate the sample variance (use VAR in the "Statistical" category) of A1:A10, A1:A100, and A1:A1000, respectively.

The table can be made more readable by formatting. Let's format the numbers so that all the proportions, probabilities, and summary statistics are displayed with three positions to the right of the decimal point.

- With the mouse select the region D10:G16. This is the region whose values are to be formatted.

- Click the Increase Decimal button on the Formatting Toolbar once. This should cause all of the values displayed in the table to be rounded to exactly two decimal places. Remember that although the values Excel displays are rounded, if the addresses of these cells were used in formulas in other cells, the values with all of Excel's precision would be used, not the rounded values.

For the proportion receiving each of the grade values and for the mean and variance, notice the pattern that exists as you move to the right. As the number of random numbers increases, the proportion that each value has is usually closer to the probability given by the probability distribution. Sometimes this doesn't happen. The exceptions generally occur when the smaller data set happened to have a proportion that was already very close to the distribution probability. Increasing the size of the data set might result in a proportion that was further from the distribution probability, but this is not what usually happens.

Similarly, as the size of a data set of random numbers increases, the mean and variance of those data generally approach the mean and variance of the probability distribution. In all cases, the values associated with 1,000 numbers should be quite close to those of the probability distribution. Increasing the number of values would bring them even closer, but it should be clear that there is not a lot of room for further improvement. Although a single value of a random variable cannot be predicted, the characteristics of a moderately large number of random variables can be predicted with a fairly high degree of accuracy.

▼ Turning Off Automatic Calculation

With this worksheet, it is easy to look at a different set of random numbers. Excel will, however, recalculate the values of all of the formulas in the workbook each time a single random number is generated. The process of picking new random numbers will be speeded up if we turn off Excel's automatic calculation.

- Open the Tools menu on the Menu Bar and choose "Options...." The Options dialog window will open.

- The Options dialog window has many tab folders. Click on the "Calculation" tab folder.

- In the top left of the dialog window is a region titled "Calculation," with several radio buttons. Click the "Manual" radio button. The dialog window should look like the picture at the top of the next page.

▼ New Random Numbers

Let's generate a new set of random numbers.

- Open the Tools menu, choose Data Analysis and Random Number Generation.

If you have done this chapter in a single session with Excel, the Random Number Generation dialog window will already have the fields filled out. If not, refer to the picture on page 91, except change the value in the Number of Random Numbers field from 1 to 1000.

- Click the "OK" button.

- Give Excel the OK to overwrite existing data.

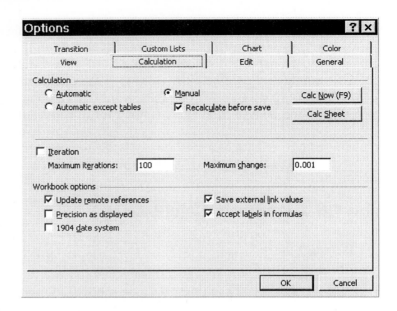

Wait until the mouse pointer is no longer in the shape of an hourglass. (If your machine is fast, the mouse pointer may not have a chance to assume the shape of an hourglass.) Notice that because you set calculation to manual, neither of the tables summarizing the random numbers will have changed until you tell Excel to do a recalculation.

- Tell Excel to recalculate by pressing the F9 function key. You should see the values in the table change.

Look at the new table. You should, of course, see some differences, but the general pattern should be the same. The larger the sample of random numbers, the closer its distribution, mean, and variance will tend to be to those of the probability distribution. You can think of the probability distribution as a description of an infinitely large set of random numbers drawn from that distribution.

▼ Exercises

1. Use the formatting buttons to enhance the appearance of the table in C9 through G16. Use formatting to set the row and column headings apart from the data in the table. Use font changes or style changes to further enhance the visual distinction between the headings and the data.

   When you are finished, print out the enhanced table with your name in the header. Here is how to print just the table (not the entire worksheet).

- Select the region C9:G16 (the new table).

- Open the File menu on the Menu Bar and choose "Print...." The Print dialog window will open.

- At the bottom left of the dialog window under "Print What," click the "Selection" radio button.

- Click the "Preview" button in the bottom left corner of the window.

- Click the "Setup..." button at the top of the Print Preview screen.

- Use the "Page" folder in the Setup dialog window to shift the Orientation from Portrait to Landscape. Increase the scaling to 200%. This will enlarge the selection to be printed so that it will fill more of the page.

- Use the "Margin" folder in the Setup dialog window to center the table horizontally and vertically.

- Use the Header/Footer folder tab to put your name and a title on the page header.

- Click the "OK" button in the dialog window.

- Click the "Print..." button at the top of the Print Preview page.

2. An investor is considering purchasing shares of newly issued stock. Suppose many companies are issuing stock this year. The percentage one-year return to each stock can be treated as an independent random number following the same distribution as shown below:

Percentage Profit	Probability
-100	.10
-60	.20
-10	.15
+10	.15
+60	.25
+100	.15

Use Excel to calculate the mean and variance of this distribution.

Use Excel's Random Number Generator to simulate the one-year return to the following different portfolios consisting of stocks with the probability distribution shown above:

- a portfolio distributed equally among five different companies' stocks.

- a portfolio distributed equally among 50 different companies' stocks.

- a portfolio of distributed equally among 500 different companies' stocks.

For each portfolio determine the proportion of stocks providing each of the six levels of profit and the mean and standard deviation of each portfolio. Create a chart comparing these proportions and summary statistics with the probability distribution like the chart prepared in this chapter. Enhance the appearance of your chart, put your name and a title on the header, and print it out. What conclusions can you draw about the effect of buying more rather than fewer stocks?

3. A city street vendor with a stand outside a large office building must determine whether to sell ice cream or soda tomorrow. The vendor believes that the profit will depend upon the weather. The payoff table is as follows:

	Strategy	
Event	Sell Soda	Sell Ice Cream
Cool Weather	+$40	+$30
Warm Weather	+$55	+$65

Based upon her past experience and the best available weather reports, the vendor estimates the probability of warm weather is .40. (Assume the weather must be either warm or cool.) Determine the expected value and the standard deviation of selling soda and of selling ice cream. Which should she decide to sell? Explain.

Chapter 4

▼

The Binomial Distribution

A number of probability distributions occur so often in practical situations that mathematical formulas for their distributions have been developed. These formulas make it easier to solve problems using these distributions, especially since Excel has built many of the most popular formulas into Excel functions. When a distribution is important enough to get this kind of special attention, it also gets a name. The distribution we will look at in this chapter is the *binomial* distribution. There is one mildly confusing feature in the way distributions are named. The name of a distribution is always singular. For example, the distribution we will look at in this chapter is always called *the* binomial distribution. In reality, however, the binomial distribution is not a single distribution in the same way as the distribution of grades discussed in a previous chapter was a single distribution. The binomial distribution is really a family of distributions. There are an infinite number of different binomial distributions. They all have certain characteristics in common, and they share a common formula.

A random number from the (or a) binomial distribution can be thought of as being generated by a random process that has two possible outcomes; one of the outcomes is of particular significance and is usually termed *success*. The other is termed *failure*. The random process occurs a fixed number of times. The probability of success each time is constant and independent of whether or not a success has occurred any of the other times. The binomially distributed random number is the count of the number of successes that have occurred.

Two things make one binomial distribution different from another. These are the probability that the random process will produce a success and the number of times that the process is repeated. These are the variables of the binomial distribution. Most statistics texts symbolize the probability of the random process resulting in success with p or π. Since the use of p may create confusion with the p value, a concept you will encounter in later chapters, the symbol used here will be π. The number of trials will be symbolized with n.

An example may make this easier to understand.

An automobile salesperson has discovered from experience that two out of every ten persons she takes for a test drive in a new automobile eventually buy a car from her. Suppose one evening she takes five people for a test drive. What is the probability that none of them purchase a car from her?

The random variable here is the number of persons who purchase a car from the salesperson out of the five taken for a test drive. The random process here is the one determining whether or not a person taken for a test drive ends up buying a car. That process has two outcomes: the person buys a car or the person does not buy a car. The outcome we want to count is the first, so we will call the outcome "buying a car" a success. The question tells us that the probability of success is two in ten or .20. In other words, $\pi = .20$. Furthermore, we know that five people are taken on a test drive, so $n = 5$.

Recall that a probability distribution tells us all the possible values that the random variable can equal and the probability associated with each of those values. What are the possible values for this random variable? In other words, what values are possible for the number of people who buy a car out of five who take a test drive? Clearly the lowest value is zero; it is possible that none of those who take a test drive will buy a car. The highest value is five; all of the people who take a test drive might buy a car. All of the integer values in between are also possible. The number of people who buy a car is thus 0, 1, 2, 3, 4, or 5. These are the possible values for the random variable (which we will symbolize as x). For this problem we are to determine the probability that $x = 0$.

Let's further explore this problem by using Excel to simulate the situation.

▼ Simulating a Binomial Problem

- Start Excel and open a new workbook.

- Open the File menu on the Menu Bar and choose "Save As...." In the dialog window that opens, find the directory containing the files for this book or, if you are using a diskette, place the diskette in the A drive and select "3½ Floppy (A:)."

- Create a new folder named "Chap_4" by using the Create New Folder button (⬚). Double click on this folder's icon after it is created.

- Save the workbook using the file name chap4.xls.

The Random Number Generation Tool will be used to simulate the random process of a test driver deciding either to buy or not to buy a car. The first step is to enter a probability distribution for this random process. To buy or not to buy; that is the first question.

Since Excel requires that the outcomes of a random process be represented as numbers, we will use "0" to represent the outcome of *not* buying a car and "1" to represent the outcome of buying a car. The probability of "1" is .20; the probability of "0" is thus .80 (1.00 − 0.20 = 0.80).

- Enter the label "Outcome" in cell H1 and "Probability" in cell I1.

- In cell H2 enter the number "1" (without quotes), which stands for buying a car, and in I2 enter the number ".20" (without quotes), which is the probability that the person taking the test drive will buy a car. This is the value of π just discussed.

- In cells H3 enter the number "0" (without quotes), which stands for not buying a car. The probability of not buying a car is $1 - \pi$. In this case that probability is 0.80, but instead of entering that number, enter the formula "=1-I2" in cell I3 so that later changes in π will cause this probability to be changed automatically. The displayed value should be 0.8.

Now let's use the Random Number Generation Tool to simulate the outcome associated with *one* person taking a test drive.

- Open the Tools menu, select "Data Analysis…," and choose "Random Number Generation." The Random Number Generation dialog window will open.

- Enter "1" for both "Number of Variables" and "Number of Random Numbers."

- Choose "Discrete" for the Distribution. In the "Value and Probability Input Range" put the address for the cell range containing the probability distribution you just entered for whether or not a test driver becomes a buyer, H2:I3.

- Choose "Output Range," and have the Random Number Generation Tool put the output in cell A1.

The completed dialog window should look like the picture at the top of the next page.

- Click the "OK" button in the dialog window.

Look in cell A1. Did the test driver buy the car (cell A1 has a "1") or not (cell A1 has a "0")?

Random Number Generation   ? ✕

Number of <u>V</u>ariables: |1 | OK

Number of Random Num<u>b</u>ers: |1 | Cancel

<u>D</u>istribution: | Discrete   ▼ | Help

┌─ Parameters ──────────────────────────────┐
│ Value and Probability <u>I</u>nput Range: │
│ |$H$2:$I$3   ▇| │
│   │
│   │
└──┘

<u>R</u>andom Seed: | |

┌─ Output options ──────────────────────────┐
│ ⊙ <u>O</u>utput Range: |$A$1   ▇| │
│ ○ New Worksheet <u>P</u>ly: | | │
│ ○ New <u>W</u>orkbook   │
└──┘

- Try another customer by opening the Tools menu again, choosing "Data Analysis," and clicking "OK" in the next three dialog windows that open. See how many times you have to do this before you find a test driver (or another test driver) who decides to buy (that is, before you get a 1 (or another 1) in cell A1.

Let's now simulate an entire evening of five test drivers.

- Open the Tools menu and choose "Data Analysis" again. Click "OK" to recall the Random Number Generation dialog window.

- Change the number "1" in the "Number of Variables" field to "5." Click "OK," and then click "OK" again in the overwrite warning window.

Five numbers will fill the range A1:E1. How many of them are 1's? Although it is not difficult to spot and count the 1's among the 0's, let's have Excel do this for us automatically. One way would be to use the COUNTIF function. A perhaps simpler method would be to simply have Excel add all five numbers together. Since the numbers must each be either 0 or 1, the sum of the five numbers will always equal the number of 1's.

- Select cell F1.

- Click the AutoSum button Σ . The formula to add A1:E1 will automatically be entered in cell F1. Press the Enter key.

Cell F1 now contains a count of the number of 1's in cells A1:E1. This number is a simulation of the number of people out of five test drivers who will buy a car. It is this number in cell F1 which is the binomially distributed random variable.

Try the simulation five to ten times by opening the Tools menu, choosing "Data Analysis" and clicking the "OK" button in the next three dialog boxes. What is the largest number of buyers you get in these simulations? What do you think is the most likely number of buyers the salesperson will get after taking five people on test drives? Your experience should convince you that often none of the five test drivers will purchase a car. Car sales is a tough business.

Rather than repeatedly simulating the purchase decisions of five test drivers, let's have Excel do this for us.

- Recall the Random Number Generation dialog window and change "Number of Random Numbers" from 1 to 1000. Click the "OK" button.

After a delay, Excel will fill the range of cells A1:E1000 with 0's and 1's. We can interpret each row in this range as a separate simulation of the purchase decision of five test drivers.

The next step is to copy the formula in cell F1, which tells the number of 1's in row 1, down column F until a similar sum is available for each row. This could be done by selecting cell F1 and dragging its fill handle down to cell F1000. This is tricky to do, however, because the region is so large. Here is an alternative.

- Click the mouse pointer in the Name Box. (See page 4 if you have forgotten where the Name Box is.) The current value will become highlighted, and you will be able to enter a new value.

- Enter "f1:f1000" (without quotation marks) in the Name Box. Press the Enter key.

The entire region F1:F1000 becomes selected.

- Open the Edit menu on the Menu Bar. Select "Fill." A cascade menu will open to the right, as shown on the next page.

- Select "Down" from the cascade menu. The menu will disappear, and the formula in F1 will be copied to all the cells in the selected region. Column F will provide the number of 1's in each of 1,000 rows. These values in column F are values for specific instances of the binomially distributed random variable, the number of people who buy cars out of five who take test drives.

The next step is to count the number of times each possible different value occurs in column F, determine the proportion of times each value occurs and the average and standard deviation of the values, and compare these with the values given by the binomial distribution functions.

The procedure we will use here is very similar to that used in the previous chapter. Two tables will be created on this worksheet. The first one will tally the number of times each possible value for the number of car buyers occurs in the first 10 rows, the first 100 rows, and the entire 1,000 rows. A second table will convert these counts to proportions and compare them to the probabilities generated by the binomial function. This table will also compare the means and standard deviations of the three groups of rows to those of the binomial distribution.

▼ Counting the Number of Car Buyers

- Prepare labels for the first table in the positions shown in the picture at the top of the next page.

The word "nights" is used in the labels to refer to the fact that the car salesperson takes five people on a test drive in an evening.

- Use the Formula Palette to create an Excel formula in cell I6 using the COUNTIF function to count the number of times the value "5" appears in the range F1:F10. Make the cell addresses in the "range" field

	H	I	J	K
5	Sales	10 nights	100 nights	1000 nights
6	5			
7	4			
8	3			
9	2			
10	1			
11	0			
12	sum			

absolute so they will not change when you copy the formula to other cells. In the "criteria" field put the cell address for the "5" in H6. Make the column reference *absolute* and the row reference *relative* so that if you copy the formula to cells in other rows, the criteria will always refer to cells in column H. The address should have a dollar sign in front of the column letter but not in front of the row number.

The number displayed in cell I6 will be an integer between 0 and 10. The most likely value is 0.

- Copy the contents of cell I6 to cells I7:I11. If the addresses have been specified properly, each cell should display the number of times the value in that row of column H occurs in the range F1:F10. Check this!

- Check the result by selecting cell I12 and clicking the AutoSum button. Press Enter. The displayed value should be 10.

- Copy the formula in cell I6 to cell J6. Double click cell J6 to edit the formula.

- Be sure the last argument of J6 is refers to cell H6 ($H6).

- Change the $F$1:$F:$10 in cell J6 to $F$1:$F:$100. This will change the function so it counts the number of times "5" appears in the first 100 random values.

- Copy cell J6 to J7:J11. These cells should display a count of the number of times each value occurs in F1:F100.

- Select cell J12, click the AutoSum button, and press the Enter key. The sum of J6:J11 should be 100.

- Copy cell J6 to K6. Double click cell K6 so that you can edit the formula.

- Change the $F$1:$F$100 in cell K6 to $F$1:$F$1000. K6 should now display the number of times the value "5" appears in all 1,000 rows of column F.

- Copy the formula in K6 to K7:K11. Each cell should show the number of times the corresponding value in row H occurs in the 1,000 rows of column F.

- Select cell K12 and use the AutoSum button to add the numbers in K6:K11. Verify that the sum is 1,000.

This table gives the results of simulating the car buying behavior of 10, 100, and 1,000 groups of five test drivers. Don't be surprised if there are no cases in which all five drivers bought cars. As we will see, the probability of all five buying a car is quite low.

The next step is to create a table where these numbers are summarized and converted to proportions and compared to the probabilities from the binomial distribution.

- Put the second table in the cells H14:L22 on your worksheet. Set up labels for this table as shown in the illustration below. Many of these labels can be easily copied from the previous table without retyping.

	H	I	J	K	L
14	Sales	10 nights	100 nights	1000 nights	binomial
15	5				
16	4				
17	3				
18	2				
19	1				
20	0				
21	mean				
22	standard deviation				

- Select cell I15. Enter in this cell the formula to divide the value of cell I6 (the number of times all five drivers purchased cars in the group of ten) by the value of cell I12 (the total size of the group of ten—10). Make the row of the address for this latter number absolute but the column relative (I$12). Press the Enter key.

- Copy the formula in cell I15 to cells I16:I20. The values of I15:I20 should sum to 1.

- With the region I15:I20 selected, drag the fill handle to the right, copying the cells in column I to columns J and K.

- Check the formula in cell K20 by selecting that cell. The Formula Bar should show its formula to be "=K11/K$12."

- Enter the formula in cell I21 to calculate the mean of F1:F10, in cell J21 to calculate the mean of F1:F100, and in cell K21 to calculate the mean of F1:F1000. Using the Excel function to do this is explained on page 50.

- Enter the formulas in cells I22, J22, and K22 to calculate the sample standard deviations for F1:F10, F1:F100, and F1:F1000, respectively. The name for the function in Excel that calculates sample standard deviations is STDEV. It can be found with the Formula Palette in the "Statistical" category. Only one argument need be supplied—the range address of the cells for which the standard deviation is to be calculated. This argument should be identical to that used in the AVERAGE function to calculate averages in row 21.

▼ Using the BINOMDIST Function

Cell L15 is to contain the probability that if five people are taken on a test drive, all five will eventually buy a car if the probability that one will buy a car is .20. Another way of saying this is that we want the probability of five successes in five trials given that the probability of success is .20.

- Select cell L15.

- Click the Edit Formula button. From the "Statistical" category choose the BINOMDIST function. Click the "Next>" button.

The BINOMDIST function has four arguments:

1. **Number_s**—short for number of successes. This is the value of the random variable for which we want a probability. Most textbooks symbolize this as x. For cell L15, this argument should be 5 (preferably a cell address of an appropriate cell containing 5) because we want the probability that all five test drivers will buy a car.

2. **Trials**—This argument is the number of trials. Most textbooks symbolize this as n. This is one of the two variables distinguishing one binomial distribution from another. For cell L15 this value should be 5 because five people test drive a car in each evening.

3. **Probability_s**—short for probability of success. Most textbooks abbreviate this either as p or as π. This is the other binomial distribution variable. For cell L15 this value should be .20 because there is a .20

probability that any one test driver will purchase a car. Rather than enter this number directly, enter the address of cell I2 where the value 0.20 was entered for use by the Random Number Generation Tool.

4. **Cumulative**—This argument determines whether Excel provides the probability that the random variable is *equal* to *x* (the value given in the first argument) or the probability that the random variable is *less than or equal* to *x*. The latter is commonly called the cumulative probability. As we will see, this is quite useful for dealing with many binomial problems. For cell L15, however, we want the probability that the number of buyers is equal to five, not less than or equal to five (which must be true). We tell Excel we don't want a cumulative probability by putting the word "false" (without quotes) or the number 0 into the argument field. If we did want a cumulative probability, we would put "true" or the number 1.

- Enter the values of the arguments in the BINOMDIST dialog window. The value in the value field in the upper right-hand corner of the window will show 0.00032 when the correct argument values are entered.

- Use the Formula Palette to enter equations using the BINOMDIST in cells L16 through L20. The arguments for BINOMDIST in each of these cases will be the same as in L15 except for the first, the number of successes. With the correct arguments, the displayed values of L16, L17, L18, L19, and L20 will be 0.0064, 0.0512, 0.2048, 0.4096, and 0.32768. If you choose to copy L16 to L16:L20, be sure you have converted the proper cell addresses in the formula in L15 to absolute.

The last step is to put the mean and the standard deviation of the binomial distribution in cells L21 and L22. If we symbolize the two variables of the binomial distribution, the number of trials, and the probability of success on a single trial, as *n* and π, respectively, the formulas for the mean and standard deviation are

$$\text{mean} = \mu = n\pi$$
$$\text{standard deviation} = \sigma = \sqrt{n\pi(1-\pi)}$$

We will later examine the effect of changes in the value of π on this worksheet, but the value of *n* will not be changed from 5. The value of π is given in cell I2.

- Enter the Excel formula in cell L21 to calculate the mean of the binomial distribution by multiplying the number 5 (*n*) by the value of cell I2 (π). The answer should be 1.

- Enter the following formula (without the quotes) in cell L22 to calculate the standard deviation of the binomial distribution: "=SQRT(5*I2*(1-I2))." The correct value is 0.894427.

- Select the range I15:L22. Use the Increase (and/or Decrease) Decimal button to have all the cells in the selected range display four digits after the decimal point.

- Save the workbook—now and often.

Examine the table. You should see the same general pattern in this table as you saw in the last chapter. As the number of nights increases, the proportion of times the numbers of buyers equaled any of the six numbers should get closer to the binomial probability shown in column L. If the value happened to be very close to the true probability for a smaller number of nights, it might diverge as the number of nights went up, but the divergence should be small. It is even more likely that the mean and standard deviation of the number of sales will get closer to the mean and standard deviation of the distribution as the number of sales goes up.

Notice that you shouldn't be surprised if in your simulation the salesperson never got all five test drivers to buy a car. As we can see from the probabilities in column L, the chance of this happening is .0003, which is less than 1 in 3,000.

The answer to the question given at the beginning of this chapter is that the probability that *none* of the five people test driving the car will purchase one from the salesperson is .3277 (in cell L20). This is the binomial probability of zero successes in five trials given a probability of success in each trial of .20.

▼ Exploring Other Binomial Distributions

Let's use this worksheet to explore a different binomial distribution, one with a different value of π.

- Because of the large amount of calculations on this worksheet, use the Options dialog window from the Tools menu to switch calculation from automatic to manual. More detail on how to do this can be found on page 99.

The great baseball player Babe Ruth came to bat 8,399 times in his illustrious career. 714 of those times he hit a home run. What is the probability that if the Babe came to bat five times in a game he would hit at least one home run?

To use the binomial distribution, we have to assume that the probability of the Babe hitting a home run was constant and independent and equal to $^{714}/_{8399}$. Counting a home run as a *success,* the probability is equivalent to the probability of one or more successes in five trials given a probability of success of $^{714}/_{8399}$.

There are two differences between this problem and the previous car salesperson problem: the value of π has changed, and the values of x for which a probability is needed have also changed. In the car salesperson problem we wanted to determine the probability that $x = 0$ (no test driver would purchase a car). In this problem we wish to determine the probability that $x \geq 1$ (at least one home run will be hit).

We will use this worksheet not only to calculate the probability, but also to simulate the Babe's batting performance in a game.

- The value of π is in cell I2. There are two ways of entering the value in the cell. Excel will allow you to enter a fraction by entering a zero, followed by a space, followed by the fraction. To do this, select cell I2 and enter "0 714/8399" without the quotes and with a space after the "0." An alternative would be to have Excel do the implied division by entering the formula "=714/8399" (no quotes, of course).

If you enter the value as a fraction, when you press the Enter key, the fraction in its reduced form (4/47) will be displayed immediately (if the cell is selected, the decimal equivalent will appear in the Formula Bar). None of the other cells have changed their value, however, because the workbook is set for manual calculation. Cell I3, which is supposed to equal $1 - \pi$, still displays 0.8.

- Recalculate the workbook by pressing the F9 function key.

This changes not only the value of cell I3 (to 0.91499) but also the binomial distribution calculations in cells L15:L22. In fact, these values are sufficient to answer the question. Let's redo the simulation, however.

- Recall the Random Number Generation dialog window from the Data Analysis list chosen from the Tools menu.

If you are still in the same Excel session you were when you generated the simulations for the car buyers, all the fields in the dialog window will already have the correct values. If they do not, look back at the illustration on page 106. Change the value in the Number of Variables field at the top to 5 and the value of the Number of Random Numbers field to 1000.

- Click the "OK" button in the Random Number Generation dialog window. When the overwrite warning window appears, click the "OK" button in it.

- After the random numbers have been generated, recalculate the workbook by pressing the F9 function key. This will update the tables that determine the number and proportion of successes and the mean and standard deviation for the first 10 simulations, the first 100 simulations, and the entire 1,000 simulations.

Look at the table again. Confirm the same general pattern you saw before. As the number of simulations increases, the statistics become closer to those of the binomial distribution given in column L.

You might notice that the displayed value for the probability that the Babe would get five home runs is .0000. Does that mean the probability is zero that he would hit a home run each time at bat? The answer is no. The probability is not zero, but it is so low that when rounded to four decimal places it displays as zero.

- Increase the width of column L to about twice its normal width.

- Click the Increase Decimal button nine times. The displayed probability in L15 is now clearly not exactly zero, but it is a small number.

- Click the UNDO button repeatedly until L15 again displays "0.0000."

What is the probability that the Babe would hit at least one home run? This probability is not directly available in the table, but it can be easily calculated. What needs to be determined is the probability that x is greater than or equal to 1 or $P(x \geq 1)$. This can also be stated as $P(x = 1$ or $x = 2$ or $x = 3$ or $x = 4$ or $x = 5)$. Since these outcomes are mutually exclusive, this probability can be calculated by adding $P(x = 1)$ plus $P(x = 2)$ and so on.

- Select cell M19. Click the AutoSum button, but do not press Enter.

When the AutoSum button is clicked, Excel makes a guess about which cells you wish to add. In this case, Excel assumes you want to add the row adjacent to cell M19 (H19:L19), which is wrong. Fortunately, Excel makes it easy for you to change the cells to be summed by "highlighting" them so that you need only enter the cell address range you want, and it will replace the one Excel guessed. In this case we want to add L15 (which is $P(x = 5)$) to L16, L17, L18, and L19.

- Select the range L15:L19 with the mouse pointer. You should see the formula in cell M19 change to "=SUM(L15:L19)."

- Now press the Enter key. The correct value, 0.3587, will be displayed in M19.

An alternative way of coming up with the same answer would have been to calculate $1 - P(x = 0) = 1 - .6413 = .3587$.

- Double click the "Sheet1" worksheet tab and change its name to "Simulate" (without quotes).

- Change Excel's calculation back to automatic. Open the Tools menu, choose "Options…," click the "Calculation" folder tab in the dialog window, and click the "Automatic" radio button in the upper left-hand corner. Click the "OK" button in the dialog window.

- Save the worksheet.

▼ Using Excel to Solve Binomial Word Problems

Most statistics texts provide binomial tables for use in solving word problems involving the binomial distribution. Instead of a table, Excel's BINOMDIST function can be used. Compared to a table, BINOMDIST is easier to use, more accurate, and can be used to solve a wider variety of problems than any binomial table. To solve a binomial word problem, however, you still must figure out what the problem is asking for, the same as you would if you were to use a table. First, you have to be sure the problem really is one requiring the binomial distribution. Next, you must come up with answers to the following three questions:

1. What is the value of π (the probability of success on a single trial) for the binomial distribution for this question?

2. What is the value of n (the number of trials) for the binomial distribution for this question?

3. For what value or values of x (the binomially distributed random variable) are we to determine a probability?

The third question is the one most likely to be answered erroneously. A systematic approach can help. Once you have determined the value of n (the answer to the second question), you know the set of possible values for x—the integers between 0 and n, including 0 and n. A useful visual aid is to write down the set of possible integers (assuming the set is not too large). Once that is done, determine which integers within the set satisfy the condition in the question for which you want to determine a probability.

There is more than one correct way of using BINOMDIST to solve any binomial word problem. The discussion below will recommend two procedures. One procedure will be used if the probability for only a single value of x is needed. The other procedure is for use when the probability of x being within a range of values is required.

▼ Using BINOMDIST with a Single *x* Value

We saw the BINOMDIST function used to calculate the actual probabilities that each possible number of test drivers would become car purchasers. Although BINOMDIST was used to determine the probabilities of six different x values (0, 1, 2, 3, 4, and 5), a probability was assigned to only a single x value. The method described below is essentially similar to that used previously.

- Double click the "Sheet2" worksheet tab. Change the worksheet's name to "1 value."

- In cell A1, enter the label "n" (without quotes). In cell A2, enter the label "pi" (also without quotes). The adjacent cells (B1 and B2) will be where you put the variables of the binomial distribution.

- In cell A4, enter the label "x." You will put the value of x for which you want a probability in cell B4.

- In cell A6, enter the label "Prob." The formula to calculate the probability will go in cell B6.

- Select cell B6, click the Edit Formula button, and choose BINOMDIST.

- The "Number_s," or number of successes, is the value of x for which we want a probability. This value will go in cell B4. Click the mouse pointer in the "Number_s" field and then click cell B4 so that its address will go in that field.

- The "Trials" field is where the binomial variable n goes. Click the mouse pointer in this field and then click cell B1 to put its address in the field.

- The "Probability_s" field is where the binomial variable π goes. Click the mouse pointer in this field and then click cell B2 to put its address in the field.

- In this case we do not want the cumulative distribution. Click the mouse pointer in the "Cumulative" field and enter the word "false" (without quotes).

- Click the "Finish" button.

Since nothing is currently entered in cells B1, B2, and B4, the BINOM-DIST function will interpret those cells as containing zeroes and will provide a result of 1, which is meaningless in this case. Let's try applying this worksheet to some specific problems.

What is the probability that the toss of two dice will result in two ones?

A "success" in this problem is getting a one. The number of trials is two, since two dice are thrown. Therefore, $n = 2$. The probability of success on a single trial is the probability that a single die will have a one when tossed. Since there are six sides to a die, and only one side has a one, the probability of rolling a one with one die is $\frac{1}{6}$. Therefore, $p = \frac{1}{6}$. The number of successes for which we want a probability is two. Therefore, $x = 2$.

- Enter (without quotes) "2" in cell B1, "0 1/6" (space after "0") in cell B2, and "2" in cell B4.

The answer, 0.027778, will appear immediately in cell B6.

Consider another problem:

A television manufacturer is considering purchasing a chassis component from an independent supplier. In order to test the supplier's quality, the TV manufacturer takes a random sample of 100 components and tests them to see how many are defective. Suppose the component manufacturer's process results in 99% of the chassis components being defect-free. What is the probability that none of the components in the sample chosen by the TV manufacturer will have a defect?

The wording of this problem is trickier than the previous problem. The first step is to decide what outcome is to be considered a "success." The second sentence of the problem suggests that finding a part to be defective is what is to be counted, that is, a defective part is a "success." The next sentence, however, tells the probability of a part being defect-free. A part is either defective or defect-free. The question can be answered by taking either of these outcomes as a "success," although that decision affects the determination of the values of n, π, and x.

Let's take the finding that a part is defective as a "success." The number of trials, n is the number of parts the TV manufacturer tests, 100. The problem tells us that 99% of the parts are defect-free. Thus 1% are defective and the probability of a part being defective (a "success"), π, is .01. We are asked the probability that none of the parts have a defect, so the value of x for which we want a probability is 0.

- Enter 100, .01, and 0 in the appropriate cells. The probability that none of the parts will be defective, .366032, will appear in cell B6.

- Observe cell B2. You entered ".01" but what is displayed is a "0" in the middle of the cell. Why is that?

When you previously entered 0 1/6 in the cell, you not only set a value for the cell, you also set a *format*. To have the cell display the number as you expected, you must change the format.

- Select cell B2.

- Open the Format menu on the Menu Bar. Select "Style...." The Style dialog window will open.

- Set the dialog window so that the Style Name displayed is "Normal." If the window does not come up with that name, click the downward pointing arrow beside the Style Name field and choose "Normal." Click the "OK" button in the window.

- Save your workbook.

Cell B2 should now display 0.01 as you expect.

▼ Using BINOMDIST with a Range of *x* Values

If the range of values includes only a few numbers, one way of determining the probability that the random variable will fall within the range would be to determine the probability associated with each value in the range and add these probabilities together. A different procedure will be used here, one that will work whether the number of values in the range is large or small. This method will use *cumulative* probabilities.

Consider the following problem:

If a fair coin is tossed ten times, what is the probability that the number of heads will be between four and six?

Remember that the outcomes of a binomial random variable are mutually exclusive. If we want the probability that an outcome will have one of several values, we want the sum of the probabilities the outcome will equal each value. In this problem, we want the probability that the number of heads is four or five or six. Although we could determine this by adding the probability that the number of heads is four to the probability that the number is five and the probability that the number is six, cumulative probabilities offer an easier method.

The cumulative probability that the number of heads is six is the probability that the number of heads is zero or one or two or three or four or five or six. This is more than we want. Since we want the probability only of four, five or six, we need to subtract the probability that the number of heads is zero, one, two or three. But this is simply the cumulative probability that the number of heads is three. The difference between the cumulative probability that the number of heads is three and the cumulative probability that the number of heads is six is the probability that the number of heads is four, five, or six.

Notice that if we want the probability of the number of heads being between four and six, we have to subtract from the cumulative probability that x is six the cumulative probability that x is *three,* one less than the lower bound of four.

- Double click the "Sheet3" worksheet tab and change its name to "Range of Values."

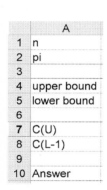

- Enter labels in column A as shown in the picture on the left.

As in the previous worksheet, the values of n and π will go in cells B1 and B2. The upper and lower bounds of the interval will go in cells B4 and B5. Cell B7 will contain the cumulative probability of the upper bound, and cell B8 will contain the cumulative probability of the lower bound *minus one.* Cell B10 will contain the difference.

- Select cell B7. Call up the Formula Palette's BINOMDIST dialog window.

- For the number of successes argument, enter the cell address for the upper bound. For the trials and probability of success arguments, enter the relevant cell address.

- Click the mouse pointer in the Cumulative field and enter the word (without quotes) "true." Click the "OK" button. The value "1" will appear in the cell.

- Select cell B8. Again call up the BINOMDIST dialog window.

- For the number of successes, you want the lower bound *minus one.* Click the mouse pointer in the "Number_s" field to put the insertion point in the field, click the cell that will contain the lower bound, and then enter "-1." The field should contain "B5-1," which instructs to Excel to take the value in cell B5 and subtract 1.

- Enter the same values in the other fields as you did for cell B4. Remember to enter "true" in the Cumulative argument field.

- Click the "Finish" button. Do not be alarmed that the cell displays the "#NUM!" Error.

- Select cell B10. Enter a formula that will take the value of cell B7 and subtract the value of cell B8. Once you press the Enter key, this cell will also display the "#NUM!" Error.

Let's put the data for this problem in the appropriate cells. In this problem we will count heads, so getting a heads from a coin toss is a "success." The coin is tossed ten times. The probability of success on each toss is .50.

- Enter the correct values for n and π in cells B1 and B2.

The range of values for which we want a probability is 4 to 6. Thus 6 is the upper bound of the range and 4 is the lower bound.

- Enter these values in the appropriate places in cells B4 and B5.

Your worksheet should look like the picture below.

	A	B
1	n	10
2	pi	0.5
3		
4	upper bound	6
5	lower bound	4
6		
7	C(U)	0.828125
8	C(L-1)	0.171875
9		
10	Answer	0.65626

The results of the calculations done on the worksheet tell us that the probability of getting six or fewer heads in ten tosses of a fair coin is .82813. The second probability shown, .17188, is the probability of getting *three* or fewer heads—remember that this is cumulative probability of the lower bound *minus one*. The probability of getting between four and six heads is thus .65625.

Consider this similar problem:

If a fair coin is tossed 100 times, what is the probability that the number of heads will be between 40 and 60?

Notice the similarity between this question and the previous question. The number of coin tosses and the range boundaries have both been multiplied by ten. The proportion of possible values within the requested range is the same for both problems. Does it seem to you that the answer to this problem will be the same as that of the previous problem?

- Change the values of *n,* the lower bound, and the upper bound to the values for this problem. The answer is 0.9648, substantially higher than that of the previous problem.

Why the difference? In the beginning of this chapter and in the previous chapter you saw that the larger a sample of random numbers, the more likely it is to resemble the probability distribution that generated the numbers. In both of these problems, the center of the range for which a probability was sought was the mean or expected value ($n \times \pi$, when $n = 10$, $n \times \pi = 5$ and when $n = 100$, $n \times \pi = 50$). A larger sample is more likely to have an actual probability closer to the mean (or expected value) than a smaller sample.

▼ Open-Ended Ranges

Sometimes the range of values for which you want a probability is open-ended. That is, only a lower bound or an upper bound is given. Consider these two questions about 100 coin tosses. "What is the probability that the number of heads will be greater than or equal to 60?" is an example of a range with no upper bound, while "What is the probability that the number of heads will be less than or equal to 45?" refers to an interval with no lower bound. For the binomial distributions, the ranges are not really unbounded, because *x* can never be less than zero or more than *n.*

The first question is equivalent to asking, "What is the probability that the number of heads is between 60 and 100?"

- Use the worksheet to answer this question by using these values for the upper and lower boundaries. The answer you should get is .028444.

Notice the two probabilities in cells B7 and B8. Cell B7 shows that the cumulative probability of the number of heads being 100 is 1. If you toss a coin 100 times, the number of heads *must* be less than or equal to 100. Cell B8 shows the probability of getting 59 or fewer heads. One minus that probability is the probability of 60 or more heads.

The second question is equivalent to asking, "What is the probability that the number of heads will be between zero and 45?"

- Put these upper and lower bounds in the appropriate place in your worksheet.

The "#NUM!" error appears as it did when you were first setting up the formulas. The reason for this error is that cell B8 calculates the cumulative probability of 1 less than the lower bound in cell B5. When cell B5 contains zero (or is blank), B8 tries to calculate the cumulative probability of −1. Since x cannot possibly equal −1, an error is generated.

What we want, of course, is the cumulative probability of 45, and this value is provided in cell B7 (.184101). We can use the worksheet to handle this type of problem, but we have to look for the answer in a different place.

▼ The Wording of Binomial Word Problems

As was mentioned at the beginning of the chapter, decoding the language of a binomial word problem is often the hardest part to solving the problem, especially when the problem is asking for the probability of a range of values for the random variable. This, of course, is not a computer problem or a statistics problem, it's an English problem. Most people taking a statistics course think English is the least of their worries, but when you are faced with solving a binomial word problem (especially on a test), it's the English that will often fail you.

The table below is meant to be an aid to help you decode word problems. When you try to solve a word problem, you must first determine the values of n, π, and the upper and lower bounds for x. The table is designed to help you with the last determination.

What is the probability that in n trials with probability of success in each trial of π, the number of success will be...

	Lower Bound	Upper Bound
...at least y.	y	n
...at most y.	0	y
...more than y.	$y + 1$	n
...fewer than y.	0	$y - 1$
...not fewer than y.	y	n
...not more than y.	0	y

▼ Exercises

1. Suppose the postal service has a delivery goal of delivering 90% of all first-class mail within the same city on the day after mailing. If this

goal is achieved, and 100 items of mail are chosen at random to test delivery time, what is the probability that...

a) at least 90 will be delivered by the next day?

b) more than 95 will be delivered by the next day?

c) all 100 pieces will have been delivered by the next day?

d) fewer than 90 will have been delivered by the next day?

2. Suppose the proportion of automobiles of a certain make that require warranty service is .15. If a particular dealer sells 500 cars...

a) what is the expected number of cars sold by that dealer which will require warranty service?

b) what is the standard deviation of the number of cars which will require warranty service?

c) what is the probability that the number of cars requiring repair will exactly equal the expected value?

d) what is the probability that the number of cars requiring repair will be within two standard deviations of the mean (more than the mean minus two times the standard deviation and less than the mean plus two times the standard deviation)?

3. Format and print out the table in the "Simulate" worksheet showing the simulated and predicted probabilities of Babe Ruth hitting different numbers of home runs for a game in which he batted five times (cells H14:L21). Put a title in the center of the header of your printout that says "Computerized Babe Ruth" (don't put quotes in your title). Put your name on the right side of the header.

4. The "Range of values" worksheet generated an error message if a lower bound of zero was used, as discussed at the end of the chapter. Figure out a way to use the IF function (in the "Logical" category) to alter your worksheet so that the correct answer appears in cell B10 when any valid value between zero and n (including zero) is put in cell B8 as the lower bound of a range.

Chapter 5

▼

The Normal Distribution

The normal distribution is important for two reasons. First, many real-world random variables are either normally distributed or have distributions that can be closely approximated by the normal distribution. Second, properties of the normal distribution place it at the foundation of traditional inferential statistics. Indeed, its importance is suggested by its name. (Another name for the normal distribution is the *Gaussian* distribution.)

Like the binomial distribution (and all other named distributions), there is not a single normal distribution. There are an infinite number of normal distributions. Any binomial distribution could be identified by the value of its variables—the number of trials (n) and the probability of success on a single trial (p or π). Similarly, any normal distribution can be completely identified by the values of two variables—μ and σ. These are the same symbols used for the mean and standard deviation of a population (or probability distribution). They are used for the variables of the normal distribution because the mean of the normal distribution *is* the value of the first variable, and the standard deviation of the normal distribution *is* the value of the second variable. Using the same symbols makes that a snap to remember.

An important difference between the normal distribution and the binomial distribution is that the normal distribution is *continuous* while the binomial distribution is *discrete*. A binomially distributed random variable must have an integer value; a normally distributed random variable can have noninteger values. Between any two integer values there are an infinite number of different values that a normally distributed random variable can equal. Like all continuous random variables, the probability that a normally distributed random variable will equal any *specific* value is zero. Nonzero probabilities can only be assigned to a *range* of values. It is thus not meaningful to ask the probability that a normally distributed random variable exactly equals 2, for instance, because 2 is a specific value and the probability is zero. We could ask the probability that a normally distributed random variable has a value between 1 and 2 or between 1.99 and 2.01. The probability associated with these ranges of values would be nonzero.

Continuous probability distributions are represented by a probability *density* function that differs from the probability *distribution* function used to represent discrete random distributions like the binomial. Probability density functions are often shown graphically. Like a discrete distribution function, the horizontal axis shows the set of values that the random variable could equal. Unlike a discrete distribution function, the vertical axis does not show probability; instead it shows density. A range of values of a continually distributed random variable would define a line segment on the horizontal axis. The *area* between the density function and that segment equals the probability that the random variable will equal a value within that range. Calculating these areas might seem difficult, but Excel provides built-in functions that will do those calculations easily. Density functions are often represented graphically, and we will see an example shortly.

In addition to being continuous, the normal distribution (*all* normal distributions) is unbounded. This means that a normally distributed random variable could take on any value from $-\infty$ to $+\infty$. As we will see, the probabilities associated with intervals far from the mean are very small. So small, in fact, that for practical purposes the distribution can be treated as bounded.

Before looking at how those calculations can be done in Excel, let's look at the shape of the normal density function and how that shape is affected by the values of the distribution's variables, μ and σ.

▼ Graphing the Normal Density Function

Although there are an infinite number of normal distributions, one is particularly important—the "standard" normal distribution, which has a mean equal to 0 and standard deviation equal to 1. Its importance comes from its usefulness in solving problems involving any normal distribution.

The following directions will direct you in preparing a chart of two normal density functions. One will be the standard normal function, whose mean and standard deviation are fixed at 0 and 1, respectively. The other will be a general normal density function with values for the mean and standard deviation that are taken from worksheet cells and that you will be able to change. In this chart the unchanging standard normal distribution will provide a benchmark that makes it easier to see how changes in the mean and standard deviation of the general normal distribution affects the shape of the distribution.

Before the chart can be drawn, a table must be created giving a set of *x* values and the density values associated with each of these *x* values.

- Start Excel with a new blank worksheet and save it in a new directory named Chap_5 as chap5.xls.

- In cell A1 enter the label "x." Column A will be used for the values of the random variables.

- In cell B1 enter the label "general." Column B will be used for the general normal density values.

- In cell C1 enter the label "standard." Column C will be used for the standard normal density values.

- Enter the label "mu" in cell D1 and "sigma" in cell D2.

- Enter the value "0" in cell E1 and "1" in cell E2. These cells will hold the variables for the general normal distribution.

These initial values for the mean and standard deviation of the general normal distribution will make it the same as the standard normal. By changing the values in these cells, however, we will be able to make our general normal distribution be any of the infinite number of normal distributions.

In column A, starting with cell A2, we will put the series of numbers starting with −5 and going to +5. Each time we move down a cell, the value will increment by 0.1. Thus cell A2 will be −4.9, cell A3 will be −4.8, and so on. How many cells will be needed? The general formula is to take the difference between the ending and starting value, divide by the increment, and add 1. Thus if we were going from *a* to *b* by increment *i*, the formula would be: $\frac{b-a}{i}+1$. For this case: $\frac{5-(-5)}{.01}+1=101$. Therefore if the series starts in cell A2, it will end in cell A102.

There are a number of ways of having Excel create the series, but since over 100 cells are involved, using the mouse could be tricky. Try the following method instead.

- Enter "-5" in cell A2.

- Click the mouse pointer in the Name Box, and then enter "a2:a102." Press the Enter key and that region will be selected. The location of the Name Box is shown on page 4.

- Open the Edit menu on the Menu Bar. Click "Fill." A cascade menu will open. Choose "Series...." These menus are shown on the next page.

- The Series dialog window will open. This window allows you to specify how you want Excel to create a series. In this case you want a *linear* series, which means the increment value will be constant, and you want the increment to be 0.1. The increment is referred to in the dialog window as "Step Value."

- Click the mouse pointer in the "Step Value" field and enter the value 0.1. The window looks like the picture below.

- Click the "OK" button and you should see the series in the selected region.

Next we will put the values for the density functions in columns B and C.

- Select cell B2. Instead of using the Formula Palette, click the Paste Function button on the Standard Toolbar: *fx*. In the "Statistical" category, choose the NORMDIST function, and click the "OK" button.

The NORMDIST function has three arguments:

1. **X**—the value of the random variable for which the density is to be determined. Enter a *relative* address for cell A2, which contains −5. The

relative address will change to refer to the cell in the same row of column A when the formula is copied down the column.

2. **Mean**—the mean of the normal distribution. Enter an *absolute* address for cell E1, which contains a 0. When the formula is copied down the column, this reference to cell E1 will remain.

3. **Standard_dev**—the standard deviation of the normal distribution. Enter an *absolute* address for cell E2, which contains a 1.

4. **Cumulative**—Enter the word "false" (without) quotes. This will cause the function to provide the density value. If the word "true" were entered, the cumulative probability would be provided.

The dialog window should look like the picture below.

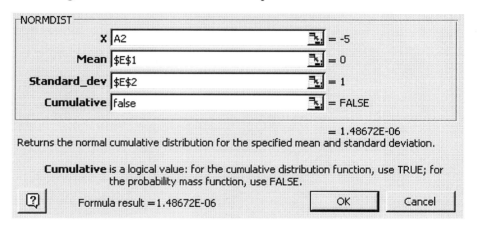

Click the "OK" button. The value that appears in cell B2 is 1.48672E-06, which could also be written as .00000148672. Remember that this very small number is *not* a probability.

The density values for the standard normal distribution will go in column C. The standard normal distribution is the normal distribution with $\mu = 0$ and $\sigma = 1$.

- Select cell C2. Use the Formula Palette and choose NORMDIST again, which will appear as the most recently used function. Use the same values in the argument fields you used above *except* enter the number 0 in the "mean" field and the number 1 in the "standard_dev" field (as shown at the top of the next page). Click the "OK" button. The same value should appear in cell C2 as appears in cell B2.

Next the formulas in cells B2 and C2 must be copied down the columns. Recall that the last value in column A is in A102. The formulas in B2 and C2 need to be copied down to row 102. The instructions which follow use a method similar to that used to generate the series in column A.

```
┌─NORMDIST──────────────────────────────────────────────────────────┐
│              X │A2                              │ �│ = -5       │
│           Mean │0                               │ ▐▄▌│ = 0          │
│   Standard_dev │1                               │ ▐▄▌│ = 1          │
│     Cumulative │false                           │ ▐▄▌│ = FALSE      │
│                                                                     │
│                                                  = 1.48672E-06      │
│  Returns the normal cumulative distribution for the specified mean and standard deviation. │
│                                                                     │
│       Cumulative is a logical value: for the cumulative distribution function, use TRUE; for │
│                 the probability mass function, use FALSE.           │
│  ┌─┐                                                                │
│  │?│    Formula result =1.48672E-06        │   OK   │   │ Cancel │  │
│  └─┘                                                                │
└─────────────────────────────────────────────────────────────────────┘
```

- Click the mouse pointer in the Name Box. Enter the range address B2:C102. Press the Enter key, and the range will be selected.

- Open the Edit menu on the Menu Bar. Choose "Fill," and a cascade menu will open. Click "Down" on the cascade menu. These menus are shown on page 108. Check row 52. Column A should display a 0. Columns B and C should both display the value 0.39894228.

- Save your worksheet now and often!

The last part is to have Excel graph the density values in columns B and C against the x values in column A. The instructions will direct you to create a graph that will share your screen with the values of μ and σ in cells E1 and E2. This will enable you to change those values and immediately see the change in the density function without scrolling your screen or changing worksheets. In an earlier chapter you saw the Histogram Tool place a chart on an existing worksheet. You can create your own chart on a worksheet by using the Chart Wizard button. It is often a good idea to select the data you want used in a chart before clicking the Chart Wizard button.

- Use the Name Box to select the region A1:C102.

- Click the Chart Wizard button 📊.

- In the Step 1 dialog window for the Chart Wizard select an XY (Scatter) plot with the data points connected by lines without markers by making the choices shown at the top of the next page. Click the "Finish" button.

To best see how the mean and standard deviation affect the general normal distribution, let's increase the size of the chart and make some formatting changes.

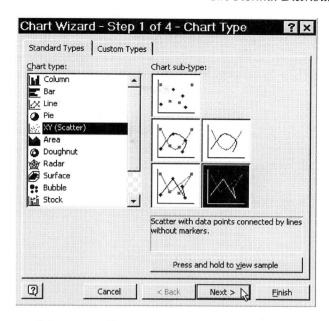

- Using the scroll bars, scroll your worksheet so that cell D1 is in the upper left corner of your screen. Columns A–C will not be visible.

- Select the chart (so that it has handles) unless it is already selected. Place the mouse pointer inside the chart boundary but not on any object in the chart. Press and hold the mouse button and slightly move the mouse. The pointer will change to a "drag" shape: ⊹.

- Drag the chart so that the upper left corner of the chart is near the upper left corner of cell D3.

- Place the mouse pointer on the handle on the lower right-hand corner of the chart. The mouse pointer will change to the object-resize shape: ↖.

- Press and hold the mouse button. Drag the handle to the lower right-hand corner of your screen. The object is to make the chart as large as possible on your screen without making it too large to be seen without scrolling and without covering the first two rows (1 and 2) of the worksheet.

Enlarging the graph has the unfortunate effect of enlarging the letters and numbers. We will reduce them next, and, while we are at it, we will make some changes in the way the chart handles axis values.

- Place your mouse pointer on the legend. Wait a second until a small window opens with "Legend" verifying the pointer is on the legend. Click the (left) mouse button. The legend should have handles indicating that it has been selected.

- Click to open the Format menu on the Menu Bar. When the menu opens, choose "Selected Legend...."

- When the Format Legend dialog window opens, click the Font folder tab at the top.

- On the right side of the dialog window is a field labeled "Size:" which controls the size of the fonts in the legend. Change the size from its present value to "8" either directly in the field or by selecting "8" from the list below the field. Click the "OK" button. The legend should appear visibly smaller.

- Place the mouse pointer on one of the numbers along the *y* (vertical) axis (such as the .45 at the top). After a second, a small window should open with "Value (Y) Axis." Click the (left) mouse pointer. This will select the *y* axis, which you can verify by seeing the handles that appear at each end of the vertical axis (in the positions shown below).

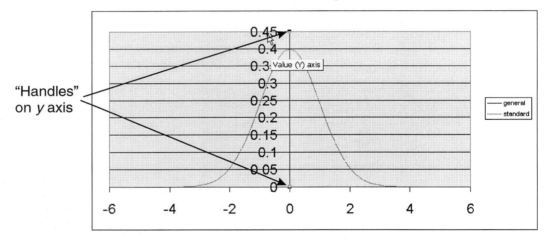

- Open the Format menu on the Menu Bar and click "Selected Axis...." Click the Scale tab. In order to ensure that the scale of the axis does not change when we change the general normal distribution curve, we want to disable the automatic determination of the axis scale. Along the left side of the dialog window is a set of check boxes that currently have check marks. Click the mouse pointer in each box so that the check marks are removed from all boxes.

- Click the Font tab. Change the font size to "8" as you did with the legend. Click the "OK" button.

The last step is to alter the *x* (horizontal) axis.

- Place the mouse pointer on one of the numbers for the *x* axis. A small window will open with "Value (X) Axis." Click the (left) mouse button to select the axis and verify that handles appear at each end of the horizontal axis.

- Open the Format menu on the Menu Bar and click "Selected Axis...."

In addition to preventing Excel from changing the values along the x axis, we will explicitly set those values to agree with the values used in the worksheet (from −5 to +5).

- Click the "Scale" folder tab. Change the values in the "Minimum:" and "Maximum:" fields to "−5" and "5," respectively. Change the "Major unit:" value to "1." This will result in values along the x axis at one-unit intervals. Remove all check marks in the window. The window should look like the picture below.

- Click the "Font" tab and change the size of the numbers to "8" as you did before.

There appears to be only one graph on your screen, but actually there are two identical charts, one on top of the other. Both are the standard normal distribution in which $\mu = 0$ and $\sigma = 1$. You may recognize the shape of the graph; it is often referred to as "bell-shaped." The peak of the graph occurs right above the value 0 on the horizontal axis.

Consider the density graph of the standard normal distribution shown on the next page. Both shaded regions have the same width on the x axis. This means that both represent equal-sized intervals of the random variable. The left region represents the interval from −3.2 to −1.6, while the central region represents the interval from −0.8 to +0.8. Both represent intervals of 1.6. The central region, however, is taller and has a much greater area than the left region. Since the area of the region equals the probability of the interval, this means that a random variable with the standard normal distribution is much more likely to have a value within the range of −0.8 to +0.8 than it is to have a value within the range −3.2 to −1.6. The places where the density function is furthest above the horizontal axis correspond to the values on the horizontal axis that are most likely to occur.

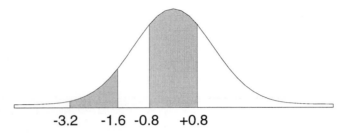

-3.2   -1.6 -0.8   +0.8

Notice on your worksheet how close the density function is to the horizontal axis to the left of −3.5 and to the right of +3.5. There doesn't seem to be any space at all between the horizontal axis and the density function line. The area of the region for the interval between 3.5 and 5.0, for example, looks like it would be zero. In fact the density function line *is* above the horizontal axis and so the region would not be exactly zero. It *would* be so small that it could practically be taken as zero. Although the standard normal distribution is unbounded, the probabilities associated with any region to the left of −3.5 or to the right of +3.5 are so very small that they can practically be treated as zero. For practical purposes, then, the standard normal distribution can be regarded as bounded between −3.5 and +3.5. Other normal distributions will also have practical (but not theoretical) boundaries.

Let's examine the effect that changes in the value of μ and σ have on the shape of the general normal density function.

- Select cell E2 (the value of σ, the standard deviation of the general normal distribution) and change the value from 1 to 1.1. The two density functions are now both clearly visible. Look at the legend to determine which is the "general" normal density function. That is the one that has changed.

- Change cell E2 from 1.1 to 2 in steps of 0.1. Observe the change in the density function with each change in σ.

Increasing the standard deviation makes the curve more "spread out." It also causes the "peak" to be less high. This second change is necessary to keep the entire area below the entire curve at a constant 1.0.

- Change cell E2 back to 1. Now change it to 0.9. Continue decreasing the value of E2 to 0.5 in steps of 0.1.

Since we have indicated in the Chart Wizard that we do not want the y axis rescaled, as the peak of the general normal distribution increases, it moves off the top of the chart on the worksheet. If the chart were taller, we would see that the plot continues to have a bell shape.

Decreasing the standard deviation makes the curve higher and more "pinched." What is the meaning of these changes? A normally distributed random variable drawn from a distribution with small standard deviation is more likely to have a value near the mean than is a normally distributed random variable drawn from a distribution with a large standard deviation. The area of an interval around the mean (like the central region in the preceding picture) will be greater the higher the curve, which happens when the standard deviation is small. The area of an interval away from the mean (like the left region in the preceding picture) will be smaller if the curve is more "pinched," as also happens with a small standard deviation.

Observe now the effect of a change in μ.

- Change the value of E2 back to 1.

- Select cell E1, which contains the mean. Change it to 0.5. Continue increasing the value of E1 by steps of 0.5 to 4.0. Observe the chart. Then change it back to 0 and decrease it by steps of −0.5 to −4.0.

As you see, changing the value of μ shifts the curve right or left. The peak is always above μ, no matter what its value. Since the peak marks the value that the random variable is most likely to be close to, you can see that the mean is always the value that normally distributed random variables are likely to be close to.

- Double click the "Sheet1" worksheet tab and change its name to "Density."

- Save the workbook.

▼ Determining Probabilities from Intervals

Most problems involving the normal distribution fall into two categories: 1) determining the probability of a normally distributed random variable having a value within a given interval, and 2) determining an interval within which the value of a normally distributed random variable will fall with given probability. The first type of problem will be considered first.

- Double click the "Sheet2" worksheet tab and change its name to "Probability."

The normal distribution has a property that made it a particularly convenient distribution to use in the pre-computer days. If we want to find the probability of a randomly distributed variable having a value within a given interval, it is an easy matter to find a corresponding interval for a different normal distribution with the same probability. The importance of this property is that once the relationship between intervals and probabilities is worked out for one particular normal distribution (that is, one particular set of values for μ and σ), a problem involving another normal distribution can be easily transformed to the one for which the probabilities have been worked out. The distribution to which all intervals are converted is the standard normal distribution we have seen, where μ = 0 and σ = 1.

Suppose we have a problem involving determining the probability of a normally distributed random variable having a value within a known interval. That interval will be defined by one or more boundary values. The process of transforming those boundary values to the equivalent values in the standard normal distribution is called the *z transformation.* If the normal distribution of concern in the problem has a mean equal to μ and a standard deviation equal to σ, the *z* transformation is given by the formula:

$$z = \frac{x - \mu}{\sigma}$$

Another name for the standard normal distribution is the *z* distribution, and the value of a standard normal interval boundary corresponding to the value of the interval boundary in a different normal distribution is called a *z* value.

With a computer program like Excel, it would be possible to avoid the *z* transformation. As you have seen, the NORMDIST function has arguments for the mean and standard deviation of the distribution that interests you. The *z* transformation is, however, easy, even trivial, in a spreadsheet. Furthermore, the use of *z* values and the *z* transformation is so deeply ingrained in modern statistical practice that the methods discussed in this book will involve calculating and using the *z* value. Its importance is sufficiently great that Excel provides separate functions for the standard normal distribution. We will use these functions because they are slightly easier to use, although we could get the same result by using the general normal distribution functions.

The discussion below will first consider determining the probabilities associated with intervals in the z distribution. This will then be expanded to an interval for any normal distribution.

▼ Determining Probabilities for *z* Intervals

All intervals for the normal distribution can be classified into one of three types or can be divided into subintervals that can each be classified into one of three types. The first type is bounded from above. It has only one boundary value and the relevant probability is the probability that a standard normal random variable will be less than that value. The second type is bounded from both sides and has two boundary values. The probability we want is the probability that a standard normal random variable falls between these two values. The third type is bounded from below. It has only one boundary value, and the probability of interest is the probability that a standard normal random variable will be greater than the boundary value. Examples of these intervals with the shaded regions whose areas equal the desired probabilities are shown in the pictures below. The "L" and "U" subscripts denote whether the boundary is lower or upper.

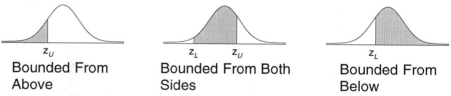

| z_U | z_L z_U | z_L |
| Bounded From Above | Bounded From Both Sides | Bounded From Below |

When you have a problem involving finding the probability of a normally distributed random variable, *you* have to figure out which of the three types of intervals is appropriate for your problem. Excel can't do this for you! The Excel functions are designed to most easily handle intervals like the leftmost one above—where the interval is bounded from above. Using the function to find the areas of other types of intervals requires some additional calculation, as will be illustrated below.

• In cell B1 enter the label "Above," in cell C1 enter the label "Both," and in cell D1 enter the label "Below." These labels correspond to the three interval types pictured above, and the column of each label will be used to calculate the probability for that interval type.

• In cells A4 and A5 enter the labels "zu" and "zl." These will correspond to the boundaries in the picture.

• In cell A7 enter the label "Prob." Row 7 will be where probabilities will be displayed.

▼ Interval Bounded from Above

Suppose that we want to determine the probability that a standard normal random variable will have a value less than −1.0. This value would be an upper bound, and the interval is bounded from above. As previously mentioned, this is the type of interval for which the Excel function is directly designed.

- Enter the number "-1" in cell B4. This is the place for the upper bound value (z_U) for a region bounded from above.

- Select cell B7. Click the Paste Function button and choose "NORMSDIST" from the "Statistical" category. Notice the "S" in the middle of this function's name. That "S" indicates that this is the function for the standard normal distribution. (We could, of course, instead use NORMDIST.)

The NORMSDIST function has only one argument, z, and the probability it provides is a cumulative probability, the probability that a standard normal variable will have a value less than or equal to the argument. This is exactly the type of probability desired in this problem.

- An insertion point should be in the "z" field. If not, click the mouse pointer in the field. Then click cell B4 (you probably will first have to move the window), and its address should appear in the field. Click the "OK" button.

The probability of a standard normal random variable being less than −1.0 is 0.158655, the value that appears in cell B7.

This is the easiest type of problem. When we have to determine a probability of a different type of interval, the way we solve it is to convert that different interval to several intervals bounded from above that can be added or subtracted from one another to get the interval we want. Let's consider an example.

▼ Interval Bounded from Both Sides

Suppose that we wanted to determine the probability that a standard normal random variable would have a value between −0.5 and 2.0. This is an example of an interval bounded from both sides. Consider the interval bounded from below by −0.5 and the interval bounded from above by 2.0. The probabilities of both these intervals can be determined using NORMSDIST as in the previous problem. The interval between −0.5 and 2.0 is simply the difference between these two intervals. This is illustrated in the picture below. The top two intervals are both bounded from above. Their difference, the bottom interval, is bounded from both sides.

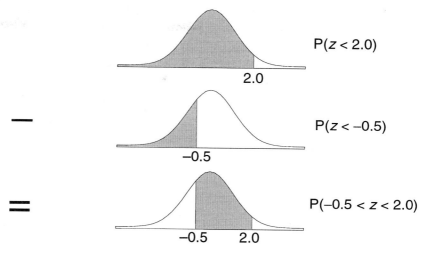

- Enter "2" and "-0.5" in the cells for the upper (zu) and lower (zl) bounds in C4 and C5 respectively. These are the upper bounds for the top two distributions in the picture above.

The NORMSDIST function is cumulative. When it is given a z value, it returns the area to the left of that z value (which equals the probability of a z variable being less than the given value). By calculating NORMSDIST of the values in C4 and C5, we will be determining the shaded areas of the top and second distributions, respectively, in the picture above.

- Click the mouse pointer in cell C7.

- Click the Edit Formula button (▤) on the Formula Palette. Select the NORMSDIST function. Move the window and click cell C4 so that its address will be entered in the z argument field. Click the "OK" button.

The Formula Bar should display "=NORMSDIST(C4)," and cell C7 should display the value "0.977249938." This is the formula to calculate the shaded area in the top distribution in the picture above, and 0.977249938 is that area. This is also the P(z < 2.0). From this we must subtract the shaded area of the middle distribution in the picture above, which equals P(z < –0.5).

- Click the mouse pointer in the Formula Bar to the right of "=NORMSDIST(C4)." An insertion point will appear to the right of the ")."

- Enter a minus sign. Click the NORMSDIST button on the Formula Palette. Click cell C5 so its address appears in the z argument field and click the "OK" button.

The Formula Bar shows that the formula in cell C7 is "=NORMSDIST(C4)-NORMSDIST(C5)." The first term, "=NORMSDIST(C4)" is the shaded area in the top distribution in the picture on page 139. The second term, "NORMSDIST(C5)," is the shaded area of the middle distribution. The formula thus calculates the difference between the two shaded regions, which gives the area of the shaded region of the bottom distribution.

The value of the formula is displayed in cell C7. The probability of a standard normal random variable having a value between −0.5 and 2.0 is 0.668712, as displayed in cell C7.

▼ Interval Bounded from Below

Suppose that we want to determine the probability that a standard normal random variable will have a value greater than 0.7. Recall that the area under the entire density function is 1.0. To determine the probability of a standard normal variable being greater than a given value, we simply subtract the probability of a standard normal variable being *less* than that value from 1.0. This is illustrated in the picture at the top of the next page.

The shaded area of the second distribution is an interval bounded from above. It, therefore, can be determined with NORMSDIST. By subtracting that area from 1.0, we can determine the shaded area of the bottom distribution, an interval bounded from below.

- Enter the value ".7" in cell D5.

- Click cell D7. Click the Edit Formula button. Enter "1-" and then click the NORMSDIST button on the Formula Palette. When the NORMSDIST dialog window opens, enter the appropriate value of the z argument.

The answer to this problem is 0.241964, and this value should appear in cell D7 in your worksheet.

- Save your workbook.

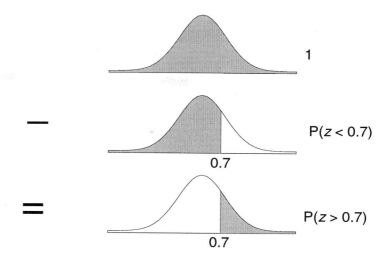

▼ Determining Probabilities for Intervals of Other Normal Distributions

Determining the probability of a normal variable with any value for the mean and standard deviation having a value within a given interval is a two-step process. The first step involves converting the boundary value or values to z values using the formula on page 136. First prepare labels for the new values that will have to be entered.

- In cells A9 and A10 enter the labels "mu" and "sigma," respectively. The adjacent cells in column B will be used to put the mean and standard deviation of the normal distribution.

- In cells A2 and A3 enter the labels "xu" and "xl," respectively. The adjacent cells in column B are where you will put the upper and lower bounds of the interval of values of the normal distribution for which a probability is wanted.

The entries in rows 4 and 5 will be changed so the upper and lower bound z values will be calculated from the corresponding upper and lower bound x values.

Consider the following problem:

Suppose Wednesday sales at a convenience store average $2,000 with a standard deviation of $500. What is the probability that sales for one Wednesday will be below $1,000?

The first step in solving a problem like this is to determine what type of interval the problem is asking for. Are we given one boundary or two? If one boundary is given, is it an upper boundary or a lower boundary? It's a good idea to sketch a picture of the distribution with the interval shown on the horizontal axis. For this problem, the picture is shown below. Clearly it is an interval bounded from above. We can use the worksheet we have already developed. Since column B has already been used for intervals bounded from above, we will use that column in this problem.

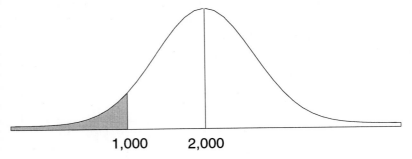

1,000   2,000

- Enter the upper bound, 1000, in cell B2.

- Enter the distribution's mean and standard deviation, 2000 and 500, in cells B9 and B10, respectively.

- Select cell B4. Enter the formula to standardize B2.

To standardize B2 (convert to a z value), you must subtract the mean (in B9) and divide the difference by the standard deviation (in B10). This is the Excel formula: "=(B2-B9)/B10." Verify that this is the z transformation shown on page 136. Press the Enter key.

The standardized value of 1,000 is -2, which appears in cell B4. The probability that sales on a single Wednesday will be less than $1,000 is the same as the probability of a standard normal random variable being less than -2. This probability is .02275, the value that appears in cell B7, since B7 already contains the formula to determine the area to the left of the z value in B4.

- Replace the numbers in C4 and C5 by formulas that will standardize the values in C2 and C3, respectively. These formulas will be similar to that in B4 and should also use the mean and standard deviation in B9 and B10. Both C2 and C3 are blank; Excel will treat their value as 0 in calculating the formulas. The standardized value of 0 in this case is -4, and that is what should be displayed in both C4 and C5 by the standardizing formula.

- Replace the number in D5 by a formula that will similarly standardize the x value in D3. It, too, should initially display -4.

Use the worksheet to solve the following problem:

An automobile manufacturer has determined that the cars in a particular model line have fuel consumption that averages 27 miles per gallon with a standard deviation of 5 miles per gallon. What proportion of cars could be expected to have fuel consumption between 25 mpg and 30 mpg?

The first step is to determine what type of interval applies to this problem (sketch a picture). Since we are given a lower and upper bound, this interval is bounded on both sides, and we can solve it using the Excel formulas in column C.

- Enter the distribution's mean and standard deviation (27 and 5) in the correct cells.

- Enter the interval boundaries (25 and 30) in the correct locations.

The correct answer, .381169 or about 38%, should appear in cell C7.

Try this problem:

A package delivery firm regularly sends trucks between two regional distribution centers. Through careful record keeping, it has discovered that the transit time is normally distributed with a mean of 10 hours and a standard deviation of 2.5 hours. What is the probability that a single truck would make the trip in less than 5 hours or more than 15 hours?

The interval described here is illustrated by the shaded areas in the diagram below. Note that this doesn't fit into any of the three categories in the worksheet. It can, however, be regarded as a combination of those three categories. Two approaches are possible:

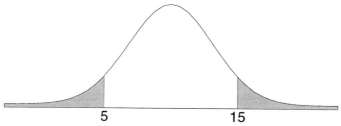

1. The shaded region could be regarded as what's left over when the central region is taken out. Using this approach, you would determine the area of the region above the interval between 5 and 15 and subtract that from 1.0. Perform this subtraction in any handy available cell by using an Excel formula. Use the cell address of the central region for your formula.

2. The shaded region could be regarded as the combination of an interval defined by an upper bound and an interval defined by a lower bound. Using this approach, you would determine the area of the left-tail region bounded from above by 5 and add that to the area of the

right-tail region bounded from below by 15. Do this addition in an available cell near that used above by using an Excel formula.

- Use both approaches to solve this problem. Verify that you get the same answer with each approach. The correct answer is .0455.

- Save your worksheet.

▼ Determining Intervals from Probabilities

A different type of problem that arises with the normal distribution (and other distributions) is one in which you want to determine an interval within which a normally distributed random variable will fall with known probability. Most problems involve one of four types of intervals (illustrated below).

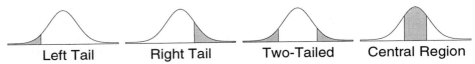

| Left Tail | Right Tail | Two-Tailed | Central Region |

The left-tail and right-tail regions are self-explanatory. An important characteristic of the two-tailed region is that *the areas of the two tails are equal*. The central region has the property that it is centered directly over the mean of the distribution. As a consequence, the two tails that lie outside the region are equal in area.

Let's set up an Excel worksheet that can handle these four cases.

- Double click the "Sheet3" worksheet tab and rename it to "Intervals."

- In the first row of cells, in B1 through E1, enter the labels "Left Tail," "Right Tail," "2-Tailed," and "Central Region."

- In the first column of cells, in A3 through A6, enter the labels "x1," "x2," "z1," and "z2." The rows with a "z" will be where the standard normal boundary values will appear. The rows with an "x" will have the z values converted to correspond with the specific normal distribution of a problem. For those areas that have a single boundary value (left and right tail), the cells adjacent to the x1 and z1 labels will be used. For the two-tail and central region areas, x1 and z1 will refer to the smaller boundary value and x2 and z2 to the larger.

- In cell A8 enter the label "Probability." We will put the probability corresponding to one of the four areas in cell B8.

- In cells A10 and A11 enter the labels "mu" and "sigma." The mean and standard deviation of a problem's normal distribution will be entered in cells B10 and B11.

Excel's NORMSDIST function is a standard normal cumulative distribution function. For problems of this type we need the inverse function, and Excel provides it in a function named NORMSINV. This function has one argument—probability. Excel interprets this as the area of a left tail and returns the corresponding z value. In the "Left Tail" diagram on the previous page, if the probability argument were equal to the area of the shaded region, the NORMSINV function would provide the z value, which is the upper bound of the shaded region. This is the inverse of the NORMSDIST function, which provides the value of the shaded area (representing a probability) when it is given z as an argument.

Suppose, for example, that we want to determine what value has the property that the probability of a standard normal random variable being less than that value is exactly .025. This situation is shown in the graph below, where the shaded left-tail area is equal to .025 and we want to know what is the value of the boundary z.

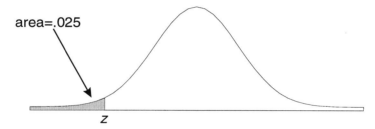

- Enter the value .025 in cell B8.

- Select cell B5 (z1 for the left-tail case), and click the Paste Function button.

- In the "Statistical" category, select NORMSINV.

- NORMSINV has a single argument, probability. Either click the mouse pointer on the cell containing the ".025" you entered above or directly enter that cell's address. Click the "OK" button.

The answer, −1.95996, appears in cell B5. Let's check this by putting this value back in the "Probability" worksheet. We will use that worksheet to have Excel determine the probability of a standard normal variable having a value less than −1.95996. If the answer to this question is ".025," we will have verified that NORMSINV worked in this case.

Although the obvious thing to do would be to simply enter the number "−1.95996" in the appropriate place, that would be only *approximately* correct. Remember that Excel rounds the values displayed in the cells. To use the full precision, we must use Excel to copy the value in B5. This raises another problem. The methods we have previously used to copy the contents of a cell won't do what we want, because B5 contains a *formula*. We don't want the formula copied, we want the *value* copied. Excel provides a way of doing this.

- Select cell B5. Click the "Copy" speed button .

- Click the "Probability" worksheet tab to return to the previous worksheet.

What we want to do is to paste the value of cell B5 (*not* the formula) as the upper bound of an interval.

- Select cell B4. This is the cell where the value is to be pasted.

- Drop down the "Edit" menu by clicking the mouse pointer on "Edit" on the Menu Bar.

- Select "Paste Special…" A small dialog box will open.

- Select "Values" as shown in the picture below. Click "OK."

The value -1.95996 will display in cell B4. Look at the Formula Bar. Does it show the cell as containing a formula or a number? Look at cell B7. This shows the probability of a normally distributed random variable being less than -1.95996. This probability is .025, confirming that -1.95996 is the correct value.

- Click the tab to select the "Intervals" worksheet again.

▼ Going from a Standard Normal Boundary to a General Normal Boundary

What if the problem involves some normal distribution other than the standard normal? Once the answer to the standard normal version of a problem is determined, it is a simple matter to convert that boundary value to a corresponding value for any normal distribution.

Consider the following problem:

The time required for a package delivery firm to deliver a package is normally distributed with a mean of 10 hours and a standard deviation of 3 hours. What delivery time will be beaten by only 2.5% of all deliveries?

A sketch might be helpful in determining which of the four interval types applies to this problem. As with the previous problem, this is a left-tail problem. If only 2.5% of deliveries take less time, the probability of a single delivery taking less time is .025. To convert a standard normal value, z, to the corresponding value, x, in a general normal distribution, the following formula can be used:

$$x = z\sigma + \mu$$

To implement this in Excel, first put the distribution's mean and standard deviation in the appropriate cells.

- Enter the value 10 in cell B10 and the value 3 in cell B11.

- Select cell B3. Enter the Excel formula that will take the z value in cell B5, multiply it by the standard deviation in cell B11, and then add the mean in cell B10.

The answer that appears in cell B3 should be 4.120117. The probability that a transit will require less than about 4.12 hours is .025.

▼ Determining the Boundaries of Other Interval Types— Right Tail

Determining the boundaries of other intervals with the NORMSINV function requires converting the probability associated with that interval into a left-tail area. The properties of the standard normal distribution make this easy: the distribution is symmetric with mean 0, the area under the entire density function is 1.0, and, in the case of the two-tailed and central region intervals, the areas of the two tails are equal.

Suppose that we had a right-tail problem, such as finding the value of z such that the probability of a standard normal variable being greater than z is exactly .25. This situation is depicted in the picture below. The shaded area is known to be .25, but what is the value of z?

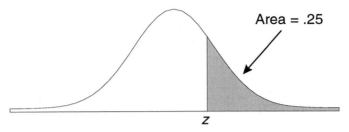

One way of solving this problem would be to subtract the known area from 1. The difference would be the area to the left of z, which is what is needed for NORMSINV. Another approach would take advantage of the symmetry of the normal density function. Consider the diagram below.

The picture on the left is the same as that above except for the addition of a vertical line at the zero mean. The picture on the right shows a normal density function with a shaded area on the left that has the same area, 0.25. How does the value of z in the picture on the left compare to that of z in the picture on the right? The symmetry of the normal density function ensures that each will be the same distance from the mean. Since the mean is zero, both z's will have the same absolute value but different signs. To find the z in the left diagram, we can use NORMSINV to find the z in the right diagram and put a minus sign in front of it to switch the sign.

Let's do this on the worksheet.

- Select cell C5. Click the Edit Formula button.

- Enter a minus sign and then click the NORMSINV button on the Formula Palette. The probability parameter should refer to cell B8. Click the "OK" button.

The value displayed in cell C5 should be 1.959961, the same as that displayed in B5, except for the sign. This is the boundary value for a probability of .025 remaining from the previous problem.

- Enter ".25" in cell B8.

The correct boundary value for this probability, 0.67449, now appears.

To solve a similar problem for a general normal distribution, this z value must be converted to an x value using the approach given on page 147.

- Enter the formula in cell C3 to convert the z value in cell C5 to the corresponding value for a normal distribution whose mean is in cell B10 and whose standard deviation is in cell B11.

The answer displayed in cell C5 should be 12.02347. Cells B10 and B11 still have the mean and standard deviation for the package delivery firm. This value can be interpreted as applying to that distribution. The probability of a delivery taking longer than 12.02347 hours is .25.

▼ Two-Tailed Intervals

The other two boundary types, the two-tailed and central region, are quite similar. Both have an upper and lower boundary that is the same distance from the mean—one above and the other below. The two types have areas (and probabilities) that are complementary—with the same pair of boundary values, they would sum to one. Finding the two boundaries, for example, that define a two-tailed area of .25 is the same as finding the two boundaries that define a central region area of .75.

Consider the two-tailed case. Since both tails have the same area, the area of the left tail is half the total. NORMSINV can easily do this:

- Select cell D5. The calculated value of the lower bound for the standard normal distribution will appear here.

- Click the Edit Formula button and then the NORMSINV button on the Formula Palette.

- Enter "B8/2" in the field for the probability argument. Cell B8 holds the probability. This expression will pass half of that as the argument to NORMSINV. You should see "0.125" in the argument values field.

- Click the "OK" button.

Cell B5 will show -1.15035, the value of z_1.

What about z_2, the boundary for the upper tail? It will have the same absolute value but the opposite sign of z_1.

- Select cell D6. Enter the formula to calculate the negative of the value in cell D5. Press the Enter key.

D6 will display 1.150349. Since there is no minus sign, an additional digit to the right of the decimal point is shown.

- Using the same approach as above (and as shown on page 147), enter the formula in cell D3 to convert the z value in cell D5 to the corresponding value in the normal distribution whose mean and standard deviation are given in cells B10 and B11.

- Enter the formula in cell D4 to similarly convert the z value in cell D6.

The value for x_1 in cell D3 should be 6.548952, and that for x_2 in cell D4 should be 13.45105. For the delivery firm, this means that there is a .25 probability that a delivery will require less than 6.548952 hours or more than 13.45105 hours. Another way of stating this is that there is a .75 (= 1 − .25) probability that a delivery will take between 6.55 and 13.45 hours.

▼ Central Regions

Finding the boundaries of a central region of known area (or probability) is very similar to finding a confidence interval, an important form of statistical inference that you will study later. An example of a problem in which the central region is known is the following:

Within what range of delivery times, symmetrically distributed about the mean, will 25% of all package deliveries fall?

If the central region has an area of .25, the two tails have an area of 1 − .25 = .75. The area of the two tails is one minus the area of the central region. The area of the left tail is half this, or .375. In this way, a central region problem can be converted to a two-tailed region problem. Recall that the lower z boundary value for a two-tailed region was found by dividing the two-tailed region area by two.

- Select cell E5.

- Click the Edit Formula button and select NORMSINV.

- In the probability argument field enter "(1-B8)/2." The argument values field should display "0.375."

Cell B8 contains the probability or area of the central region. This expression will determine the area of the left tail and pass the result as an argument to NORMSINV.

- Click the OK button.

The value of z_1, -0.31864, will appear in cell E5. The upper bound, z_2, will have the same absolute value, but opposite sign, as z_1.

- Enter the formula in E6 to calculate the negative of the number in E5.

The last step is to convert the standard normal values z_1 and z_2 to general normal values x_1 and x_2 using the mean and standard deviation in cells B10 and B11.

- Enter the formulas in cells E3 and E4 to convert the values in E5 and E6, respectively.

The value displayed in E3 should be 9.044082, and that in E4 should be 10.95592. Since the probability in E8 is still .25, the probability of a delivery taking between approximately 9.0 and 10.9 hours is .25. We would expect 25% of delivery times to fall within that range.

- Save your workbook.

▼ The Normal Distribution as an Approximation to the Binomial

One of the reasons for the popularity of the normal distribution is that it can approximate many other distributions, including distributions that are inconvenient to work with without a computer. One of the distributions that has traditionally been approximated by the normal distribution is the binomial distribution. This approximation underlies the traditional approach to making statistical inferences about a population proportion. Although the use of computer programs like Excel makes this unnecessary, this approach still dominates in introductory statistics textbooks. In this section we will use Excel's graphics to compare various binomial probability distribution functions with their approximations using the normal distribution.

The variables of the binomial distribution are n and π (or p), the number of trials and the probability of success on a single trial, respectively. These must be converted to values for the normal distribution's μ and σ using the formulas for the mean and standard deviation of the binomial distribution:

$$\mu = n\pi$$
$$\sigma = \sqrt{n\pi(1-\pi)}$$

We will proceed by creating a binomial table for the case when $n = 100$ and $\pi = .2$, add the corresponding normal approximation for each value of x and then graph the two distributions.

- Open the "Insert" menu on the Menu Bar and select "Worksheet." When the new worksheet is created, change its name to "Binom Approx."

- Place the following labels in the newly renamed worksheet.: "x" in A1, "Binomial" in B1, "Normal" in C1, "n" in D1, "pi" in D2, "mu" in D3, and "sigma" in D4.

- Enter the initial value for n (100) in cell E1 and the initial value for π (.2) in cell E2.

- Enter the Excel formula in cell E3 to calculate μ as shown in the formula on the previous page.

- Enter the Excel formula in cell E4 to calculate σ as shown in the formula on the previous page. You will need to use the SQRT function, which can be found in the "Math & Trig" category.

At this point your worksheet should look like the one below. Be sure E3 and E4 contain formulas (and not just numbers), because we will be changing the values of n and π, and μ and σ need to automatically recalculate.

	A	B	C	D	E
1	x	Binomial	Normal	n	100
2				pi	0.2
3				mu	20
4				sigma	4

The values of x (which go from 0 to n) are to be placed in column A.

- Place the series of integers from 0 to 100 in the range A2:A102. The easiest way to do this is to first enter a "0" in A2, then select the region A2:A102 using the Name Box, then drop the "Edit" menu on the Menu Bar, choose "Fill," then "Series...," and select a "Step Value" of 1. This same procedure was used earlier and described in more detail on page 127.

Each cell in column B will contain the binomial probability of getting the number of successes indicated by the value in that row in column A given the value of n in cell E1 and the value of π in cell E2. This is most easily done by entering a formula in B2 that uses a relative address to refer to x and absolute addresses to refer to n and π. The formula can then be copied to cells B3:B1001.

- Select cell B2.

- Click the Paste Function button. Choose the BINOMDIST function in the "Statistical" category.

- The "number_s" argument is x and should have a *relative* address reference to cell A2.

- The "trials" argument is n and should have an *absolute* address reference to cell E1.

- The "probability_s" argument is π and should have an *absolute* address reference to cell E2.

- Enter the word "false" in the "cumulative" argument field so Excel will provide the probability for a single x value.

- Click the "OK" button.

The value appearing in cell B2 should be 2.03704E-10. This is a very small number, reflecting the fact that it is extremely unlikely that no success would occur in 100 trials if the probability of success in each trial were .2.

- Copy the formula in cell B2 down through cell B102. The easiest way to do this is to use a method similar to that used to generate the series in column A. Select cells B2:B102 using the Name Box. Open the "Edit" menu on the Menu Bar, and choose "Fill." Select "Down" (instead of "Series...").

Examine the probabilities. As you move down the list, the probabilities should first increase. The largest probability will correspond to a value for x of 20 (in cell B22). That probability is 0.099300215. Check to be sure you have this value in your worksheet. If you do not, then you have made an error somewhere and need to recheck and redo the values in columns A and B.

Since the normal distribution is continuous, the probability of a normally distributed random variable equaling any specific value is always zero. In order to approximate a single binomial value, the corresponding range of values from the previous integer to the desired integer is used. For example, if we wanted to approximate the probability of getting exactly 15 successes, we would use the probability of a normally distributed random variable having a value greater than 14 and less than 15. This can be implemented using Excel's cumulative distribution functions by subtracting the probability the normal variable is less than 14 from the probability it is less than 15. The approximation could be improved (but seldom is) by using the "correction for continuity" discussed in an exercise at the end of the chapter.

In order to enter a formula in which Excel subtracts the probability of a value being less than $x - 1$ from the probability of a value being less than x, we will start with cell C3. This is the first cell for which there is a value in the worksheet for $x - 1$. This cell will contain the probability of a normally distributed random variable (with the same values for μ and σ as the binomial distribution being approximated) having a value less than 1 and more than 0.

We want to be careful in the use of *relative* and *absolute* cell addresses so that the formula in cell C3 can be copied down to the other cells in column C. The references to the "x" values should be relative, since we want those to differ for each formula in column C. The references to μ and σ, however, should be absolute. The mean of the normal distribution is in cell E3 and the standard deviation is in cell E4, and those addresses must be fixed for all the formulas in column C.

Since the formula we want to enter must calculate the difference between two normal probabilities, the Paste Function must be used *within* an equation rather than as the whole equation.

- Click the Edit Formula button. Select the NORMDIST function.

- Set the "x" argument to be a *relative* reference to cell A3.

- Set the "mean" argument to be an *absolute* reference to cell E3, and the "standard_dev" argument to be an *absolute* reference to cell E4.

- Enter the word "true" in the field for the "cumulative" argument.

- Click the mouse pointer to the right of the formula being written in the Formula Bar. With the insertion point on the right of the formula, enter a minus sign.

- Click the NORMDIST button on the Formula Palette again. A new dialog window will open. Enter the same arguments as you did previously except the "x" argument should be a relative reference to cell A2. Click "OK."

The *value* displayed in cell C3 will be 7.31223E-07, but the *formula* in the Formula Bar should be "=NORMDIST(A3,$E$3,$E$4,TRUE) - NORMDIST(A2,$E$3,$E$4,TRUE)." This calculates the probability of being less than 1 (in A3) and subtracts the probability of being less than 0 (in A2). This is the probability of a normally distributed random variable with mean 20 and standard deviation 4 having a value between 0 and 1. This value, like the value it approximates in cell B3, is very close to 0.

- Copy cell C3 to cells C4 through C102. Like other massive copies, this is best done by entering the range C3:C102 in the Name Box and then using the "Edit...Fill...Down" menus sequence. Use the Name Box to select cell A1.

The easiest way to evaluate the approximation is to look at a graph that charts both the values in column B and those in column C.

- Click the Chart Wizard button.

- In the Step 1 dialog window, select the "Custom Types" folder tab. In the "Chart Type" list select "Line - Column" (you will have to scroll down the list to see this choice. This choice will make the binomial distribution a vertical bar chart with the normal approximation superimposed as a line chart. Click the "Next>" button.

- In the Step 2 dialog window, we need to tell the Chart Wizard which data to use in the chart. Click the "Data Range" folder tab (it may already be on top) and replace the values in the "Data range:" field with the address for the data in columns B and C. This is most easily done either by using the mouse to select the data region or by first clicking cell B1 and then, while pressing the Shift key, pressing the right arrow key, the End key, and the down arrow key. The contents of the field should be "='Binom Approx'!$B$1:$C$102." Click the "Finish" button.

Excel has placed the chart too low on the worksheet.

- Move the chart so that its upper left-hand corner is in cell D5. One way of doing this is to click the Cut button, enter "D5" into the Name Box, press the Enter key, and click the Paste button.

- Scroll your worksheet so that cell D1 is in the upper left corner (columns A-C should not be visible). Place the chart so that it is on the left side of the screen just below row 5. Increase the height and width of the chart so that it extends to the lower right corner of your screen.

This arrangement of your worksheet will allow you to change the values in cells D1 through D4 and see their effect on the chart without scrolling. Your worksheet should look approximately like the picture at the top of the next page.

If the approximation were perfect, each point on the line would lie on the top of a bar. A close inspection should convince you that the line plot looks as if it had been shifted slightly to the right of the bar chart.

- Select cell E2 (which contains the value of π). Change the ".2" to ".5." Notice how this changes both the graph and the values of μ and σ (in cells E3 and E4).

- Experiment with other values of π, going from very small values (such as .001) to very large values (.999). Notice the extent to which the normal line closely follows the binomial bar chart.

The normal distribution generally does a better job of approximating the binomial distribution the closer π is to .50. It also works better for larger values of *n*.

Try now an even smaller value for *n*.

- Change the value of π to .5, and change the value of *n* to 20.

- Correct the horizontal dimension of the chart by selecting the chart (single click the mouse button with the mouse pointer inside the chart boundary on the white margin) and then click the Chart Wizard button. Click the "Next>" button to go to the Step 2 dialog window.

- Change the "$C$102" at the end of the "Data range:" field to "$C$22." This will cause the chart to show just the binomial and normal approximations for values of *x* between 0 and 20. Click the "Finish" button.

For smaller sizes of *n* the normal distribution is a poorer approximation of the binomial.

- Experiment with different values for π when $n = 20$. Verify that the approximation seems best when π is close to .5.

▼ Exercises

Answer problems 1 through 4 on a new, blank worksheet. The objective of the lesson was not to provide you with a worksheet to use to solve these problems but to enable you to learn how to use Excel to implement standard statistical concepts. In answering Problem 5, however, you should use the "Binom Approx" worksheet developed in the lesson.

1. The scores on an exam are approximately normally distributed with a mean of 75 and a standard deviation of 10. If the professor wants 10% of the class to receive the grade of A, then what is the minimum score a student can get and receive an A on the exam?

2. The weight of a loaf of bread produced by a bakery is normally distributed with a mean of 18 ounces and a standard deviation of .9 ounces. The bread is packaged with a wrapper that describes it as weighing 16 ounces. What proportion of the loaves of bread can be expected to weigh less than the amount shown on the package?

3. A company that produces fasteners for the automotive industry is evaluating a new bolt-making machine that makes a particular style bolt with a weight that is normally distributed with a mean of 28 grams and a standard deviation of 1.16 grams. Within what interval, symmetrically distributed about the mean, will the weight of 95% of the bolts fall?

4. The speed of cars traveling a section of the interstate was found to be normally distributed with a mean of 62 mph and a standard deviation of 4.8 mph. What is the probability that a single car is exceeding the posted speed (55 mph)?

5. In examining the normal distribution as an approximation for the binomial, we did not use the correction for continuity. To approximate the binomial probability of receiving exactly x successes, the normal probability of getting a value between $x - 1$ and x was calculated. This was done by subtracting the cumulative probability of $x - 1$ from the cumulative probability of x. If the correction for continuity were used, the binomial probability of receiving exactly x successes would be approximated by the normal probability of getting a value between $x - 0.5$ and $x + 0.5$.

   Print the chart you got showing the relationship between the binomial and normal approximations distributions *without* using the correction for continuity when $n = 10$ and $\pi = .2$. Put headings on the printout that identify this printout as *not* using the correction for continuity.

   Consider the formula in cell C3. It currently calculates the cumulative normal probability of 1 (in cell A3) or less and subtracts the cumulative normal probability of 0 (in cell A2) or less. Thus the approximation of the binomial probability that x equals 1 is the normal probability that x is between 0 and 1. The correction for continuity would instead use the normal probability that x is between ½ and 1½. Instead of using A3 and A2 in the x fields of NORMDIST, use A3 + 0.5 and A3 − 0.5 to incorporate the correction for continuity. Similarly, change the other formulas in column C. Print the resulting chart, this time with a heading that identifies it as using the correction for continuity. What difference does the correction for continuity seem to make? (To print only the chart, first select it, then click the Print Preview button:).

Chapter 6

The Sampling Distribution of the Mean

Sampling distributions are the foundation of inferential statistics. The object of inferential statistics is to take data from a sample and gain knowledge about the population from which the sample was drawn. A good example is a TV rating service, such as Nielsen, which tracks the TV watching behavior of a sample of viewers and makes inferences about the popularity of shows to all television viewers. A potential problem with this, which has occurred to anyone whose favorite show was canceled because of "low ratings," is that the sample might somehow not be "representative" of the population. How sure can we be that a couple of thousand viewers are going to be similar to the population of millions of television viewers? It's an obvious question. The answer comes from understanding sampling distributions.

What we want to know about a population is usually a descriptive statistic, such as the mean or the proportion of the population that fits into a certain category. A population descriptive statistic is called a *parameter*. A parameter is a number. It's easy to imagine calculating this descriptive statistic if all the population data were available. Because of difficulty or expense, collecting all the population data is not done. Instead, a sample is drawn from the population, and a descriptive statistic is calculated from the sample data. In the jargon of inferential statistics, the number calculated from the sample is a *statistic*. Once a sample is drawn and a statistic is calculated from the sample, that statistic becomes an *estimator* for the population parameter that we want to know. Since a sample may not be representative of the population, we need to know whether the sample statistic is likely to be a good estimator of the population parameter.

There are a number of techniques for selecting samples from a population. Unfortunately, many methods are not statistically valid in the sense that a statistic calculated from a sample should not be used to make an inference about the population parameter. Among those sampling techniques from which valid inferences can be made, the simplest is known as *simple random sampling*. In this technique, all items in the population have an equal probability of being chosen. Depending on the nature of the data to be analyzed, other valid techniques, such as stratified sampling, may make it possible to make equally valid inferences from smaller samples. They sometimes complicate the mathematics of the analysis, however, and for introductory statistics it is best to keep things as simple as possible.

With simple random sampling (or any other valid sampling technique), any value taken from a member of a sample is a random number since that member is chosen by a random process. Any sample statistic calculated from the sample values is also going to be a random number. A random number has a distribution. If we knew that distribution, we would have good information on the likelihood of a sample statistic being a good estimator of a parameter.

Sampling can be done *with replacement* and *without replacement*. When a sample is drawn with replacement, once an item is chosen for the sample from the population, that same item is replaced before a second item is selected for the sample. It is possible that the same population item might be chosen twice for the sample. When sampling is drawn without replacement, this cannot happen. If the population is very large compared to the sample, both techniques result in essentially equivalent samples, but this is not the case if the sample is close in size to the population. Suppose a sample of ten people were chosen from the entire U.S. population. It wouldn't matter if the sampling were done with or without replacement, because it is unlikely that the same person could be chosen twice if sampling were done with replacement. On the other hand, if a sample of ten people were chosen from a class of thirty, it is very likely that someone would be chosen more than once if sampling were done with replacement. In practice, sampling is almost always done without replacement. With small populations this permits smaller samples to be used to make equally valid inferences. The simplest analysis, however, occurs if sampling is done *with replacement*. So that technique will be the one we will assume is used whenever it might make a difference.

▼ Simulating the Sampling Distribution of the Mean

Most people find the concept of a sampling distribution a little tricky when they first encounter it. It often seems a little nebulous or abstract. It is really a very concrete concept, however. We will investigate it here by using Excel to help us look at a specific sampling distribution of the mean.

Ideally, this would be done by calculating a mean from every possible sample that could be drawn from a population. Unfortunately, for even moderately large samples drawn from moderately large populations, the number of possible samples is astronomical. For example, suppose we were interested in estimating the average lifetime of a specific lot of 100 light bulbs by choosing and testing a sample of ten light bulbs. How many different samples are there in total?

How many different choices do we have for the first member of the sample? Any of the 100 bulbs in the population could be chosen. What about the second member? If the sampling is done with replacement, there are 100 choices for the second as well. The total number of distinct samples would be the product of 100 multiplied by itself 10 times, or 100^{10}. This is a huge number which could be written as a 1 followed by 20 zeroes! If we correct for the fact that some of these samples would be identical except for order, we still would have left so many samples that their number would have 14 digits to the left of the decimal point! If the sample size or population sizes were large, the number of samples would grow even faster.

Our approach will be to look at the means of a large enough number of samples that we can get a good notion of what the distribution of all sample means would look like.

▼ Drawing Samples with Excel

Excel has a sampling tool included with its Analysis Tools. Unfortunately, this tool will not take multiple samples. Taking a thousand samples one at a time is impractical. By installing the Excel Add-Ins included on the data diskette for this book, you will add this capability to your Excel. Instructions for installing the Add-In are given in Appendix C.

- If you have not already done so, start Excel with a new blank workbook. If the workbook that displays is not empty, click the New button on the Standard Toolbar: ▯ .

- Save the new workbook in a file named chap6.xls. (Note: this file should be saved on a hard disk or network drive; it will become too large for a diskette. For a method of storing it on diskette at the end of your session, see Appendix F.)

- In cell A1, enter the label "Population."

- In cells A2 through A6, enter five different numbers. Use any numbers you like, but be sure all five are different.

- In cell C1, enter the label "Samples."

For the purposes of seeing how a sample can be chosen, the five numbers you have entered in cells A2 through A6 will be regarded as a population, and we will see how the Excel Add-In can be used to select values from this population.

- Open the Tools menu on the Menu Bar. Select "Learning Business Statistics." A submenu will open (as shown below). Select "Multiple Random Samples." If "Learning Business Statistics" does not appear on your Tools menu, you have not installed the Add-Ins for this book. Follow the instructions in Appendix C before proceeding.

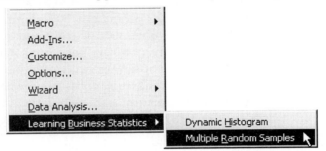

- The Multiple Random Samples dialog window will open. In the "Population Range:" field, enter the range address of the population values you have entered. In the "Sample Size:" and "Number of Samples:" fields, enter the number "1." In the "Output Range:" field, enter "C2." Click the "OK" button.

Cell C2 should now contain a value chosen randomly from the five values in column A.

- Recall the Multiple Random Samples dialog window and click the "OK" button. Try this several times, observing the value in cell C2.

Sometimes the same value will be chosen twice, but usually you should see a new value in cell C2 each time the Multiple Random Samples tool is run.

- Recall the Multiple Random Samples dialog window. Change the value in the "Sample Size:" field from "1" to "5." Click the "OK" button.

- Rerun the Multiple Random Samples tool several times and observe the changes in the sample.

When a sample contains more than one value, the Multiple Random Samples Tool places the sample values in a row. Your observation should confirm that the sampling is done with replacement since the samples will usually contain the same value more than once.

- Recall the Multiple Random Samples dialog window and change the "Number of Samples:" field from "1" to "3." Click "OK" and observe the values written by the tool

When more than one sample is drawn, each sample is written in a separate row. The random samples each contain five values (the length of a row) and there are three samples (the number of rows).

We are now ready to use the Multiple Random Samples tool to investigate the sampling distribution of the mean.

▼ Setting Up a Population

- Double click the "Sheet2" worksheet tab and change its name to "Population."

Once we have the workbook set up, it will be easy to change the population from which the samples will be drawn. To begin with, a very simple population will be used—all of the numbers divisible by .5 between .5 and 100.

- Enter the number ".5" in cell A1.

- Enter the number "1.0" in cell A2.

- Select the region A1:A200. The easiest way to do this is probably to enter "a1:a200" in the Name Box and press the Enter key.

- With A1:A200 selected, open the "Edit" menu on the Menu Bar. From the menu that drops down, select "Fill." A cascade menu will open. Select "Series…" from that menu. The Series dialog window will open.

- Just to the left of the center of the dialog window is a region titled "Type," which contains four selections with radio buttons. These selections are "Linear," "Growth," "Date," and "AutoFill." Select "AutoFill" by clicking the mouse pointer on the radio button just to the left of that choice. Click the "OK" button in the box.

The selected region A1:A200 should automatically fill with the series of numbers from .5 to 100, with each cell having a value that is .5 greater than the cell above it. The effect of using Series Fill with "AutoFill" is the same as if A1:A2 were selected and the mouse used to drag the fill handle to cell A200. When large regions (such as this) are involved, using the mouse is often not easy because of the difficulty of controlling Excel's scrolling.

▼ Setting Up a Dynamic Histogram

In order to better see the shape of the distribution of the population we have just created, it would be useful to have a histogram. In Chapter 2 you learned how to use the Histogram Tool. That is the simplest way of producing a histogram in Excel. Like all the output prepared by the analysis tools, the histogram tool is *static*—changes to the data are not immediately reflected in the histogram. To see the effect of changes in the data, the Histogram Tool would have to be rerun.

Instead of using the Histogram Tool, the Add-Ins included with this book provide a Dynamic Histogram Tool. It is very similar in use to the Histogram Tool but has a few differences. For example, you must provide a "Bins" range for the Dynamic Histogram Tool. The Dynamic Histogram Tool does not produce a "More" bin. A chart is always produced. The major difference, however, is that the relationship between the histogram (both chart and table) and input data is *dynamic*. If the input data changes, the histogram will automatically reflect those changes.

The first step is to set up the "bins," the intervals that each bar in the histogram will represent. Since the population values all fall between 0 and 100, let's use ten intervals whose upper bounds are 10, 20, 30, etc.

- In cells B1 through B10, enter the values 10, 20, 30, ..., 100. Remember that one easy way of doing this is to enter "10" in cell B1 and "20" in cell B2. Then use the mouse to select cells B1:B2. After the two cells are selected, the fill handle can be dragged down to cell B10. When it is released, the series will be completed.

- Open the Tools Menu, click "Learning Business Statistics," and select "Dynamic Histogram."

- In the "Input Range" field, enter the address of the data that the histogram is to summarize: A1:A200.

- In the "Bin Range" field, enter the address of the bins: B1:B10.

- In the "Output Range" field, enter B12. Click the "OK" button.

The histogram for this population should consist of ten bars of equal height with that height corresponding to 20.

The last thing to put on this worksheet is the population mean and standard deviation.

- Delete the values in cells B1:B10

- Enter the Label "Mean" in cell B1 and "Standard Deviation" in cell B2.

- Enter the formula in cell C1 to calculate the mean of the numbers in A1:A200. The Excel function has the name AVERAGE. The value displayed should be 50.25.

- Enter the formula in cell C2 to calculate the standard deviation of the numbers in A1:A200. Since these numbers constitute a population, you need to use the population standard deviation formula rather than the sample standard deviation formula. The Excel function to calculate a population standard deviation is STDEVP. The value displayed should be 28.86715.

- Save your workbook, now and often!

▼ Drawing the Samples

Double click the "Sheet3" worksheet tab and change its name to "Samples." On this worksheet we will have Excel draw 1,000 different samples of size 30 from the population of 200 on the "Population" worksheet.

Open the Tools menu on the Menu Bar. Select "Learning Business Statistics" and then click "Multiple Random Samples."

- In the "Population Range:" field, you should enter the address of the population on the Population worksheet. This is best done with the mouse since the worksheet name must be part of the address, and this is done automatically when you use the mouse.

- Enter "30" for Sample Size and "1000" for Number of Samples.

- Click the "Output Range:" field so an insertion point is visible and click cell A1 on the Samples worksheet. The dialog window should look like the picture at the top of the next page. Notice how Excel includes the worksheet name in the name range. Click the "OK" button.

Be patient! Depending (of course) on the speed of your computer, the selection of 1,000 samples of size 30 could take several minutes.

▼ Calculate the Sample Means

The Samples worksheet now has 1,000 rows of numbers, each of which is 30 numbers long. Each row is a separate sample drawn from the population on the Population worksheet. The next step is to calculate the mean of each of the 1,000 samples.

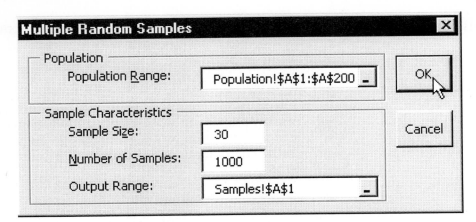

- Select the last value of the first sample by doing the following. First click any cell in the first row (A1 is fine). Press and release the End key. Then press the right arrow key. The active cell should now be AD1.

Excel uses letters of the alphabet to name columns. After the 26th column, two letters are used. The 27th columns is AA followed by AB, AC, and AD. Since the samples require 30 columns, the last number is in the fourth column after the first 26 columns, which is AD. After 26 columns in which the first letter is A, Excel has another 26 columns in which the first letter is B.

- Select cell AF1, either by using the scroll bars to scroll your worksheet or by using the name box. The average of the first sample will be calculated in this cell.

- Click the Paste Function button and select the AVERAGE function from the "Statistical" category. When the dialog window appears, Excel will assume you want the average of the cells in the row to the left of AF1. Since we are keeping AE1 blank, the range in the Number1 parameter field should be A1:AD1. Be sure the address is relative so that it will update when copied.

The expected (in the statistical sense) value of a sample mean is the population mean. We already determined the population mean to be 50.25. It would be surprising if the sample mean were exactly this value, but it is likely to be close to this value. The means of the next 999 samples will be determined by copying the contents of this cell downward.

- Copy cell AF1 down through AF1000. A good way to do this would be to use the Name Box to select the region and to use Fill on the Edit menu.

▼ The Theoretical Distribution of Sample Means

We now have a set of 1,000 sample means. With a population of 200 and a sample size of 30 (sampling with replacement) there are 200^{30} different samples. The distribution of all 200^{30} means would be the sampling distribution of the mean. The 1,000 means we have generated can be thought of as a sample drawn from the entire population of samples. It's a big enough sample that by looking at the distribution of the 1,000 numbers we have, we should get a pretty good idea of the characteristics of the distribution of all sample means.

Statistical theory tells us that the distribution of sample means should have a mean that is itself equal to the population mean:

$$\mu_{\bar{x}} = \mu$$

and a standard deviation that is related to the population standard deviation by the following formula:

$$\sigma_{\bar{x}} = \frac{\sigma}{\sqrt{n}}$$

Note that n is the size of each of the samples, not the total number of samples. For our case, $n = 30$ (*not* 1,000).

The preceding two equations hold strictly for the entire set of sample means. The mean and standard deviation of the 1,000 values we have drawn might differ. Still, it would be interesting to see how close the mean and standard deviations of the sample means just generated are to the values that theoretically would hold for the entire set of sample means. Let's create a table for these values.

- In cell AG1 enter the label "Sampling Distribution." In cell AG3 enter the label "Theoretical." In cell AG4 enter the label "These Samples."

- Increase the width of column AG so that it is wide enough to hold the label in AG4.

- In cell AH2 enter the label "Mean," and in cell AI2 enter the label "Standard Deviation."

- In cell AH3, enter a formula that reads the population mean from the Population worksheet. Do this by making AH3 active. Then enter an equal sign to tell Excel you are beginning a formula. Then click the Population worksheet tab with the mouse pointer. Then click the cell containing the population mean (C1). Press the Enter key.

Pressing the Enter key will cause your display to shift back to the Samples worksheet with the value 50.25 displayed in AH3.

- Again make AH3 active and observe the formula in the Formula Bar. Verify that it is "=Population!C1."

Once again we see the use of a worksheet name in a cell range address, necessary if the range is not on the current worksheet. If you were to change the name of a worksheet, Excel would automatically change all formulas in the workbook that referred to cells on that worksheet.

The next step is to enter the formula that will calculate the theoretical standard deviation of sample means from the population standard deviation. This requires taking the population standard deviation and dividing it by the square root of the size of the samples. For the samples we have just generated, the size is 30. Rather than use that number, we will use Excel's COUNT function to actually count the number of values in a row. That way the formula will still work when we generate samples with fewer than 30 values.

- Select cell AI3. Click the Edit Formula button. An equal sign will appear in the Formula Bar. Move the Formula Palette down to the middle of your screen so that you can see the column headers and the first two rows.

- Switch to the Population worksheet and click the cell with the population standard deviation. The Formula Bar should now have "=Population!C2," which represents the population standard deviation. We must complete the formula by telling it to divide this by the square root of the sample size.

- Enter the division symbol ("/"). It should appear at the end of the Formula Bar, which now should be "=Population!C2/."

- Click the arrow to the left of the Formula Bar, which opens the list of recently used functions. Click SQRT if it appears on the list. If it does not, click "More Functions..." and select SQRT from the "Math & Trig" category. The SQRT dialog window will open with an insertion point in the Number argument field.

Instead of entering a number whose square root we want taken, we need to enter an Excel function that will count the number of values in one of the samples.

- Click the arrow to the left of the Formula Bar, which opens the list of functions. Select the function COUNT from the "Statistical" category.

Only the Value1 argument field of COUNT will be used. We need to put there the range address of one of the 1,000 samples. Since all are the same size, any of the samples will do. Let's arbitrarily use the first sample.

- Select the Samples worksheet. Click the cell with the last value of the first sample (AD1). Press and hold the Shift key. While pressing the Shift key, press and release the End key then the left arrow key.

The Value1 argument field of COUNT should contain "Samples!A1:AD1." Look at the place in the dialog window where the function result is shown (just below and to the right of the Value2 argument field). It should show "30," which is a count of the numbers in the range A1:AD1.

- Click the "OK" button. Cell AI3 should display 5.270397. This is the theoretical value of the standard deviation of the means of samples of size 30 selected from the population on the Population worksheet. This value is often called the *standard error of the mean* or just the *standard error*.

The next step is to add the formulas to calculate the mean and standard deviation of the sample means that are in the cell range AF1:AF1000. We expect these values to be close to the theoretical values for the mean and standard deviation in AH3 and AI3, respectively. They won't be exactly the same because the 1,000 sample means on this worksheet are only a sample of the (huge) set of all possible sample means.

- Select cell AH4. Enter the Excel formula that calculates the average of the numbers in the range AF1:AF1000.

- Select cell AI4. Enter the Excel formula that calculates the standard deviation of the numbers in the range AF1:AF1000. In this case you should use the *sample* standard deviation (STDEV) because the 1,000 sample means represent a sample of the huge set of all possible sample means.

The theoretical mean and standard deviation should be very close (but not identical) to the mean and standard deviation of the 1,000 sample means. An increased number of samples (more than 1,000) should result in values even closer to the theoretical values.

▼ Examining the Distribution of Sample Means

We will use a histogram to investigate the distribution of the 1,000 sample means. Their distribution will be compared to theoretical normal distribution by modifying the histogram to show a superimposed normal distribution, similar to the one used in chapter 4.

In order to provide more detail, 20 bars will be used for the histogram of sample means compared to the 10 bars used for the population histogram. This means 20 "bins" (or categories) must be created. Cells AG6:AG25 will be used for this. These bins will go from 5 to 100 by 5.

- Enter the series of numbers 5, 10, 15, ..., 100 in AG6:AG25. This is easiest if you use the Fill handle or the Fill Menu.

- Select "Learning Business Statistics" from the "Tools" menu and click "Dynamic Histogram"

- In the "Input Range" field put the range address of the 1,000 sample means on your worksheet.

- In the "Bins Range" field, put the range address of the bin values you have just entered: AG6:AG25.

- Enter "AG6" in the "Output Range" field. This will cause the histogram table to overwrite the bin values you previously entered, but since the table shows those values, nothing will be lost. Click the "OK" button.

The histogram chart should have only about a half dozen bars, and they should all be in the center of the horizontal axis. Although we specified 20 bins for this chart, most of them are empty. Compare the histogram of the 1,000 sample means on the "Samples" worksheet with the histogram of the population on the "Population" worksheet. Clearly their shapes are very different! The fact that all the bars are clustered together provides visual confirmation that the standard deviation of sample means (the standard error) is less than the standard deviation of the population.

We will explore this distribution further in two ways. First we will compare the frequencies with those that would have been expected if the distribution of sample means was the normal distribution. Then we will change the bin ranges so that we can more closely examine the range of values for which the frequencies are non-zero.

▼ The Normal Distribution and the Central Limit Theorem

According to the Central Limit Theorem, the distribution of sample means should be approximately normal if the samples are large enough. The size of the samples required for this depends on the population distribution. According to a widely used rule of thumb, sample sizes of at least 30 are sufficiently large to assume the distribution of sample means is normal. We will look at that by comparing the distribution of sample means with that which would occur if the sample means were normally distributed. Since the 1,000 sample means we are looking at are a tiny proportion of all the sample means, some mismatch between the actual distribution of the 1,000 sample means and the number predicted by the normal distribution is to be expected. The central limit theorem doesn't assure us that any 1,000 samples will be distributed *exactly* as predicted by the normal distribution, but the distribution should be close.

The range AI7:AI26 will be used for the values predicted by the normal distribution. In each cell we will calculate the probability of a normally distributed random variable with μ given by the value in AH3 and σ given by the value in AI3 falling within an interval determined by the bin value in that row in column AG. This probability will be multiplied by 1,000 giving the expected number of the 1,000 samples falling within the bins interval.

Since we have to calculate normal probabilities for a *range* of values, the first normal probability will be calculated for the *second* bin. Cell AI8 will take the probability of a normal random variable being less than the value given in AG8 minus the probability of it being less than the value in AG7 and multiply that difference by 1,000. The difference in the two probabilities equals the probability of the random variable being greater than the value in AG7 and less than the value in AG8. The formulas in the rest of the range will be similar to that of AG8. By the judicious use of absolute and relative addresses, we will be able to copy AG8 through the rest of the range.

The probabilities will be calculated using Excel's NORMDIST function, which (unlike the NORMSDIST function) allows us to specify a value for the mean and standard deviation. An argument value controls whether this function provides the density or cumulative probability. We will use it to provide cumulative probability.

- Move the histogram chart to the right, if needed, so that it does not cover column AI. Enter the label "Normal Expected" in cell AI6.

- Select cell AI8. Click the Edit Formula button. Enter "1000*(" in the Formula Bar.

This will multiply the normal probability by 1,000. Inside parenthesis just opened we will calculate the probability of a normal variable being less than the bin value in AG8 minus the probability of a normal variable being less than the bin value in AG7.

- Click the downward pointing arrow on the Formula Palette, which opens the list of recently used functions. The function you want is

NORMDIST (*not* NORMSDIST). If it is not on the list, select "More functions..." and look for it in the "Statistical" category.

- The value for the "x" argument is the value in cell AG8. Be sure to use the *address* AG8 (and not just the displayed value). Be sure the address is relative.

- Cells AH3 and AI3 contain the theoretical mean and standard deviation of the distribution of sample means. Put these addresses in the argument fields for "mean" and "standard_dev," respectively. These addresses should be *absolute*. Enter the word "true" in the "cumulative" argument field.

Look at the Formula Bar. At this point it should contain "=1000*(NORMDIST(AG8,$AH$3,$AI$3,true)." The NORMDIST function in this formula will determine the probability of a normal random variable being less than the bin value in AG8. We need to subtract from that the probability of a normal variable being less than the bin value in AG7.

- Click the mouse pointer in the Formula Bar to the right of its current contents. An insertion point should appear. Enter a minus sign ("-"). As soon as you enter it, the NORMDIST dialog window will close.

- Since NORMDIST was the most recently used function, its name should appear on the most-recently-used-function button to the left of the Formula Bar. Click it and a new NORMDIST dialog window will appear.

- This time the "x" argument field should contain the relative address of AG7. The "mean" and "standard_dev" argument fields should contain absolute addresses for AH3 and AI3, respectively, as before. Again enter the word "true" in the "cumulative" argument field.

- Click the mouse pointer on the right side of the Formula Bar so that an insertion point appears. Enter a right parenthesis (")"). This closes the parenthesis entered after the "1000*" within which the difference between the two normal probabilities was calculated. Click the "OK" button on the Formula Palette.

The value 1.12133E-11 should be displayed in cell AI8, and the Formula Palette should contain "=1000*(NORMDIST(AG8,$AH$3,$AI$3,TRUE)-NORMDIST(AG7,$AH$3,$AI$3,TRUE))"

- Copy the formula in AI8 to AI9 through AI26. The value displayed in cell AI16 should be 321.4897797.

If the actual distribution of the sample means is approximately normal, the expected values displayed in column AI should be close to the actual counts in the same rows in column AH. You should be able to verify that as you go down both columns, both sets of values increase and then decrease. The comparison would be much easier, however, if it could be made graphically.

▼ Adding the Normal Expected Values to the Histogram

We already have a chart showing the distribution of the actual 1,000 sample means—the histogram chart. Excel makes it easy to modify this chart so that it also shows the normal expected values.

- Select the region AI6:AI26. This contains the normal values and the heading.

- Click the Copy button on the Standard Toolbar: 📋.

- Place the mouse pointer in the center of the histogram. You can put it either in the gray plot area or directly on one of the bars. Click the (left) mouse button so that either the plot area or the bars are selected.

- Click the Paste button on the Standard Toolbar: 📋.

You should immediately see a new set of bars on the histogram, and the chart should be selected. These two bars chart the normal expected values. The comparison can be made clearer by changing the chart type.

- Open the "Chart" menu on the Menu Bar. Select "Chart Type...."

- In the Chart Type dialog window, click the "Custom Types" folder tab. Scroll down through the list of chart types until you find ⌷⌷ Line - Column . Select it by clicking the mouse pointer directly on it. Click the "OK" button.

As indicated by the legend, the values predicted by the normal distribution are represented by dots connected by a line. The actual values in the 1,000 samples are shown by bars. If the actual values were precisely predicted by the normal expected values, each dot would lie exactly on the top of a bar.

The comparison between the actual and expected values would be clearer if we altered the bins so that they provided more detail in the central region of values where the nonzero values lie. Rather than having the bins go from 5 to 100, let's have them go from 32 to 70.

- Enter the number "32" in cell AG7 and "34" in AG8. Select the range AG7:AG8. Place the mouse pointer over the Fill Handle and drag it down to cell AG26. The bins values in AG7:AG26 should now contain the series of number from 32 to 70 with an increment of 2.

The chart should show more bars and comparing the normal expected values with the actual values of the 1,000 sample means should be easier. Enlarging the chart will also make the comparison easier.

- Scroll your worksheet so that the upper left corner of the chart is in the upper left corner of your screen. Click on an empty part of the chart and use the handles to resize the chart so that it fills the screen.

Let's compare the distribution of a different set of 1,000 sample means with the expected values.

- Click the mouse pointer on the worksheet (to deselect the chart). Open the Tools menu on the Menu Bar, select "Learning Business Statistics," and click "Multiple Random Samples."

- If you are in the same Excel session as when you last ran the Multiple Random Samples Tools, the fields in the dialog window will already be filled out. If they are empty, look at the picture on page 166 to see what values should be entered. Click the "OK" button. Remember that it may take several minutes for the new samples to be generated.

Once the new sample is generated, the worksheet will automatically calculate the new set of means and show their distribution on the revised histogram. By doing this a few times you can develop a feel for the relationship between the distribution of 1,000 sample means and the normal distribution.

▼ Nonuniform Population

The uniform population that we have been using is quite different from the normal distribution of the sample means, although it is symmetric. Suppose the population distribution differs even more from the normal distribution. Let's first try a bimodal distribution with no values near the mean.

- Click the "Population" worksheet tab.

In order to minimize the changes a new population would require of the workbook, the new population should have a mean close to that of the current population (about 50). We're going to use Excel's built-in Random Number Generation Tool as a handy method for quickly generating a large number of numbers, which we will use as our population. This tool was used previously in Chapters 3 and 4.

- With the "Population" worksheet active, open the "Tools" menu on the Menu Bar. When the Menu Bar drops down, select "Data Analysis." The "Data Analysis" window will open enabling you to choose among the tools. If "Data Analysis" does not appear in your Tools menu, see Appendix B.

- Select the "Random Number Generation" tool. This will require scrolling down the list. One way of scrolling is to press the key for the first letter of the item you want ("r" in this case).

Recall that in the first two fields of this tool, you indicate the number of columns and the number of rows in the range of cells in which you want the tool to enter numbers. Put the number of columns in the field that is labeled "Number of Variables" and the number of rows you want filled in the field labeled "Number of Random Numbers." For this exercise, we will select 200 numbers to be our population. All of them will go in column A, but we will use the Random Number Generation Tool to choose 100 numbers twice, rather than choosing all 200 at once.

- Enter the number "1" in the "Number of Variables" field and the number "100" in the "Number of Random Numbers" field.

- In the "Distribution" field select "Uniform." This selection will cause the next two fields to change.

When "Uniform" is chosen, the Random Number Generation Tool will generate values that are between the two values entered in the fields in the "Parameters" section labeled "Between" and "and." These values will be continuous, not integers.

- Enter values so that the Random Number Generation Tool will generate numbers between 0 and 20.

- Select the radio button beside "Output Range," and using either the mouse pointer or the keyboard, indicate that the numbers should start in cell A1. The window should look like that shown at the top of the next page.

- Click the "OK" button. Click the "OK" button on the window warning that you are about to overwrite some data. Column A (A1:A100) will fill with numbers.

The first half of our new population contains values between 0 and 20. Let's make the second half consist of values between 80 and 100.

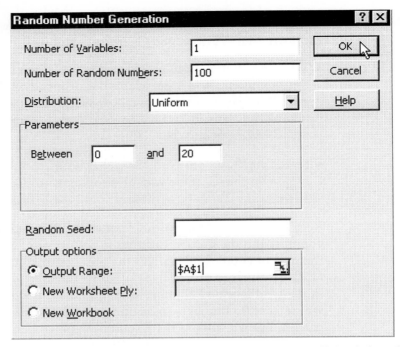

- Recall the Random Number Generation Tool. You will find that the dialog box contains the values you previously entered. Three fields need to be changed. Make the two changes so that the tool will generate random numbers between 80 and 100. Change the "Output Range" field so that the numbers will start in cell A101 instead of A1. That will cause the numbers selected this time to be put in column A *after* the previous set of numbers between 0 and 20.

- Click all the "OK" buttons necessary to get Excel to generate the numbers chosen.

- Scroll your worksheet up so that the population histogram is visible.

The population histogram should show only four bars, two at the left and two at the right, reflecting the fact that the new population has no values between 20 and 80.

- Open the Tools menu and select Multiple Random Samples from "Learning Business Statistics." If the dialog window's fields are already filled out, click "OK." If not, use the picture on page 166 and set the values of the fields before clicking "OK."

The mean of this new population will be very close to the mean of the previous population, and the chart should thus appear centered about as it did before. This population, however, has a larger standard deviation than did the previous population and so does the distribution of sample means. If you look at the "tails" of the distribution on each side of the histogram, you will see that they are above the horizontal axis. A slight increase in the range of values shown on the *x* axis would be desirable but is not absolutely necessary.

- Recall the Multiple Random Samples Tool and draw a new set of samples. Do this a couple of times. How well do the sample means from this population fit the normal curve compared to the means of samples previously drawn from the uniform population?

You should see little or no difference. In other words, samples of size 30 drawn from this nonuniform population have means that seem normally distributed, as do samples of the same size drawn from a uniform population. Despite the sharp difference in the shapes of the population distribution, the sample means have distributions that are the same shape!

Both of the populations we have considered are symmetric, as is the normal distribution. Will the same relationship hold if the population is sharply skewed?

▼ Skewed Population

We will use the Random Number Generation Tool to help create a skewed population. The procedure below is designed to create a skewed population whose mean is close to 50.

- Click the "Population" worksheet tab.

- Run the Random Number Generation Tool four times. Several things will be the same each time the tool is used. The "Number of Variables" should always be 1. The "Distribution" should always be "Uniform." The radio button beside "Output Range" should be selected although the address will change. The fields which should be changed each run are the "Number of Random Numbers," the two fields giving the beginning and end values for the uniform random variables ("Between" and "and"), and the address for the "Output Range" field. The values are summarized in the table at the top of the next page.

These four sets of random numbers will completely overwrite your previous population in column A with a new set of numbers.

The population histogram should clearly show that the data are left (or negatively) skewed. As you look from left to right, there should be a clear tendency for the histogram bars to get taller, although sometimes a bar may be slightly lower than the one to its left. An example of one of these population histograms is shown on the next page. Yours will differ somewhat since it will be based on different random numbers.

Run	"Number of Random Numbers"	"Between"	"and"	"Output Range"
1	20	0	20	A1
2	40	20	40	A21
3	60	40	60	A61
4	80	60	80	A121

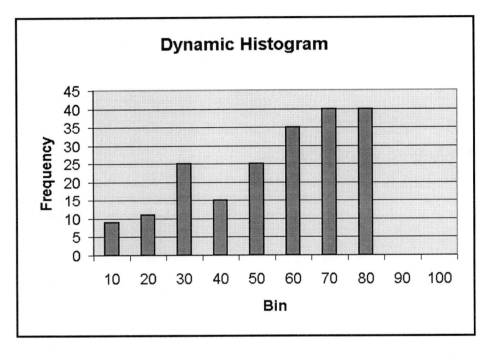

- Recall the Multiple Random Samples Tool and run it to draw samples from this new population. Click the "Samples" worksheet tab and look at the histogram of the sample means.

This population has a smaller standard deviation (and smaller standard error) than the previous population. A fairly large number of the bars in the sample means histogram thus appear to have zero height.

- Use the Multiple Random Samples Tool several times and observe the "fit" between the sample means histogram and the normal distribution line. Compare this to the fits you saw in the previous two populations.

Skewed populations require the largest sample sizes for sample means to be approximately normally distributed. If the population's skewness were to affect the distribution of sample means, there would be a tendency for the histogram bars to the right of the mean to go above the normal line while those to the left of the mean would have a tendency to lie entirely below the normal line. Although this population is quite skewed, there should be little or no sign of that in the distribution of sample means. It is, however, not difficult to create a distribution so severely skewed that the distributions of the means of samples of size 30 are also clearly skewed. Such distributions are rarely encountered with real data. The rule of thumb that samples of size 30 are large enough for the assumption of normality of the distribution of sample means is just that—a rule of thumb.

Let's see how well the distribution of the means of smaller samples fits the normal approximation.

- First erase the current sample values. Use the Name Box to select the region A1:AD1000 (on the Samples worksheet). Press the Delete or Del key. Erasing the sample values will result in error codes appearing in many cells of the worksheet, but this is not a problem.

- Recall the Multiple Random Samples Tool. Change the value in the "Sample Size" field from "30" to "10." Click the "OK" button.

The smaller sample size increases the standard error (standard deviation of the sample means). This means the chart tends to be more "spread out," less concentrated in the center than was the case with samples of size 30. If the population skew is affecting the sample means, the chart of the sample means should show a tendency for the bars to the right of the center to be above the normal expected values while those on the left will tend to be below. Do you see such a tendency?

- Rerun the Multiple Random Samples Tool several times and examine the chart of sample means to see if there is a tendency for the population skew to be reflected in the distribution of the means of the 1,000 samples.

- Save the workbook.

- Open the File menu on the Menu Bar. Select "Close." This will close the chap6.xls workbook. Open the File menu again and select "New." Click "OK" in the dialog window, which asks if you want a new workbook. This will provide you with a new blank workbook.

▼ The *t* Distribution

In the great majority of situations where the sampling distribution of the mean is applied, the population standard deviation is unknown. Instead, the standard deviation of a single sample must be used. Although the *expected value* of a sample standard deviation is the population standard deviation, a sample standard deviation is a random number, and its use can be thought of as adding uncertainty to the sampling distribution.

In the early part of the century William S. Gosset, a British industrial research scientist who worked for the Irish brewer Guinness, showed that better results were obtained when the sampling distribution of the mean was treated not as following the normal distribution but as following a similar distribution, which he termed the *t* distribution. The use of a different probability distribution in Excel would cause little difficulty except for the fact that Excel is inconsistent in its treatment of continuous probability distributions.

As you know, the normal distribution has two variables, μ and σ. An important property of that distribution is that a problem involving any normal distribution can be converted to a problem involving the standard normal distribution (which has $\mu = 0$ and $\sigma = 1$) by using the standardization formula (which converts x to z, or vice versa).

The *t* distribution is used in place of the *z* distribution when the population standard deviation is unknown. While the *z* distribution is a specific instance of the normal distribution, the *t* distribution has a variable called the *degrees of freedom* or *dof*. For problems involving the sampling distribution of the mean, the value of the degrees of freedom is $n - 1$ where n is the size of the sample from which the standard deviation was calculated.

Before using the *t* distribution, the value of the sample mean must be transformed in a way identical to that used to standardize the sample mean to a z variable: subtract the population mean and divide by the standard error (calculated, in this case, from the sample's standard deviation). The transformed value can be treated as a random variable following the *t* distribution with $n - 1$ degrees of freedom.

Excel provides four functions to handle the normal distribution: NORMDIST, NORMSDIST, NORMINV, and NORMSINV. The first two are distribution functions, and the second two are inverse distribution functions. The two with an "S" in the name are for the standard normal distribution while the other two work for any normal distribution (and require that the values for μ and σ be given as arguments). All of these functions are cumulative; the probability they associate with a value for the random variable is the probability of a random variable being less than or equal to that value.

By contrast, there are two functions for the *t* distribution, TDIST and TINV. The first is a probability distribution function and the second is an inverse distribution function. Both provide a relationship only for stand-ardized *t* values. They both take the value of the degrees of freedom as an argument. Neither of them are cumulative. Furthermore, both of them handle only positive *t* values. Despite these differences, we can get the same information from these two functions as we did from the nor-mal functions. We just have to keep in mind how what we want relates to what the functions provide.

Consider the diagram below showing the density function for a standard *t* distribution. If an argument of TDIST is set equal to the value of *t* in the diagram, TDIST will return either the area of both shaded regions or the area of just the shaded region to the right, depending on the value of another argument. Notice that the two regions are always equal in size, so that if TDIST is asked to give the area of both regions, the result is ex-actly twice what it would be if TDIST were asked to give the area of just one region. The value of *t* must be positive, a negative value for *t* will re-sult in an error message. Since the *t* distribution is symmetric (and has mean 0), the value for the upper boundary of the left tail will have the same absolute value (but negative sign) as the lower boundary of the right tail.

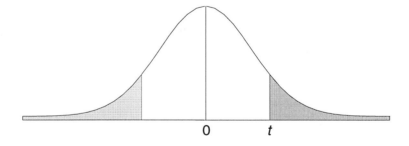

Suppose we want to determine the probability of a *t* variable being be-tween two values, both of which are positive or both of which are negative. We can use two calls to TDIST, each of which uses the absolute value of the boundary values, to determine the one-tail probability. The difference between the two one-tail probabilities is the value we want. Unfortunately, whether we want the one-tail area of the right-most value minus the left-most value, or vice versa, depends on whether the values are both positive or both negative. Since the answer is a probability, and probabilities must be positive, this problem can be solved by taking the absolute value of the difference.

TINV has an argument set equal to a probability. It interprets that prob-ability as the area of *both* tails, and it returns the value of *t* shown in the diagram. Unlike TDIST, TINV has no argument allowing us to indicate that our problem involves only the area of one tail. Since the area of one tail is always merely half the area of two, this is not a serious problem. Notice that the *t* value returned is always positive.

▼ Looking at the *t* Distribution

To better understand the *t* distribution, we will compare it to the *z* distribution using the same approach we used to compare the distribution of the sample of sample means with the normal distribution for all sample means.

- Save the new workbook as chap6b.xls.

- Double click the Sheet1 worksheet tab and change its name to "t vs z."

- In the row of cells A1:D1, enter the labels "Value," "z," "t," and "dof."

- In cell E1 enter the number "10." This will be the initial value for the degrees of freedom of the *t* distribution we plot.

- In the column A2:A82 enter the series of numbers that goes from -4 to 4 with an increment of 0.1.

The first *z* and *t* probabilities will go in row 3. In column B we will calculate the probability of a *z* value falling between the value in that row in column A (–3.9) and the value in the *previous* row of column A (–4).

- Select cell B3. Click the Edit Formula button.

Since Excel's NORMSDIST function is cumulative, the formula to be entered here is easy: the probability of a standard normal variable being less than –3.9 minus the probability of a standard normal variable being less than –4. Since –3.9 is to the right of –4, the area to the left of –3.9 includes the area to the left of –4. In other words, the probability of being less than –3.9 must be greater than the probability of being less than –4. Consequently, the former probability minus the second probability must be positive.

- Select the NORMSDIST function either from the list of most recently used functions or from the "Statistical" category.

- In the "z" argument field, enter a relative address for the –3.9 in column A: A3.

- Click the mouse pointer on the right side of the Formula Bar. Enter a minus sign ("-"). The NORMSDIST dialog window will close.

- Since NORMSDIST was the last function used, its name will appear on the button to the left of the Formula Bar. Click that button.

- Enter a relative address for the –4 in the previous row of column A: A2. Click the "OK" button.

The value displayed in cell B3 should be 1.64295E-05, and the Formula Bar should show "=NORMSDIST(A3)-NORMSDIST(A2)."

- Copy the formula in cell B3 to cells B4:B82. Check your work by examining the displayed value in cell B42. It should be 0.039827895.

In column C we will use Excel to calculate the same probabilities for the *t* distribution whose degrees of freedom is given in cell E1 (currently 10). We will use Excel's TDIST function. If TDIST provided cumulative probabilities like NORMSDIST, the formulas in column C would be almost identical to those in column B except for the substitution of TDIST for NORMSDIST. Unfortunately, TDIST does not provide cumulative probabilities, and this will complicate its use. Consider the formula to go in cell C3.

The formula in cell C3 should calculate the probability of a *t* distributed random variable having a value between –3.9 (the value in A3) and –4 (the value in A2). Refer to the picture on page 181. To solve this problem, we will have TDIST provide a one-tail probability. This means that TDIST will provide the probability of a *t*-distributed random variable having a value *greater* than the given value. (Remember that NORMSDIST provided the probability that the random variable would be *less* than the given value.) Furthermore, the value given TDIST *must* be non-negative. Thus rather than asking TDIST for the probability of a random variable being less than –4, we must ask for the probability of a random variable being *greater* than +4. Fortunately, since the *t* distribution is symmetric, these two probabilities are equal.

One way to solve the problem of TDIST requiring a positive value is to use the absolute value function (ABS). Instead of giving TDIST a reference to cell A3 (for examples) we will have it use the absolute value of the value in cell A3.

Remember that we want the formula in cell C3 to calculate the probability of a *t* variable being between the value given in A3 and that in A2. Telling TDIST to provide the probability associated with the absolute value of the value in A3 will result in it providing the probability of a random variable being greater than 3.9. Subtracting from this the probability of a random variable being greater than the absolute value of the number in A2 will give us the probability of a variable being between +3.9 and +4. Because of the *t* distribution's symmetry, this is the same as the probability of being between –3.9 and –4—the answer we want.

Unfortunately, we will run into a problem when we copy this formula into cells where the corresponding values in column A are positive. Consider the formula we want to go in cell C45. This formula should calculate the probability of a *t* random variable being between 0.3 (the value in A45) and 0.2 (the value in A44). If we simply copied the formula just described for cell C3 to cell C45, it would calculate the probability of a random variable being greater than 0.3 (the absolute value of the value in A45) minus the probability of the random variable being greater than 0.2. Unfortunately, since 0.3 is greater than 0.2, the probability of being greater than 0.3 is *less* than the probability of being greater than 0.2. Thus, the first probability minus the second probability would be negative—a nonsense result since no probability can be negative.

A solution to this problem is to take the absolute value of the difference, which would convert the negative difference to a positive value. Although this is not necessary for cell C3 (and other cells where the corresponding values in column A are negative), it won't do any harm and will allow a single formula entered in cell C3 to provide the correct answer when it is copied to all the other cells.

In summary, the formula to be entered in cell C3 will take the absolute value of a difference between two probabilities. The first probability is the one returned by TDIST when it is given the absolute value of the value given in A3. The second probability is the one returned by TDIST when given the absolute value of A2.

- Select cell C3. Click the Edit Formula button. Select the ABS function (in the "Math & Trig" category if not in the list of recently used functions).

- ABS has only one argument field—"Number." With an insertion point in that field, select the TDIST function (in the "Statistical" category). At this point the Formula Bar should contain "=ABS(TDIST())."

The TDIST dialog window shows three arguments:

1. **X**—the value of the random variable for which you want a probability. TDIST gives the probability of a *t* variable exceeding this value. This value *must* be non-negative.

2. **Deg_freedom**—the value of the degrees of freedom for the standard *t* variable given as the *x* argument.

3. **Tails**—either the number "1" or the number "2," depending on whether you want the probability (area) of one or both tails.

What we want initially is for the "X" argument to refer to the absolute value of A3, the "Deg_freedom" argument to refer to the value in E1, and the "Tails" argument to be "1."

- With an insertion point in the "x" argument field, recall the ABS function. Since it was just used, it will be the second in the list of recently used functions. As soon as the ABS dialog window appears, the Formula Bar will contain "=ABS(TDIST(ABS()))."

- With an insertion point in the "Number" argument of the ABS dialog window, click the mouse pointer in cell A3. The Formula Bar should now contain "=ABS(TDIST(ABS(A3)))."

- Place the mouse pointer in the Formula Bar directly over "TDIST" and click the (left) mouse button. This will recall the TDIST dialog window, and the "X" argument field will contain "ABS(A3)."

- Click the mouse pointer in the "Deg_freedom" argument field. Enter an *absolute* address for the cell containing the degrees of freedom (E1).

- Click the "Tails" argument field. Enter "1" (without quotes). At this point the Formula Bar should contain "=ABS(TDIST(ABS(A3),$E$1,1))."

- Place the mouse pointer in the Formula Bar directly over ABS and click the (left) mouse button. This will recall the ABS dialog window, and the "Number" argument field will contain "TDIST(ABS(A3),$E$1,1)."

The expression in the "Number" argument field will return the probability of *t* variable having a value greater than the absolute value of A3 (3.9). We need to subtract from this the probability of a *t* variable having a value greater than the absolute value of A2 (4).

- Click the mouse pointer in the "Number" argument field to the right of the expression currently there. Enter a minus sign ("-"). Notice that a minus sign appears in the Formula Bar between the last two right parentheses.

- Open the list of recently used functions and select TDIST (which should be second on the list. The Formula Bar should contain "=ABS(TDIST(ABS(A3),$E$1,1)-TDIST())."

- All of the argument fields in the TDIST dialog window should be blank. Click the mouse pointer in the "X" argument field so that an insertion point is there.

- Open the list of recently used functions and select ABS (second in the list). When the ABS dialog window opens and an insertion point is in the "Number" argument field, click cell A2. The Formula Bar should contain "=ABS(TDIST(ABS(A3),$E$1,1)-TDIST(ABS(A2)))."

- Click the mouse pointer on the *rightmost* TDIST in the Formula Bar. The TDIST dialog window should open and "ABS(A2)" should be in the "X" argument field.

- Click the mouse pointer in the "Deg_freedom" argument field. Enter an absolute address for the degrees of freedom (10) in cell E1. Enter the number "1" (without quotes) in the "Tails" argument field. Click the "OK" button.

The value displayed in cell C3 should be 0.000221338. This is the probability of a random variable with the *t* distribution with 10 degrees of freedom having a value between –3.9 and –4. The formula in C3 (shown in the Formula Bar) should be "=ABS(TDIST(ABS(A3),$E$1,1)-TDIST(ABS(A2),$E$1,1))."

- Copy the formula in cell C3 to C4:C82. Check your work by looking at the value displayed in cell C45. It should be 0.037584292, which is the probability of a *t* distributed variable (10 dof) falling between 0.3 and 0.2.

▼ Plotting the *t* and the *z* Distributions

The values in columns B and C are probabilities associated with small intervals (0.1). The plots of these probabilities will have shapes that are very close approximations to the shapes which the density functions would have. The values along the horizontal axis correspond to values that the random variable might equal. The closer the plot is to the horizontal axis, the less likely are those values to occur. By comparing the plots of the *t* and *z* distributions, we can tell which values are more likely to occur in one distribution rather than the other by seeing which distribution's plot is higher above the section of the horizontal axis corresponding to those values.

- Select the region B1:C82. This is most easily done by entering that address range in the Name Box and pressing Enter.

- Click the Chart Wizard button.

- In the Step 1 dialog window select the "Standard Types" folder tab. Under "Chart type" select "⟨ Line." Under "Chart sub-type" select the choice in the upper left-hand corner. Click the "Next>" button.

The *t* and *z* values are correctly charted, but the values shown on the *x* axis are not correct. This can be fixed in the Step 2 dialog window.

- Click the "Series" folder tab. Click the mouse pointer in the "Category (X) axis labels:" field. Click the mouse pointer in cell A2. Press and hold the Shift key and, while pressing the shift key, press and release the End key and then press and release the down arrow key. This action should result in "='t vs z'!$A$2:$A$82" being placed in the field. This tells Excel to use the values in that range to label the horizontal (*x*) axis.

- Click the "Finish" button.

- Move the chart so that the upper left corner is in cell D2. Scroll your screen so that cell D1 is in the upper left corner. Select the chart (unless it is already selected) so that it is surrounded by "handles." Drag the lower right handle to the lower right corner of your screen. The objective is to make the chart as large as possible but small enough to view without scrolling and small enough that cells D1 and E1 are also visible.

- Enlarging the chart may have made the values along the axis too large. If so, click one of the numbers along the horizontal axis. When the axis is selected, open the Format menu on the Menu Bar and select "Selected Axis...." When the dialog window opens, click the "Font" folder tab and change the size to 8. Click one of the numbers on the vertical axis and follow the same procedure to change the font size to 8.

- Change the value of the degrees of freedom by changing the number in cell E1. Start by reducing the value to 8, then to 5, then to 2, then to 1. Does reducing the value of the degrees of freedom make the two plots more alike or less alike?

- Increase the value of the degrees of freedom. Try 20, 100, 1000, 10000, and 100,000. It may seem that the line for the *z* plot completely disappears. Actually, it is simply becoming better covered by the *t* plot line. Look carefully at the places where the plot curves most sharply and you may see indications that the two lines are not perfectly superimposed. If you can't tell a difference, scroll the worksheet back to where you can see the numbers in columns B and C. If the two plots were identical, the numbers would be identical. If you can't see a difference between the numbers in columns B and C, increase the widths of those columns. This will enable Excel to display the numbers with more precision, making the (slight) difference clearer.

As you can see, as the degrees of freedom increases, the *t* distribution becomes more like the normal distribution.

- Change the degrees of freedom back to 1.

When the degrees of freedom is 1, the *t* distribution is most unlike the normal. The difference is similar for other values of the degrees of freedom. The tails are "fatter" for the *t* distribution than they are for the normal. The *t* distribution appears more spread out than the normal distribution. Since the tails are higher and the peak is lower, how would the width of an interval symmetrically distributed around the mean with given area compare for the standard *t* and *z* distributions? This issue will be discussed again below.

▼ Using Excel to Solve Distribution of Sample Means Problems

Solving distribution of sample means problems is not important because these problems are useful. It is important to help you connect an understanding of the normal distribution with an understanding of confidence intervals and hypothesis tests, highly useful tools of statistical inference. There are two classes of problems concerning the distribution of sample means: those for which the population standard deviation (or variance) is known, and those for which only a sample standard deviation is known. The first class of problems is solved much like the very similar normal distribution problems. The primary difference is that the standard error (standard deviation of sample means) must be calculated from the equation $\sigma_{\bar{x}} = \dfrac{\sigma}{\sqrt{n}}$. Consider the following example:

A soft drink bottling machine fills each bottle with an average of 2.05 liters with a standard deviation of .03 liters. Within what region symmetrically distributed around the mean will 95% of the means of samples of 50 bottles fall?

- Double click the Sheet2 worksheet tab. Change its name to "sigma known."

- Enter the following labels in cells A1:A9: "Mu," "Sigma," "n," "Standard Error," "Prob," "zL," "zH," "x bar L," and "x bar H."

- Enter the values from the problem above in cells B1:B3 adjacent to the labels in column A.

- Enter an Excel formula in cell B4 that will divide the value of the standard deviation by the square root of *n*. The displayed value should be 0.004243.

- Enter the number ".95" in cell B5.

- Using the same technique used in Chapter 5, enter the formulas in cells B6 and B7 that will display upper and lower z values for the central interval with area .95. This will require using the NORMSINV function. B6 will display -1.95996, and B7 will display 1.959961.

- Enter the formulas in cells B8 and B9 that will convert the z values in cells B6 and B7 to $\bar{x}$ values. This conversion should be done using the following formula:

$$\bar{x} = \mu + z\sigma_{\bar{x}}$$

The difference between this formula and that used in Chapter 5 is that the z value is multiplied by the standard error rather than by the population standard deviation. The displayed value for cell B8 should be 2.041685, while that for B9 should be 2.058315. Thus 95% of the means of sample of size 50 will lie between 2.041685 and 2.058315.

Now consider the following problem:

A soft drink bottler has selected a random sample of 10 bottles from a bottle-filling machine designed to fill bottles with an average of 2.05 liters. The average fill in the sample was 2.00 liters with a standard deviation of .12 liters. If the machine was actually putting an average of 2.05 liters in all bottles, what is the probability that a sample of 10 bottles could be selected with a sample average of 2.00 or less?

This problem requires the t distribution because the only standard deviation known is that of a single sample.

- Double click the Sheet3 worksheet tab to display this blank worksheet. Change its name to "sigma unknown."

- Enter the following labels in cells A1:A8: "mu," "s," "n," "standard error," "x bar," "t," "TDIST," "Answer."

- In cells B1:B3 enter the population mean (2.05), the sample standard deviation (.12), and the sample size (10). In cell B5 enter the value for $\bar{x}$ (2.00). These are the data provided by the problem.

- In cell B4 enter the formula that will calculate the standard error. The standard error is calculated from the sample standard deviation just as it was from a population standard deviation; divide the standard deviation by the square root of *n*. The displayed value should be 0.037947.

- In cell B6 enter the formula that will standardize the number in cell B5. The formula to standardize the x value is the same as that used in the previous problem, although the symbols are usually slightly different:

$$t = \frac{\bar{x} - \mu}{s_{\bar{x}}}$$

The symbol t is used instead of z because sample means will be treated as following the t distribution. The symbol for the denominator is $s_{\bar{x}}$ instead of $\sigma_{\bar{x}}$ to indicate that the standard error used here is derived from a sample standard deviation (s) instead of a population standard deviation (σ). When the correct formula is entered in B6, it will display the value -1.31762.

Before using TDIST, it is helpful to have a clear picture of what area in the density function corresponds to the probability we want to determine. For this problem, the density function and the area are shown below:

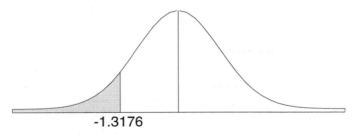

-1.3176

Compare this diagram with that shown on page 181. If we give TDIST the absolute value of -1.31762 and ask for the one-tail probability, it will return the area of the tail to the right of (+)1.31762. But the area of this tail is the same as the one above, which we want.

- Select cell B7, click the Edit Formula button, and choose TDIST.

- In the "X" argument field, enter the expression that will take the absolute value of the number in cell B6.

- In the "Deg_freedom" argument field, enter an expression that will subtract 1 from the number in cell B3. The degrees of freedom equals $n - 1$.

- Enter the number "1" in the "Tails" argument field. The number 0.11009272 will appear immediately as the "Formula Result." Click the "OK" button, and the same number will appear in cell B7.

- Since this is the value we want, enter a formula in cell B8 that will make the contents of that cell equal the value of cell B7. The probability of a sample of ten bottles having an average fill less than 2.00 liters is .110093.

Consider this problem:

A soft drink bottler has selected a random sample of 12 bottles from a bottle-filling machine. The average fill in the sample was 2.00 liters with a standard deviation of .09 liters. What is the probability that the average fill for a sample of 12 bottles will be within .05 liters of the actual average fill for all bottles?

A diagram of the density function with the relevant area is shown below. The smallest value a sample mean can have and be on the boundary of the area is $\mu - .05$. The largest value a sample mean can have is $\mu + .05$.

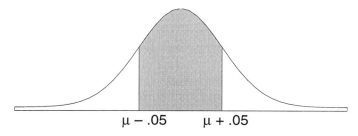

$$\mu - .05 \qquad \mu + .05$$

In this problem we are given a value for s and n, but we don't have a numeric for the two $\bar{x}$ values, and we don't have a value for μ. The expressions that are given for $\bar{x}$ ($\mu \pm .05$) will enable us to find the corresponding t values because the value for μ will cancel out.

- Enter the values for s and n in the appropriate places on the worksheet. The standard error will be calculated automatically from these values and should be displayed as 0.025981.

The calculation the t value corresponding to the x value of $\mu + .05$ is:

$$t = \frac{\bar{x} - \mu}{s_{\bar{x}}} = \frac{(\mu + .05) - \mu}{s_{\bar{x}}} = \frac{.05}{s_{\bar{x}}} .$$

Notice that μ is not present in the final expression.

- Select cell B6. Enter the formula that will divide the number .05 by the standard error in cell B4. The displayed value should be 1.924501.

How do we use TDIST with this problem? Compare the diagram above with the one showing the probability given by TDIST on page 181. The center region above is the complement of the two shaded tails shown on page 181. The shaded area above can be calculated by having TDIST determine the two-tail probability associated with the positive t value and subtracting that probability from 1.

The formula currently in cell B7 determines the one-tail area associated with the t value. Let's change it to the two-tail area:

- Select cell B7. Click the Mouse pointer on "TDIST" in the Formula Bar. Click TDIST on the most recently used function button. The TDIST dialog window will appear with the argument fields filled out as they were when the formula in B7 was created.

- Change the "1" in the "Tails" argument to "2." Click the "Finish" button. The value displayed in cell B7 should be 0.080535.

- Select cell B8. Enter the Excel function that subtracts the value in cell B7 from 1.

The answer to the problem, as displayed in cell B8, shows that the probability that the mean of a sample of 12 bottles will be within .05 liters of the mean of all bottles is .919465.

Let's examine the use of the TINV function to solve a couple of problems:

An advertising agency wants to determine whether a new campaign for Crunch-O cereal has increased consumption among 8- to 12-year-olds who eat cold cereal. Prior to the campaign, those in the population group consumed an average of 12 oz of Crunch-O per month. If the campaign had no effect, average consumption would remain at 12 oz. A sample of 15 children was chosen whose consumption after the campaign averaged 13.9 oz with a standard deviation of 3.1 oz. Assuming the campaign had no effect (and the population average remained at 12 oz.), what sample average would be exceeded by only 5% of all samples?

A diagram of this situation is shown below. The shaded area to the right has a given area of .05. The problem is to determine the boundary value, $\bar{x}$ for that area. This is done by first using TINV to determine the value of t such that the probability of a standard t having a greater value is .05, and then converting that t value to an $\bar{x}$ value.

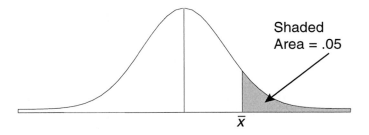

- Enter the following labels in cells D1:D8: "mu," "s," "n," "standard error," "upper tail," "TINV Prob," "t," "x bar."

- In cells E1:E3, enter the values given in the problem: $\mu = 12$, $s = 3.1$, and $n = 15$.

- In cell E4 enter the formula to calculate the standard error. The displayed value should be 0.800417.

- Enter the upper tail area, .05, in cell E5.

Refer back to the picture on page 181. In order to use TINV, we must determine the *two-tail* probability which would give us the *t* value corresponding to the $\bar{x}$ value in the picture on page 192. If we were to add a left tail to the picture corresponding to the area to the left of $-\bar{x}$, the area of that tail would also be .05 because of the symmetry of the *t* distribution. Thus the two-tail area is exactly twice the one-tail area.

- Enter the formula in cell E6 that will double the value in cell E5. The displayed value should be 0.1.

- Select cell E7. Click the Edit Formula button. Select TINV from the "Statistical" category. Move to the TINV dialog box.

- In the "Probability" argument field, put the address for the two-tail probability you have just calculated. In the "Deg_freedom" argument field, enter an expression that will subtract 1 from the value in cell E3. Click the "Finish" button. The displayed value should be 1.761309. This *t* value needs to be converted to an $\bar{x}$ value.

The formula for converting a *t* value to an $\bar{x}$ value is very similar to that used to convert a *z* value to an *x* value:

$$\bar{x} = \mu + t s_{\bar{x}}$$

- Enter the formula in cell E8 that will add the mean (in cell E1) to the product of the *t* value (in cell E7) and the standard error (in cell E4).

The answer, 13.40978 oz., is the sample average amount of cereal that would be exceeded by only 5% of the sample of 15 children assuming that the average amount eaten by all children was 12 oz.

Let's consider a slightly different version of the problem:

An advertising agency wants to determine whether a new campaign for Crunch-O cereal has increased consumption among 8- to 12-year-olds who eat cold cereal. Prior to the campaign, those in the population group consumed an average of 12 oz. of Crunch-O per month. If the campaign had no effect, average consumption would remain at 12 oz. A sample of 15 children was chosen whose consumption after the campaign averaged 13.9 oz. with a standard deviation of 3.1 oz. Assuming the campaign had no effect (and the population average remained at 12 oz.), within what interval, symmetrically distributed about the mean, would 95% of sample means fall?

The diagram for this problem is shown below. The shaded central region has an area of .95, and the values of $\bar{x}_L$ and $\bar{x}_H$ must be determined.

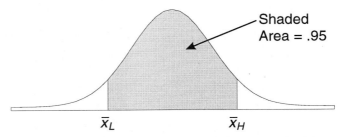

- Since the mean, sample size, and standard deviation for this problem are the same as those for the previous problem, copy the region D1:E4 to G1:H4. An easy way to do this is to select D1:E4, place the mouse pointer on the boundary of the selected region, and press and hold the Ctrl key while dragging the boundary to the new location.

- Add the following labels to cells G5:G10: "Mid Prob," "TINV Prob," "t," "x bar L," "x bar H," and "width."

- In cell H5 enter the given probability of a sample mean having a value in the central region, .95.

Compare the shaded region shown in the diagram above with that required by TINV (shown in the diagram on page 181). The probability required by TINV is the *complement* of that given in the problem, and is shown in the diagram above by the nonshaded region under the density function. Since the area under the entire density function is 1, the area of the nonshaded region is 1 minus the area of the shaded region.

- Enter the formula in cell H6 that will calculate 1 minus the value in cell H5. The displayed number should be 0.05.

- Select cell H7. Click the Edit Formula button. Select TINV and go to the dialog window.

- In the "Probability" field enter the address for the TINV probability, H6. In the "Deg_freedom" field enter the expression that will subtract 1 from the value given in the cell where the number of observations is (H3). Click the "Finish" button. The value displayed in H7 should be 2.144789.

This t value is the t value corresponding to $\bar{x}_H$. There is also a negative t value corresponding to $\bar{x}_L$. Since both have the same absolute value, the negative t value must be −2.144789.

- Enter the formula in cell H9 that adds the product of the positive *t* value (in H7) and the standard error (H4) to the mean (H1). The displayed value should be 13.71672.

- Enter the formula in H8 that will do the same as the one in H9, except with the negative *t* value. Since the standard error is (always) positive, adding the product of the negative *t* value and standard error is the same as subtracting the product of the positive *t* value and standard error. The displayed value should be 10.28328.

- In cell H10 enter the formula that will calculate the difference between the value in cell H9 and that in cell H8. The displayed value should be 3.433449.

The answer to this problem is that 95% of the means of samples of size 15 will be between 10.28328 and 13.71672.

Let's consider the effect of the degrees of freedom on the width of this interval by determining the change in the width of the interval that would occur if the sample had a size different from 15 (but with the same standard deviation).

- Change the value of *n* (H3) to 10. Observe what happens to the *t* value (H7), the standard error (H4), and the interval width (H10). (With a sample of size 10, the interval width should be 4.435216.) Switch the value in H3 back and forth between 15 and 10 until you have determined the way all three of these values change.

When the sample size goes down, the degrees of freedom also decreases. This causes the *t* value to increase (to 2.262159 when *n* is 10). Refer again to the diagram on page 181. As the value of *t* goes up, the boundary moves further from the mean, 0, of a standard *t* distribution. Since the *t* value of the boundary for the left tail has the same absolute value (but negative sign), it too moves away from the mean and the interval becomes larger. Conversely, if the sample size (and degrees of freedom) becomes larger, the width of the interval containing the central 95% of *t* values decreases. Since the *z* distribution is the limit of the *t* distribution as the degrees of freedom increases toward infinity, the width of the interval containing 95% of *z* values must be narrower than the corresponding interval for any *t* distribution.

When the number of observations goes down, the standard error goes up. This reinforces the effect of the change in the *t* value caused by the change in degrees of freedom. Conversely, an increase in sample size causes the standard error to go down, which reduces the width of the central interval. The impact of the change in the standard error is much larger than the impact of the change in the degrees of freedom of the *t* distribution.

▼ Exercises

1. A bottle-filling machine is designed to fill bottles with an average fill of 2.02 liters. A sample of 20 bottles is selected. The average fill of the bottles in the sample is 1.99 liters, and the standard deviation is .09 liters. Assume that the machine is operating properly and really is filling *all* bottles with an average fill of 2.02. What is the probability that a random sample of 20 bottles could have a sample average fill of 1.99 or less? Assume that the filling process is normally distributed.

2. For the question above, determine an interval symmetrically distributed about the population mean of 2.02 liters within which would fall 90% of the means of samples of 20 bottles.

3. The average time required for students to complete the registration process at a university has been 55 minutes. A university administrator is trying a new procedure. Under this procedure, the registration times of 25 randomly selected students are recorded, resulting in a sample mean of 50.2 minutes and a sample standard deviation of 8.7 minutes. Assuming that there has been no improvement in the average time with the new procedure, determine the probability that the mean time for 25 students would be 50.2 minutes or less. Assume that student registration times are normally distributed.

4. A bolt-making machine is designed to produce bolts whose length is normally distributed with an average of 2 inches and a standard deviation of .1 inches. If the machine is working properly, what is the probability that a sample of 10 bolts would have an average length of 2.05 inches or more?

5. For the problem above, determine the value of the length of the bolts such that only 5% of the samples of 20 bolts would have means less than that length.

6. Decreasing the number of degrees of freedom causes the shape of the standard *t* density function to change. The function goes up in the tails and down in the middle. This change is similar to that which happens with the normal density function when the value of the standard deviation is increased. Is it the same? Investigate this by changing the "t vs z" worksheet. Change column B so that NORMDIST is used rather than NORMSDIST so that you can vary the value for the standard deviation. Use a low value (1 to 4) for the

degrees of freedom of the standard t distribution. Now change the standard deviation of the normal curve so that the tops of the two curves are the same height. Are the two curves identical? If not, describe the differences. Print the plot showing the two curves with the same heights. Put your name on the header and use the title to document the value for the dof of the t curve and the value of σ for the z curve.

7. When samples of size 30 are chosen, the distribution of sample means is fairly close to the normal distribution, even when the population follows the skewed distribution we tried last. According to the standard rule of thumb for the central limit theorem, this should not be the case for smaller sample sizes. Investigate the case of samples of size 15. Reload the chap6.xls spreadsheet, but be sure to turn off automatic recalculation *before* you open it. Change the formulas in column AF so that they calculate the average of the first 15 cells in each row instead of the first 30. Also change the standard deviation of the normal curve (cell AI3) so that it reflects the new sample size. Although it is not necessary, it might speed up recalculation if you deleted the second 15 in each row. If the population's skew comes through in the distribution of sample means, you should tend to see bars on the right side of the distribution above the normal line, while those on the left are below the normal curve. Recalculate the spreadsheet several times to check if this is the case. Rescale the horizontal axis so that you can see more of the plots. Print out some of the plots to show what you have seen.

Chapter 7

▼

Confidence Intervals on a Population Mean

Inferential statistics generally involves a straightforward application of the concepts of a sampling distribution. One of the techniques of inferential statistics is interval estimation. Suppose you need to know the mean of a population, but only data from a (properly drawn) sample is available. How can you take information from a sample and use it to *infer* information about a population? The best single-value (or *point*) estimate you can give for a population mean is the sample mean. It is best in the sense that no other calculation can be made of the data in the sample yielding a single number that is likely to be as close to the population mean as is the sample mean.

Using the sample mean as an estimate of the population mean has one drawback—it is certain to be wrong! A sample mean, as we saw in the previous chapter, is a continuous random variable. A population mean, on the other hand, is not a random variable. It is a fixed value, even though it is unknown. The probability that a continuous random variable will ever precisely equal a fixed value is zero. Therefore, the probability that any sample mean will ever precisely equal the population mean is zero. Clearly statistics needs a technique for providing estimates of a population mean that can sometimes be correct.

The sampling distribution of the mean provides a technique for determining intervals within which a sample mean may lie with nonzero probability. These problems, examples of which were worked in the previous chapter, are worded like this, "Find an interval symmetrically distributed around the population mean that will contain $x\%$ of sample means." By using the t distribution, it is possible to use a sample standard deviation to solve this type of problem. The interval boundaries are found by evaluating the following expression:

$$\mu \pm ts_{\bar{x}}$$

The center of this interval is μ, the population mean. The lower bound is below μ by an amount equal to $ts_{\bar{x}}$, while the upper bound is above μ by the same amount. The value of t is determined by the size of the $x\%$ in the problem and by the size of the sample (degrees of freedom). The value of the standard error, $s_{\bar{x}}$, is determined by the sample standard deviation (s) and the sample size (n).

In most situations the value of μ is unknown. If we knew μ, there would be no point to estimating it with a sample! If we don't know the value of μ, there's no way we can calculate the boundaries of an interval symmetrically distributed around μ, which contains a given percentage of sample means. Even though its value is unknown, both μ and the interval around μ still exist. If we pick a sample, there is no way of knowing whether or not the mean of that sample lies within the interval. But we do know the *probability* that it lies within the interval. How can this be used? Consider the diagram below of a density function of a sampling distribution of the mean.

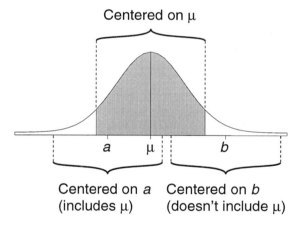

Centered on μ

a μ b

Centered on a Centered on b
(includes μ)   (doesn't include μ)

Suppose the shaded central region, which is centered on μ, has an area of .95. The portion of the horizontal axis below the shaded region represents the range of values, symmetrically distributed about the mean, within which a single sample mean has a .95 probability of falling. If we know nothing about the population, then we can't know the actual values of the boundaries of that range. If a sample is drawn and its mean is calculated, we cannot know for sure if that mean lies within the range of values (as does a in the diagram) or outside the range (like b). But we know it has a 95% chance of being inside the range and only a 5% chance of being outside the range.

Suppose we construct an interval of the same width as the unknown interval around this sample mean. We can do this by adding and subtracting $ts_{\bar{x}}$ from the sample mean, which we can calculate entirely from the data of the sample. This value, $ts_{\bar{x}}$, is called the *sampling error.* Notice that if the sample mean lies with the range containing 95% of the sample means (like *a*), the interval centered on it will include μ. If the sample mean lies outside the range containing 95% of the sample, then the interval centered on it will not contain μ. Since there is a 95% probability that the sample mean does lie within the range, there is a 95% probability that this interval centered on the sample mean will include the unknown value of μ. Such an interval is called a *95% confidence interval*. Intervals can be constructed to other confidence levels, such as 80%, 90%, or 99%, by using the appropriate value for *t* in the expression for the sampling error.

▼ Using Excel to Determine Confidence Intervals

- Start Excel with a new blank workbook and save it in a file named chap7.xls.

- Double click the "Sheet1" worksheet tab and change its name to "CI on Mu."

Consider the following problem:

A manufacturer wants to test a batch of light bulbs for lumen output. A sample of light bulbs was tested with the following results:

1326, 1336, 1351, 1365, 1209, 1343, 1259, 1365, 1308, 1349

Determine a 95% confidence interval estimate for the mean lumen output of all light bulbs in the batch. The lumen output of all bulbs can be assumed to be normally distributed.

- In cell A1 enter the label "Data." In cells C1:C9 enter the following labels in the order given: "n," "mean," "std dev," "std err," "conf level," "t," "samp error," "lower bnd," "upper bnd."

Column D will contain the statistics given by the labels in the same row of column C.

- In cells A2:A11, enter the data from the problem.

Many of Excel's built-in functions will automatically ignore blank cells. This will be used to create a worksheet that can determine confidence intervals for samples of varying size.

- Select cell D1. Click the Edit Formula button. Select the COUNT function ("Statistical" category).

- When the dialog window opens, be certain an insertion point is in the "Value1" argument field. If it is not, click the mouse pointer in that field.

- Click the mouse pointer on the column heading of column A. (The column heading is the gray square at the top of the column with the letter "A" in it.) The argument field will contain "A:A." Doing this is equivalent to selecting the entire column, including the label and all of the blank cells. This style of addressing can be used in any function and in the Name Box to refer to entire columns. Multiple columns can be selected by giving the starting and ending column letters. "C:E," for example, would refer to all of columns C, D, and E.

- Click the "OK" button. Cell D1 will display "10," which is the number of data items in column A, the size of the sample.

The COUNT function counts only cells displaying numbers. It ignores labels and blank cells. It will include functions if they display a number. Many of the other Excel functions designed to do calculations behave the same way.

- Observe the behavior of the COUNT function by entering the number "0" in cell A14. Then delete that number so that the value displayed in D1 is "10."

- Using the "A:A" addressing style, enter the formula in cell D2 to calculate the mean of the numbers in column A. The displayed value should be 1321.1.

- Enter the formula in cell D3 to calculate the standard deviation of all the numbers in column A. The displayed value should be 50.38397.

- Enter the formula in cell D4 to calculate the standard error. Recall that the standard error is the standard deviation (in cell D3) divided by the square root of the sample size (in cell D1). The value displayed in D4 should be 15.93281.

- Enter "95%" in cell D5. Be sure to enter the percent symbol "%."

Excel regards the percent symbol as a type of cell format. Entering a number followed by a percent sign is equivalent to first entering the number as a proportion between 0 and 1 and then clicking the Percent Style button to set that cell's format.

- To see the effect of the percent style, select D5 again and click the comma style button: **,** . The cell will display 0.95, the actual value in the cell. Select the cell again and click the percent style button: **%** . Now it again displays 95%. When this cell is used in a formula, the value Excel will use in calculations is 0.95.

The formula to be entered in cell D6 will determine the *t* value corresponding to the level of confidence (.95 for this problem) and the degrees of freedom. The TINV function will convert a probability to a *t* value, but the probability it expects is not the area of the central region corresponding to the confidence level. Refer to the diagram on page 181. TINV must be given the two-tail probability represented by the two shaded regions. The confidence level corresponds to the area of the un-shaded region in the center. These two areas are complementary; they must sum to one. To determine the tail areas, simply subtract the confidence level from one.

- Select cell D6. Click the Edit Formula button and select the TINV function.

- In the "Probability" argument field, enter an expression that will subtract the confidence level in cell D5 from one. Check the value displayed to the right of the argument field. It should show the value "0.05."

- In the "Deg_freedom" argument field, enter the expression that will subtract one from the sample size in cell D1. The value displayed to the right of the field should be "9." Click the "OK" button. The value displayed in cell D6 should be 2.262159.

- Enter the formula in cell D7 to calculate the sampling error. The sampling error, $ts_{\bar{x}}$, is the product of the *t* value and the standard error. The displayed value should be 36.04255.

- Enter the formulas in cells D8 and D9 to calculate the lower and upper bounds of the confidence interval. The lower bound is the sample mean minus the sampling error while the upper bound is the sample mean plus the sampling error. The displayed values should be 1285.057 and 1357.143, respectively.

The 95% confidence interval on the population mean can be written as

$$1285.057 < \mu < 1357.143$$

You can determine the 80% confidence interval on the mean by entering ".80" (or "80%") in cell D5. You should get this result:

$$1299.064 < \mu < 1343.136$$

Similarly the 99% confidence interval should be

$$1269.321 < \mu < 1372.879$$

Notice that the higher the level of confidence, the lower the value of the lower bound and the higher the value of the upper bound. Higher levels of confidence are associated with larger sampling errors and wider intervals than lower levels of confidence. It is desirable for a confidence interval to have as high a level of confidence as possible, but it is also desirable for it to be narrow. What answer do you get from Excel when you ask for a 100% confidence interval (the correct answer is $-\infty < \mu < +\infty$)?

▼ Using Excel to Determine Required Sample Size

The only practical way of reducing the sampling error without decreasing the level of confidence is to increase the size of the sample. As n increases, the standard error will decrease. The higher degrees of freedom will also slightly reduce the t value associated with a particular confidence level. Larger samples are more expensive to collect and thus some tradeoff between the sample size and the size of sampling error is often needed. In order to investigate that tradeoff, users of confidence intervals will often want to determine the sample size needed to obtain a target sampling error. Since the sampling error, $ts_{\bar{x}}$, requires a standard deviation, it is not really possible to determine the relationship between sample size and sampling error before drawing a sample. It's tough to draw a sample before knowing the sample size required. This problem is so important, however, that we have to assume that some information about the population standard deviation is known. Perhaps historical data can be used or a pilot sample drawn. Assuming that we know something about the *population* standard deviation also sidesteps another issue. If we don't know the size of the sample, what value for the degrees of freedom should be used for the t in the sampling error? Using a value for the population standard deviation enables us to use the z distribution rather than the t distribution for the distribution of sample means. The sampling error in this case is $z\sigma_{\bar{x}}$ rather than $ts_{\bar{x}}$. If we symbolize the sampling error as e, this equation can be written as

$$e = z\sigma_{\bar{x}}$$
$$= z\frac{\sigma}{\sqrt{n}}$$

Solving for n yields

$$n = \frac{z^2\sigma^2}{e^2} = \left(\frac{z\sigma}{e}\right)^2$$

If the value for n is not an integer, the convention is to *round up* to the nearest integer. This formula, including the rounding, is easily evaluated by Excel.

- Double click the "Sheet2" worksheet tab and rename it "n" (the symbol for the size of a sample).

Consider the following problem:

Owners of a fast-food restaurant want to estimate the average amount spent by customers during the lunch hour. A 92% confidence interval is desired with a sampling error of no more than ±$2.00. Based on past experience, they believe the standard deviation of customer expenditures is no more than $5.00. What sample size is needed to achieve this sampling error?

- Enter the following labels in the range A1:A6 of your worksheet: "samp error," "conf level," "z," "sigma," "n1," "n2."

- In cell B1 enter the desired sampling error from the problem, 2. In cell B2 enter the desired confidence level, .92 (or 92%). In cell B4 enter the assumed value for σ, 5.

Cell B3 must contain the z value corresponding to the confidence level in B2. This will involve using the NORMSINV function, which converts a *left-tail* probability to a z value. Furthermore, if you convert the area of the central region corresponding to a confidence interval to the area of the tail to the left of the central region, the z value you get will be negative. You want the value displayed in cell B3 to be positive. Refer to Chapter 5, particularly the section beginning on page 150, to review the technique for determining the z value you need.

- Enter the formula in cell B3 to convert the confidence level in cell B2 to the appropriate positive z value. When the correct formula is entered, the displayed value corresponding to a 92% confidence level is 1.750686.

- Enter the Excel formula in cell B5 that will calculate the value for n given in the formula on page 203. Recall that " ^ " is the Excel symbol to raise a number to a power. The expression to square the value of cell B3 would be "B3 ^ 2." When the correct formula is entered, cell B4 should display the value 19.15564.

- Enter the Excel formula in cell B6 that will round the value in cell B4 up to the next integer. Use the CEILING function (Math & Trig category) for this with the number "1" as the value of the "Significance" argument. Cell B6 should display the value 20.

This worksheet allows us to easily investigate the trade-offs between decreased sampling error and increased sample size. Suppose, for example, that we wanted to reduce the sampling error by half.

- Change the desired value of the sampling error in cell B1 from "2" to "1." This should cause the required sample size (n_2) to be 77.

Reducing the required sampling error by half more than tripled (or almost quadrupled) the required sample size.

- Reduce the desired sampling error again by half from ±1.00 to ±0.5. This should cause the needed sampling size to nearly quadruple again to 307.

As the sampling error gets smaller, it becomes increasingly more expensive (in terms of sample size) to achieve additional reduction.

▼ Simulating the Accuracy of Confidence Intervals

In order to better understand the accuracy of confidence intervals, we will look at the results of drawing 1,000 samples from a known population and constructing a confidence interval from each sample. Of course, when confidence intervals are actually used, the population is never known, otherwise there would be no point in estimating the population mean—we could calculate it directly. As a result, we never know for sure whether a confidence interval is really correct or not. Although artificial, this exercise will give us better insight into the meaning of "confidence level."

- Save and close the chap7.xls worksheet.

Consider the following problem:

A large woodworking company is offered the opportunity to purchase a lot of 1,275 radial saw blades from a new supplier at what seems like a very good price. Critical to the decision of whether or not to buy the blades is their quality, and a critical aspect is the blades' useful lifetime, since a low price on a blade that won't last is no bargain. The only way of determining the lifetime of a blade is to destructively test it—use it to cut wood in a testing situation until it wears out. Clearly a sampling procedure is necessary, and the company has decided to estimate a 95% confidence interval of the average life of the blades in the lot.

- Open the workbook SawBlades.xls located in the Chap_7 folder of the data diskette for this book. Open the File menu on the Menu Bar and click "Save As...." Save the workbook on a hard disk or network drive because it will become too large to fit on a diskette.

There are three worksheets in this workbook: "Population," "Samples," and "Conf Intervals." The "Population" worksheet shows the actual lifetime of each of the 1,275 blades. Think of this information as arising from pedagogical magic—neither the company nor the supplier can really know this information. We will use the Multiple Random Samples tool to draw 1,000 samples and place them on the "Samples" worksheet. There are already three samples there that we will use to develop the confidence interval calculations. The actual confidence intervals will be calculated on the remaining worksheet. Let's do this now for the first sample provided.

- Click the "Conf Intervals" worksheet tab and select cell A2. We will enter a formula to calculate the mean of the first sample here.

- Click the Edit Formula button. Select the "Average" function (Statistical category). With an insertion point in the "Number1" field, click the "Samples" worksheet.

- Move the Formula Palette down so that you can see the second row on the worksheet. Click the row header for the second row. In the "Number1" field you should see "Samples!2:2." This form of address refers to the entire second row of the "Samples" worksheet. Since all cells in that row are blank except for the sample values, this address will work for all of the functions calculating sample statistics. Click the "OK" button. The value displayed in cell A2 of the "Conf Intervals" worksheet should be 98.93333

- Select cell B2. Enter a formula which will calculate the sample standard deviation of all values on row 2 of the "Samples" worksheet. The displayed value will be 17.87843.

- Select cell C2. Enter a formula using the COUNT function that will determine the number of values on row 2 of the "Samples" worksheet. The displayed value should be 15.

- Enter a formula in cell D2 to calculate the standard errors, using relative addresses for B2 and C2. This displayed value should be 4.61619.

- Use an absolute address to the value in cell K1 and a relative address to the value in cell C2 in a formula entered in cell E2 to calculate the t value. The displayed value should be 2.144789.

- Use relative addresses to calculate the sampling error in cell F2. The displayed value should be 9.900751.

- Use relative addresses to calculate the upper and lower bounds of the confidence interval in cells G2 and H2. The displayed values should be 89.03258254 and 108.8340841, respectively.

Based on this sample, the 95% confidence interval on the mean is: $89.0326 < \mu < 108.8341$. Is this correct? A common error in confidence intervals is to say that this statement has a 95% probability of being correct. Probability can only be used when discussing random variables. The boundaries of the confidence interval of this sample are not random numbers—we have determined exactly what their value is. The population mean is also not a random number, although we haven't figured it out yet. Let's do that now.

- Switch to the "Population" worksheet. In cell G1 enter the label "Population Mean." In cell G2 enter a formula to calculate the average of the population numbers in A2:E256. The displayed value should be 100.

- Switch to the "Conf Intervals" worksheet.

Does the confidence interval contain the true population mean? The answer is yes. There is no probability associated with it. If we were to draw another sample, would it also contain the true population mean? Of that we cannot be certain. The confidence interval boundaries of a new sample are random numbers (until the sample is drawn). We therefore can speak of the probability that those boundaries will bracket the true population mean. What is that probability? Is it 95%? We will examine this by drawing 1,000 samples and determining the proportion of the 1,000 resulting confidence intervals that do correctly bracket the population mean. The expected value of that proportion is the probability of a sample having correct confidence interval boundaries. Of course, it is likely the proportion will differ somewhat from its expected value, but it should be close.

Before drawing the 1,000 samples, let's put a formula in cell I2 that will automatically tell us if the confidence interval is correct. We can use Excel functions to display the word "Yes" if the confidence interval is correct and "No" if it is not. This formula will have to examine the values in G2 and H2 and display "Yes" if and only if the value in G2 is less than the population mean and the value in H2 is greater than the population mean.

- Select cell I2. Click the Edit Formula button. Choose the IF function ("Logical" category).

The IF function has three arguments. In the "Logical_test" argument field, we will put an expression that is either true or false. If the expression is true, the IF function will display the value of the "Value_if_true" argument field. Otherwise it will display the value of the "Value_if_false" argument field. The expression we want is one that says that the value of G2 is less than the population mean *and* the value of H2 is less than the population mean. The fact that we have two conditions, both of which must be true, means we have to use another Excel function.

- With the insertion point in the "Logical_test" field, open the list of functions and select the AND function from the "Logical" category.

The AND function has two or more arguments. Each argument must contain an expression that is either true or false. If all arguments are true, the AND function returns the value of true. If any argument is false (even if others are true) the AND function returns the value false. In the "Logical1" argument field we will enter an expression that the value of G2 is less than the population mean, and in the "Logical2" argument field we will enter an expression that the value of H2 is greater than the population mean. The AND function (and the value of the IF function's "Logical_Test" argument) will thus be true if and only if the confidence interval correctly brackets the population mean.

- With the insertion point in the "Logical1" argument field, click the mouse pointer in cell G2. This address should be *relative*. Enter the "less than" symbol ("<"). Click on the "Population" worksheet and then click on cell G2, where the true population mean is. Make this address *absolute*. The argument field should contain "G2<Population!$G$2." Immediately to the right of the argument field you should see "=TRUE" for the value of the field.

- Click the "Logical2" argument field to put the insertion point there. Click cell H2 on the "Conf Intervals" worksheet. Enter a "greater than" symbol (">"). Click cell G2 on the "Population" worksheet and make the address *absolute*. The field should contain "H2>Population!$G$2." To the right of the field you should see "=TRUE," and just below you should also see "=TRUE" for the resulting value of the function. The Formula Bar should contain "=IF(AND(G2<Population!$G$2,H2>Population!$G$2))."

- Click the mouse pointer on the "IF" in the Formula Bar. The IF function dialog window should reappear with the "Logical_test" argument field filled.

- Enter the word "Yes" in the "Value_if_true" argument field and the word "No" in the "Value_if_false" argument field. Click the "OK" button. The word "Yes" should display in cell I2.

- Test the worksheet by copying the formulas in row 2 (A2:I2) down to rows 3 and 4. Check the displayed results with the picture below. If your values are not the same, change only the formulas in row 2 and recopy those formulas to rows 3 and 4 until your results agree.

	A	B	C	D	E	F	G	H	I
1	Mean	Std Dev	Count	Std Err	t value	Samp Err	Lower Bound	Upper Bound	Correct?
2	98.93333	17.87843	15	4.61619	2.144789	9.900751	89.03258254	108.834084	Yes
3	105.8	16.83194	15	4.345989	2.144789	9.321227	96.47877269	115.121227	Yes
4	91	14.14719	15	3.652788	2.144789	7.834457	83.16554284	98.8344572	No
5									

Let's now check the accuracy of 1,000 different confidence intervals.

- Open the "Tools" menu on the Menu Bar. Select "Learning Business Statistics" and "Multiple Random Samples." If "Learning Business Statistics" is not on the Tools menu, you haven't installed the Add-Ins for this book. See Appendix C.

- Use the mouse to enter the address of the population (to ensure the worksheet name is included). Enter "15" for the sample size and "1000" for the number of samples. Click the "Output Range:" field and then click the mouse pointer in cell A2 of the "Samples" worksheet. The dialog window should look like the picture below.

- Click the "OK" button. Note that this will replace the three samples already on the worksheet, as well as generate 997 additional samples.

- Switch to the "Samples" worksheet and verify that all the rows between 2 and 1001 contain numbers.

- Switch to the "Conf Intervals" worksheet. Select the region A2:I1002. This is probably most easily done using the Name Box.

- Open the Edit menu on the Menu Bar. Select "Fill" and then "Down." This should copy the formulas in the first row to the next 999.

- Look at the values displayed on the worksheet. Since the samples have all been separately drawn, you should see different numbers as you look down each column, with the exception of columns C and E. Most of the cells in column I should display "Yes," but you should find a few No's as you scroll down through the column.

In order to more easily determine the number of confidence intervals that are correct and incorrect, we will construct a table in which Excel will automatically tabulate the number of times "Yes" and "No" appears in column I.

- In cells J4:J6 enter the labels "Correct," "Incorrect," and "Total." In cells K3:L3 enter the labels "Number," and "Percent."

Excel has a function, COUNTIF, that will scan a range of cells and count the number of times a particular value (including a particular word) appears.

- Select cell K4. Click the Edit Formula button and choose the COUNTIF function from the "Statistical" category.

COUNTIF has two arguments: "Range," where the range address to be scanned is entered, and "Criteria" where a value can be put that is to be counted.

- With the insertion point in the "Range" argument field, click the header for column I. "I:I" will appear in the argument field. Enter "Yes" in the "Criteria" argument field. Click the "OK" button. Cell K4 will display a number which should not be greater than 1,000 and should be close to 950. This is the number of times the word "Yes" appears in column I.

- Select cell K5. Enter a formula using COUNTIF, which will count the number of times "No" appears in column I.

- Select cell K6. Click the AutoSum button on the Main Toolbar: Σ. Press the Enter key. K6 should display 1000.

- Enter formulas in L4 and L5 that will take the corresponding numbers in K4 and K5 and convert them to proportions by dividing by the number in K6.

- Select L6 and enter the formula that will sum the numbers in L4 and L5. The displayed value should be 1.

- Select cells L4:L6. Click the Percent Style button (%)to display the proportions as percentage. Then click the Increase Decimal button (⊞) so that the percentages show two values to the right of the decimal points.

Recall that when the confidence level is increased, the sampling error (and the width of the confidence interval) increases. Every sample whose 95% confidence interval included the mean will still include the mean when the confidence level increases to 99%. Some of the samples whose 95% confidence intervals did not include the mean will now include the mean because those intervals are wider.

- Experiment with lower confidence levels, including 80%, 50%, and 25%. Compare the value of the confidence level with the percentage of the 1,000 samples whose confidence intervals are correct.

The confidence level and the percentage of the 1,000 samples with correct confidence intervals should always be close in value, regardless of the value of the confidence level. So what does the confidence level mean? If we choose a sample and construct a 95% confidence interval from that sample, is it correct to say that there is a 95% chance that the population mean lies within the confidence interval?

No. Once a sample is chosen, a 95% confidence interval either contains the population mean or does not contain the population mean. Since we usually don't know the population mean (and wouldn't need a confidence interval if we did) we don't know whether or not the interval does contain the population mean. Not knowing doesn't change the fact that everything is determined and a probability statement is inappropriate.

The confidence level tells us the probability that a randomly chosen sample will have a correct confidence interval. If we construct a 95% confidence interval, there is a 95% probability that we will choose a sample whose confidence interval will be correct. The distinction here is subtle. It is the sample and the confidence interval boundaries calculated from that sample that are random. The confidence level tells us the probability that the confidence interval procedure will result in a correct interval. Once a particular interval is calculated, its boundaries are no longer random; they are fixed. The population mean is also not random; it too is a fixed value. Before the sample was chosen, there was a probability, given by the confidence level, that that sample would result in a correct confidence interval. After the sample is chosen, the confidence interval is either correct or incorrect, and our ignorance of that state does not make the issue random or probabilistic.

▼ Exercises

Close your worksheets before doing the exercises. Your objective in using Excel to determine confidence intervals is not to use the worksheets you have developed in this lesson but to understand the process of forming confidence intervals well enough that you can always develop your own worksheet in response to any problem you encounter.

Sometimes the data we wish to analyze are provided on a diskette or in another form that can be directly read by a computer. It is a good idea to have Excel read such data because it reduces the chance for error. Data provided on a diskette can come in a variety of formats. The easiest for

Excel is for the data to be in the form of an Excel workbook. Other formats are common, however, and we often have no control over the formats in which data we want to use are provided.

Besides Excel workbooks, Excel has no difficulty reading data provided in the formats of competing spreadsheet products like Quattro Pro and 1-2-3. The format used by early versions of 1-2-3 has become a popular way to distribute data because this format can now be read by most spreadsheet programs. Files written in this format typically have names which end in .WKS or .WK1.

The most universal format for data is ASCII text. Data in this form can be read by most computer programs. Data in this form can be in a file with any name, although common endings for files with ASCII data include .TXT, .DAT., and .PRN. There is nothing in the ASCII format that corresponds to the notion of spreadsheet cells. Although Excel can read ASCII text, it needs help determining exactly what items go into individual cells. In most cases, this is easily done.

 In these exercises we will use a set of data collected by a battery manufacturer testing the life of a particular model battery. These data are in the file named Battery.txt, and instructions will be given on how to read them. The first step is the same as that used for reading an Excel workbook.

- Click the Open button 🖼 and display the directory where the data files for this book are located (probably Chap_7 on the drive A: diskette).

The Open dialog window will initially show only files containing Excel workbooks (and directories or folders). To get the window to show other files (including ASCII files) a setting must be changed.

- Near the bottom left of the Open dialog window, locate the field named "Files of type:". Click the small downward-pointing arrow to open the list as shown by the picture below. Select "All Files (*.*)" The list will close and "All Files (*.*)" will appear in the field.

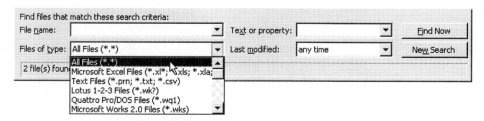

This setting will cause the Open dialog window to show all of the files in the displayed directory.

- Select "Battery.txt" from the list of files and click the "Open" button on the right side of the dialog window.

Excel will recognize that the data in the file are in the ASCII format. Because this format can be harder for Excel to interpret than other formats, Excel automatically starts the Text Import Wizard and opens the first dialog window. You will notice that the window shows some of the first few lines of the data. Most of the difficulties with using ASCII files occur when there is more than one number in each line. With this file, however, each line has only a single number. Excel has no difficulty with such a file.

- Click the "Finish" button.

Excel tries to treat the ASCII file as a workbook. If you look on Excel's Title Bar you will see the name "Battery.txt." Notice that the workbook has only a single worksheet. If you were to make changes on that worksheet and then try to save them, Excel would do its best to write the changed workbook as an ASCII file and would replace the existing Battery.txt with the file it wrote. To avoid this, it is necessary to do the following.

- Click "File" on the Menu Bar. Select "Save As...." The Save As dialog window will open.

- At the bottom of the window is a selection field titled "Save File as Type." You will probably recognize it as similar to the "List Files as Type" field in the Open dialog window.

- The current selection is "Text (Tab delimited) (*.txt)." Click the down arrow to the right of the field and choose "Microsoft Excel Workbook (*.xls)." Notice that the name of the file in the "File Name" field changes from "BATTERY.TXT" to "BATTERY.xls."

- Click the "Save" button. This will save the file in the same folder as Battery.txt. Notice that the Excel Title Bar now has the name BATTERY.xls.

1. Based on the data in the worksheet, calculate a 95% confidence interval on the average battery life of all batteries of this type.

2. Suppose the manufacturer wanted future 95% confidence intervals to have a sampling error of, at most, 0.5 hr. Assuming that future population variances are the same as the current sample variance, determine how large a sample would be needed to achieve this sampling error.

3. Produce a chart that shows the relationship between sampling error and required sample size, assuming the population has the same

standard deviation as this sample of batteries. Do this by creating a series of numbers that goes from 2 to .1 by increments of –0.05. In an adjacent column, determine the sample size required to achieve that sampling error with a 95% confidence interval. Produce a line plot with desired sampling error on the *x* (horizontal) axis and required sample size on the *y* (vertical) axis. Give the chart an appropriate title and print it. Be sure your name is in a header or footer. Describe in words the relationship the chart shows between reduced sampling error and increases in the required sample size.

4. Develop a chart showing the relationship between confidence level and sampling error for a confidence interval of the population mean battery life. First add a new worksheet to your workbook by opening the "Insert" menu on the Menu Bar and selecting "Worksheet." A new worksheet will be created with the name "Sheet2," although Excel will place it in front of the existing "Sheet1." Copy cells A1:A36 from "Sheet1" to the new worksheet. Copy also the cells you used in answering Exercise 1 to the new worksheet. Create a column with the series of confidence levels from 10% to 95% with increments of 5%. In a column to the right enter the formula which will calculate the sampling error associated with each confidence level. Plot this relationship on a line chart with confidence level on the *x* axis and sampling error on the *y* axis. Print the chart with an appropriate title and your name in either the header or footer. Describe this relationship and contrast it with the relationship between sampling error and sample size you determined in response to Exercise 3.

5. Use the Descriptive Statistics Tool to analyze the Battery Life data. In the "Output Options" area select "Summary Statistics" and "Confidence Level for Mean" and put "95%" in the field to the right. The output written by the tool will include a number labeled "Confidence Level(95.0%)." What name has been used in this chapter for that number?

The data for the following problems can be found in the workbook Exercises.xls in the folder containing the data for this chapter.

6. A detergent-box filling machine fills empty boxes with detergent. A sample of boxes filled by the machine was selected, and the weight of the detergent (in ounces) placed in each box was measured. The measurements are:

    55.67, 47.28, 54.55, 48.19, 46.94, 52.34, 49.62, 51.48, 49.77, 49.71, 48.09, 49.78, 48.39, 49.81, 53.83, 48.41, 47.30, 46.68, 48.40, 48.85, 47.97, 49.98, 51.20, 51.57, 55.81

Determine a 95% confidence interval for the mean amount of detergent placed in all boxes. How large a sample would you estimate would be required to reduce the sampling error to 0.75 ounces?

7. A bank office wishes to estimate the amount of time required to approve a home equity line of credit measured from the original application. A sample of applications was selected, and the amount of time (in working days) required to approve each application was determined. The values are:

8, 16, 17, 12, 11, 16, 16, 21, 18, 11, 16, 18

Determine a 90% confidence interval for the average amount of time required to approve all home equity lines of credit. How large a sample do you estimate would be required to reduce the sampling error to 1 day?

8. A ball bearing manufacturer wants to determine the diameter of a particular ball bearing. A sample of bearings was selected and the diameter of each bearing (in cm) was measured. Those numbers were:

9.66, 8.34, 11.09, 9.53, 9.22, 10.10, 11.51, 10.13, 8.62, 9.62, 9.29, 10.66, 12.28, 10.06, 11.63, 9.42, 9.24, 9.31, 9.29, 11.75

Determine the sampling error associated with 99%, 95%, and 90% confidence intervals of the mean. How large a sample would you estimate would be required for a 99% confidence interval sampling error of 0.50 cm?

9. A large university offers many sections of undergraduate statistics. A sample of sections for the past five years was chosen, and the section GPA was calculated. These data are:

1.8, 1.8, 2.2, 2.4, 3.2, 1.6, 3.1, 3.0, 1.5, 2.4

Based upon these data, determine a 95% confidence interval for the average section GPA for all sections for the past five years. How large a sample would you estimate would be required to reduce the sampling error to 0.1?

10. A manufacturer of aircraft control cable makes a particular cable designed to have a breaking strength of 1,000 kg. A sample of cable was chosen and tested to determine breaking strength. The measured breaking strength of the sample cables (in kg) were:

996, 993, 990, 1010, 995, 989, 999, 1011, 981, 1000, 980, 994, 1003, 990, 999

Based upon these data, determine a 90% confidence interval estimate for the mean breaking strength of all cable. How large a sample would you estimate would be required to reduce the sampling error to 2 kg?

Chapter 8

▼

Understanding Hypothesis Testing

Hypothesis testing is a technique that lets sample data be used to determine whether or not a characteristic of a population is true. It is used when the need is to answer a yes/no question about the population rather than to determine an estimate of a population parameter. This arises, for example, in quality control when the yes/no question may be, "Is our production system operating properly?" It is used in marketing when the yes/no question might be, "Does the proposed new package lead to higher sales than the old package?"

Hypothesis testing often seems confusing at first to the beginning student, although it is as straightforward an application of sampling distributions as confidence intervals. This chapter will give you a better sense of what hypothesis testing is and what it does. You will use Excel to explore the relationship between the characteristics of a population and those of samples within the framework of hypothesis testing in a way that could not easily be done without a computer. The example used here will be a hypothesis test on a population mean, but the concepts apply equally to all hypothesis tests. The next chapter will deal with the ways you can use Excel to solve hypothesis testing problems and should be read only after you understand what hypothesis testing is about.

There are several steps to solving the typical hypothesis testing word problem. The first step requires setting up the Null and Alternative Hypotheses and determining the appropriate sample descriptive statistics to use in the later calculations. This is often the hardest step, because it is difficult to set up the two hypotheses before you fully understand what hypothesis testing is and what its capabilities and limitations are. Once you understand how hypothesis testing works, you will find it easier to formulate Null and Alternative Hypotheses.

Consider the following quality control example. This problem is a little simpler than the typical hypothesis testing problem in most textbooks, but it's a good starting point to see how hypothesis testing works.

A division of a cereal manufacturer is responsible for packaging the product. When the packaging process is working correctly, the amount of cereal in each box is normally distributed with an average fill of 16 ounces and a standard deviation of 0.50 ounces. In order to check the fill of a large shipment sent to a grocery store chain, a sample of 10 boxes is chosen, and the average weight of the 10 boxes is 15.43 ounces. Does this provide evidence that the packaging process is working incorrectly?

Although it is unrealistic to assume that we could know anything about the distribution of the weights of *all* the cereal boxes, this example will be easier to explore if we take the population standard deviation as 0.50 ounces and the population distribution as normal. The question to be determined through hypothesis testing is whether or not the population mean is really 16 ounces.

▼ The Population and the Null Hypothesis

For this particular problem, the Null Hypothesis is: $H_0: \mu = 16$, and the Alternate Hypothesis is $H_A: \mu \neq 16$. The Null and Alternate Hypotheses are always statements about a population parameter; they are never statements about a sample statistic. They are always constructed so that one of them *must* be true and the other *must* be false. The Null Hypothesis *always* contains an equal sign (including =, ≤, or ≥). The Alternate Hypothesis *never* contains an equal sign. The relational symbol in the Alternate Hypothesis must be ≠, <, or >.

The object of the hypothesis test is to decide whether or not the Null Hypothesis is true. Let's begin by provisionally assuming that it *is* true, and the average fill of all boxes is really 16 ounces. We'll then look at the characteristics of the samples you could expect to get from the population described by the Null Hypothesis by having Excel simulate the choosing of such samples. Finally, we'll decide whether or not the sample described in the problem (with a sample mean of 15.43) is like those samples. If it is, that's evidence that the sample in the problem is *consistent* with the Null Hypothesis. If it's not, that indicates the sample is *inconsistent* with the Null Hypothesis and provides evidence that the Null Hypothesis is not true.

When we say the average fill is 16 ounces, we're making a statement about the population—all the boxes being filled (which we generally cannot measure directly). The statement also tells something about the weight of any single box of cereal we might measure. If the average weight of all the boxes is 16 ounces, we *expect* the weight of any randomly chosen box to also be 16 ounces. The word "expect" is used here in its statistical sense, not its everyday sense. There is going to be some variation in the weight of individual boxes; no box-filling process can be absolutely perfectly precise. If we regard the actual weight of any box of cereal to be a continuous random number, then the probability is zero that a single box will turn out to have a fill that exactly equals 16 ounces. Most boxes will have a fill close to 16 ounces, and the average fill of boxes chosen will tend to be closer to 16 ounces as the number of boxes chosen increases.

Similarly, if the average weight of all boxes filled is 16 ounces, we *expect* the average weight of a random sample of ten boxes to also be 16 ounces. Just as in the case of an individual box, the average fill of a sample will almost certainly differ from 16 ounces just because of the random nature of the filling process. Finding a sample whose average fill differs a little from 16 does not provide evidence that something has gone wrong with the average fill of all boxes. Finding a sample whose average is very far from 16 would, however, be suspicious. As we saw in Chapter 6, the distribution of sample means has the same mean as the population but a smaller standard deviation. It is thus unlikely that the difference between a sample mean and the population mean will be great. A small difference could well be due to normal random fluctuations, but a large difference probably indicates some problem with the population.

▼ Formulating the Null and Alternate Hypotheses

To solve a typical hypothesis testing word problem, you have to first determine the Null and Alternate Hypotheses. One principle to keep in mind is that the Null Hypothesis must describe the population and must give an expected value for the sample. A Null Hypothesis must have an equal sign ($=$); it cannot have a not equal ($\neq$) or a greater than ($>$) or a less than ($<$) sign. Most statistics texts formulate one-tailed Null Hypotheses with greater than or equal to ($\geq$) or less than or equal to ($\leq$) signs. In practice, these are treated as equal signs when the tests are performed (a few statistics texts use equal signs even in one-tailed Null Hypotheses). The reason for these restrictions on the relationships expressed by the Null Hypothesis is that the Null Hypothesis must tell what the population *is*, not what it *is not*. It would have been impossible to generate the simulated samples in this chapter without a specific value from the Null Hypothesis for the average fill of all boxes.

If a problem asks for evidence of a particular situation, that situation is formulated as the *Alternate* Hypothesis. This is because you only come to a conclusion in hypothesis testing when you *reject* the Null Hypothesis.

If you reject the Null Hypothesis, you have evidence of the Alternate Hypothesis. For this reason, many students find it easier to formulate the Alternate Hypothesis first, and the Null Hypothesis as the logical opposite of the Alternate Hypothesis.

▼ How Small a Difference Is Small?

In the example given here, the sample of ten boxes had a mean of 15.43 ounces. This differs from the expected amount by 0.57 ounces. Is this the kind of small difference we expected to happen by chance in a sample of boxes chosen when the average of all (population) is 16? Or is 0.57 ounces too large a difference to explain by chance variability? A small difference would be *consistent* with a population mean of 16, while a large difference would be *inconsistent* with a population mean of 16. If we decide that 0.57 ounces is large, we will conclude that the average fill of all the boxes is not 16. In that case something is wrong with the box-filling process, and it will have to have attention.

Let's examine the question by taking a population of boxes in which the filling process *is* working properly and drawing several samples of 10 boxes and determining the sample average for each sample. By doing this, we will be able to see whether or not a sample whose average differs from 16 by 0.57 ounces (or more) is unusual. In other words, we will be able to determine if 0.57 is a large difference.

- Start Excel if you have not already done so, and open the workbook in the file named Cereal.xls (in the Chap_8) folder. Open the File menu on the Menu Bar, click "Save as…," and save the workbook on a hard disk or network drive because it will grow too large to fit on a diskette. Appendix F provides instructions for storing the large file on a diskette at the end of your computer session.

- Select the "Population_I" worksheet. In cell F1, enter the label "Population Mean" and increase the column width to hold this label. In cell G1 enter the formula that will calculate the average of the values on this worksheet (A2:E256). The average is 16.

- Switch to the "Samples_I" worksheet. One sample is already present on the worksheet.

- In cell K2 enter the formula to calculate the sample mean (use relative addressing). In cell L2 enter a formula (using absolute addressing) that will display the value shown in cell G1 if the "Population_I" worksheet. In cell M2 enter a formula that will calculate the absolute value of the difference between the values displayed in cells K2 and L2. Cells

K2:M2 should display 15.90, 16, and 0.103. If cell M2 displays "-0.103," correct the cell's formula so that it takes the *absolute value* of the difference.

- Open the Tools menu on the Menu Bar, select "Learning Business Statistics" and click "Multiple Random Samples." If "Learning Business Statistics is not on your Tools menu, refer to Appendix C.

- Fill out the dialog window of the Multiple Random Samples tool so that it will select values from the population on the "Population_I" worksheet (A2:E256), select samples of size 10, select 1,000 samples, and will write the samples on the "Samples_I" worksheet beginning in cell A2 (thus overwriting the sample already there).

- Copy the formulas you entered in cells K2:M2 to all the cells below them through row 1001. (Enter K2:M1001 in the Name Box, then click the menus "Edit"…"Fill"…"Down.") The values displayed in columns K and M will differ, but column L should display "16" in all cells.

Column M shows the amount each sample mean differs from 16. Since there are 1,000 different sample means, looking through them all to find those that exceed 0.57 would be a little tedious. One way of making this easier would be to resort the samples on the worksheet by the value in column M.

- Select the region A1:M1001. Open the Data menu on the Menu Bar and select "Sort…." The Sort dialog window will open.

In the dialog window we will tell Excel which column to sort the region by. We also will ask for a descending sort. This will put the samples with the largest differences at the top since those are the ones we are most interested in.

- At the bottom of the dialog window there is a region titled "My list has" with two choices selected by radio buttons. Select "Header row." This will cause the columns to be identified by the labels in the first row rather than by the column letter.

- Open the list under "Sort by" and choose "Absolute Difference," which will be at the bottom of the list. Click the "Descending" radio button. The dialog window should look like the picture at the top of the next page. If so, click the "OK" button.

Arrange your worksheet so that you can see the values at the top of column M, the difference column. In the entire set of 1,000 samples that Excel simulated, the one with the mean furthest from 16 is now in row 2. The difference between that sample's mean and 16 is shown in cell M2. Is it greater than or equal to 0.57? If not, then none of the 1,000 samples had a mean that differed from 16 by as much as the one in the problem. Perhaps the value in cell M2 is greater than 0.57. If so, see how many of the values in cells below M2 are also greater than 0.57. It is very unlikely (though not impossible) that there are more than three or four samples out of 1,000 with means which differ from 16 by as much as 0.57, and it is very likely that none of the 1,000 samples had a mean that differed from 16 by so much.

▼ An Unusual Sample or a Process Gone Bad?

What has this exercise shown? If the average fill were 16 and 1,000 samples of ten boxes were chosen, none or few of the samples would have means that differed from 16 by 0.57 or more. Thus a difference in a sample mean of 0.57 is *not* the kind of difference you would expect from a randomly drawn sample. It is not a small difference. It is a large difference—one very unlikely to occur by chance. A sample of ten boxes having a mean of 15.43 is thus *not* consistent with all boxes being filled, on average, with 16 ounces.

Knowing this, what do we conclude if, one day, a sample of ten boxes is drawn with a mean of 15.43? Although it is *possible* that the difference is due to chance, the probability of this is very low. There is another explanation, however. If something has gone wrong with the filling process, the population mean might no longer be 16. If the population mean had fallen, say, to 15.40, a sample mean of 15.43 might not be surprising at all. In this case, of course, something has gone wrong that needs correcting. Since a sample mean of 15.43 is so unlikely if nothing has gone wrong, it would be reasonable to conclude from such a sample mean that something has gone wrong. In this case we would *reject* the Null Hypothesis that the population mean (μ) equaled 16, and conclude that the Alternate Hypothesis ($\mu \neq 16$) is correct.

Suppose the sample of ten boxes instead had an average weight of 15.89 ounces? The difference from 16 in this case is 0.11. Scroll through the values in column M until you find a value less than 0.11. What row is this value in? All of the numbers above it are greater than .11. Since the largest number is in row M2, the total number of values in column M that exceed 0.11 is the row number of the first number less than 0.11 minus 1. How many of the thousand samples have means greater than 0.11? What proportion of the thousand samples does that represent?

This proportion is liable to be at least .40, probably more. This shows that there is a high probability that a sample mean can differ from 16 by 0.11 or more. This is a difference that could likely occur by chance; it is thus a *small* difference that is *consistent* with all boxes being filled, on average, with 16 ounces. With such a sample we would *not* conclude that something has gone wrong with the process. We would *fail to reject* the Null Hypothesis.

▼ Summary

Here's a quick summary of the steps we went through in determining that something had gone wrong with the process of filling cereal boxes:

1. The Null Hypothesis was assumed to be correct ($\mu = 16$).

2. Under that assumption, Excel simulated the drawing of 1,000 samples. The assumption was used when the Random Generation Number Tool was told to generate numbers with a mean of 16.

3. The mean of each sample was calculated.

4. The difference between each sample mean and the *expected* value of the sample means (16) was calculated.

5. The differences were sorted from highest to lowest so we could easily determine how many of the samples had means that differed from the population by at least as much as the sample described in the problem.

Had we calculated the proportion of the 1,000 samples with differences at least as great as that of the sample in the problem (0.57), we would have been approximating a probability, and that probability would have been close to zero. This is the probability that a single sample of ten boxes chosen when the process was working perfectly would have a mean further from 16 than the sample mean given in the problem (15.43). This probability, called the *p* value, can be calculated precisely from the distribution of sample means using the techniques explored in

Chapter 6, and it is a far easier process than generating a thousand samples.

▼ Determining the *p* Value

The diagram below shows the distribution of the means of samples of size 10 drawn from a normally distributed population with mean 16 and standard deviation 0.05. The shaded areas show the probability that a sample mean will differ from 16 by at least as much as 15.43 differs from 16. This combined area equals the *p* value.

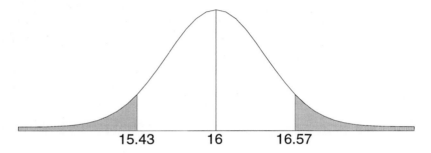

| 15.43 | 16 | 16.57 |

Since we know the population standard deviation, the normal distribution should be used for the distribution of sample means. In most hypothesis testing problems we will *not* know the population standard deviation and instead will know the standard deviation of a single sample. In that case, (which we will consider below), the *t* distribution will be used.

- Switch to the "Population_I" worksheet. In cells F2:F7, enter the following labels: "Population Standard Deviation," "Sample Size," "Standard Error," "Sample Mean," "z value," and "p value." Adjust the width of column F to hold the labels.

- In cell G2 enter a formula that will calculate the standard deviation of the population data on the worksheet (A2:E256). Be sure not to use the sample standard deviation function! The displayed value should be 0.5. (0.500196 is wrong!)

- In cell G3 enter the sample size (10), and in cell G4 enter the formula to calculate the standard error from the population standard deviation and the sample size. The displayed value should be 0.158114.

- In cell G5 enter the sample mean for this problem (15.43) and in cell G6 enter the formula that will convert this value to a *z* value using the mean and standard deviation of the distribution of sample means. The displayed value should be –3.605. Recall that the mean of this distribution is the same as the population mean and that the standard deviation is the standard error.

The result in cell G6 means that the z value corresponding to the sample mean value of 15.43 in the diagram on page 224 is −3.605 and the z value corresponding to 16.57 is +3.605

- Use the NORMSDIST function in cell G7 to calculate the p value. Remember that the p value equals the area of both shaded tails in the diagram on page 224. The displayed value should be 0.000312.

This p value means that if a sample of size 10 were drawn from the population on the "Population_I" worksheet, the probability that the mean of the sample would differ from 16 by as much as 15.43 differs from 15 is 0.000312. This is less than 1 in 1,000—a bit more than 3 in 10,000. You shouldn't be surprised if none of the 1,000 samples you drew had a sample whose mean differed from 16 by 0.57 or more; if one or more your samples had such means you were lucky. This confirms our finding that a sample mean of 15.43 is *not* consistent with the claim that all the cereal boxes, on average, are filled to 16 ounces. With this sample we would *reject* the Null Hypothesis.

Suppose the sample mean had been 15.89 rather than 15.43? What would the p value have been then? You can quickly determine this by replacing the 15.43 in cell G5 with 15.89. The p value becomes .486616. In other words, if all boxes were filled with an average of 16 ounces, just under half of all samples of ten boxes would have means that differed from 16 by as much or more as 15.89 differs from 16. Is this close to the proportion you determined for your 1,000 samples? This is a high proportion and makes it reasonable to conclude that the average fill of all boxes might really be 16 and that the sample's average of 15.89 was due to chance. In this case, we would *fail to reject* the Null Hypothesis. Note that this is not the same as concluding that the Null Hypothesis is true. The fact that the sample is consistent with the Null Hypothesis does not mean that we have shown that it is true, a point that will be explored more later.

▼ From *p* Value to Conclusion

Hypothesis testing is essentially a process that determines whether or not the sample selected has characteristics that make it likely to have been drawn from a population described by the Null Hypothesis. The p value quantifies this relationship between the sample and the Null Hypothesis.

A small p value is evidence that the sample is not the kind of sample that would be expected from the population described from the Null Hypothesis. This leads to the conclusion that the population must be different from that described by the Null Hypothesis. The Null Hypothesis is rejected.

Since chance can cause small differences between the actual and expected value of a sample statistic, a small difference could occur by chance with a large probability. The p value for a small difference between the analysis sample's mean and the Null's expected mean would be large. A *small* difference can occur with a *large* probability.

A large p value is evidence that the difference between sample and population mean is likely to have occurred by chance. In that case the Null Hypothesis would not be rejected. Instead we would conclude that the difference between the analysis sample's actual mean and the expected mean given by the Null Hypothesis is due to chance. The Null Hypothesis is *not* rejected.

The p value provides a measure of the difference between the actual sample statistic of the test sample and the expected value of the sample statistic implied by the Null Hypothesis. The p value is the probability that if the Null Hypothesis were true, another sample of the same size as that used for the analysis would have a statistic (such as sample mean) at least as different from the population parameter (population mean) as the analysis sample.

Whether or not a sample leads to rejection of the Null Hypothesis depends on how low the p value is. In the example given here, the p value was extremely low. In many, perhaps most, problems, the question is bound to arise of how low the p value must be before the Null Hypothesis is rejected. In many of the hypothesis testing problems that beginning students encounter, the problem will provide a significance level, also referred to as α. For that problem, the significance level is the threshold. If the p value is less than the significance level, the Null Hypothesis is rejected. If the p value is greater, the Null is not rejected. Providing a significance level neatly solves the problem of how low a p value is low, but it begs the larger question of what the value of the significance level *should* be.

▼ The Consequences of Error—Type I versus Type II

Hypothesis testing can never be an infallible method of determining the characteristics of a population. Depending on a sample to provide evidence about a population is always risky since we can never be certain the sample isn't unrepresentative. It's good to remember that the benefit of hypothesis testing also comes from the fact that it depends on a sample, because analyzing the entire population may be impossible or prohibitively expensive. Hypothesis testing is often the only practical way of investigating a population. The investigator using it, however, must explicitly consider the consequences of the unavoidable error that might occur with a hypothesis test.

Consider the problem just analyzed. A cereal packaging division wants to be sure that the average fill of cereal in all boxes is exactly 16 ounces. They monitor this process by selecting a sample and performing a hypothesis test. If the hypothesis test reveals a problem, the company does whatever is necessary to correct the problem. Suppose the hypothesis test gives them the wrong answer? What impact does that have?

There are two types of wrong answers. One possibility is that the filling process is working properly, but by sheer bad luck the company happens to select a sample that is not representative and which leads to the erroneous conclusion that something is wrong. The consequence of this error is needless expense. Equipment may be taken out of service for expensive testing; perhaps the production of cereal may be stopped or slowed until the cause of the problem is determined. The company's revenue may suffer. These costs would be gladly paid to fix a problem, but if there is no problem they are needless. Concluding that there is a problem when, in fact, there is no problem, is an example of *Type I* error.

The other possibility is that the filling process has broken, and the average fill of cereal boxes is either too high or too low, but again by sheer bad luck the company happens to select a sample that is not representative and that leads to the erroneous conclusion that something is *not* wrong. In this case, the company continues to incorrectly fill the boxes, unaware of the need for correction. Depending on whether the boxes are underfilled or overfilled, this could result in product waste, higher than expected production costs, regulatory troubles, or loss of confidence by consumers. These are potentially costly problems that the company also wants to avoid. Concluding that there is no problem when one really exists is an example of *Type II* error.

Ideally, of course, the company wants to avoid, or at least minimize, both types of error. The only way to reduce the likelihood of both types of error is to collect more data and use larger samples. This is itself a costly action. If Type I and Type II errors are very rare, it may make more sense to accept the risk of bearing the costs associated with them than to bear the costs of additional testing. We will assume that the company has decided that it can't afford to test samples of more than ten boxes, although the cost of additional data collection should be balanced against the costs of errors. In this chapter you will explore the relationship between the significance level and the balancing of Type I and Type II errors.

▼ Simulating Type I Errors

We will explore Type I and Type II errors by looking at the accuracy of hypothesis tests in a way similar to that used in Chapter 7 to look at the accuracy of confidence intervals. Just as for a confidence interval, when a hypothesis test is done on an unknown population there is no way to be certain whether the outcome of the test is correct or not. We will look at the accuracy of hypothesis testing by selecting samples from known populations. The first population will be the one on the "Population_I" worksheet just used.

For all the populations we will do the same hypothesis test, "Is there evidence that the population mean differs from 16?" This also is the same test just considered, and the Null and Alternate Hypotheses are:

$$H_0: \mu = 16 \text{ and } H_A: \mu \neq 16$$

This time, however, all the data used in the test will come from the sample. This means that the standard error will be calculated from the sample standard deviation rather than from the population standard deviation. The t distribution will then be used instead of the z distribution for the distribution of sample means.

We know that the mean of Population_I is 16. A sample drawn from that population will have a correct hypothesis test if the test fails to reject the Null Hypothesis and concludes there is no evidence the population mean differs from 16. If a sample results in a hypothesis test that rejects the Null and concludes that there *is* evidence the population mean differs from 16, the test will be in error, and the error will be Type I error.

- Select the "Summary" worksheet. Information common to the tests on all populations will be placed here, as will a table summarizing the results of all the hypothesis tests.

- In cell B1 enter the *hypothesized* population mean. This is the population mean that the Null Hypothesis provides. For all populations we will be testing the Null Hypothesis that $\mu = 16$. Therefore B2 should contain "16" (without quotes).

- Cell B3 will contain the significance level. Recall that the significance level sets how low the p value must be to conclude the sample must not have been drawn from a population described by the Null Hypothesis (reject the Null Hypothesis). Enter the value ".05" in B3 for the initial value.

- Switch to the "Type_I" worksheet. This worksheet contains three samples. The first sample will be used to develop the hypothesis testing formulas and the others will be used to test those formulas.

- In cells K2 and L2 enter formulas to calculate the sample mean and standard deviation for the sample in row 2. Use relative addressing. The displayed values should be 15.969 and 0.450443, respectively.

- Use the COUNT function in cell M2 to determine the number of values in the sample (A2:J2). Use relative addressing. The displayed value should be 10.

- Enter a formula in cell N2 to calculate the standard error from the sample standard deviation and sample size. Use relative addresses. The displayed value should be 0.142443.

- Enter a formula in cell O2 to calculate the sample *t* value. The *t* value is calculated from the formula $t = \dfrac{\bar{x} - \mu}{s_{\bar{x}}}$. The value of $\bar{x}$ is the sample mean given in cell K2. The value of μ is the *hypothesized* population mean given in cell B1 of the "Summary" worksheet, and it should be referred to with an *absolute* address. The denominator, $s_{\bar{x}}$, is the standard error calculated from the sample standard deviation and should be referred to with a *relative* address. The Excel equation appearing in the Formula Bar should be "=(K2-Summary!$B$1)/N2." If you use a mouse to enter the cell addresses, the denominator will be "Type_I!N2." Edit the Formula Bar to remove the "Type_I!" from the formula. It won't have any effect on this worksheet, but will cause problems later. The displayed value should be –0.21763.

- Enter the formula in cell P2 to calculate the (2 tail) *p* value. Use the TDIST function. Remember that you must use the ABS function to ensure that the *t* value used in TDIST's X argument is positive. The degrees of freedom is sample size minus 1. The displayed value should be 0.83257.

- Enter a formula in cell Q2 using Excel's IF function to display "Reject the Null" if the *p* value in cell P2 is less than the significance level in cell B3 of the "Summary" worksheet, and "Fail to Reject" if it is not. Be sure to use *absolute* addressing in referring to the significance level. The cell should display "Fail to Reject."

- Copy the formulas in the range K2:Q2 down to rows 3 and 4. Check the displayed values with the picture on the next page. If the values in your worksheet differ, change only the formulas in row 2. If row 2 shows the correct values but rows 3 or 4 do not, check the relative and absolute addressing.

	K	L	M	N	O	P	Q
1	Sample Mean	Sample Standard Deviation	Sample Size	Standard Error	Sample t Value	p Value	Conclusion
2	15.969	0.450443	10	0.142443	-0.21763	0.83257	Fail to Reject
3	16.425	0.464166	10	0.146782	2.895447	0.017726	Reject the Null
4	16.149	0.630634	10	0.199424	0.747152	0.474038	Fail to Reject

Now let's look at the results of hypothesis tests on 1,000 different samples drawn from this population.

- Use the Multiple Random Samples Tool to draw 1,000 samples of size 10 from the "Population_I" worksheet (A2:E256) and write the samples beginning in cell A2 of the "Type_I" worksheet. This will overwrite the three samples previously there and change the values in the cells in the previous picture.

- Copy the formulas in cells K4:Q4 down to row 1001. Adjust the width of column Q so that it is wide enough to hold the displayed text.

Column P shows the p values for each of the 1,000 hypothesis tests, and column Q shows the conclusion we would draw from each test at the .05 level of significance. Although it should be clear that far more samples result in "Fail to Reject" than in "Reject the Null," the exact number in each category will change when we change the significance level. Since the number falling into each category depends in part on the significance level, we will construct a table that will provide a count of the samples resulting in each conclusion.

- Enter the labels shown in the picture below in the range R1:T4.

	R	S	T
1		Count	Proportion
2	Reject the Null		
3	Fail to Reject		
4	Total		

- Enter a formula in cell S2 that will provide a count of the number of times "Reject the Null appears in cells Q2:Q1001. Use the COUNTIF function in the "Statistical" category. In the "Criteria" field put "Reject the Null" *and use quotation marks* in the field. If the displayed value is zero, your formula has not been correctly formed.

- Enter a similar formula in cell S3 that will provide a count of the number of hypothesis with "Fail to Reject."

- Use the AutoSum button in cell S4 to add the values in cells T2 and T3. The displayed value should be 1,000.

- Use cells T2:T3 to convert the values in S2:S3 to proportions by dividing each number by the total in S4. Use the AutoSum button in S4 to verify that the two proportions sum to one.

▼ Significance Level and Type I Error

Since the Population_I data has a population mean exactly equal to 16, a sample's hypothesis test is correct if the conclusion is "Fail to Reject." Those samples that conclude "Reject the Null" have Type I error. Thus the proportion of samples with Type I error is the value displayed in cell T2.

- Remember that the current significance level is .05. Note the current proportion of Type I error. Change the significance level (on the "Summary" worksheet) to the following values: .01, .10, .20, .25, and note in each case the proportion of samples with Type I error (cell T3). What is the relationship between the significance level and the proportion of samples with Type I error?

As the significance level increases, so does the proportion of samples with Type I error. In fact, the two should be approximately equal. The *expected* proportion of samples with Type I error is the same as the significance level.

If we *knew* that the Null Hypothesis test were true, then choosing a very small significance level would increase the likelihood that a hypothesis test would yield the correct conclusion. Of course, if we *knew* the Null Hypothesis were true, there would be no reason to use a sample to test it! What if the Null Hypothesis were false or unknown?

- Change the significance level on the "Summary" worksheet back to .05.

▼ Simulating Type II Errors

A Type II error can occur only if the Null Hypothesis is wrong. The Null Hypothesis specifies a particular value for a population mean ($\mu = 16$ for the case we have been considering). If the population parameter is any other value, the Null is wrong, and any test that fails to reject the Null Hypothesis will have Type II error.

We can simulate Type II error by simply drawing samples from a different population—one in which we know the mean does not equal 15. The simulation will be easy compared to the one for Type I errors because we have already entered all the formulas required to do hypothesis tests.

- On the "Type_I" worksheet, select cells K1:T4. These contain the labels and formulas to perform hypothesis tests on the first three samples and the table counting the results of the tests.

- Copy the contents of K1:T4 to cell K1 on the "Type_IIL" worksheet. One easy way of doing this is to click the Copy button ( ) on the Standard Toolbar after selecting the cells on the "Type_I" worksheet to be copied. Then select cell K1 on the "Type_IIL" worksheet and click the Paste button: .

- Adjust the width of columns Q and R. Range K1:T4 should look like the picture below. Pay particular attention to the numbers in K2:P2. The error codes in rows 3 and 4 are there because there are no sample values in that row. If your values are the same except for the Sample t and p Value, you may have a reference to the "Type_I" worksheet in your formulas. Reread the instructions on page 229

	K	L	M	N	O	P	Q	R	S	T
1	Sample Mean	Sample Standard Deviation	Sample Size	Standard Error	Sample t Value	p Value	Conclusion		Count	Proportion
2	15.178	0.428688	10	0.135563	-6.0636	0.000187	Reject the Null	Reject the Null	1	1
3	#DIV/0!	#DIV/0!	0	#DIV/0!	#DIV/0!	#DIV/0!	#DIV/0!	Fail to Reject	0	0
4	#DIV/0!	#DIV/0!	0	#DIV/0!	#DIV/0!	#DIV/0!	#DIV/0!	Total	1	1

- Use the Multiple Random Samples Tool to draw 1,000 samples of size 10 from the "Population_II" worksheet (A2:E256) to the "Type_IIL" worksheet (A2), overwriting the sample currently there. The error codes in rows 3 and 4 will be replaced.

- Copy the formulas in row 4 of columns K through Q down to row 1001. The table in R1:T4 will automatically update and the value in S4 should be 1,000. Look at the values in this table.

Unlike the table in the "Type_I" worksheet, the great majority of samples from Population_II should result in rejection of the Null Hypothesis. In other words, most of the samples would lead to the conclusion that there *is* evidence that the population mean differs from 16. A few samples, however, should lead to the opposite conclusion that there is *not* evidence that the population mean differs from 16. Which conclusion is correct?

- Switch to the "Population_II" worksheet. In cell G1 enter a formula that will calculate the mean of the data on the worksheet. The displayed value should be 15.3.

Since the population mean is 15.3 (and not 16), the Null Hypothesis is *incorrect*. Therefore hypothesis tests that reject the Null Hypothesis are correct while those that fail to reject are in error, Type II error in this case. Based our examination of Population_I and Population_II, it seems that the result of hypothesis testing is very likely to provide the correct result. Unfortunately, this is not always the case.

▼ Hypothesis Testing—a Difficult Population

Let's take a look at one last population, the one in the "Population_III" worksheet. We will use the "Type_IIS" worksheet to hold samples from that population and tabulate the results of hypothesis tests from those samples. The procedure is very much like that we have just used.

- Copy the formulas in K1:T4 of the "Type_IIL" worksheet to cell K1 of the Type_IIS worksheet. Adjust columns Q and R. The displayed values should be as shown below:

	K	L	M	N	O	P	Q	R	S	T
1	Sample Mean	Sample Standard Deviation	Sample Size	Standard Error	Sample *t* Value	*p* Value	Conclusion		Count	Proportion
2	15.983	0.325783	10	0.103022	-0.16501	0.872580	Fail to Reject	Reject the Null	0	0
3	#DIV/0!	#DIV/0!	0	#DIV/0!	#DIV/0!	#DIV/0!	#DIV/0!	Fail to Reject	1	1
4	#DIV/0!	#DIV/0!	0	#DIV/0!	#DIV/0!	#DIV/0!	#DIV/0!	Total	1	1

- Use the Multiple Random Samples Tool to select 1,000 samples of size 10 from the Population_III worksheet. Have the Tool write the samples starting in cell A2 of the "Type_IIS" worksheet.

- Copy the formulas in K4:Q4 down through row 1001. The table in R1:T4 will update and cell S4 should display 1000. Examine the table.

Most of the samples should result in "Fail to Reject," but a fairly large minority of samples should result in "Reject the Null." Since most samples indicate that the Null should not be rejected, isn't it reasonable to believe that the population mean probably is 16 as indicated by the Null Hypothesis?

- Switch to the "Population_III" worksheet and enter a formula in cell G1 to calculate the mean of the data on that worksheet. The result should be 15.8.

Is the Null Hypothesis correct? No. The population mean is 15.8, not 16. Certainly 15.8 is closer to 16 than is 15.3, the mean of the Population_II worksheet, but the assertion that the mean is 16 is wrong in both cases. The correct conclusion in both cases is to reject the Null and those samples that fail to reject have Type II error. The data in Population_III are troublesome because *most* of the samples result in error. What effect does significance level have on this error?

▼ Significance Level and Errors in Hypothesis Tests

Let's summarize the results of the hypothesis tests on the three populations on the "Summary" worksheet so that we can easily change the significance level and see the effect on the number of samples that result in erroneous conclusions.

- Select the "Summary" worksheet. The labels have already been entered in A4:G8. The data will come from the worksheets whose name abbreviates the column labels in row 5. Type I errors can occur only if the Null is correct, while Type II errors can occur only if the Null is incorrect. The large and small "Difference" refers to the difference between the actual population mean and that given by the Null Hypothesis. The hypothesized mean is always 16. The "large" difference is the one between 16 and 15.3, and the "small" difference is the one between 16 and 15.8.

- Select cell B6. This will contain the number of correct tests from the "Type_I" worksheet. Click the Edit Formula button. Select the "Type_I" worksheet tab. These samples were drawn from a population where the mean is 16. The correct result is "Fail to Reject," so click cell S3. The Formula Bar should contain "=Type_I!S3." Press the Enter key and the screen will return to the "Summary" worksheet with the correct value displayed in B6.

- Select B7. Click the Edit Formula button and then click cell S2 in the "Type_I" worksheet. Press the Enter key.

- Select C6. Click the Edit Formula button. Click the "Type_IIL" worksheet and click the cell that contains the count of samples whose tests reject the Null Hypothesis (S2), the correct result for this population in which the mean is 15.3 and not 16.

- Using the same procedure, make cell C7 display the count of samples in the "Type_IIL" worksheet that come to the wrong conclusion.

- Using the same procedure, have D6:D7 show the number of correct and incorrect tests for the samples in the "Type_IIS" worksheet.

- Select B8:D8 and click the AutoSum button. The correct formulas summing each column will automatically be entered in each cell. In all three cases, the sum should be 1,000.

- Enter formulas in cells E6:G7 that will display the proportion of correct and incorrect tests. Either calculate these from the values in B6:D7 or display the values from the samples worksheets.

- Using the AutoSum button in E8:G8, verify that the proportions sum to 1.

We can now look at the effect of significance level on the likelihood of a sample resulting in a correct or incorrect test. This effect will be clearest if you look at the proportions part of the table

- First confirm the result seen earlier with Type I errors. Change the significance level first to .01 and then to .10 and notice the effect on the values in E6 and E7. The proportion of incorrect tests in the Type I column should approximate the significance level; lower significance levels increase the proportion of correct tests.

- Look next at each of the Type II columns as the significance level changes from .01 to .10 (and back).

In the case of Type II errors, lower significance levels *decrease* the proportion of correct tests, the opposite of the situation with Type I errors. Choosing a significance level involves balancing the likelihood of Type I and Type II errors.

▼ Type II Errors and the Power of a Test

For the Type_IIL population, the hypothesis test was quite accurate in its ability to reject an incorrect Null hypothesis. For the Type_IIS population, however, the same test did a very poor job of rejecting an incorrect Null. The ability of a hypothesis test to come to the correct conclusion including rejecting an incorrect Null Hypothesis is termed the *power* of the test. When the Null is wrong, a test's power depends (among other things) on the difference between the value of the population parameter hypothesized by the Null and the population's actual value for that parameter. Tests of incorrect Nulls are always more powerful when the population is very different from the Null hypothesis than when it is similar. We considered two populations in which the Null Hypothesis was incorrect. These are two of a potentially infinite number of populations, since there are an infinite number of possible values the population mean can have not equal to the hypothesized mean.

It is possible to develop a relationship between the actual population mean and the hypothesized population mean (or other parameter) on the one hand and the probability of correctly rejecting an incorrect Null Hypothesis on the other hand. This relationship is termed the test's *power curve*. The power of a hypothesis test can generally be improved by choosing larger samples. This, of course, is often expensive.

As we have seen, tests of incorrect hypotheses are less likely to be accurate if the population differs only slightly from the value hypothesized by the Null than if the population differs significantly. It may be that, for a given situation, this will not be unacceptable. Consider the case we have been investigating. Suppose the process the cereal packaging division is using to fill packages is not, in fact, filling boxes with an average of exactly 16 ounces. What is the consequence? As discussed before, this probably depends on whether the boxes are being overfilled or underfilled, but, in either case, it is reasonable to expect that those consequences are less severe if the error is slight than if it is large. Some increased inaccuracy in a test's ability to detect small errors may be acceptable. In a case where this issue is important, a complete analysis of a test's power curve is the best way to determine the appropriate sample size required to achieve an acceptable level of power.

▼ Failing to Reject versus Accepting a Null Hypothesis

The two standard conclusions arising from a hypothesis test are to *reject* the Null Hypothesis or to *fail to reject*. These are not, of course, exact opposites. The opposite of rejecting the Null would be to *accept* the Null. Why isn't that wording used?

Examine the table we have just constructed. You have conducted a test on a single sample, but you have no clear idea from which of the three populations (among others) the sample was drawn. Suppose the test results in your rejecting the Null Hypothesis. That conclusion may be wrong, in which case you have Type I error. The advantage of Type I error is that you have control over the probability of Type I error by setting the significance level. You can't be sure that your conclusion is correct, but you do know the probability that you have selected a sample with Type I error. You know this *only if you reject the Null Hypothesis*.

Suppose instead that your test results in failing to reject the Null hypothesis. Could that conclusion be wrong? Certainly. The problem here is that you have absolutely no way of knowing the probability that you are wrong. If your population is like that on the "Population_IIS" worksheet, the probability of an error is very low. If, on the other hand, the population is like that on the "Population_IIL" worksheet, the probability is very high (over 50%) that your conclusion is wrong. Since you can't know which population (among others) you drew from, you have no way of knowing the probability of being wrong. In a sense, failing to reject the Null is a much less comfortable place to be than rejecting the Null because of the inability of knowing the probability of being wrong. Statisticians prefer the lack of commitment in the phrase "fail to reject" over the much stronger "accept" when it comes to hypothesis testing.

▼ Exercises

In performing the first hypothesis test discussed in this chapter, we were concerned with the probability that the mean of a sample of ten boxes would differ from 16 by more than 0.57 (the amount by which the sample mean given in the problem, 15.43, differed from 16). That probability was estimated empirically by actually looking at 1,000 sample means and seeing how many had means that differed from 16 by more than .57. It was also determined analytically by calculating the p value.

1. If another 1,000 samples were drawn, what is the probability that the number of means that differ from 16 by more than 0.57 would be exactly 0? Exactly 1? Exactly 2? Three or more? Given these answers, do you think your set of 1,000 samples was typical of all the possible sets of 1,000 samples? Why or why not? (Hint: Use the binomial distribution to answer this question. The number of trials is 1,000, and the probability of success is the p value.)

2. Using the Population_I sheet of your workbook, find a value for the sample mean (cell G5) that will produce a p value of exactly .01. Start with 15.4, and increase the digit in the tenths place (initially "4"—the digit just to the right of the decimal point) until the p value switches to a value greater than .01. Then reduce the tenths place by one so the p value is again less than .01 and add a "5" to the hundredths place (the digit just to the right of the tenths place). Adjust the "5" up and down until you find the value for the hundredths place that keeps the p value just below .01. Then add a "5" to the thousandths place (just to the right of the hundredths) and make the same adjustment, continuing to the right until the p value that appears in your worksheet displays exactly as .01. What is the z value associated with this sample mean? This z value is the *critical z* for a significance level of .01. Suppose you were given a problem just like that given at the beginning of this chapter, but with a different sample mean. What values for that sample mean would result in a p value less than .01? Explain.

3. (advanced) Use NORMSINV to determine the precise z values that would produce a p value of .01. Using the population mean and the standard errors, convert the z values to critical values. One will be the same as the one determined in response to question 2. The other one will be greater than 16. What will its value be?

4. Produce a table showing the results on your "Summary" worksheets for significance levels of .01, .05, and .10. Do the first one by entering the label in cell A10 "Significance=.01." Next, copy the labels in A5:A7 to A11:A13. Set the significance level (B2) to .01. Select cells E5:G8 and click the Copy button on the Standard Toolbar. Select cell B11. Open the "Edit" menu on the Menu Bar. Select "Paste Special...." When the Paste Special dialog window opens, click the "Values" radio button under "Paste." Repeat the "Paste Special" operation and paste "Formats." This creates a table for a significance level of .01 which will not change when you change the value of cell B2. Use a similar method to create labeled tables for significance levels of .05 and .10. Print the three tables together and alone on a single sheet of paper by first selecting the region containing the three tables. Open the "File" menu on the Menu Bar and select "Print...." Under "Print what" click the "Selection" radio button and then click the "Preview" button. Add a heading with an appropriate title and your name.

5. (advanced) Use the distribution of sample means to determine precisely the probability of Type II error for samples of 10 drawn from Populations II and III. Use a significance level of .05. To do this you will need to first determine the population standard deviation. Then determine the critical values for the test ($H_0: \mu = 16$, $H_A: \mu \neq 16$). Finally, use the actual population mean to determine the probability of a sample mean falling between the two critical values.

Chapter 9

Hypothesis Testing of a Population Mean

Excel provides powerful tools that make it easy to perform hypothesis tests on a population mean. This chapter will provide you with instructions and exercises to help you gain proficiency in using Excel for this, but it does assume you have a basic understanding of the procedures involved in performing a hypothesis test. The chapter will provide examples of problems for which the t distribution is appropriate and problems for which the z distribution is appropriate. Examples of tests of both one- and two-tail hypotheses will be given. In addition, the use of critical values as well as z values will be discussed.

In considering these different types of hypothesis testing problems, you will develop a workbook that is very versatile in its ability to solve all the different types of problems involving hypothesis tests of a population mean. This workbook, however, is not the objective of the chapter. When you use Excel to work on the exercises at the end of the chapter (or on other exercises), you should always start with a new blank workbook and enter the labels and formulas needed to solve the problem at hand.

▼ Classifying the Problem

When you face a statistical problem, you need to determine the type of problem you are facing before you start to solve it. Since we are dealing in this chapter with hypothesis tests on a population mean, it is reasonable to conclude that all problems here will be of that type. Once you consider other types of hypothesis testing problems, however, you will have to determine exactly which population parameter is to be tested. Once a problem is identified as one requiring a hypothesis test of a population mean, you still have other issues to resolve.

1. **Will the test be one- or two-tailed?** A one-tailed test is one in which you are concerned with the question of whether the population mean exceeds a particular value or is less than a particular value. A two-

tailed test is one in which you are concerned with whether the population mean simply differs from a specified value; it does not matter if the mean is above or below that value. The hypothesis tests used in the previous chapter were two-tailed.

This determination must be made before the Null and Alternate Hypotheses can be specified, and they determine the relational symbols used. For a two-tailed test, the Null Hypothesis always has an equal sign (=) and the Alternate Hypothesis always has a not equal sign (≠). For a one-tailed test, the Null Hypothesis will always have a greater-than-or-equal sign (≥) or a less-than-or-equal sign (≤). The Alternate Hypothesis will have either a greater than or less than sign (> or <).

2. **Should the *z* or *t* distribution be used?** If you know the standard deviation of the population, it is appropriate to treat the distribution of sample means as following the *z* distribution. If you only know the standard deviation of a sample, the *t* distribution should be used.

Because traditional *t* tables are less satisfactory than *z* tables, traditional statistical practice has favored using the *z* distribution as a substitute for the *t* distribution in situations where large samples (and thus a large value for degrees of freedom) were used, even if the only known standard deviation came from a sample. The *t* distribution with a large value for the degrees of freedom is very close to the *z* distribution and using it will introduce very little error. With computers (and Excel), the advantage of the *z* distribution disappears, and it is always appropriate to use the *t* distribution when the population standard deviation is unknown.

3. **Should the decision be made with critical values or the *p* value?** This decision is primarily one of taste. The critical value approach is more traditional and will be preferred by those who are used to using it. Some day you may work with people with that preference. One characteristic of that approach is that it is often more suited to be used with statistical tables than the *p* value approach. The use of computers has greatly increased the popularity of the *p* value approach because it is easier for computers to report. A *p* value's magnitude is more intuitive than that of a critical value. Since both methods give the same answer, choose the method you prefer and use it consistently. The worksheets developed in this chapter will use both methods, but you needn't do that with exercises or other problems unless there is a specific reason.

▼ Two-Tail Tests on a Population Mean, σ Known

Consider the following problem:

A manufacturing firm purchases sheet metal from a supplier who maintains that the average thickness of the metal sheets is 15 mils and that the standard deviation of the metal sheets is .1 mils. The manufacturing firm selects a sample of 50 sheets and determines that the sample mean is 14.982 mils. At the .05 level of significance, is there evidence that the population average claimed by the supplier is incorrect?

Since the supplier's claim is incorrect if the population mean is either more or less than 15 mils, a two-tailed test is appropriate. The Null Hypothesis must have an equal sign, and the Alternate Hypothesis must have a not equal sign.

We are asked to look for evidence that the supplier is incorrect, and the assertion that he is incorrect becomes the Alternate Hypothesis. The Null Hypothesis is: $H_0: \mu = 15$, and the Alternate Hypothesis is $H_A: \mu \neq 15$. We will find evidence that the supplier is incorrect if the Null Hypothesis is rejected.

No sample standard deviation is given by the problem. Instead we have the claim of the supplier that the population standard deviation, σ, equals .1. This is a two-tailed test using the z distribution. We will prepare a worksheet with labels for this type of problem.

- Open Excel with a new blank workbook.

- Under the "File" menu choose "Save As," and save the worksheet as chap9.xls.

- Double click the "Sheet1" worksheet tab at the bottom of the Excel window and rename it "2-Tail, Sigma Known."

The first step in setting up a worksheet is to enter labels for the data provided by the problem and for the values that will be calculated from that data. There are three types of data that the problem must provide: data about the population, data about the test sample, and the significance level. The objective of the calculations is to determine if a sample whose mean differs from the hypothesized population mean by as much or more as the test sample's could be drawn from this population with a probability less than the significance level. If the answer is "yes," we conclude that the sample could not have been drawn by chance. It is inconsistent with the Null Hypothesis, and we reject the Null Hypothesis. If the answer is "no," we conclude the sample is consistent with the Null Hypothesis and fail to reject it.

In performing a hypothesis test, we always assume the Null Hypothesis is true. This assumption provides one piece of data about the population, the population mean. In this problem we also know the population standard deviation.

We have two pieces of information about the test sample: the sample mean and the sample size.

From the sample size and the (population) standard deviation, we will calculate the standard error. The standard error is actually the standard deviation of all sample means. In a sense it is data about neither the population nor the test sample; it is a measure of the population of samples. We will include it under the category of test statistic since it is integral to the calculation of that statistic.

After the standard error is calculated, it is used with the population mean to convert the sample mean to a *z* value. This *z* value is the *sample z*. The larger the absolute value of the sample *z*, the lower the probability that a sample could be drawn by chance with a sample mean differing from the hypothesized population mean by as much as the test sample's. To determine whether that probability is less than the significance level, we can either convert the sample *z* to a probability and compare it with the significance level, or we can convert the significance level to a critical *z* and compare it with the sample *z*. Both methods are discussed below.

Enter the labels in the worksheet shown in the picture below. The large labels are 14 point. First enter the label and reselect the cell containing the label. Click the arrow to the right of the font size tool on the Formatting Toolbar ($\boxed{10 \blacktriangledown}$) and select "14." You can make the *z*'s and *p*'s italic by selecting them in the Formula Bar and then clicking the Italic button on the Formatting Toolbar.

	A	B	C	D	E	F	G	H
1	Population Data			Sample Data			Test Statistic	
2	Hypothesized Mean			Mean			Standard Error	
3	Standard Deviation			*n*			Sample *z*	
4								
5	Significance Level			*p* Value			Critical *z* Values	
6	Alpha			2 Tail			Upper	
7							Lower	

Next enter the data values from the problem.

- In cell B2, enter the population mean given by the Null Hypothesis.

- In cell B3, enter the population standard deviation.

- In cell E2, enter the sample mean, 14.982.

- In cell E3, enter the size of the sample, 50.

- In cell B6, enter the significance level (α), .05.

The remaining cells contain formulas performing calculations on these values.

The formula for the standard error is

$$\text{SE}(\bar{x}) = \sigma_{\bar{x}} = \frac{\sigma}{\sqrt{n}}$$

- In cell H2 enter the Excel formula to calculate the standard error. The displayed value should be 0.014142.

- The formula for the sample z is

$$z = \frac{\bar{x} - \mu}{\sigma_{\bar{x}}}$$

In cell H3, enter the Excel formula for the sample z. The displayed value should be -1.27279.

This sample has a mean of 14.982. Is that close enough to 15 that it is reasonable to believe the difference is due to chance, or is it so far from 15 that such a sample is unlikely to have been drawn from a population with mean 15? To reject the Null Hypothesis, the probability of a randomly chosen sample having a mean that differs from 15 by at least as much as 14.982 differs from 15 must be less than the significance level (.05 in this case). In that case we decide the difference is too great to be due to chance and the difference must be due to the population mean being different from 15. If the probability is greater than the significance level, we conclude that the Null Hypothesis could be true and the different sample mean could be the result of chance.

The decision of whether or not to reject the Null Hypothesis thus involves a comparison between the sample z and the significance level. Before this comparison can be done, either the sample z must be converted to a probability (the p value approach), or the significance level must converted to a z value (the critical value approach).

▼ The *p* Value Approach

The p value approach involves converting the sample z to the probability that a z value will have an absolute value that exceeds the absolute value of the sample z. For this problem, that probability is represented by the shaded area in the density function depicted in the picture at the top of the next page.

Excel's NORMSDIST function can be used to determine this area. NORMSDIST has a single argument and provides the probability of a standard normal variable having a value less than that argument. This is represented as the area to the left of the argument on the probability den-

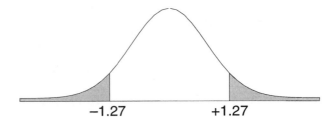

-1.27   +1.27

sity function. If the argument for NORMSDIST were -1.27279 (the sample *z* for this case), the area of the left shaded tail in the density function above would be returned. If NORMSDIST were given the positive value 1.27279, the area to the left of that value would be returned. This would be equivalent to 1.0 minus the area of the right shaded tail. What we want here is the area of *both* shaded tails. An easy way to get that would be to double the value NORMSDIST would return if given a negative parameter, -1.27279 in this case.

Although the sample *z* in this case *is* a negative number, the formula for the *p* value should be one that would work even if the sample *z* were positive. A way to ensure that the parameter given NORMSDIST is negative is to take the negative of the absolute value of the sample *z*.

• Select cell E6. Click the Edit Formula button. Since we want to double the value that will be returned by NORMSDIST, enter "2*" and then select NORMSDIST (Statistical Category). When the NORMSDIST dialog window appears, enter a minus sign in the Z argument field. Use the recent function button to select ABS (Math & Trig). In the Number field enter the address of the sample *z*. Click the "OK" button. The displayed value will be 0.203092.

The *p* value is over .20, clearly greater than the significance level. That means that the test sample might well have been drawn by chance from a population whose mean was 15. The sample is consistent with the Null Hypothesis. We will fail to reject the Null and conclude that there is not evidence that the supplier is incorrect.

What if the mean had been further from 15? Select cell E2 and enter 14.95, which is further from 15 than is 14.982. Notice how the value of the sample *z* increases (in absolute value) to -3.53553, and the *p* value decreases to .000407, which is less than the significance level. If the sample mean had been 14.95, we would have concluded that the sample could not have been drawn from a population whose mean was 15. The Null Hypothesis would have been rejected, and we would have concluded that there was evidence that the supplier is incorrect.

Change the value of E2 back to 14.982. Let's now consider how Excel can be used to test a Null Hypothesis using the critical *z* approach.

▼ The Critical Value Approach

Rather than converting the sample z to a probability, the critical value approach converts the significance level to a z value. These z values define "rejection regions," as shown in the diagram below.

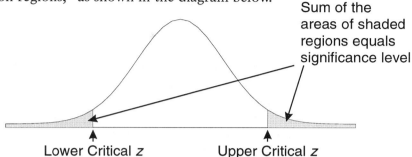

Sum of the areas of shaded regions equals significance level

Lower Critical z Upper Critical z

The rejection regions are those z values that are greater than the upper critical z or lower than the lower critical z. The probability of a z value falling within the rejection region is equal to the shaded area that is equal to the significance level. Notice that the area of each tail for a two-tail critical region is half the significance level.

The determination of a critical value requires an inverse distribution function. For the z distribution this is NORMSINV. We will do the lower critical z first since it is slightly easier.

- Select cell H7 and click the Edit Formula button. Select the NORMSINV function ("Statistical" category).

The dialog window for the NORMSINV function has only one parameter, "Probability," the probability of getting a z value less than the value the function returns. For the lower critical z in the diagram above, that probability is the area of the left tail. Since the area of both tails is given by the significance level (in cell B7), the correct probability for the lower critical z is half that.

- Enter in the "Probability" field of the dialog box an Excel expression that will divide the value of cell B6 by 2. Click the "OK" button. The lower critical z value, -1.95996, should appear in cell H7.

- Select cell H6. Enter an Excel formula to determine the value of the upper critical z. There are several acceptable ways of doing this. All will result in cell H6 displaying a positive number with the same absolute value as that displayed in H7.

Since it is always the case that the upper and lower critical z's have the same absolute values, it is common for just the positive value to be referred to as the critical z.

We can now determine whether or not to reject the Null Hypothesis by comparing two z values, the test statistic and the critical z. If the test statistic lies within the critical region, the Null Hypothesis is rejected. The test statistic will lie within the critical region if its absolute value exceeds the absolute value of a critical z (both of which have the same absolute value). The sample z, –1.27279, does *not* lie within the rejection region since it is not to the left of the lower critical z (–1.95996). We thus fail to reject the Null Hypothesis and conclude that there is not evidence that the supplier is incorrect. This, of course, is the same conclusion arrived at with the p value.

Again, change the sample mean in cell E2 from 14.982 to 14.95. The test statistic changes to -3.53553. This value *does* lie within the rejection region since it lies to the left of the lower critical z, which remains unchanged. In this case we would reject the Null Hypothesis and conclude that there *is* evidence that the supplier is incorrect. The critical value approach will always give the same answer as the p value approach.

This worksheet will enable you to perform any two-tail hypothesis test when sigma is known, by simply setting the values of cells B2, B3, E2, and E3 to the values appropriate for that problem. Consider the following problem:

A quality control inspector wants to check the manufacturing process in a plant that makes scales for home use. The scales are tested by having them weigh a precise reference weight, which weighs 120 pounds. When the manufacturing process is working properly, the measured weight given by all scales averages 120 pounds with a standard deviation of .015 pounds. The inspector chooses 30 scales and weighs the reference weight with each of them. The average weight reported by this sample of scales is 120.01 pounds. Does the inspector have evidence at the .01 level of significance that the manufacturing process is not working properly?

The Null and Alternate Hypotheses for this problem are $H_0: \mu = 120$ and $H_A: \mu \neq 120$.

- Enter the hypothesized population mean, population standard deviation, sample size, sample mean, and significance level in the appropriate cells. When you have done this correctly, the sample z will be 3.651484, the p value will be .000261, and the upper critical z will be 2.575835.

The Null Hypothesis is rejected. Yes, the inspector does have evidence that the manufacturing process is not working properly.

▼ One-Tail Tests on a Population Mean, σ Known

- Double click on worksheet tab "Sheet2" and rename it "1-Tail, Sigma Known."

Consider the following problem:

A mail-order furniture company has been receiving complaints from customers concerning delays in receipt of merchandise shipped to them. The furniture company suspects the fault lies with the trucking firm it employs to ship the furniture to its customers. The trucking firm assures the furniture company that the average time from shipment to delivery is no more than 15 days, with a standard deviation of 4 days. The furniture company decides to check this by selecting a random sample of 50 shipments and determining the precise time between shipment and delivery. The furniture company decides that a significance level of .02 is appropriate for this issue.

The concern here is that the average delivery time may exceed the 15-day standard. There is no concern that the average may be less than 15 days. This makes a one-tail test appropriate here. When the furniture company takes its sample, it will calculate the sample mean. If the sample mean is less than 15 days, there would be no reason to do any further calculations. A sample mean that is less than 15 cannot possibly provide evidence that the population mean exceeds 15. If, however, the sample mean exceeds 15, a procedure is followed to determine if the high sample mean could be due to chance.

Many statisticians would formulate the Null and Alternate Hypotheses as follows:

$$H_0: \mu \leq 15$$
$$H_A: \mu > 15$$

Other statisticians, however, while keeping the Alternate Hypothesis the same as that shown above, would formulate the Null Hypothesis as:

$$H_0: \mu = 15$$

If it is necessary to calculate a test statistic, the value for the population mean (μ) used in the calculation would be the one given by the second form of the hypothesis test. In other words, for the purposes of calculating a test statistic, an inequality in the Null Hypothesis is treated as an equality.

Suppose the furniture company selects a sample, and the sample mean is 17. Since this value exceeds 15, further computation is necessary to determine if chance can be excluded as an explanation for the high sample mean. The data and calculations for this problem are so similar to those for the previous problem that we will copy the labels and formulas from that worksheet.

- Copy the range A1:H7 from the "2-Tail, Sigma Known" worksheet to cell A1 of the "1-Tail, Sigma Known" worksheet. Adjust the width of columns A and G.

Change the data in the worksheet to reflect the values for the current problem:

- In cells B2:B3 enter the hypothesized population mean and the population standard deviation given in the problem.

- In cell E2 enter the sample mean, 17.

- In cell E3 enter the sample size, 50.

- In cell B7 enter the significance level, .02.

The formula for the sample z is the same for one- and two-tail tests, and the correct value, 3.535534, should appear in cell H2.

The differences between a one-tail and a two-tail test are in the formulas for the p value and for the critical z values. One label also needs to be changed.

- Change the label "2 Tail" in cell D7 to "1 Tail."

- Select cell E7 and examine the current formula: "=2*NORMSDIST(-ABS(H2))." This formula doubles the area of one tail, which is appropriate in the two-tail test case. For a one-tail test, the doubling should be removed.

- Use the mouse cursor to select the "2*" in the Formula Bar. With that (and only that) selected, press the Delete key. The displayed value should be 0.000204.

The critical z values for a two-tail test divide the significance level in two parts. The two critical z values define two tails whose *combined* areas equals the significance level. A one-tail critical z defines a single tail whose area equals the significance level.

- Select cell H7 and observe its contents in the Formula Bar.

The current formula, =NORMSINV(B6/2), divides the significance in cell B6 by 2. For a one-tail critical value, the division by two should be removed.

- Remove the "/2" from the formula. The displayed value should be -2.05375.

- Make any necessary changes to cell H8 so that its value will be the positive number with the same absolute value as that of cell H7.

In a one-tail test, only one of the two critical z's is correct for that test. If the sample data are not consistent with the Null Hypothesis, the correct critical z will have the same sign as the sample z.

The formulas for the decision rules are the same for one- and two-tail tests. The p value is much lower than the significance level, and the absolute value of the sample z exceeds the absolute value of the critical z. The Null Hypothesis is rejected. This result indicates that the furniture company should conclude that the trucking firm's claims are not accurate and that the average delivery time for all shipments exceeds 15 days. If the population mean were 15, the probability of a random sample of 50 deliveries having a mean delivery time of 17 or more is low enough that chance is excluded as an explanation for the high sample mean. If the sample mean were closer to 15, this would not have been the case.

Change the value of cell E2 to 16 (be sure to press the Enter key). The p value increases to .03885, greater than the significance level of .02. The sample z falls to 1.767767, less than the critical z and no longer in the rejection region. A sample mean of 16 is close enough to 15 that it could have happened by chance and the trucking firm's claim cannot be rejected. What would happen if the significance level were .05? The result would clearly change since the p value is below the significance level. To see how this would work with the critical value approach, change cell B7 to .05 and observe the effect on the critical z. Change B7 back to .02 before proceeding.

▼ A Warning About One-Tail Tests

Earlier you created an Excel worksheet that completely automates a two-tail test. This is not, however, the case with the worksheet for a one-tail test.

Consider, for example, the possibility that the average delivery time for the sample of 50 chosen by the furniture company was 13 days. Enter the value 13 for the sample mean in cell E2. The p value is much less than the significance level. Should the Null Hypothesis be rejected? No. A sample mean of 13 days is *consistent* with the trucking firm's claim that the average of all delivery times is less than 15 days. That assertion cannot be rejected by a sample that is consistent with the claim. For such a sample, no calculations of p values or critical z by Excel are needed. In the case of one-tail tests, the Excel worksheet should be used *only when the sample statistic is consistent with the Alternate Hypothesis.*

▼ Hypothesis Tests on a Population Mean When σ Is Unknown

In the great majority of real hypothesis tests on a population mean, no information about the population, including the population standard deviation, is available. In these cases a sample standard deviation, s, must be used, and the t distribution is used instead of the normal distribution (although the error in using the normal distribution is minuscule when the sample size is large).

Textbook problems concerning hypothesis tests on a population mean when σ is unknown sometimes provide the sample mean and standard deviation, but sometimes the sample data are provided instead. Determining the mean and standard deviation becomes part of the problem—a more realistic situation. Excel can, of course, easily determine these sample statistics. Some textbooks provide the data for problems on a diskette. In this section we will cover the use of such data.

Although you have produced separate worksheets for the one- and two-tail tests for the case when σ was known, you have seen that the differences were very small. We will combine one- and two-tail tests in a single worksheet by including both one- and two tail p values and critical t's. Keep in mind that Excel cannot determine for you whether a one-tail or two-tail test is appropriate for a particular problem. Furthermore, in a one-tail test, Excel cannot determine for you if the sample is inconsistent with the Alternate Hypothesis. As you saw earlier, if the sample is inconsistent with the Alternate Hypothesis, calculated p values and critical values are incorrect, and it would be incorrect to reject the Null Hypothesis. The use of Excel, or any other computing tool, can never substitute for an understanding of basic statistical principles.

- Double click the worksheet tab "Sheet3" and rename it "Sigma Unknown."

- Return to the previous worksheet, "1-Tail, Sigma Known."

- Copy cells A1:H6 from this worksheet to the the "Sigma Unknown" worksheet. Adjust the widths of columns A and G.

Several modifications need to be made in the new worksheet. Either select each cell in turn and make the changes in the Formula Bar or double click and make the changes in the cells.

- Change the "z" in cells G3 and G5 to "t."

- Select cell A5. From the "Insert" menu choose "Rows." One blank row will be inserted in your worksheet below row 5. This will move the text "Significance Level" from row 5 to row 6.

Since the standard deviation will come from a sample rather than from a population, move the cells referring to the standard deviation (A3:B3) from "Population Data" to "Sample Data." By using a move operation, Excel will automatically update the formula in cell H2 to refer to the new location, and H2 should continue to display the previous value. You can move a cell by using the "drag-and-drop" method (page 32) or by using Cut and Paste (Edit menu of Standard Toolbar buttons).

- In cell D8, enter the text "2 Tail."

- Copy the labels "1 Tail" and "2 Tail" from D7:D8 to G7:G8.

- Erase the formulas from E7 and H7:H8. These will have to be changed to accommodate the *t* distribution.

At the completion of these steps, your worksheet should look like the picture below:

	A	B	C	D	E	F	G	H
1	Population Data			Sample Data			Test Statistic	
2	Hypothesized Mean	15		Mean	13		Standard Error	0.56569
3				*n*	50		Sample *t*	-3.53553
4				Standard Deviation	4			
5								
6	Significance Level			*p* Value			Critical *t* Values	
7	Alpha	0.02		1 Tail			1 Tail	
8				2 Tail			2 Tail	

The calculations for the standard error and for the test statistic (sample *t*) are correct. Using a sample standard deviation does not change the way they are computed except that the standard deviation comes from a sample rather than from a population.

The next step is to enter formulas for the *p* values and critical *t* values that will use the *t* distribution. Excel's *t* distribution functions differ enough from the *z* distribution that we cannot simply change a formula name and must completely reenter new formulas.

For the *p* value functions, we must use TDIST. One of the arguments of TDIST ("X") is the value of a *t*-distributed random variable for which we want a probability. The value of the argument *must* be nonnegative. The exact probability TDIST returns is explained on page 181 and depends on the value of the "Tails" argument.

- Select cell E7. Click the Edit Formula button and use TDIST to determine the probability of a *t*-distributed random variable having a value greater than the absolute value of the number distributed in cell H3. The degrees of freedom is one less than the value in cell E3. The displayed value should be 0.00045.

- Select cell E8. Enter a formula that will calculate the probability of a *t* distributed random variable (with $n - 1$ degrees of freedom) having a value that is either greater than the absolute value of the number displayed in cell H3 or less than the negative of the absolute value of that number. The displayed value should be 0.0009.

Notice that the two-tailed *p* value is always twice the one-tailed *p* value.

The last change that needs to be made will change the calculation of the critical values so that the significance level is converted to a *t* value rather than the *z* distribution. This can be done using the TINV function in Excel. It is slightly easier to use TINV to determine the two-tailed critical *t*, so we will start there.

- Select cell H8. Click the Edit Formula button and choose the TINV function (Statistical category).

The TINV function has two arguments: "Probability" and "Deg_freedom." The second argument is, of course, the degrees of freedom, equal to $n - 1$. The TINV function, unlike TDIST, has no "Tails" argument defining exactly what the value of the "Probability" argument represents. For TINV, the probability is always interpreted as a *two-tailed* probability, and the value returned by TINV is always positive, the boundary for the upper tail. This is shown in the diagram below.

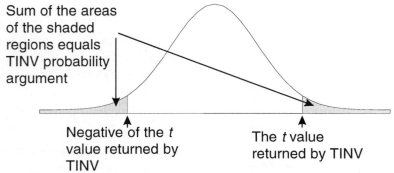

Sum of the areas of the shaded regions equals TINV probability argument

Negative of the *t* value returned by TINV

The *t* value returned by TINV

If the value of the "Probability" argument is the significance level (and the right value for the degrees of freedom is used), TINV returns the correct two-tailed critical *t* value.

- Enter the cell address for the significance level in the "Probability" argument field, and enter the correct formula in the "Deg_freedom" argument field. Click "OK." The displayed value in cell H7 should be 2.404886.

To calculate a one-tailed critical *t*, TINV's "Probability" argument has to be set equal to a value such that one of the tails in the picture above has an area that equals the significance level. If one of the tails has an area equal to the significance level, then the area of both tails is exactly twice the significance level. This is the value which should be used in the "Probability" argument.

- Select cell H7, click the Edit Formula button, and select TINV. Enter a formula in the "Probability" argument field that calculates twice the significance level. Enter the formula in the "Deg_freedom" field to calculate the correct degrees of freedom. Click "OK." The displayed value should be 2.109873.

There is no simple relation between the one-tail critical *t* and the two-tail critical *t* as there was in the case of *p* values. The two-tail critical *t* is not twice the one-tail critical *t*. The inverse probability function (TINV) must be used to calculate both.

In the previous worksheets, two critical *z* values were given for two-tail tests. The lower value was always negative and always had the same absolute value as the upper value. For this worksheet, only the absolute value is shown, which is the standard convention in statistics.

▼ Using the Worksheet

Consider the following problem:

The average balance in a particular type of savings account in a large, multibranch bank has been $2,500. A new branch has opened, and the manager wants to determine if the average balance for this type of account in the branch differs from $2,500. A random sample of 30 accounts is chosen. The sample mean is $2,399, and the sample standard deviation is $250. At the .05 level of significance, does the manager have evidence that the average balance at the new branch differs from $2,500?

A two-tail hypothesis test is appropriate for this problem. The Null and Alternate Hypotheses are

$$H_0: \mu = 2,500$$
$$H_A: \mu \neq 2,500$$

- Enter the hypothesized population mean, $2,500, in cell B2.

- Enter the sample data (mean = $2,399, n = 30, and standard deviation = $250) in the appropriate cells in column E. Note that it is perfectly acceptable to enter numbers with dollar signs and commas. ($2,399 and 2399 are both acceptable).

- Enter the significance level, .05, in cell B8.

If entered correctly, the p value (two-tail) should be 0.034939, and the critical t (also two-tail) should be 2.045231. Since 0.034939 (the p value) is less than the significance level (.05), we would conclude that this sample is too unlikely to be drawn from the population described by the Null Hypothesis to believe that this is what happened. So we reject the Null Hypothesis and conclude yes, there is evidence that the average balance at the new branch differs from $2,500.

▼ Using Named Ranges

So far, all of the Excel formulas in this book have used actual cell addresses to refer to the values in a worksheet. It is also possible to use names rather than cell addresses in formulas. Using names provides two advantages: it makes the formulas more readable, and, by redefining the names, it makes it possible to change the data used by a set of formulas without changing the formulas. Within a worksheet, it is often possible to use row and column labels to refer to data. Although convenient to use, this feature can cause problems if the same label appears in more than one location, and the problems can be difficult to trace.

Another method is to explicitly assign a name to a range of cells. This method will be explored here.

Often a hypothesis testing problem will provide the complete sample data rather than the sample statistics. It is a simple matter for Excel to compute these statistics directly. A feature in Excel allows you to give a name to a range of cell addresses. This can increase the versatility of worksheets designed to solve a class of problems.

Consider the following problem:

The manager of a firm in the business of telephone solicitation is interested in determining if the installation of new telephone equipment has increased the average sales per worker. Last year, average sales per worker for the month of July were $3,987. As soon as the month of July ended this year, the manager selected a sample of 10 workers and determined the level of sales per worker. These were

$2,958, $2,215, $4,146, $6,138, $2,893, $2,085, $2,588, $2,218, $3,341, $1,283

Based on this sample, does the manager have evidence, at the .05 level of significance, that average sales for all workers this July exceeded the average of July of last year?

The correct test for this problem is one-tail, and the Null and Alternate Hypotheses are

$$H_0: \mu \leq \$3{,}987 \text{ or } H_0: \mu = \$3{,}987$$

$$H_A: \mu > \$3{,}987$$

- Open the Insert menu on the Menu Bar and click "Worksheet." A new worksheet, "Sheet4" will be added to your workbook.

- Rename the "Sheet4" worksheet to "Data."

- Move the "Data" worksheet to the end of the worksheets by first placing the mouse pointer on the worksheet tab (where its name is). Press and hold the left mouse button and drag the tab to the right. The mouse cursor will change to this shape ▨, and a small triangle will appear above and between the worksheet tabs. Move the cursor to the right until the triangle is to the right of the last worksheet ("Sigma Unknown"): ▨ ⬋. Release the mouse button and the worksheet will be moved.

- Enter the sample data in column A of the "Data" worksheet. Select the set of sample data (A1:A10). Click the cursor in the Name Box (which should show a cell address for one of the numbers in the sample–probably A1 or A10).

- Replace the cell address in the Name Box with the name "data," and press the Enter key. This will give a *range* name to the sample data that can be used in worksheet formulas.

- Switch to the "Sigma Unknown" worksheet. Enter the hypothesized mean, $3,987, in cell B2.

We will now replace the numbers under "Sample Data" with formulas to calculate the appropriate statistics.

- In cell E2 enter the formula "=average(data)." Notice that this formula refers to the range name of the sample data on the next worksheet. The value that appears in this cell should be $2,987. Notice that Excel continues to use the same *format* (dollar signs and commas) used previously.

- In cell E3, enter the formula "=count(data)." The COUNT function determines the number of numeric values in the range, which is the same as the sample size, n. The value should be 10.

- In cell E4, enter the formula "=stdev(data)." This calculates the sample standard deviation of the data. The value should be 1352.809.

What is the conclusion in this case? The p value is 0.022056, which is certainly less than the significance level (.05). This suggests that the Null Hypothesis should be rejected. This conclusion, however, is wrong. The reason can be found in the sample mean, which is $2,987 (2986.5). Since this sample value is less than $3,987, it cannot be used to reject the Null Hypothesis and accept the Alternate Hypothesis because it is consistent with the Null, not the Alternate Hypothesis. *A necessary condition for rejecting the Null Hypothesis (and concluding that there was evidence that the average sales for all workers exceeded $3,987) is that the sample mean must exceed $3,987.* Thus the correct conclusion is to fail to reject the Null Hypothesis and to conclude that there is no evidence that the average sales of all workers exceeds $3,987. Whenever sample data are consistent with the Null Hypothesis, it is always correct to fail to reject the Null Hypothesis regardless of the p value or the critical t.

Using a name range has an important advantage. Suppose that the manager chooses a larger sample than indicated in the problem. Suppose that the sample was of size 15, and, in addition to the ten values given above, the following five values were also chosen:

$$\$4,200, \ \$3,900, \ \$2,800, \ \$4,400, \ \$2,910$$

- Select the "Data" worksheet, and add these five values in column A *after* the ten values already there. The new values should go into cells A11:A15.

- Open the Insert menu on the Menu Bar and select "Name." A cascade menu will open. Select "Define..." from that menu. The Define Name dialog window will open.

- Under "Names in Workbook" you should see the name "data." Click that name with the mouse pointer, and the word "data" should then appear in the top field of the dialog window.

- The bottom field of the dialog window is titled "Refers to:." That field should contain the cell addresses of the range with the name "data" ("=Data!$A$1:$A$10"). Move the mouse pointer across that address so that it is "highlighted." The dialog window should look like that shown at the top of the next page.

- Place the mouse pointer on cell A1 and select the range containing all of the data by pressing the (left) mouse button and dragging the pointer down to cell A15. The contents of the "Refers to:" field should change to "=Data!$A$1:$A$15", the addresses you have just selected with the mouse. You have redefined the address of the range of cells with the name "data."

- Click the "OK" button and return to the "Sigma Unknown" worksheet. Notice that the sample statistics have changed. The sample mean is now $3,205, n is now 15, and the sample standard deviation is $1,198 (1198.224).

Once you redefined the "data" range name, all of the formulas referring to that name automatically changed to reflect the new definition. You can thus use this worksheet to do hypothesis tests on any amount of data without revision as long as you enter the data somewhere in the workbook and give the range containing the data the name "data."

▼ Using Data on a Diskette

You can also read data from a file and bring the file into the worksheet. The simplest way of doing this is to read the file into a workbook and then copy the data from that workbook to the current one.

Consider the following problem:

A car manufacturer has launched a special ad campaign for a particular model car. The manufacturer wants to determine if average sales per dealer for this model exceed 60 during the month following the campaign. A random sample of dealers was surveyed. Respondents were asked how many of that particular model were sold in the month. The responses were coded and are available in the file Cars.txt.

Based on the response to the survey, does the manufacturer have evidence (at the .05 level of significance) that average sales for all dealers during the month exceeded 60?

The test for this problem would be one-tail. The Null and Alternate Hypotheses are

$$H_0: \mu \le 60 \text{ or } H_0: \mu = 60$$
$$H_A: \mu > 60$$

- Enter "60" into the cell on the "Sigma Unknown" worksheet for the hypothesized sample mean (B2). Be sure the significance level (cell B8) is .05.

- Click the Open button on the Standard Toolbar . A dialog window will open where you will locate the Cars.txt file.

There are two fields that you need to adjust: "Look in:," and "Files of type."

- First find the directory containing the data. Click the "Up One Level" button first: 🗀. If the data are located on a diskette, select "3½ Floppy (A:)" first and then choose the "Chap_9" folder. Change the "Files of type" to "All files (*.*)" Double click "Cars.txt," which should be in the list of files. Excel will open the first Text Import Wizard dialog window.

- As you will see in that first window, this file contains only one data number per line with a label on the first line. Since the label has three words with spaces, we do not want Excel to regard the space character as a delimiter.

- Click the "Next>" button. Be sure the small square to the left of "Space" in the group of delimiters *does not* have a check in it. Click the "Finish" button.

Excel will create a new workbook with the name (on the Name Bar) "Cars.txt." The data will be in column A with the label in the first row.

- Select the entire set of data. An easy way of doing this is to select cell A1. Press the Shift key on your keyboard, and, while pressing the Shift key, press and release the End key, and then press and release the key with the downward pointing arrow. This should select cells A1:A51.

- Click the Copy button.

- Open the "Window" menu on the Menu Bar.

At the bottom of the menu is a list of the open workbooks. This list should include "Cars.txt" (with a check mark in front of it) and "chap - 9.xls," the workbook with the hypothesis testing formulas. Click the mouse pointer on the name "chap9.xls." Your screen should immediately display that workbook.

- Click the "Data" worksheet tab to bring it to the top.

- On the "Data" worksheet, select cell A1.

- Click the Paste button. The data on the number of cars sold will be copied to column A of the "Data" worksheet.

- Open the "Insert" menu and select "Name..." then "Define."

When the Define Name dialog window appears, it is ready to define a new name, "Number_of_Cars." Excel gets this name from the label in A1, except that blanks are replaced by underscores. Although this makes it easy to give the new data that name, we want to redefine the "data" named range.

- Click "data" in the list in the dialog window and redefine the range it refers to to A1:A51

- Return to the "Sigma Unknown" worksheet by clicking its worksheet tab.

The sample mean shown on the worksheet should be 62.64. Because of the previous formatting, the value may appear as $63.

- Remove the dollar signs from cells B2, E2, and E4 (if they are present) by selecting each cell and then clicking the Comma Style button 🮲.

- Increase the number of displayed decimal places for cells E2 and E4 by using the Increase Decimal button 🮲.

Is there evidence that the average number of cars for all dealers exceeded 60? Notice that the sample mean, *62.64, is* greater than 60 and is thus consistent with the Alternate Hypothesis. The calculations appearing on the worksheet enable us to determine whether or not chance is a likely explanation for the high sample value. An examination of the one-tail p value (0.020569) shows that probability to be less than the significance level, and thus the decision is to reject the Null Hypothesis.

The Null Hypothesis is rejected. Yes, there is evidence at the .05 level of significance that the average sales for all dealers that month exceeded 60.

▼ Exercises

Close the worksheet you have developed in this chapter before working the problems below. Use a new, blank worksheet with them. For each problem, state the Null and Alternate Hypotheses and, determine the p value or critical t. State whether you reject or fail to reject the Null Hypothesis and give a yes or no answer to the question asked. Copies of the data for the problems can be found in the workbook Exercises.xls.

1. A milk bottle-filling machine is operating properly when the average amount of milk placed in each bottle is exactly 1 gallon with a standard deviation of .02 gallons. A random sample of 50 bottles was chosen, and the average amount of milk in the sample was 1.01 gallons. At the .01 level of significance, is there evidence that the machine is not working properly?

2. A testing agency wishes to test the effectiveness of a new brake design in a particular automobile. The brakes are claimed to be able, with an average driver, to stop an automobile traveling at 40 mph in less than 50 feet. A random sample of drivers is chosen to test the brakes and the stopping distances are as follows:

   49, 42, 46, 29, 48, 55, 43, 48, 50, 46, 41, 46, 37, 40, 39

   Based on this sample, is there evidence at the .05 level of significance that the average stopping distance for all drivers is less than 50 feet?

3. The director of retail operations wants to assign enough tellers to a group of bank branches that the average amount of time any customer will have to spend waiting in line will be less than 120 seconds during peak hours. A random sample of customers was chosen during those peak hours, and the amount of time spent waiting in line by each customer was carefully measured in seconds. The data are coded in the file bank.txt. Based on these data, is there evidence at the .01 level of significance that the average amount of time spent by all customers is less than 120 seconds?

4. A random sample of students from a local college was selected and each person's height was measured. The results (in inches) were

   62, 59, 73, 56, 71, 68, 54, 53, 64, 69

   Is there evidence (at the $\alpha = .05$ level of significance) that the average height of all students is less than 68 inches?

5. A winery claims that the acidity level of a particular wine is normally distributed with an average pH level of 6.10. A random sample of 10

bottles is selected and the sample average acidity level as measured by pH is 6.03 with a sample standard deviation of .125. Is there evidence that the claim of an average pH level of 6.10 is not valid? Use $\alpha = .01$.

6. A random sample of students from a local college was selected and each person's height was measured. The results (in inches) were

   62, 59, 73, 56, 71, 68, 54, 53, 64, 69

   Is there evidence (at the $\alpha = .05$ level of significance) that the average height of all students is more than 68 inches?

7. A random sample of students from a local college was selected and each person's height was measured. The results (in inches) were

   62, 59, 73, 56, 71, 68, 54, 53, 64, 69

   Is there evidence (at the $\alpha = .05$ level of significance) that the average height of all students differs from 68 inches?

Chapter 10

Inferences on a Population Proportion

Some types of data cannot be averaged. In the period prior to an election, polls are taken to measure support for the various candidates. Imagine that you are involved in conducting such a poll for a particular candidate who is hoping to win an election. The first step would be to select a random sample. Once the sample is selected, data would be collected from each person in the sample to determine whether or not that person intends to vote for your candidate. The simplest type of data we might have for each member of the sample is a "yes" or "no." The entire set of data would be a collection of yes's and no's. How can you take an average of data like these? You can't. Instead, you describe the sample by calculating the proportion of people in the sample who said "yes." You can then use the sample proportion to make inferences about the proportion of people in the population who support the candidate, much as you used sample data to make inferences about a population mean when the data were of the type that could be averaged.

Once you have a basic understanding of confidence intervals and hypothesis tests of a population mean, you are most of the way to also understanding inferences on a population proportion. The concepts are the same, but some of the mechanics are a little different. Inferences on a population mean are based on the distribution of sample means. Inferences on a population proportion are based on the distribution of sample proportions.

Inferences on proportions are made on "binomial" data—the same kind of data encountered with the binomial distribution. Each individual observation can have only two values, traditionally called "success" or "failure." When the proportion of a sample that falls into a certain category is calculated, an observation in that category is a "success." The rest are "failures." Even though an election (and a poll) may have more than two choices, whenever the proportion favoring a certain outcome is determined, an observation either favors that outcome or does not favor that outcome.

▼ Sampling Distribution of the Proportion

The sampling distribution of the proportion comes directly from the binomial distribution. In the binomial distribution, the random variable is the "number" of successes. In the sampling distribution of the proportion, the random variable is the "proportion" of successes. When a sample is chosen from a population, the sample size, *n*, can also be thought of as the binomial *n* trials. The population proportion of successes (π) is also the probability that a single observation selected from the population will be a success and is thus the same as the binomial π. The binomial random variable—number of successes or *x*—is converted to the proportion of successes (p_s—not to be confused with *p* value) by dividing by *n*.

The simple conversion of the binomial random variable to the sample proportion of successes makes it easy to determine the mean and standard deviation (standard error) of sample proportions. The mean of sample proportions is the binomial mean divided by *n*, and the standard deviation of sample proportions is the binomial standard deviation divided by *n*, which results in the following:

$$\mu_{p_s} = \pi$$
$$\sigma_{p_s} = \sqrt{\frac{\pi(1-\pi)}{n}}$$

As we saw in Chapter 4, under certain conditions (large *n*, π not too far from 0.50), the normal distribution approximates the binomial distribution. Subject to the same limitations, it also approximates the distribution of sample proportions and is traditionally used for this. As we will see, in the case of hypothesis testing it is possible to use the binomial distribution directly, which will give somewhat more accurate results.

▼ Confidence Intervals on a Population Proportion

As was noted in chapter 7 (see the discussion beginning on page 198), determining a confidence interval is closely related to the sampling distribution problem where an interval symmetrically distributed around the mean containing a given percentage of sample values is determined. For example, suppose we knew the population π and wanted to determine the interval around π which would contain a desired percentage of all the sample p_s's. Using the normal approximation, the boundaries would be $\mu_{p_s} \pm z\sigma_{p_s} = \pi \pm z\sqrt{\dfrac{\pi(1-\pi)}{n}}$. If we wanted the interval containing 95% of the values of sample proportions, the appropriate z value would be approximately 1.96.

A confidence interval on a population proportion would be centered on a single sample proportion, but would have the same width ($\pm z\sigma_{p_s}$) as the interval above. There is, however, a problem. The value of σ_{p_s} is dependent on π, and π is unknown (its value is being estimated with the confidence interval). The traditional solution is to substitute the value of p_s from the sample. One justification for doing this is that the value of $\pm z\sigma_{p_s}$ is not highly sensitive to small changes in the value of π (a proposition that will be explored more in an exercise). Therefore, if p_s is reasonably close to π, using it in place of π to calculate σ_{p_s} should be acceptable. The formula for a confidence interval on π is thus:

$$p_s \pm z\sqrt{\dfrac{p_s(1-p_s)}{n}}$$

This can be easily implemented with Excel.

- Start Excel with a new blank workbook and save it as chap10.xls.

- Change the name of the "Sheet1" worksheet to "CI on Pi."

- Enter labels so your worksheet looks like the picture below. The larger labels are 14-point font and the smaller are in 10-point font. Adjust the column width so that the columns are wide enough to accommodate the 10-point labels. Allow the larger labels to continue to the unused adjacent cells.

	A	B	C	D	E
1	Sample Data			Confidence Interval	
2	n			standard error	
3	proportion of successes			level	
4				z value	
5				sampling error	
6				lower bound	
7				upper bound	
8					

Consider the following problem:

A candy manufacturer wants to estimate the impact of an advertising campaign in a metropolitan area by measuring brand recognition for a new confection marketed for children. A random sample of 350 children from the area was chosen, and the children were asked if they knew of the new brand. Of these, 112 recognized the new brand. Based on this sample, provide a 95% confidence interval estimate of the proportion of all children in the area who would recognize the new brand.

- Enter the value of n, 350, in cell B2.

- Have Excel calculate the value of p_s in cell B3 by entering a formula that divides 112 by 350. Then "highlight" the formula by dragging the mouse cursor across it on the Formula Bar (with the left mouse button pressed). After the formula is "highlighted," press the F9 function key. The formula will be replaced by its value, 0.32.

- Enter the formula in D2 to calculate the standard error as $\sqrt{\dfrac{p_s(1-p_s)}{n}}$.

  One way of doing this is to use the Edit Formula button and display the dialog window from the SQRT function ("Math & Trig" category). Enter the expression for $\dfrac{p_s(1-p_s)}{n}$ in the "Number" argument field. Be sure to include the parentheses, and remember that multiplication must be shown explicitly with "*." If the formula is entered correctly, the displayed value will be 0.024934.

- Enter "95%" (without quotes) in cell E3. Be sure to include the percent sign, which will cause Excel to interpret the value as 0.95.

The z value in cell E3 is the absolute value of the boundaries of a region in the center of the standard normal distribution whose area is given in cell E2. This is illustrated in the picture below. The shaded central region has an area equal to the confidence level. The two boundaries are labeled z and $-z$. Both have the same absolute value, and it is this value that is needed in E3.

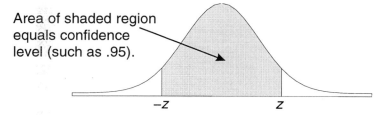

Area of shaded region equals confidence level (such as .95).

$-z$ z

Determining the z value requires using the NORMSINV function. That function has a single argument: "probability," and provides the z value for which the area to the left in the density function equals the "probability" argument. There are two different ways of doing this. One way would be to enter an expression for the "probability" argument that would calculate the area of the left tail from the value of E2. This is a simple expression, but the value returned by NORMSINV would be $-z$, a negative number. This means the formula in E4 would have to convert the negative value provided by NORMSINV to a positive value, perhaps by using the ABS function. Another way would involve putting an expression in the "probability" argument, which adds the area of the central region to the area of the left tail. That sum is the area to the left of the positive *z* value on the right in the picture. With this area for a probability, NORMSINV would return the positive *z* value.

- Enter a formula in cell E4 that will determine the *z* value for the confidence level in E3. With 95% in E3, the displayed value will be 1.959961. Be sure this is displayed as a positive number.

- The sampling error is the product of the *z* value (in E4) and the standard error (in E2). Enter the formula in E5 to calculate this. This displayed value will be 0.04887.

- The lower bound is the value of p_s minus the sampling error, and the upper bound is p_s plus the sampling error. Enter the formulas in cells E6 and E7, respectively. The displayed values will be 0.27113 and 0.36887.

The 95% confidence interval on the proportion of all children in the area who recognize the brand name is between 0.27113 and 0.36887.

- Check the worksheet by changing the value of *n* to 275, the confidence level to 99%, and the value of p_s to .45. The lower bound of the 99% confidence interval is 0.372725, and the upper bound is 0.527275. Be sure cells E5 and E6 of your worksheet display these values.

▼ Determining Sample Size for a Desired Sampling Error

Larger samples generally result in narrower confidence intervals. Although it's desirable for confidence intervals to be as narrow as possible, sample size is usually the primary factor determining the cost of a statistical study. As a result, it is not uncommon for researchers to want to know how big a sample will be required to obtain a confidence interval of a certain width or a certain sampling error (the sampling error is half the width of the confidence interval).

The formula for the sampling error is $e = z\sqrt{\dfrac{\pi(1-\pi)}{n}}$, although p_s must be used in place of π. Solving for *n* yields: $n = \pi(1-\pi)\dfrac{z^2}{e^2}$.

When the value of n obtained from this formula is not an integer, the convention is to round *up* to the next larger integer.

Since the sample size determination must be made prior to selecting the sample, we generally do not have a value for π or even a value for p_s. This situation is analogous to that faced when determining the sample size required for a given confidence interval on a population mean. In that case, it was σ that was unknown. The problem here turns out not to be as difficult as it was in that case, however. Unlike σ, π is bounded—its value must be between 0 and 1. Once the confidence level (which determines z) and the desired sampling error are determined, the value of n is determined by $\pi(1-\pi)$. The closer π is to 0.50, the larger this expression. If we have no idea of the actual value of π, we simply use the value 0.50. The sample size we would calculate from this value might be too large—which means the actual sampling error obtained from the sample cannot possibly be larger than the desired value. It's better to discover that your estimate is more accurate than you expected rather than less accurate. On the other hand, if we are certain that π cannot possibly equal 0.50, choosing another value which is still closer to 0.50 than π will reduce the calculated value of n (thus saving money), and *still* ensure a sampling error no larger than the desired level.

- Change the name of the "Sheet2" worksheet to "n" and switch to it.

- Enter labels to your worksheet so that it looks like the picture below.

	A	B	C
1	Sample Size Determination		
2	pi		
3	confidence level		
4	sampling error		
5	z		
6	n1		
7	n		

Consider the following problem:

A computer manufacturer wants to survey individuals who have bought a new model of a home computer to determine the proportion who report that they are satisfied with their purchase. For past models, the proportion has always been at least 80%. The manufacturer has strong reason to believe that no fewer than 70% could possibly report being satisfied. If the manufacturer wants to be able to estimate a 99% confidence interval with a sampling error of ±2%, how big a sample would be required?

Since the data in this problem are expressed as percentages, we will enter them in Excel as percentages. Remember that to Excel the difference between a percentage and a proportion is formatting, so that entering a number with a percent sign causes the actual number stored in the cell to be the corresponding proportion.

- Enter "70%" as the value of π in cell B2 and "99%" as the confidence level in cell B3. Enter "2%" for the sampling error in cell B4.

The z value needed in cell B5 is the same type of z value used in the previous worksheet. It is the absolute value of the boundaries of the central region of a normal density function whose area equals the confidence level.

- Enter a formula in cell B5 that will determine the z value for the confidence level in B3. With 99% in B3, cell B5 should display the value 2.575835.

Cell B6 will contain the formula for n shown on the previous page. The value obtained from this formula will not be an integer. Cell B7 will be used for a formula that rounds the value of cell B6 up to the next integer.

- Enter the Excel formula that will calculate $\pi(1-\pi)\dfrac{z^2}{e^2}$. In place of π, z, and e, you will use cell references to their locations in the worksheets. Remember that you must explicitly tell Excel where to multiply by using Excel's multiplication symbol (the asterisk). To square a number (or raise it to any other power), you use the exponentiation symbol, "$\wedge$." The value that should be displayed in B6 is 3483.335.

To round a number up to the next integer, use the CEILING function in the "Math & Trig" category. That function has two arguments. The "number" argument should refer to B6. The "significance" argument is the value you want the answer to be divisible by. This should be set equal to the number "1," indicating that you want the answer to be an integer (divisible by 1).

- Enter a formula using the CEILING function in cell B7 that will round the value displayed in cell B6 up to the next integer. The displayed value should be 3484.

Remember that the sample size is the primary factor determining the cost of a statistical study. Let's see how some of the factors determined by the computer manufacturer in this problem affect the sample size.

What effect does the sampling error have on the sample size? Smaller sampling errors mean more precise estimates, so the computer manufacturer would like them to be as small as possible.

- Change the sampling error from 2% to 1%. The needed sampling size will shoot up to 13,934.

Reducing the sampling error by half approximately quadruples the sample size. The value of *n* (before rounding up) will exactly quadruple.

- Change the value of π from 70% to 30%. Notice this has no effect on the size of *n*.

Since π enters the determination of *n* only through the expression $\pi(1-\pi)$, there is no difference between using 70% (.70) and 30% (which is $1-.70$). In both cases the value .70 will be multiplied by the value .30.

Change π to 50%. The required size of *n* will increase. Can you find another value for π that will increase *n* further?

- Change the confidence level from 99% to 90%. The lower confidence level reduces the required sample size by more than half to 6764 ($\pi = 50\%$).

▼ Hypothesis Tests on a Population Proportion

When the normal approximation is used for the distribution of sample proportions, hypothesis tests on a population proportion are very similar to hypothesis tests on a population mean. Somewhat greater accuracy can be achieved by converting a hypothesis test on a population proportion to a binomial problem and using the binomial distribution. Without computers it would be quite difficult to use the binomial approach, and few textbooks cover it for this reason. With Excel, the binomial distribution is no more difficult to use than any other probability distribution. Since it is the traditional approach, the normal approximation for the distribution of sample proportions will be explored first.

▼ Hypothesis Tests on π Using the Normal Approximation

- Switch to the "Sheet3" worksheet and change its name to "Hyp Test on pi."

- Prepare your worksheet by making it look like the picture on the next page. This involves using 14-point font for the large labels, using italic face for *z* and *p*, where appropriate, and manually adjusting column widths to hold the 10-point labels. The line below "Normal Approximation" can be made by selecting the region A6:I6, clicking the small downward pointing arrow beside the Borders button on the Format-ting Toolbar, and then clicking the button showing a dark underline.

	A	B	C	D	E	F	G	H	I
1	Population Data			Sample Data			Significance Level		
2	Hypothesized pi			Proportion			Alpha		
3				n					
4				Standard Error					
5									
6	Normal Approximation								
7	Test Statistic			Approximate p Value			Critical z Values		
8	Approximate Sample z			1 tail			1 tail		
9				2 tail			2 tail		
10									

Let's consider the following problem:

An airline has established an on-time goal that requires that at least 95% of its flights will arrive on time. A random sample of 120 flights for the current week was chosen, and 110 of those flights arrived on time. Is there evidence at the .05 level of significance that the goal is not being met?

The first step, as in all hypothesis testing problems, is to formulate the Null and Alternate Hypotheses.

$$H_0: \pi \geq .95 \text{ and } H_A: \pi < .95$$

This is a one-tail test. The next step is to determine whether the sample is consistent with the Null Hypothesis. It would be consistent if the pro-portion of planes that arrived on time in the sample were greater than or equal to .95. The sample proportion $p_s = \dfrac{110}{120} = .9167$. The sample is thus *not* consistent with the Null Hypothesis. We must then determine whether this low sample proportion might reasonably be due to chance. Similar to the case of a hypothesis test on a population mean, this is done by determining the answer to the following question: "If the Null Hy-pothesis were true, what is the probability that a sample this size would have a sample proportion at least as far from what was expected as this sample?" If that probability is low (less than the significance level), we conclude that chance is not a reasonable explanation, and the Null Hy-pothesis is rejected. If that probability exceeds the significance level, we conclude that chance might be the explanation and fail to reject the Null Hypothesis. In assuming that the Null Hypothesis is true, we assume that $\pi = .95$, since this is the value given by the Null most likely to result in a sample proportion less than .95. If $\pi = .95$, we would also expect (in the statistical sense) that $p_s = .95$.

- Enter the value for the population proportion assuming the Null Hy-pothesis is true in cell B2.

- Enter the significance level for this problem in cell H2.

- Enter the sample proportion in cell E2. Do not simply enter ".9167." Instead, have Excel divide 110 by 120 and then convert the answer to a number. This will improve the accuracy with which this number is represented. Although the gain is small, there is no reason not to take advantage of it.

- Enter the sample size, n, in cell E3.

- Enter the formula in cell E4 that will calculate the standard error, the standard deviation of sample proportions σ_{p_s}, using the formula on page 263. In this case use the hypothesized population proportion in B2 for π rather than the sample proportion. The displayed value should be 0.019896.

- In cell B8 calculate the sample z from the formula $z = \dfrac{p_s - \mu_{p_s}}{\sigma_{p_s}}$. As shown by the formula on page 263, $\mu_{p_s} = \pi$. Use the hypothesized value for π in cell B2. The displayed value should be -1.67542.

The p value is the probability that a standard normal random variable will have a value less than -1.67542. If this were a two-tail test, this probability would be multiplied by 2. For this problem, the sample z is negative. For other problems, the sample z may be positive. To use Excel's NORMSDIST function to get a tail area, the value of the argument *must be* negative. (This is discussed in more detail in the context of a two-tail test starting on page 243.)

The NORMSDIST function has one argument named "z," referring to the upper bound of the left tail of the standard normal distribution for which an area is desired. For this problem, the value is that shown in cell B8. We must put an expression in the "z" argument field that will make the value in that field negative regardless of the sign on B8.

- Select cell E8, click the Edit Formula button, and choose NORMSDIST. In the "z" argument field enter an expression that takes the negative of the absolute value of cell B8. The Excel ABS function can be used to take the absolute value. The displayed value should be 0.046926.

- Enter the formula in cell E9 that doubles the value in cell E8. The displayed value should be 0.093853.

The calculation of critical values is the same as was given in the discussions starting on pages 245 and 248. An abbreviated explanation follows.

To calculate the critical z values, use NORMSINV to convert the significance level to a z value. Always display a positive value. The NORMSINV function has a single argument ("probability"). Since NORMSINV is cumulative, it returns the upper bound of the lower tail region whose area equals the value of that argument. That means that if you set the argument equal to the significance level (which is less than .50), the z value returned will be negative. What you want is the absolute value of that negative number. There are several ways of doing this. One approach is to set the "probability" argument equal to the significance level and invert the sign of the returned z value (by preceding it with a minus sign or by nesting it in the ABS function). The other approach would be to set the "probability" argument equal to 1 minus the significance level.

- Using any acceptable method, enter a formula in cell H8 that will display a positive one-tail critical z for the significance level shown in H2. The displayed value for the .05 significance level should be 1.644853.

To determine the two-tail critical value, the "probability" argument should be half the significance level. Here also, the z value should be a positive number.

- Enter a formula in cell H9 that will determine the two-tail z value for the significance level in H2. The displayed value should be 1.959961.

With the information on the worksheet, we can now determine the answer to the problem. Since the (one-tailed) p value is less than the significance level, the Null Hypothesis should be rejected. The same result can be deduced from the fact that the absolute value of the sample z exceeds the (one-tailed) critical z. Yes, there is evidence at the .05 level of significance that the airline's on-time goal is not being met.

It is interesting to note that if the test had been two-tailed, that is, if we were looking for evidence that the on-time proportion *differed* from .95, we would have failed to reject the Null Hypothesis. Paradoxically, our sample supports the assertion that the airline's total on-time proportion is below .95 but does not support the assertion that it differs from .95, when both tests are done at the .05 level of significance.

Our conclusion that there is evidence the airline is not achieving 95% on-time performance is based on the normal distribution approximating the binomial, and the approximation could be a source of error. The fact that the p value is so close to the significance level (and that the absolute value of the sample z is so close to the critical z) is a source of concern. This sample is so close to the "Reject"/"Fail to Reject" margin, that we cannot have great confidence in any conclusion. We can, however, eliminate the error associated with the normal approximation by using the binomial distribution to analyze this problem.

▼ Using the Binomial Distribution to Test Hypotheses on π

Reread the problem on page 270. If $\pi \geq .95$, the expected number of on-time flights in a random sample of 120 would be $\pi \times n$, which would be an amount greater than or equal to 114. In this sample, however, only 110 flights were on time, less than expected if the Null Hypothesis were true. The p value is the probability that if the Null Hypothesis is true ($\pi = .95$), a random sample of 120 flights would by chance have a number of on-time flights as different or more different from what was expected as did this sample. In other words, if the probability of a single flight being on time is .95, what is the probability that in 120 flights the number of on-time flights would be 110 or less?

If the probability of a flight's being on time is independent (which was implicitly assumed in using the normal approximation), the number of on-time flights in a sample of 120 is binomially distributed. If the normal distribution is used to approximate the binomial, the probability is 0.046926, the same as the one-tail p value obtained using the normal distribution as an approximation for the distribution of sample proportions. With Excel it is as easy to use the binomial distribution as the normal distribution. The probability given by the binomial distribution is the correct p value, while that given by the normal distribution is only an approximation.

We will add to the current worksheet so that it can be used to handle the binomial distribution approach for all hypothesis tests on a population proportion. The first step is to add the labels shown in the picture below. Carefully note the row numbers; these labels go below the portion of the worksheet you have already used.

	A	B	C	D	E	F	G	H
12	**Binomial Approach**							
13	**Number of Successes**			**Probability of x**			**Exact *p* Values**	
14	Sample			< or = Sample			1 tail	
15	Expected			> or = Sample			2 tail	

- Enter the number of successes for this sample in cell B14. For this problem, a success is a flight arriving on time. The number of successes is the number of flights that arrived on time in the sample of 120.

- Enter the formula in cell B15 that will calculate the expected number of successes, which is $n \times \pi$. Use the cell addresses for n and the hypothesized value for π located in the upper portion of the worksheet. The value displayed in cell B15 should be 114.

If the Null Hypothesis were true, the expected number of on-time flights would be 114 (or more). The actual number of on-time flights was 110. The p value is the probability, assuming that π really is 0.95, that in another sample of 120 flights the number of on-time flights would differ from the expected value by as much or more than it did for this sample. Since the expected value was 114 (or more), the number of on-time flights in a second sample would differ as much or more if it were 110 *or less*. The p value is the binomial probability that the number of successes will be less than or equal to 110, given 120 trials and a probability of success on each trial of 0.95. The formula for this binomial probability will be entered in cell E14.

- Select cell E14, click the Edit Formula button, and select the BINOM-DIST function from the "Statistical" category. Enter the word "true" in the last ("Cumulative") argument field, and the value returned by the function will be a *cumulative* probability, that is, the probability of obtaining a number of successes less than or equal to the value referred to by the "Number_s" argument, which should refer to the cell containing the number of successes in the sample. The "Trials" argument should refer to the cell in the worksheet with the value of n and the "Probability_s" argument should refer to the cell with the hypothesized value of π. When the correct references have been entered in the argument field, the value appearing in the dialog window below and to the right of the argument fields will be 0.078629947. The displayed value in the cell will be this same value rounded. Click "OK."

The value displayed in cell E17 is the exact (one-tailed) p value for this problem.

In some hypothesis tests of a population proportion, the expected number of successes will be less than those obtained in the sample. Assuming the sample is not consistent with the Null Hypothesis, a one-tail p value would be the binomial probability that another sample would have a number of successes greater than or equal to the number in this sample. To enable this worksheet to be used for these problems it will be necessary to calculate that binomial probability. This can be determined by calculating one minus the cumulative probability of the number of successes being one less than the number of successes in this sample. In other words, the probability of 110 successes *or more* is one minus the probability of 109 successes *or less*.

- Enter the formula in cell E15 that will calculate the binomial probability of a number of successes greater than or equal to the value given in cell B14. The number of trials and the probability of success on each trial are the same for this calculation as they were for the previous calculation. The value displayed in cell E15 should be 0.96155.

The one-tail p value for any problem will be either the value in cell E17 or the value in cell E18. How can we know which is the correct one? Unless the number of successes in the sample happens to be exactly the expected number, one of those two values will be less than .5 and the other will be greater than .5. If the number of successes in the sample is not consistent with the Null Hypothesis, the p value must be less than .5. As was the case with hypothesis tests on a population mean, the worksheet can't determine if the sample is or is not consistent with the Null. If the sample is consistent, there is no need to calculate a p or critical value because the Null Hypothesis cannot be rejected. Our calculation of the p value can, therefore, reasonably assume that the sample is *not* consistent with the Null Hypothesis.

- Enter a formula in cell H14 that gives that cell the value in E14 if E14 is smaller than E15, and the value in E18 otherwise. The value displayed in cell H14 should be .07863.

The p value for a two-tail hypothesis test using the binomial approach will be exactly double the one-tail p value.

- Enter a formula in cell H15 that display a number twice the one displayed in cell H14. The displayed value should be .15726.

All that is left is the decision under the binomial approach, which is exactly the same as the p value decision used in the normal approximation approach except that the exact p values determined by the binomial distribution rather than the approximate p values determined by the normal approach are compared to the significance level.

An important difference between the p value used in the binomial approach and that used in the normal approximation is that the binomial p value is *greater than* the significance level. The conclusion, therefore, changes. With this p value we would fail to reject the Null Hypothesis. No, there is not evidence that the proportion of all on-time flights is less than .95.

▼ Which Approach Is Correct, Binomial or Normal?

With different results from the binomial and normal approximation, it is natural to ask, "Which approach is correct?"

The answer, of course, is that the *p* value determined by the binomial approach, .07863, is correct, not the *p* value determined by the normal approximation approach, .046926. The latter value is an *approximation* of the former, not a very good approximation since the error is over half the approximate value. Why was the error so bad?

As we explored in the chapter on the normal distribution, the normal distribution approximates the binomial best if *n* is large and if π is close to 0.5. The value for π for this problem, 0.95, seems far from 0.5, but many textbooks give the rule of thumb that it is safe to use the normal approximation if $n \times \pi > 5$ and $n \times (1-\pi) > 5$. Did the values for this problem meet that test?

Another factor that caused the normal approximation to lead to the wrong conclusion in this problem is that the *p* value is close to the significance level. Had the *p* value been further in value from the significance level, the error involved with the normal approximation might not have mattered.

While it can be argued that the use of the binomial distribution usually adds little to the result obtained with the normal distribution, the obvious rejoinder is to question why any procedure, like the use of the normal approximation to test hypotheses of population proportions, that introduces error should be used in preference to a procedure giving a more accurate answer. Virtually all textbooks teach the normal approximation because it is easier to use that procedure with statistical tables. With computer programs like Excel, that advantage disappears.

▼ Exercises

Use the Excel worksheets you have developed to answer the following questions. In the case of hypothesis testing questions, state the Null and Alternate Hypotheses and determine the approximate *p* value using the normal distribution as well as the precise *p* value using the binomial distribution. Indicate whether or not you reject the Null Hypothesis and provide a yes or no answer to the question asked.

1. A large magazine wants to estimate the proportion of readers who are female. How large a sample would be needed to provide a 95% confidence interval estimate with a sampling error of ±1.00%?

2. A surreptitious survey at a convenience store revealed that out of 120 persons purchasing cigarettes, 43 appeared to be under the age of 27. Using these data as a random sample, calculate a 90% confi-

dence interval estimate on the proportion of all cigarette purchasers at the store who appear to be under 27.

3. A political polling firm has conducted a poll to measure support for the incumbent political candidate. Out of 1,243 randomly selected voters likely to vote in the next election, 560 indicated an intention to vote for the candidate. Based on this survey, provide a 95% confidence interval estimate of the proportion of the entire electorate who will vote for the incumbent. What sample size should the firm choose next time if they wished to reduce the sampling error to ±1.5%?

4. A soft drink manufacturer is considering introducing a new soft drink by dispensing free samples at grocery stores. Some grocery store shoppers, however, are known to refuse to accept free samples. The manufacturer wants to determine if there is evidence of a difference between the proportion of weekday shoppers who will accept free samples versus the proportion of weekend shoppers who will accept samples. A random sample of 375 weekday shoppers are selected and 290 are found to accept free samples. A random sample of 346 weekend shoppers are selected and and 284 are found to accept free samples. Construct a 95% confidence interval of the proportion of all weekday and all weekend shoppers who will accept samples. Based on these intervals, would you say there is good evidence of a difference between the proportion of the two groups of shoppers who accept free samples?

5. A grocer wants to determine the proportion of apples in a shipment which have spoiled and cannot be sold. He randomly selects 250 apples from the shipment and finds 42 to be spoiled. Determine a 99% confidence interval estimate of the proportion of apples in the entire shipment that have spoiled. Suppose he wished to reduce the sampling error to ±.05. Estimate the required sample size.

6. The tourist office of a Caribbean island wants to issue tourists a guarantee that in a 14-day stay, at least 12 days will be sunny. To determine if this is feasible, 150 days during the tourist season are monitored. 125 of them were sunny. Determine a 90% confidence interval estimate for the proportion of all days during the tourist season that are sunny.

7. The management of a baseball stadium is interested in determining whether or not a new ad campaign has been successful in convincing more than 20% of people attending a game to purchase hot dogs. A sample of 200 people at the game was surveyed, and 33 reported

having bought hot dogs. At the .05 level of significance, is there evidence that the ad campaign was successful?

8. An advertising firm wants to determine the proportion of children aged 10 to 15 who report that Coke is their favorite soft drink. They want to be able to develop a 95% confidence interval estimate on this proportion with a sampling error of at most ±0.015. The firm is uncertain about what that proportion will be; past studies have found values ranging between 0.40 and 0.70. How large a sample should the firm choose? Report the effect of the assumed value of the true proportion by answering this question for the following assumed values for π: 0.40, 0.50, 0.60, and 0.70. If the firm has no idea which value is correct, which would you recommend they use and why?

9. An administrator of an institution that was previously a women's college and is now coeducational claims that at least half of the current students are male. A random sample of 200 students was selected, and 90 of them were male. At the .05 level of significance, is there evidence that the administrator's claim is invalid?

10. A city council wants to estimate the impact that a local professional hockey team has on the local economy by estimating the proportion of fans attending a game who live outside of the county in which the city is located. A random sample of 150 fans was chosen, and 25 of these were found to live outside the county. Based on this result, provide a 99% confidence interval estimate on the proportion of all fans who live outside the county.

11. A manufacturing firm's quality control process involves measuring the proportion of product coming off a particular assembly line that is defective. Quality standards require that that proportion be no higher than 0.005. If evidence indicates that the proportion of defectives is higher than that amount, the equipment used on that assembly line may be failing and the line must be stopped and the equipment must be inspected. A random sample of 500 product items was taken off the line, and four of them were found to be defective. At the .05 level of significance, should the firm stop the line and inspect its equipment?

12. A confidential survey of all seniors attending a particular university 20 years ago found that 29% of them admitted to having cheated at some point in their college career. In order to determine if there has been a change in behavior, the student newspaper interviewed a random sample of 120 seniors and found that 24 of those admitted to having cheated at some point in their college career. At the .05 level

of significance, is there evidence that the proportion of seniors who admit to having cheated has changed from the value found 20 years ago?

13. The management of a baseball stadium is interested in determining whether a new ad campaign has been successful in convincing more than 20% of people attending a game to purchase hot dogs. A sample of 200 people at the game were surveyed and 49 reported having bought hot dogs. At the .05 level of significance, is there evidence that the ad campaign was successful?

Chapter 11

Inferences on a Population Variance

In Chapter 7 we considered the problem of determining the required sample size to achieve a desired sampling error for a confidence interval on a population mean. In order to determine the sample size, it is necessary to have some information about the population standard deviation. One way this might be done is through a pilot study. In such a study a sample is drawn and from that sample an inference about the population standard deviation is made. (Since the standard deviation is simply the square root of the variance, the same inferences can be applied either to a population variance or standard deviation.)

Quality control is another area where inferences about a population variance are important. In any production process some degree of process deviation is inevitable. Maintaining high quality requires that variability be kept within acceptable limits. Consider, for example, a firm that manufactures cables used in airplanes to control the flight control surfaces, such as the ailerons, rudder, and elevator. If one of these cables were to break, it could have serious consequences on the pilot's ability to control the airplane. We would naturally expect that an important dimension of quality in these cables would be their strength. The manufacturer of the cables will undoubtedly have an ongoing quality control program involving sampling cable from the manufacturing processing and testing the strength of the sample cable. From such a sample, inferences on the mean strength of all cable can be made, ensuring that the average strength of all cable is sufficient for the job.

Ensuring that the cable is sufficiently strong, *on average*, is not enough. Even if the average strength is sufficient, if the variance in the strength of the cable is large, some of the cable that is manufactured will be far stronger than needed, while other cable will be too weak. If your airplane happened to be the one whose cables broke because they were too weak, you would probably not be consoled by the knowledge that the *average* strength of all the cable made by that manufacturer was sufficient! The way for the manufacturer to avoid this is to monitor not only the average strength but also the *variance* of the strength of the cable being manufactured. If the variance is kept low enough (and the mean is kept high enough), the manufacturer can be reasonably assured that *all* the cable is strong enough to depend on.

The standard procedure for inferences on a population variance differs from the others we have seen. Rather than being based on the sampling distribution of the variance, it is based on the sampling distribution of another statistic. This statistic is called the "chi square" statistic and is calculated according to the following formula: $\chi^2 = \dfrac{(n-1)s^2}{\sigma^2}$.

In this formula, s^2 is a sample variance, which, like all sample statistics, is a random number. Since s^2 is random, so is χ^2. Under the restrictive assumption that the population is normally distributed, the distribution of the χ^2 random number is easier to work with than would be the distribution of the s^2 random number, and this is the reason for its use. Notice that χ^2 cannot be negative, since both s^2 and σ^2 must be positive, and, since n cannot be less than 1, $(n-1)$ must also be positive.

If the population is normally distributed, the chi square statistic follows a distribution that is called the *chi square* distribution. The same term is used to refer to the statistic and to the distribution. The chi square distribution has only a single variable—the degrees of freedom. The degrees of freedom for the problems we will be concerned with will always be $n-1$, where n is the size of the sample.

Excel has two built-in functions for using the chi square distribution, CHIDIST and CHIINV. CHIDIST converts a value of the chi square statistic to a probability, and CHIINV converts a probability to a value of the chi square statistic. In this way they are like the NORMSDIST and NORMSINV functions (and TDIST and TINV). Unlike the normal distribution functions, the two chi square functions are not cumulative. Whereas the NORMSDIST function gives the probability of a standard normal variable being *less than* the value given in its argument, the CHIDIST function gives the probability of a chi square variable with the specified degrees of freedom being *greater* than the value given in its argument. Similarly, the NORMSINV function returns a z value for which the probability of a standard normal variable being *less* equals the probability given in the function's argument. The CHIINV function returns a χ^2 value for which the probability of the chi square variable being *greater* equals the probability given in the function's argument.

There are a few other differences between using the chi square distribution and the other continuous distributions we have investigated. Some of these differences will be easier to understand after examining the shape of the density function. We can do this by having Excel prepare a chart of the distribution function for very small intervals. This has the same shape as the density function.

- Start Excel with a new workbook and save it as chap11.xls.

- Rename the "Sheet1" worksheet to "Chart."

- Enter the series of numbers 0, 1, 2, etc., up to 100 in column A.

- Enter the label "DOF" in cell D1. Cell E1 will be used for the chi square distribution's only variable, the degrees of freedom.

- Enter the number "25" in cell E1. This will be the first value for the degrees of freedom we will try.

Column B will be used to enter the probability of a chi square variable having a value between the value given on the same row of column A and that of the previous row. For example, row 6 has "5" in column A. In column B we will enter a formula that will display the probability of a chi square variable having a value between the "5" in A6 and the "4" in A5. One way of doing this is to subtract the probability of a chi square variable being less than 4 (that is, the cumulative probability of 4) from the probability of a chi square variable being less than 5. The difference is the probability of being between 4 and 5.

The CHIDIST function, however, is not cumulative. Rather than provide the probability of a chi square variable being *less* than the value we give it, it provides the probability of a chi square variable being *greater* than the value we give it. The probability that CHIDIST returns for the chi square value of 4 will be greater than the probability it returns for the chi square value of 5. To get the probability of being between 4 and 5, we do the opposite of what would be done with a cumulative probability function; that is, we subtract the probability associated with 5 from the probability associated with 4. Let's start with the value 1.

- Select cell B2. Click the Edit Formula button. Select the CHIDIST function ("Statistical" category).

The function has two arguments: "X" is the value for which the function will provide the probability of a chi square variable being larger, and "Degrees_freedom" is the degrees of freedom of the chi square distribution for which we want the probability.

- In the "X" argument field enter a *relative* address reference to the cell in the previous row in column A. That cell contains a zero. In the "Degrees_freedom" argument field, enter an *absolute* address reference to the cell where we have placed the degrees of freedom (initially, 25).

Notice that the function result, shown in the dialog window below the argument fields, is "1." The probability of a chi square variable being greater than zero is 1. Remember that a chi square variable must be positive.

- Click the mouse pointer in the Formula Bar to the right of its current contents so that an insertion point appears at the end. Enter a minus sign.

- Click the CHIDIST button (most recently used function). A new CHIDIST dialog window will appear.

- This time, enter a *relative* address reference to the cell in the same row in column A (which contains the number "1"). Enter an *absolute* reference to the cell containing the degrees of freedom, as in the previous case. Although the value given this time (1) is different from that given last time, the probability appearing in the "Value" field will again be 1. That value is actually very slightly less than 1, but so slight that Excel expresses it as a 1. Click the "OK" button. The value "6.36158E-14" will display in B2. This is an extremely small number, but still greater than 0.

- Copy the formula in cell B2 down to cell B101. Since the two uses of CHIDIST in the formula in cell B2 use relative addresses for "x," those addresses should change as the formula is copied. The address of the degrees of freedom, however, should not change since an absolute address was used in the "degrees_freedom" argument. If error values appear in the cells to which you copied the formula, check to be sure you have the correct cell references in B2.

We can treat the values in column A as chi square values, and we will next chart the probabilities in column B against those values.

- Select the range A1:B101. Click the Chart Wizard button. Select "XY (Scatter)" from the "Standard" chart types. Choose the subtype shown on the bottom right, which will connect the data points with lines and without markers. Click the "Next" button twice.

- Use the Chart Wizard to add the title "Chi Square Distribution" to the chart and to eliminate the legend. Click "Finish."

- Position and resize the chart so that it lies just below the first row (so that you can see and change the value in E1 and so that the chart fills as much of the screen as possible). Reduce the font size of the values shown on the axis and of the title so as to increase the size of the plot.

Your worksheet should look much like the picture at the top of the next page.

Notice that although the graph is bell-shaped, it is not symmetric. The degrees of freedom of the chi square distribution is also the mean. The mean of the distribution on your screen is, therefore, 25.

Where exactly is the point on the graph directly above the mean? In the case of the normal and *t* distributions, the peak of the graph lies directly above the mean. To check whether this is also true of the chi square distribution, let's have Excel put the vertical axis on the value 25.

- Click the mouse pointer on one of the values on the horizontal axis so as to select the horizontal axis. (When it is selected there will be "handles" on each end of the axis.") Open the Format menu on the Menu Bar (or click the right mouse button) and choose "Selected Axis."

- Click the "Scale" file folder tab.

- Change the "0" in the field labeled "Value (Y) Axis Crosses at " to "25." Set the "Maximum" value (in the second field) to "100." Click the "OK" button.

With the *y* axis drawn directly above 25, it is clear that the point on the graph directly above the mean is not at the peak but to the right of the peak. The positive or right skew of the chi square distribution causes the extreme positive values to pull the mean to the right.

- Change the value for the degrees of freedom to other values. Try a number of values between 2 and 90. Change the position of the *y* axis so that it lies above the mean (the degrees of freedom) in each case.

Pay attention to the effect these changes have on the apparent skewness of the chart and to the range of values for which the probabilities are clearly nonzero. You will notice that for larger values, not all of the density function will appear on your graph, given the range of chi square values we are showing. The mean should always appear to the right of the plot's peak, but as the degrees of freedom increases, it should be closer.

The fact that the density function of the chi square distribution is not symmetric and is not centered on zero will affect the nature of confidence intervals using this distribution.

▼ Confidence Intervals on a Population Variance

- Rename the "Sheet2" worksheet to "CI on Var" and switch to it.

- Enter the labels and adjust font sizes and column lengths so that your worksheet looks like the picture below.

	A	B	C	D	E
1	**Sample Statistics**			**Chi Square Values**	
2	*n*			Confidence Level	
3	Standard Deviation			Larger	
4				Smaller	
5	**Confidence Interval**				
6	Upper Variance				
7	Lower Variance				
8	Upper Standard Deviation				
9	Lower Standard Deviation				
10					

Consider the following problem:

A large bakery produces a national brand of cookies. Experience has shown that the temperature at which the cookies are baked affects their taste. It is important to maintain as little variation as possible in the baking temperature so as to maintain the consistency required of a national brand. A random sample of 25 batches of cookies was selected, and the standard deviation of the temperature at which those cookies were baked was 2.13° F. Based on this result, and assuming the distribution of temperatures is normal, construct a 95% confidence interval on the standard deviation in the baking temperature of all batches of cookies.

- Enter the values for *n*, the sample standard deviation, and the confidence level (as a proportion or with a percent sign) in cells B2, B3, and E2, respectively.

When we determined a confidence interval from a statistic that followed the normal or t distribution, the first step was to determine the z or t values corresponding to the confidence level desired. Similarly, when determining a confidence interval for a population variance or standard deviation, the first step is to determine the χ^2 values corresponding to the confidence level. For the t and z distributions, the two values always had the same absolute values and differed only in sign. This is not the case with the chi square distribution, however.

Consider the chi square density function in the illustration below, which shows the two values as χ_L^2 and χ_R^2. If these correspond to the values for the 95% confidence interval, the area of the white region between them must be .95. The area of each shaded tail region is .025. Unlike the case with the t and z distributions, the two values are not equidistant from the mean because the distribution is not symmetric.

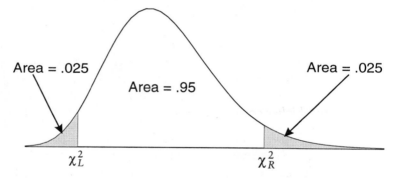

To find the values for χ_L^2 and χ_R^2, use the CHIINV function. This function requires that we provide it with the area to the *right* of the value it returns. For the 95% confidence interval, the area to the right of χ_R^2 is .025, and the area to the right of χ_L^2 is .95 + .025 = .975. We will need to provide CHIINV with expressions that will work even if the confidence level in cell E2 is changed. The central area is always equal to the level of confidence (expressed as a proportion). The sum of both tail areas is one minus the central area, and each tail is half the sum. The area to the right of χ_R^2 is the area of one tail. The area to the right of χ_L^2 can be calculated either as the area of the right tail plus the central area or as one minus the area of the left tail.

- Select cell E3, which will contain the formula to determine the value of χ_R^2. Click the Edit Formula button and select the CHIINV function in the "Statistical" category.

- The dialog window shows two arguments. In the "Probability" argument field, enter an expression that will calculate the area of the right tail in the picture on page 286, given the confidence level (the area of the central region).

- In the "Deg_freedom" argument field, enter an expression that will subtract one from the sample size given on the worksheet. Click the "OK" button. The displayed value in cell E3 should be 39.36406.

- Select cell E4, click the Edit Formula button, and again select CHIINV. Enter an expression in the "probability" argument field that will calculate the area to the right of χ_L^2 from the confidence level in the worksheet. Enter the same expression in the "degrees_freedom" argument field used in E3. Click "Finish." The value displayed in E4 should be 12.40115.

Taking the formula for the chi square statistic on page 281 and solving for σ^2 gives: $\sigma^2 = \dfrac{(n-1)s^2}{\chi^2}$.

The sample data in the numerator of this formula are known for this problem. The confidence interval on σ^2 is found by evaluating the formula for each of the two chi square values corresponding to the confidence level. Note that since we are dividing by the chi square value, the *higher* confidence level limit is found when we use the *lower* chi square value, and vice versa.

- Select cell B6. Enter the Excel formula that will calculate σ^2 according to the formula above, using the lower chi square value in E4. Notice that the formula requires the sample variance (s^2), while the worksheet contains the sample standard deviation (s). The displayed value should be 8.780285.

- Select cell B8 and enter the Excel formula to calculate the lower bound of the confidence interval on the variance by using the higher chi square value in E3. The displayed value should be 2.766117.

- Enter formulas in cells B9 and B10 that will determine the boundaries of the confidence interval on the population standard deviation. Each boundary is simply the square root of the corresponding variance boundary. The displayed values should be 2.963155 and 1.663165.

The 95% confidence interval on the variance of the temperature for all batches of cookies is 2.8 to 8.8, while the 95% confidence interval on the standard deviation of the temperature is approximately 1.7 to 3.0.

Check your worksheet by using it to solve the following problem:

A manufacturer of light bulbs is monitoring the life of 60-watt bulbs made under a new process. A sample of 150 bulbs was chosen, and the standard deviation in the life of those bulbs was 23.5 hours. Based on this result, and assuming the life of light bulbs is normally distributed, determine a 90% confidence interval on the standard deviation of all bulbs produced by that process.

Your worksheet should show that the 90% confidence interval is from 21.47137 hours to 25.99324 hours.

▼ Hypothesis Tests on a Population Variance

Prepare a worksheet for hypothesis tests on a population variance.

- Switch to the "Sheet3" worksheet and rename it "Hyp Test on Var."

- Enter labels on the worksheet so that it looks like the picture below.

	A	B	C	D	E	F	G	H
1	Population Data			Sample Data			Significance Level	
2	Hypothesized Sigma			n			Alpha	
3				s				
4				Test Statistic				
5								
6	p Values			Critical Chi Square				
7	1 tail			1 tail	upper			
8	2 tail				lower			
9				2 tail	upper			
10					lower			
11								

Probably the most common hypothesis test on a population variance tests whether the variance has exceeded some target level. This is the type of test that would arise in quality control since the object there is to keep the variance as low as possible. The tests for whether a population variance is below a certain value or differs from a certain value (two-tail) is similar. We will develop a worksheet for all types of tests, but the first example will be a typical quality-control type problem.

A laundry detergent company packages its product in boxes labeled as containing 64 oz. Although some variation in the amount of detergent placed in each box in unavoidable, it is desirable for that variation to be kept as low as possible. If too much detergent is placed into the box, it may spill over and be wasted. If too little is placed into the box, customers may be unhappy and the company may face regulatory difficulties. Given the characteristics of current filling technology, a standard deviation in the amount of fill in each box of 1.6 ounces is normal and unavoidable. A higher standard deviation, however, indicates a problem with the process. In order to monitor the process, the firm carefully measures the amount of detergent in a random sample of 50 boxes chosen from each batch. In a recent sample, the measured sample standard deviation was 1.9 oz. At the .05 level of significance, does the company have evidence that the standard deviation in the fill of all boxes exceeds 1.6 oz?

The Null Hypothesis for this problem is $H_0: \sigma \leq 1.6$, and the Alternate Hypothesis is $H_A: \sigma > 1.6$. For this sample, the sample standard deviation s is 1.9, which is greater than 1.6. Therefore, the sample is not consistent with the Null Hypothesis, and we have to determine if this might be due to chance.

As indicated by the labels, the worksheet we are developing is designed to accept standard deviations (rather than variances) as input. This is an essentially arbitrary choice, but is consistent with the wording of this problem, which refers to standard deviations rather than variances.

- Enter the values from the problem in the appropriate places in the worksheet. The value for σ from the Null Hypothesis goes in cell B2, the sample size and sample standard deviation go in cells E2 and E3, and the significance level goes in cell H2.

- Enter an Excel formula in cell E4 that will calculate the value of the chi square statistic for this sample, assuming that σ has the value given by the Null Hypothesis (in B2). The formula for the chi square statistic (χ^2) can be found on page 281. The value displayed in cell E4 should be 69.09766.

If the Null Hypothesis is true (interpreted as $\sigma = 1.6$), the expected value of a sample standard deviation would also be 1.6, and the expected value of the chi square statistic would be 49 (the degrees of freedom or $n-1$). The probability that a sample would have a sample standard deviation of 1.9 or more is the same as the probability that a sample would have a chi square statistic of 69.09766 or more. That probability is the p value and can be determined by using the CHIDIST function. The p value equals the shaded area of the graph of the density function (shown below) for the chi square distribution with 49 degrees of freedom.

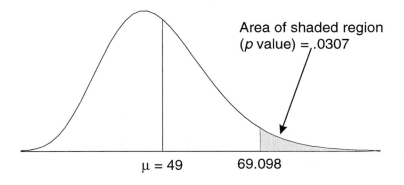

- Select cell B7. Click the Edit Formula button and choose CHIDIST. Since the CHIDIST function returns the probability of a chi square statistic *greater* than that given as the "X" argument, the cell address of the sample chi square statistic should be put in the "X" argument field. The "Deg_freedom" field should contain an expression that will calculate $n - 1$. The value displayed as the p value should be .030749.

Since this p value is less than the significance level, we conclude that this sample could not have been drawn from a population described by the Null Hypothesis (with $\sigma = 1.6$). The Null Hypothesis is rejected. Yes, there is evidence that the standard deviation in the fill of all boxes exceeds 1.6 oz. The company should investigate the package-filling process to determine what has gone wrong.

The test could also be done using a critical value. For this problem, the critical chi square would be the value for which the probability of a greater chi square exactly equals the significance level. To convert the significance level (a probability) to a chi square value, use the CHIINV function.

- Select cell F7, click the Edit Formula button and select the CHIINV function. The "Probability" argument field should have the address of the significance level, and the "Deg_freedom" field should contain an expression that will calculate $n - 1$ as before. The critical chi square for this problem is 66.33865, which should display in cell F7.

The rejection region lies above 66.33865. Since the sample chi square (69.09766) is greater, and therefore is in the rejection region, the critical value approach (as it must) also leads to a rejection of the Null Hypothesis, the same conclusion found with the p value.

▼ Two-Tail Test on Population Standard Deviation (or Variance)

Although this is not generally the concern of quality control, suppose the question to be determined was whether or not the sample provided evidence at the .05 level of significance that the standard deviation of detergent fill was *different* from 1.6 ounces. In this case the Null Hypothesis would be $H_0 : \sigma = 1.6$, and the Alternate Hypothesis would be $H_A : \sigma \neq 1.6$. This Null Hypothesis could be rejected if the sample standard deviation was less than 1.6, while the one-tail test just considered could be rejected only if the sample standard deviation exceeded 1.6.

As in other hypothesis tests, the two-tail p value is twice the one-tail p value.

- Enter the formula in cell B8 that doubles the one-tail p value in cell B7.

Since the two-tail p value is .061499, which exceeds .05, we fail to reject the two-tail Null Hypothesis. It may seem puzzling that at the same significance level we can find evidence that the population standard deviation *exceeds* 1.6 oz, but we can't find evidence that it *differs* from 1.6. Remember, though, that a sample with a standard deviation below 1.6 could not possibly lead to the conclusion that the population standard deviation exceeds 1.6 oz but could lead to the conclusion that the population standard deviation differs from 1.6 oz. The significance level is the probability of committing Type I error. *If* the true population standard deviation is 1.6 (the Null Hypothesis is true), the probability of incorrectly rejecting that Null will be .05 for both one- and two-tail cases.

Determining the critical chi square values for a two-tail test is almost exactly the same as determining the chi square values for a confidence interval. To translate a significance level to the corresponding confidence level, subtract it from one. In this case, the significance level is 0.05. The critical chi square values are the same as those for a $1 - 0.05 = 0.95$ or 95% confidence interval. Look at the diagram on page 286. The two values, shown there as χ_L^2 and χ_R^2, define two tails with equal areas that sum to 0.05. These are the critical chi square values for a hypothesis test at the 0.05 significance level. The values can be determined by using the CHIINV function and providing that function with the area to the right of each critical value. The area to the right of χ_R^2 is half the significance level, 0.025. The area to the right of χ_L^2 is one minus half the significance level.

- Select cell F9. Use the CHIINV function to determine the upper critical value, χ_R^2, for the significance level and sample size entered on the worksheet. The value displayed in cell F9 should be 70.22236.

- Select cell F10 and use the CHIINV function to determine the value of the lower critical chi square, χ_L^2. The displayed value should be 31.55493.

The critical chi square values are 31.55493 and 70.22236. Since the sample chi square, 69.09766, lies between these two values, the sample is not in the rejection region, and we would fail to reject the Null Hypothesis, the same result obtained with the two-tail p value.

▼ Test on a Population Variance Being Below a Given Value

The remaining hypothesis test to consider is one in which we look for evidence that the population variance is below a given value. Consider the following problem:

The laundry detergent company is evaluating a new package-filling process developed by a group of its engineers. The new process promises to increase quality by reducing the standard deviation of the fill placed into each box. Under the old process, the standard deviation was 1.6 oz. The new process was put into operation and a random sample of 50 boxes filled by that process was chosen. The standard deviation in the fill of those 50 boxes was 1.35 oz. At the .05 level of significance, does the company have evidence that the standard deviation of all boxes filled by the new process is less than 1.6 oz?

The Null Hypothesis for this problem is $H_0: \sigma \geq 1.6$, and the Alternate Hypothesis is $H_A: \sigma < 1.6$. The sample standard deviation is 1.35, not consistent with the Null Hypothesis, so we have to determine if this could be due to chance.

- The only change in the values from the previous problem is the sample standard deviation. Change the appropriate cell in the worksheet to reflect this change.

The worksheet immediately updates. The correct sample chi square value in this case is 34.88379, as is shown in the worksheet. The *p* value shown in the worksheet, 0.936075, is wrong, however. The situation is shown in the diagram at the top of the next page.

The *p* value for this problem is the probability that if the population variance equaled 1.6 oz (the Null Hypothesis were true), a sample of 50 boxes could be chosen whose sample variance by chance was 1.35 or less. This is identical to the probability that the sample's chi square statistic would be 34.88379 or less. It is this probability that is illustrated in the diagram on the next page of the density function of the chi square statistic.

Compare this diagram with that shown on page 289. In that case, the *p* value was equal to the area to the *right* of the sample chi square. In this case it is equal to the area to the *left* of the sample chi square. The problem with the formula in cell E6 calculating the *p* value is that it is calculating the area to the right of 34.884 instead of the area to the left. The correct *p* value is not .936075 but one minus .936075.

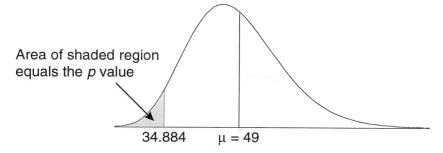

Area of shaded region
equals the *p* value

34.884   μ = 49

In other words, the CHIDIST function returns the correct *p* value for problems like the previous one-tail problem where the *p* value is the area of a right tail. To get the *p* value for problems like this one, when a left tail area is desired, we must calculate one minus the probability returned by CHIDIST. Is there a way we can enter a formula which will determine whether the *p* value is the value returned by CHIDIST or one minus the value returned by CHIDIST?

If we calculate both the area to the right of the sample chi square (the value returned by CHIDIST), and the area to the left of the sample chi square (one minus the value returned by CHIDIST), the correct value is always the smaller. As long as we remember that the *p* value given by the worksheet is only meaningful if the sample is not consistent with the Null Hypothesis, the *p* value can never exceed .5.

Excel has a built-in function, MIN ("Statistical" category), which takes two or more arguments and returns the value of the smallest. We can use this to have the correct formula for the *p* value chosen automatically.

- Select cell B7. Look at the expression in the Formula Bar. One of the arguments of MIN will be that expression, and the other will be one minus that expression. Use the mouse pointer to highlight the expression (don't include the equal sign) and click the Copy button on the Standard Toolbar.

- Erase the contents of cell B7. We are now ready to enter a new formula.

- With B7 selected, click the Edit Formula button, and select MIN.

- The dialog box for MIN shows two arguments: "Number1" and "Number2." Click the mouse pointer in the "Number1" argument field and click the Paste button. In the value field to the right of the argument field you should see the number that used to be displayed in B7, .936075. This is the probability of a random chi square variable *exceeding* the sample chi square value.

- Click the mouse pointer in the "Number2" argument field. Notice how this causes a "Number3" argument field to appear (which we won't use). The MIN function doesn't have a fixed number of arguments, and whenever you use the last one in the dialog window, a new one will appear until the maximum of 30 arguments have been used.

In the "Number2" argument field, you should enter an expression that will calculate one minus the probability of a chi square variable being greater than the sample chi square.

- Begin the expression by entering "1-" (without quotes) in the "Number2" argument field. Click the Paste button. The number appearing in the value field is 0.063924595, which is 1 minus 0.936075405. This is the probability of a random chi square variable being *less* than the sample chi square value

- Click the "OK" button. Cell B7 will display the value 0.063925, which is the smaller of the values in each of MIN's arguments.

Since this p value exceeds the significance level, the Null Hypothesis is not rejected. The manufacturer does not have evidence at the .05 level of significance that the new filling process reduces the standard deviation (or variance) of the fill in all detergent boxes.

All that remains is to determine the critical chi square value for the lower one-tail test. This is the chi square value for which the area under the density function to the left of the value equals the significance level. Since CHIINV interprets the probability given it as the area to the right of the value it is to return, we must convert the significance level to the corresponding right area by subtracting one.

- Select cell F8. Click the Edit Formula button and choose the CHIINV function. In the "Probability" field, enter an expression that calculates one minus the significance level. In the "Deg_freedom" field, enter an expression that calculates $n - 1$. Click "OK." The value appearing in I7 is 33.93029.

Since the sample chi square exceeds the critical chi square, the sample does not lie in the rejection region.

▼ Exercises

Close your current workbook. The workbook in Exercises.xls in the Chap_11 folder contains the data for these problems.

1. A detergent-box filling machine fills empty boxes with empty detergent. A sample of boxes filled by the machine was selected, and the weight of the detergent (in ounces) placed in each box was measured. The measurements are

   55.67, 47.28, 54.55, 48.19, 46.94, 52.34, 49.62, 51.48, 49.77, 49.71, 48.09, 49.78, 48.39, 49.81, 53.83, 48.41, 47.30, 46.68, 48.40, 48.85, 47.97, 49.98, 51.20, 51.57, 55.81

   Determine a 95% confidence interval for the standard deviation of the amount of detergent placed in each box in the population.

2. A bank office wished to estimate the amount of time required to approve a home equity line of credit measured from the original application. A sample of applications were selected, and the amount of time (in working days) required to approve each application was determined. The values are

   8, 16, 17, 12, 11, 16, 16, 21, 18, 11, 16, 18

   Determine a 90% confidence interval for the variance of the amount of time required to approve all home equity lines of credit.

3. A ball bearing manufacturer wants to determine the diameter of a particular ball bearing. A sample of bearings was selected, and the diameter of each bearing (in cm) was measured. Those numbers were

   9.66, 8.34, 11.09, 9.53, 9.22, 10.10, 11.51, 10.13, 8.62, 9.62, 9.29, 10.66, 12.28, 10.06, 11.63, 9.42, 9.24, 9.31, 9.29, 11.75

   Determine 99%, 95%, and 90% confidence intervals of the standard deviation.

4. A large university offers many sections of undergraduate statistics. A sample of sections for the past five years was chosen, and the section GPA was calculated. These data are

   1.8, 1.8, 2.2, 2.4, 3.2, 1.6, 3.1, 3.0, 1.5, 2.4

   Based upon these data, determine a 95% confidence interval for the variance in all sections' GPA's for the past five years.

5. A manufacturer of aircraft control cable makes a particular cable designed to have a breaking strength of 1,000 kg. A sample of cable was chosen and tested to determine breaking strength. The measured breaking strengths of the sample cables (in kg) were

   996, 993, 990, 1010, 995, 989, 999, 1011, 981, 1000, 980, 994, 1003, 990, 999

Based upon these data, determine a 75% confidence interval estimate for the variance of the breaking strength of all cable.

6. A machine is designed to fill cereal boxes so that the average fill is 16 oz with a standard deviation of 1.1 oz. A sample of 15 boxes of cereal was selected and measured. The following measurements were recorded.

16.81, 11.18, 17.36, 14.55, 15.64, 17.29, 20.8, 17.26, 16.07, 14.86, 13.95, 14.51, 17.65, 14.91, 18.41

At the .01 level of significance, is there evidence that the machine is not meeting specifications with respect to variation?

7. Experience has shown that variability in the output of a bolt-making machine increases shortly before a machine failure. Amalgamated Bolts has determined that properly operating machines produce an average of 1,000 bolts per hour, with a variance of 25.0. In order to anticipate a possible breakdown, the output of each bolt-making machine is monitored. As part of this program, the output of one particular bolt-making machine was monitored this week during a random sample of 20 hours. The measurements were as follows:

1001, 1005, 997, 1000, 994, 1001, 999, 1006, 994, 1004, 998, 1000, 1001, 994, 996, 1000, 1008, 996, 994, 1002

Based on this sample, is there evidence at the .10 level of significance that this machine is about to break down?

8. A specialty light bulb used by the manufacturer of a computer projection system is supposed to have an average life of 200 hours with a standard deviation of 12 hours. A new supplier of the bulbs has promised the projection system manufacturer light bulbs that have less variation in their life. In order to test this, the projection system manufacturer selected a random sample of 12 bulbs and subjected them to testing. The lifetimes of the 12 bulbs were

180.6, 211.9, 175.1, 181.4, 196.5, 188.9, 206.3, 189.7, 223.3, 180.0, 211.3, 193.7

Based on this sample, does the projection system manufacturer have evidence (at the .05 level of significance) that supports the new supplier's claims?

Chapter 12

▼

Inferences on Two Population Means

All of the inferential statistics investigated so far have been *univariate*—they were concerned with only a single variable. Techniques that are concerned with more than a single statistic add an important dimension to inferential statistics—the investigation of relationships among two or more variables. The techniques explored in this chapter do not enable the investigation of as many different types of relationships as those in later chapters. The one type of relationship they do handle, however, is an important one: the relationship between the mean of an observation and which of two groups that observation is in. This is a relationship between two variables, one of which is discrete, with exactly two, values and the other of which is continuous.

All of the techniques considered here have certain features in common. There are always two samples, each drawn from a different population. A sample mean is computed from each of the two samples, and the difference between those two means is calculated. This difference is a random number, like all sample statistics considered earlier, and its distribution is used to make inferences about the difference between the two population means. These inferences can be either confidence intervals or hypothesis tests, but the Excel procedures we will examine have been created with hypothesis testing in mind. Although the hypothesized difference between the two population means can be any value, by far the most common value is zero. A Null Hypothesis with a difference of zero between the means is appropriate for a question that asks, "Is there evidence of a difference in the two population means?" or, for the one-tail case, "Is there evidence that the mean of one of the populations exceeds the mean of the other?"

There are two different ways in which data can be collected for these tests, and they require different analysis techniques. One method is the *paired samples approach.* and the other method is the *independent samples approach*. In the paired sample approach, each observation in one sample is linked to a matching observation in the other sample. The observations are matched so that, ideally, they are identical in all

297

characteristics that might affect the variable whose means are being compared *except* for the difference in the populations from which each is drawn. Since each observation in one sample is matched to an observation in the other sample, the two samples must be the same size. In the independent samples approach, no attempt to match characteristics between observations is made: The two samples are each randomly drawn from their respective populations. The samples may or may not be the same size.

It is always more difficult to select paired samples than independent samples, but the test for paired samples is more sensitive, and, for this reason, is preferable to the independent samples approach. It frequently is the case, however, that the paired samples approach is simply impossible. The paired samples approach is most often used when the data are to be collected from a future experiment over which the investigator has some control. The issue of matching samples is part of a much larger topic called *experimental design,* which is very important in laboratory science, where the investigator has considerable control over the process generating the data. Sometimes this is the case in business and economics, but more often it is not.

▼ Inferences from Paired Samples

Consider the following problem:

A tire manufacturer wants to determine if a new rubber formulation will improve tread wear. One set of 12 tires was manufactured with the old formulation, and another set was manufactured with the new formulation. Both sets of tires were identical in all respects except for the rubber. Six test cars and drivers were chosen for the test. Each car received two tires with the old rubber formulation and two with the new. One of each was placed on the front and one of each was placed on the rear. Each car drove until a tire wore out. That tire's mileage was recorded, and the car continued driving until all of the test tires had worn out. The mileage each tire received is shown in the table on the next page.

Based on the data in that table, does the manufacturer have evidence at the .05 level of significance that the average tread life of all tires made with the new rubber formulation exceeds the average tread life of all tires made with the old rubber formulation?

The Null Hypothesis for these data is $H_0: \mu_{new} \leq \mu_{old}$, and the Alternate Hypothesis is $H_A: \mu_{new} > \mu_{old}$. Because of the methods used with inferences on two population means, it is common to formulate the hypotheses in terms of the difference between the two population means.

Car	Tire Location	Total Tread Life in Miles	
		Old Rubber	New Rubber
1	Front	37,661	31,902
	Rear	42,342	41,203
2	Front	31,108	38,816
	Rear	41,239	43,305
3	Front	32,903	35,375
	Rear	42,658	52,353
4	Front	29,829	30,883
	Rear	39,616	49,424
5	Front	34,625	38,724
	Rear	42,650	43,234
6	Front	31,923	34,565
	Rear	39,990	43,861

If $\mu_D = \mu_{new} - \mu_{old}$, an alternative formulation for the Null Hypothesis is $H_0: \mu_D \leq 0$, and for the Alternative Hypothesis: $H_A: \mu_D > 0$. These samples are clearly paired because each tire with the old rubber formulation has a corresponding tire with the new formulation.

The data for this problem are provided in an Excel workbook named "tires.xls" in the subdirectory for this chapter.

- Open the workbook "tires.xls." After opening it, select "Save As..." from the "File" menu on the Menu Bar and give the workbook the name "chap12.xls." Alternatively, you can open a new workbook and enter the labels "Old" and "New" in cells A1 and B1 and enter the data in the two rightmost columns of the table below their respective labels. Save this workbook under the name "chap12.xls."

- Change the name of the "Sheet1" worksheet to "Paired."

- Enter the label "Difference" in cell C1. In cells C2 through C13, enter formulas that will calculate the value in each row in column B (the mileage with the new formulation) minus the value in column A (the mileage with the old formulation). The value displayed in cell C13 should be 3,871. If you used the tires.xls workbook, you will notice that the cell formatting shows negative numbers in parentheses rather than with a minus sign. The value in C2, for example, will display as (5,759).

Each of these values is a random number. Think of them as being selected from a population of differences. Imagine that each tire in the
population of tires made with the new rubber formulation was paired
with a corresponding tire in the population of tires made with the old
formulation and the difference in the mileage of the two pairs was calculated. This would be the population of differences. The formulation of
the Null and Alternate Hypotheses, which use "μ_D," are referring to the
mean of this population of differences. The values you have in column C
are a sample from that population and can be used to test hypotheses on
the population mean, μ_D. The methods described below are identical to
those used in Chapter 9. You may wish to review the methods of testing
a hypothesis on a population mean in that chapter.

- Enter the label "Mean" in cell B14, "Standard Deviation" in cell B15,
  "Standard Error" in cell B16, "t" in cell B17, and "p value" in cell
  B18. Adjust the width of column B.

- Enter formulas in cell C14 and C15 to calculate the average and standard deviation, respectively, of the numbers in C2:C13. The displayed
  values will be 3092 and 4471.701.

Notice that since the sample mean is positive, it is not consistent with the
Null Hypothesis. It will be necessary to calculate a sample t and determine from it if the positive sample mean could reasonably be due to
chance.

- Enter a formula in C16 to calculate the standard error by dividing the
  sample standard deviation by the square root of the sample size. The
  displayed value should be 1290.87.

- Enter the formula in C17 to calculate the sample t for the Null Hypothesis that the population mean is less than or equal to zero. Enter
  the formula in cell C18 to calculate the one-tail p value from that sample t value. The displayed value should be 0.01777.

Since this p value is less than the significance level, we would reject the
Null Hypothesis and conclude that there is evidence that the average
tread life of all tires made with the new rubber formulation exceeds that
of all tires made with the old formulation.

Notice that the standard error and means you have calculated could also
be used to calculate a confidence interval on the difference between the
average tread life of the two populations of tires.

▼ Using the Analysis Tool for a Paired Samples Test

Although analyzing data from paired samples is very straightforward, Excel provides an Analysis Tool for this very task. The Analysis Tool automatically does all of the calculations and produces an output. The output, however, is in the form of numbers rather than formulas. As a result, the tool must be used each time the data change. It is not possible using an Analysis Tool to develop a worksheet that will automatically recalculate when the data change.

- Open the "Tools" menu on the Menu Bar and click "Data Analysis...." If "Data Analysis..." is not present on your Tools menu, see Appendix B.

- When the Data Analysis dialog window opens, scroll down through the list of Analysis Tools and choose "t-Test: Paired Two Sample for Means." The dialog window for this tool will open.

- In the fields for the "Variable 1 Range" and "Variable 2 Range," enter the cell address ranges for the columns with the mileage for the "Old" and "New" rubber formulations, respectively. Include in these ranges the cells in the first row containing the labels "Old" and "New."

- In the "Hypothesized Mean Difference" field, enter the number "0."

- Click the small box beside the word "Labels" so that a check appears. By doing this you tell the analysis that the first cell in the variable ranges contains a label. It is always good to do this because it enables the Analysis Tool to use your labels in the output.

- The "Alpha" field should contain the significance level, 0.05. The Excel Analysis Tools generally seem to start assuming this is the significance level you want, but you can change it to another value.

- Click the button to the left of "Output Range" and enter the address D1. The output of the Analysis Tool will be placed immediately to the right of the data already entered in the worksheet.

- Click the "OK" button. The output will be written to columns D, E, and F, and the cells containing that output will be selected. As with all the output of all the Analysis Tools, the column widths are not adjusted to fit the output, which you must do next.

- Open the "Format" menu on the Menu Bar. Select "Column" and, from the submenu that opens, select "AutoFit Selection." This will adjust the widths of the columns so that you can see the output of the Analysis Tool.

As you examine the output of the Analysis Tool, you will notice that it provides a number of statistics, such as the means of each sample, which we did not calculate before, and omits some (such as the mean sample difference) that were calculated before. These means are useful because they help you determine how the tool made its calculations. Look, for example, at the sample t (labeled "t Stat") in cell E10. It has the same absolute value as the sample t earlier calculated in cell C17, but a different sign. The differences in column C were calculated by subtracting the values in column A from those in column B (that is, $B - A$). However, the Analysis Tool calculated the differences as $A - B$. In the case of one-tail tests, it is important to check the means of each sample to ensure that the sample data are not consistent with the Null Hypothesis. It is also wise to include labels with the data analyzed so that the output will be clearly labeled.

In addition to giving both one-tail and two-tail p values, the output of the Analysis Tool also includes critical t values. The value given in the tool's dialog window is used to determine these values. Notice that the output does not indicate if the Null Hypothesis is rejected. When you use an Analysis Tool to do a hypothesis test, you must still determine if the Null Hypothesis is rejected, including whether or not the sample is consistent with the Null Hypothesis (for one-tail tests). Notice also that the output does not include a standard error of the mean of the differences. It cannot, therefore, be used to derive confidence intervals.

▼ Tests of the Difference of Means for Independent Samples

When samples drawn from two populations are not paired, they are called *independent* samples. Such samples need not be the same size. Excel provides three different Analysis Tools for hypothesis tests on independent samples. The appropriate one to use depends on the information you have on the variances of the two populations. There are three possibilities, and each requires different calculations.

1. You know the two population variances. This situation arises primarily in statistics texts since the usual situation is one in which you know nothing about the populations. In this case, a sample statistic with a z distribution can be calculated from the data in the two samples.

2. You don't know the population variances, but you believe they are equal or are willing to assume they are equal. Even if the two population variances are equal, the two sample variances will differ purely by chance. Each sample variance is an estimate of the same popula-

tion variance, and the appropriate approach is to combine the two sample variances so as to get a better estimate of that common population variance. This estimate is referred to as the *pooled sample variance*. From the two sample means and the pooled sample variance, a sample statistic with a *t* distribution can be calculated. The degrees of freedom of the *t* distribution is $n_1 + n_2 - 2$, where n_1 and n_2 are the sizes of the two samples.

3. You don't know the population variances, but you believe they are unequal or do not want to assume they are equal. This situation is what statisticians refer to as the Behrens-Fisher problem. A sample statistic is calculated from the sample data. This statistic approximately follows the *t* distribution, and for this reason some texts refer to it as *t´*, although Excel's output simply designates it as "t Stat." The degrees of freedom is calculated by a formula known as Satterthwaite's approximation and is rounded to the nearest integer. This is then used to determine both *p* values and critical values using the *t* distribution.

Let's consider the realistic case where you do not know the variances of the two populations. In this case you must use options 2 or 3 above. It is very likely that you may be uncertain as to whether the population variances are equal or unequal. It is reasonable, therefore, to use both procedures in all problems involving hypothesis tests on the equality of means when the data are independent samples. Although the two tests will result in different *p* values, in most cases the two *p* values will be close. Either both will be greater than the significance level or both will be less than the significance level, and they will therefore be in agreement on the rejection of the Null Hypothesis. In this case, doing both procedures establishes that the result of a hypothesis test does not depend on the equality or inequality of population variances.

What if both procedures are done and they lead to different conclusions on whether or not the Null Hypothesis should be rejected? Although rare, this *can* happen. The decision on whether the two populations have equal means in this case depends on whether they have equal variances. There is an Analysis Tool within Excel that tests for the equality of two population variances. This test may be inconclusive, however, and a final conclusion may elude the investigator who really has no additional data on the populations. Fortunately, this is a rare situation whose primary use is to worry students of statistics.

Consider the following problem:

A firm supplying computer display projectors is considering switching to a new supplier of specialty bulbs because of that supplier's claim that its bulbs last longer. The firm has data from tests of sample bulbs of its old supplier and has recently acquired and tested a sample of bulbs from the potential new supplier. Based on these data, does the firm have evidence at the .05 level of significance that the bulbs from the new supplier have a longer average life than bulbs from the old supplier?

The Null Hypothesis for this problem is $H_0: \mu_{new} \leq \mu_{old}$, and the Alternate Hypothesis is $H_A: \mu_{new} > \mu_{old}$. A necessary condition for the rejection of the Null Hypothesis is that $\bar{x}_{new} > \bar{x}_{old}$ (the sample is not consistent with the Null Hypothesis).

- Select the "Sheet2" worksheet. The data on bulb life are located there, with the sample data for bulbs from the old supplier in column A and those from the new supplier in column B. The first sample is larger than the first.

- Rename the "Sheet2" worksheet to "Independent."

We will first use the Tool that performs the test that assumes that the two populations have equal variances. The output from that test will enable us to check whether or not the sample data are consistent with the Null Hypothesis. If they are not, we will also use the tool for the analysis, assuming the population variances are unequal.

- Click on "Data Analysis…" on the "Tools" menu. On the Data Analysis dialog window, select "t-Test: Two-Sample Assuming Equal Variance."

- Enter the range address of the "Old" data in the "Variable 1" field. Include the address of the cell containing the label "Old."

- Enter the range address of the "New" data in the "Variable 2" field, also including the address of the label.

- Enter the number "0" in the "Hypothesized Mean Difference" field and click the box beside "Labels" so a check mark appears.

- Click the radio button beside "Output Range" so it is selected and enter the address C1 in the "Output Range" field. Click "OK."

- When the tool has completed writing the output, and the range containing the output is selected, click the "Format" menu on the Menu Bar, select "Column" and then "AutoFit Selection" to adjust the column width so the output can be seen.

The first row of the output, labeled "Mean," gives the value of the sample means. You should have 47.5 for the mean of the sample of bulbs from the old supplier and 52.41666667 for the mean of the sample from the new supplier. This means that $\bar{x}_{new} > \bar{x}_{old}$. Since the Null Hypothesis is $\mu_{new} \leq \mu_{old}$, the sample is *not* consistent with the Null and the reported p values are therefore valid.

Notice the output gives the estimated "Pooled Variance," and it is between the two sample variances.

The most important part of the output is the reported p values. The one-tail p value is .051746314. This is slightly greater than the significance level (.05). On that basis we would fail to reject the Null Hypothesis and conclude that there is not evidence at the .05 level of significance that bulbs from the new supplier outlast those from the old supplier.

Let's now see if the results are different if we assume the two populations have different variances.

- Recall the Data Analysis dialog window. Choose "t-Test: Two-Sample Assuming Unequal Variance" (immediately below the previous choice).

- The dialog window for this tool looks like that of the previous tool except for the title bar, which has the words "Assuming Unequal Variance." Complete the fields of this dialog window exactly as you did the one for the previous tool except direct the output to cell C16, which will put it directly below the previous tool's output. Click "OK."

The output of this tool is similar to that of the previous one. A good check to be sure you haven't made an error is to verify that the reported sample means on this output are the same as they were for the output above it. No "Pooled Variance" is reported since none is calculated if the population variances are believed unequal.

The one-tail p value on this output is .025783329, which is less than the 0.05 significance level. Although in most cases these two outputs will lead to the same conclusion, they do not for this problem. The small p value in this procedure indicates that the Null Hypothesis should be rejected, and that we should conclude at the 0.05 level of significance that there *is* evidence that bulbs from the new supplier outlast those from the old! When the two procedures come to different conclusions, how are we to choose?

▼ Testing for a Difference in the Variance of Two Populations

The decision for this problem depends on whether or not the variance in the life of the population of bulbs from the old supplier equals the variance in the life of the population of bulbs from the new supplier. With our samples from each population, we do have some information on this issue. Both outputs provide the sample variances. Take a look at them.

For the sample of bulbs from the old supplier, the variance is a bit less than 90.55. For the sample of bulbs from the new supplier, the variance is just under 21.54. This seems like a substantial difference. Is it possible that such a difference in sample variances could arise if the samples were drawn from populations with the same variance? It certainly is *possible*, but it would be interesting to know how likely such a result would be. If this seems like a hypothesis testing question, good for you! This is exactly what we can do. Excel provides with a method of determining whether or not these samples provide evidence that the two populations have different variance.

To look for evidence of a difference in population variances we can test the Null Hypothesis $H_{0:}\ \sigma^2_{new} = \sigma^2_{old}$ against the Alternate Hypothesis $H_{A:}\ \sigma^2_{new} \neq \sigma^2_{old}$. The sample statistic in this case is the ratio of the two sample variances which, under the assumption of population normality, follows the F distribution. If the Null Hypothesis is rejected, we have evidence that the population variances differ. If they differ, the second t-Test output is the correct one for testing the equality of population means.

- Recall the Data Analysis dialog window and select "F-Test Two-Sample for Variances." The dialog window for this tool is very similar to those you have filled out for the two procedures testing the equality of means. The major difference is that this tool's dialog window has no field for "Hypothesized Mean Difference." Enter the same cell addresses in the "Variable" fields here as you did for the previous tools. Select the "Output Range" radio button and direct the output to cell C30, placing it below both previous outputs. Click "OK."

The output from this tool testing the equality of variances is similar to that of the two previous outputs testing the equality of means. Like the others, it provides the two sample means. Check to be sure the sample means in this output are identical to those of the other outputs, verifying that the correct data were used for the analysis. The sample statistic calculated in this analysis is the sample F, 4.204110346. The most important part of the output is the p value (labeled "P(F<=f) one-tail"), which in this case is slightly over .0088. Unfortunately, the Null Hypothesis we want to test ($H_{0:}\ \sigma^2_{new} = \sigma^2_{old}$) requires a *two-tail* test, and this output gives only a *one-tail* p value (and critical value). Fortunately, it is easy to convert a one-tail p value to its two-tail counterpart: multiply by two. This must always be done when Excel's F test is used in the context of choosing between the two t tests on the equality of two population means.

- Select the region containing the last row of the output (C39:E39). Use the mouse to move that region down one row so that the row below the one-tail p value is blank.

- In (now blank) cell C39, enter the label "2-tail p value." In cell D39 enter a formula that will multiply the value of cell D38 by two. The displayed value will be 0.017676129.

This is a fairly small p value. At the 5% or 2% significance level (but not 1%), we would reject the Null Hypothesis that the population variances are equal and conclude that we have evidence that they are unequal. This, in turn, implies that the proper procedure for testing the equality of the means is the second procedure, which assumes the population variances are different. The low p value from this procedure (just under .026) led to the conclusion that there is evidence that the average life of bulbs from the new supplier exceeded that of the old supplier. This would be the ultimate conclusion from our analysis of the data.

In most cases the need to test a hypothesis about two population means will not require a test of equality of the two population variances because both procedures testing the means will yield the same result. Only in cases where they differ can an F test possibly be useful determining which means test procedure should be relied upon. In the example discussed here, the small p value in the F test led to a rejection of the Null Hypothesis of equal variances—a clear indication that the assumption of unequal variances is the correct choice. But what if the p value in the F test were large and the Null Hypothesis could not be rejected? As we saw in Chapter 8, failing to reject the Null Hypothesis is not the same as *accepting* it because we cannot determine the probability of committing Type II error. A failure to reject the Null Hypothesis that the population variances are equal is therefore *not* a solid justification for choosing to assume they are equal and using that assumption to test the population means. In fact, the only reliable guidance the F test can give us is to choose the assumption of unequal variances. It can't tell us to assume the assumption of equal variances. If a decision on the test of population means depends on the equality of variances (and it usually doesn't), and if the F test results in a p value too large to conclude the variances are unequal, we are left in a kind of statistical limbo. Without additional information it would be difficult to draw any conclusion.

▼ Exercises

1. The paired samples approach was described as being more *sensitive* than the independent samples approach. What, exactly, does this

mean? In the paired-samples problem on tire life, the average tread life of the tires made with the new compound was 3,091.75 miles greater than the average tread life of the tires made with the old compound (40,304 miles versus 37,212 miles). This difference was great enough to conclude the new rubber compound made a significant difference. Suppose we had the same sample data but from independent samples. Would we then have found evidence of a difference? Check this by analyzing the tire data using the two independent samples approaches. Explain why this makes the paired samples approach more *sensitive*.

The data for the problems given below can be found in an Excel workbook in the file named Exercises.xls. The questions below indicate which worksheet has the data for each problem.

2. A manufacturing firm has plants in two different states and wants to compare the productivity of workers in one plant with workers in the other plant. The managers of each plant were asked to provide output per worker for a sample of 31 days. The resulting data are on the worksheet "Plants A & B." Based on these data, is there evidence (at the 0.10 level of significance) of a difference between average worker productivity (measured as output per worker) in the two plants? Provide the Null and Alternate Hypotheses for this test, give your reasons for rejecting or not rejecting the Null, and provide a yes or no answer to the question of whether there is evidence of difference in average productivity.

3. A long-distance trucking firm wants to determine whether increased maintenance will increase the gas mileage of trucks. A random sample of 25 trucks and drivers who repeatedly drive the same routes was placed on the standard maintenance routine for one week and the intensive maintenance routine for another week. The average gas mileage for each truck under each routine was collected and is presented in the worksheet named "Maintenance," in which the data for each truck are in one row. Based on these data, is there evidence (at the 0.01 level of significance) that the intensive maintenance increases gas mileage? Provide the Null and Alternate Hypotheses, the basis for rejecting or not rejecting the Null, and a yes or no answer to the question of whether intensive maintenance increases mileage.

4. The sales department of a firm is considering enrolling their salespeople in a program in positive sales motivation offered by a national consultant. In order to determine the effectiveness of the program, the firm sends a random sample of 30 salespersons to attend their program and measures their sales over the following month. A control group of 30 salespersons who did not attend the program is also

chosen at random, and their sales are also measured during the same month. Total monthly sales for each sample are on the "Motivation" worksheet. Based on these data, is there evidence that attending the program would increase the average sales of all salespeople? Provide the Null and Alternate Hypotheses, the basis for rejecting or failing to reject the Null, and a yes or no answer to the question of whether there is evidence that program attendance would increase average sales.

Chapter 13

Analysis of Variance

Analysis of variance (or *ANOVA*) is another technique for testing the equality of different population means. Its name comes from the fact that it uses variance-like measures to make inferences about population means. One of the most useful characteristics of the analysis of variance technique is that it can be extended to any number of populations. Excel's Data Analysis Tools provide three different analysis of variance techniques. These techniques are appropriate for different types of data collection—analogous to the difference between paired samples and independent samples used in the *t* test for differences in two population means.

All of these techniques have certain things in common, however. All of them are designed to test the Null Hypothesis that all the populations from which the samples were drawn have equal means. The Alternate Hypothesis is that at least one of the population means differs from the others. If there are n different samples (drawn from n different populations) the Null Hypothesis can be symbolized as $H_0: \mu_1 = \mu_2 = \ldots = \mu_n$. There is no succinct way of expressing the Alternate Hypothesis (except as *not* the Null Hypothesis). The Alternate Hypothesis is true if many different conditions are met including, among many others, none of the population means being equal or all of the population means being equal except one. Analysis of variance techniques also share assumptions about the data. In addition to assuming the samples are random, they also assume the populations are normally distributed and have equal variance.

▼ Single-Factor Analysis of Variance

The (mathematically) simplest form of analysis of variance is the single-factor analysis (also frequently called *one-way* analysis of variance). It is used when the data are like those used in the independent sample approach to a test of the equality of two population means. The only difference accounted for in the sample observations is the different populations from which each observation came. Since, like all ANOVA techniques, the populations are assumed to have equal variance, this technique is an alternative to the t test for the equality of two population means assuming equal population variances. It is more versatile than that test because it is not restricted to two populations. When used with two populations, it gives exactly the same (two-tail) results.

In addition to single-factor analysis of variance, Excel has tools for two other types of ANOVA. They are all conceptually similar, and we will take a close look at how single-factor ANOVA works to gain an understanding of the essentials of any ANOVA procedure.

Let's consider the following problem:

A company is considering two competing sales training courses for new salespersons. In order to compare their effectiveness, with each other and with no course, three groups of five randomly chosen new salespersons are selected. One group is sent to sales training course "A," the second is sent to sales training course "B," and the third receives no training at all. After the two groups have completed their training, sales records for each salesperson for the next two-week period are collected, and the results for each group are shown in the table below.

Course A	Course B	No Course
$2,058	$3,339	$2,228
$2,176	$2,777	$2,578
$3,449	$3,020	$1,227
$2,517	$2,437	$2,044
$944	$3,067	$1,681

Based on the data in the table, is there evidence at the 0.10 level of significance that there would be a difference in the means of all salespersons if they were sent to a training course?

What characteristics of these sample data would lead us to find evidence of a difference in the population means?

First, a large difference in sample means is more likely to lead to the conclusion of a difference in population means than would a small difference in sample means. Sample means are randomly distributed around their population means. The means of any set of samples might be closer together or might be further apart than the population means, but sample means are unbiased estimates of population means. Sample means that are far apart are more consistent with differing population means than with identical population means.

Second, small sample variance is also more likely to lead to the conclusion that the population means differ than is large sample variance. Small sample variance is consistent with small population variance, and if the population variance is small, the sample means are likely to be close in value to the population means. Differences in sample means are less likely to be the result of chance and more likely to be the result of a difference in population means. We can get a sense of both the difference in sample means and the sample variance by making a chart of the data.

The chart we will make will be a type of scatterplot in which the data for each sample will be displayed as points in a vertical array. The three samples will be shown side by side, with the group and grand means. This chart will make it easy to visually compare the locations and variances of the three samples and to see how each sample clusters around its sample mean and the grand mean.

- Open the Excel workbook in the file anova.xls in the Chap_13 folder.

- The data for this problem are on the "Sheet1" worksheet in the range B1:D6. Change that worksheet's name to "Sales Course." Change the name of the "Sheet2" worksheet to "Calc."

- Select cells B6:D6 in the "Sales Course" worksheet. Click the arrow beside the "Borders" button on the Formatting Toolbar and choose the button from the set that opens, which will draw a dark underline below the selected cells.

- In cell A7 enter the label "means," and in cell A8 enter the label "grand mean."

- In cells B7:D7 enter formulas that will calculate the average of each column of five numbers. The values appearing in B7 through D7, respectively, should be 2228.8, 2928, and 1951.6.

- Enter the formula in cell D8 that will calculate the average of 15 numbers in B1:D6. The displayed value should be 2369.467.

In order to make the chart discussed above, we need a reorganized copy of the data in which all data values are placed in a column. Other columns will contain the group number for each of the values, that value's group mean, and the grand mean. This copy will be constructed so that changes in the original will automatically update the copy. One way of doing this would be to use a simple equation setting the value of each copy equal to the original. The procedure shown on the next page is equivalent, and you may find it easier.

- Switch to the "Calc" worksheet. Enter the labels "Sample" in cell A1, "x" in cell B1, "Sample Mean" in cell C1, and "Grand Mean" in cell D1. Adjust the column widths to hold the labels.

- Place a dark underline below the labels in A1:D1 with the "Borders" button. The heavy underline selection you made earlier will be the choice displayed on the button for the rest of the session until you make another choice. As long as you want heavy underline in this session, you need only click the button on the toolbar.

- Return to the "Sales Course" worksheet. Select cells B2:B6 (the "Course A" data) and click the Copy Button ⌷ on the Standard Toolbar.

- Go to the "Calc" Worksheet. Select cell B2. Open the "Edit" menu on the Menu Bar. Select "Paste Special…." When the dialog window opens, click the "Paste Link" button on the right side (shown below). The numbers will appear to have been copied, but the Formula Bar will show that each cell contains an equation referring to cells in the "Sales Course" worksheet. Changing the values there will cause the corresponding values in the "Calc" worksheet also to change.

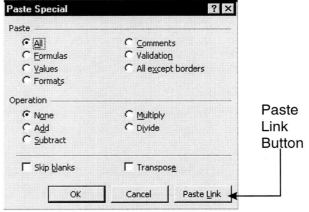

- Select cell B7 in "Sales Course" (the mean of "Course A") and click the Copy button again.

- Return to "Calc" and select the cell range C2:C6. Open the "Edit" menu on the Menu Bar, select "Paste Special…," and, when the dialog window opens, again click the "Paste Link" button. Each of the cells in C2:C6 will display the number 2228.8, but will actually contain a formula referring to cell B7 in "Sales Course."

- Enter the number "1" in cell A2 and then copy it down to cells A3:A6.

We now have the beginning of a table containing each value (in column B), the sample number in column A, and the sample mean in column C.

The same data for the other two samples will appear in the same columns immediately below the data just entered.

- Go to the "Sales Course" worksheet and select cells C2:C6. Click the Copy button. Switch to "Calc." Select cell B7, click "Paste Special…" off the "Edit Menu," and click the "Paste Link" button in the dialog window. The data from "Course B" will now appear directly below that of "Course A."

- Return to "Sales Course." Select cell B7 (the mean of "Course B"), click the Copy button, switch to "Calc," select the range C7:C11, and again make a "Paste Link" by opening the "Edit" menu, clicking "Paste Special…," and then clicking the "Paste Link" button.

- Enter the number "2" in cells A7:A11.

The data for the second sample now appear directly below the first. The third sample will be placed below the second.

- Using the same procedures as before, create a "Paste Link" reference in cells B12:B16 in the "Calc" worksheet to cells D2:D6 (the "No Course" sample) in the "Sales Course" worksheet. Check the Formula Bar for a cell in the range B12:B16 to be sure it contains a formula referring to a cell in the "Sales Course" worksheet and not simply a number.

- Create a "Paste Link" in cells C12:C16 of "Calc" to the mean of the "No Course" sample in cell D7 of "Sales Course." Each of the cells in C12:C16 should display the value 1951.6, but should show a formula in the Formula Bar.

- Enter the number "3" in cells A12:A16 of "Calc."

The last step is for each of the cells in column D of the table to refer to the "Grand Mean" of all the samples.

- Select cell D8 in the "Sales Course" worksheet, which contains the average of all 15 numbers, and click the Copy button. Go to the "Calc" worksheet. Select cells D2:D16, open the "Edit" menu, click "Paste Special…," and then click the "Paste Link" button. Each of the cells in D2:D16 will display the 15-number mean but will contain an equation referring to cell D8 in "Sales Course."

▼ Charting the Sample Values and the Means

The next step will be to produce a scatter plot that graphically displays the sample values, the sample means, and the grand mean.

We will initially create the chart on the "Calc" worksheet that ontains the data in a form that can be used by the Chart Wizard, and then it will be moved to the "Sales Course" worksheet. We will then be able to change the data on that worksheet and see how those changes affect the chart.

- Select the region A1:D16 on the "Calc" worksheet and click the Chart Wizard button.

- In the "Step 1" Chart Wizard dialog window, select "XY (Scatter)" from the "Standard Types" and choose the chart subtype at the top that shows data points with no lines.

- Click the "Next>" button three times so that you are at "Step 4." In that step have the chart placed in the "Sales Course" worksheet by selecting that worksheet as shown below.

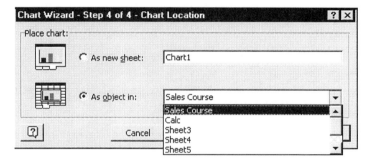

- Click the "Finish" button. The chart will be placed on the "Sales Course" worksheet.

- Enlarge the chart and arrange the worksheet so that both the entire chart and the numbers are visible without scrolling the worksheet.

We will make a few editing changes to improve the chart. These will include connecting the sample means and grand means points with separate lines and eliminating the horizontal axis. Let's first deal with the means.

- Place the mouse pointer directly on one of the three points showing the grand mean. If you have the pointer correctly placed and leave it for a second, a marker will appear identifying the point as being in the "Series 'Grand Mean'" followed by the horizontal and vertical axis values. Click the (left) mouse button once. All three grand mean points will change color indicating that they have been selected.

- Open the Format menu on the Menu Bar and click "Selected Data Series...." When the "Format Data Series" dialog window appears, click the "Patterns" folder tab, unless it is already on top.

The left side of the dialog window allows you to determine if a line connects the points and, if so, the color and other characteristics of that line. The right side of the window allows you to determine the appearance of the markers that show the position of the data points. We want to connect the points with a line and have no markers at all.

- In the left side of the dialog window in the "Line" area, click the "Custom" radio button and select a solid line "style." You may change the color and weight of the line if you wish.

- On the right side of the dialog window in the "Marker" area, click the "None" radio button. Click the "OK" button. Click on a blank portion of the chart to remove the selection of the grand mean points. The next step will give a similar treatment to the sample means.

- Select the sample means by placing the mouse pointer on one of them and clicking the (left) mouse button. Format the series so that it has a line connecting the points that differs in style (not solid) and color from that connecting the grand mean. Eliminate the markers for the sample means as you did for the grand mean.

The last step involves eliminating the present horizontal axis and substituting character labels to identify the three samples. This is a cosmetic change.

- Select the horizontal axis by clicking the mouse pointer on one of the numbers on that axis. You should see "handles" at each end of the axis.

- Open the Format menu on the Menu Bar and click "Selected Axis...." An alternative is to click the right mouse button and select "Format Axis" on the pop-up menu.

- Click the "Patterns" folder tab. On the left side of the dialog window is the "axis" region. Click the "None" radio button. On the bottom right side is the "Tick mark labels" region. Click the "None" radio button here as well. Click "OK."

- Place the labels "Course A," "Course B," and "No Course" below the horizontal axis by entering each label's text in the Formula Bar, pressing the Enter key, and then moving the label into position. For more details on this process, refer to page 50.

- Adjust the font sizes of the text on the chart to give the graphics more space, if needed.

Your completed chart should look like the picture at the top of the next page.

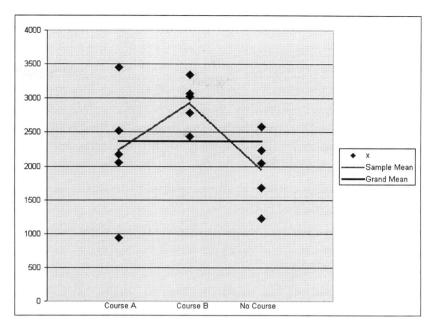

It is clear from the chart that those who took course "B" did better on average than either of the other groups, and those who took no course did the worst, on average. This suggests that the sales courses do make a difference. A statistical test will enable us to determine if this pattern could reasonably have arisen by random chance. The test, single-factor ANOVA, is discussed below.

▼ Determining the Sum of Squares

A population variance is the average sum of squared deviations from the mean. A sample variance is an unbiased estimator of a population variance. To be unbiased, the sum of squared deviations must be divided by the degrees of freedom rather than by the number of observations. An analysis of variance involves calculating several variance-like measures. Each of them is a sum of squared deviations around some measure divided by the degrees of freedom. We will extend the table in the "Calc" worksheet to calculate these measures. Once this worksheet is finished, the results will be placed back on the "Sales Course" worksheet. We will then experiment with samples drawn from different populations to see how the chart and the statistical tests reflect those changes.

• Select the "Calc" worksheet.

Most of the calculations will be done in additional columns added to the present table. Row 1 will contain labels for these columns. In those labels we will use "s bar" to refer to the *sample* means, which differ for each sample, and "g bar" to refer to the *grand* mean, which is the same for all samples.

- Enter the following labels in row 1, columns E through J: "x-s bar" in E1, "(x-s bar)^2" in F1, "s bar-g bar" in G1, "(s bar-g bar)^2" in H1, "x-g bar" in I1, and "(x-g bar)^2" in J1. Adjust the column widths. A quick way of adjusting them all at once is to select cells F1:J1 (E1 should already have enough room), and open the "Format" menu on the Menu Bar. Select "Column," then select "AutoFit Selection."

- Place a heavy underline under these cells like the one under the labels entered previously.

In all of the formulas below, use *relative* addresses. First, enter the formulas for the first row. A simple copy will generate the formulas for the rest of the cells.

- In cell E2, enter a formula to calculate the difference between the *x* value in that row (column B) and the sample mean for that row (column C). The displayed value should be -170.8. In the language of ANOVA, this is a *deviation* from the sample mean.

- In cell F2, enter a formula that will calculate the square of the number in cell E2. This value (29172.64) is a *squared deviation*.

- In cell G2, enter a formula to calculate the difference between the sample mean in that row (column C) and the grand mean (column D). This value, -140.6667, is the *deviation* of the sample mean from the grand mean.

- In cell H2, enter a formula to square the value in G2. This value, 19787.11111, is another *squared deviation*.

- In cell I2, enter a formula to calculate the deviation of the *x* value in that row from the grand mean. The displayed value should be −311.467.

- In cell J2, enter a formula to calculate the squared deviation of the *x* value in that row from the grand mean by squaring the value in I2. The displayed value should be 97011.48.

The next step is to copy these formulas down their columns.

- Select cells E2:J2. Place the mouse pointer over the fill handle in the lower right corner of J2. When the pointer changes to a black cross, press and hold the (left) mouse button and drag the outline border down until it includes row 16. Release the mouse button, and the rest of the table will be filled with numbers.

- Use the "Borders" button to put heavy underlines beneath the last cell in each of the three columns of squared deviations: F16, H16, and J16.

- Enter the label "Sums" in cell A17, "SSW" in cell E17, "SSB" in G17, and "SST" in I17. "SSW" stands for "Sum of Squares Within," "SSB" for "Sum of Squares Between," and "SST" for "Sum of Squares Total."

- In cell F17, use the AutoSum button to enter a formula to add the numbers in column F. The value is 4790788. The numbers in column F are squared deviations, and F17 is a *sum of squared deviations* or a *sum of squares*. Since it is based on the difference between each value and that value's sample mean, it is the sum of squares within each group (or sample), SSW.

- Using the AutoSum button (or other means), enter formulas in cells H17 and J17 to calculate the sum of squares for their respective columns. H17 will display 2531795.733, and J17 will display 7322584.

H17 is the sum of squares between groups (SSB), and J17 is the total sum of squares (SST). The three sums of squares will be used for calculations in the *ANOVA table*

▼ Preparing the ANOVA Table

- Switch to the "Sales Course" worksheet.

- The ANOVA table will be put in the region of cells A10:F13. Scroll your worksheet and enter labels for the table as shown in the picture below.

	A	B	C	D	E	F
10		SS	df	MS	F	*p* value
11	Between					
12	Within					
13	Total					

The "SS" label stands for "Sum of Squares." The first step will be to create a link between each of the three cells in that column and the corresponding sum of squares in the "Calc" worksheet.

- In cell B11, enter a formula that refers directly to the value of SSB in the "Calc" worksheet (H17). One way of doing this is to use Copy, Paste Special, and Paste Link, as was done in setting up the Calc worksheet.

- Using the same procedure, create links for "SS Within" and "SS Total" in the "Sales Course" worksheet to the corresponding values (SSW and SST) in row 17 of the "Calc" worksheet.

The degrees of freedom of SST is the sum of the sample sizes minus 1. If all the samples were drawn from a single population and were combined into a single sample, this would be the degrees of freedom of the variance of that single sample. In this case there are three samples each of size 5. The degrees of freedom of SST is $5 + 5 + 5 - 1 = 14$.

- Enter the number "14" in cell C13 of "Sales Course."

If a separate variance were calculated from each sample, the degrees of freedom for each sample would be the sample size minus 1. The degrees of freedom of SSW is the sum of the degrees of freedom of each sample. This is the sum of the sample sizes minus the number of samples. For this problem there are three samples. The degrees of freedom of SSW is $5 + 5 + 5 - 3 = 12$.

- Enter the number "12" in cell C12.

The variance of SSB is the variance of sample means around the grand mean. There are only as many sample means as there are samples. The degrees of freedom is the number of samples minus one. For this problem there are three samples. The degrees of freedom of SSB is $3 - 1 = 2$.

- Enter the number "2" in cell C11.

Notice in the table that the total sum of squares is the sum of the two sum of squares above it, and the degree of freedom of the total sum of squares is the sum of the two degrees of freedom above it.

Dividing a sum of squares by the appropriate degrees of freedom results in a variance-like measure. It is traditional in ANOVA to do this only for the within-groups and between-groups measures.

- Enter formulas in cells D11 and D12 to divide the sum of squares in each row by its degrees of freedom. The displayed values should be 1265898 (D11) and 399232.3 (D12).

- In cell E11 enter the formula that will take the value in cell D11 and divide it by the value in cell D12. The displayed value will be 3.17083.

This number, essentially a ratio of two variances, is a random number distributed under the F distribution. The F distribution is the ratio of two independent chi square distributions, each of which is divided by its degrees of freedom. The assumption of equal values for σ in all populations will cause this to simplify to a ratio of sample variances in many cases. A large value for the between-groups variance compared to the within-groups variance indicates that the sample values are relatively closer to the sample means (small sample variation) than the sample means are to the grand mean (large difference in sample means). This is the kind of result that would be expected if the samples were drawn from populations with different means. A p value can be determined by using the F distribution function in Excel to determine the probability that a value as high or higher than that in cell E11 could occur by chance.

- Select cell F11. Click the Edit Formula button. In the "Statistical" function category, choose FDIST. There are three arguments for this function.

The "X" argument field should have the cell address of the value for which we want the probability that an F distributed random variable will exceed E11. The two "Deg_freedom" arguments are the degrees of freedom of the numerator variance (in C11) and the denominator variance (in C12).

- Enter the appropriate cell references in the FDIST argument fields and click the "OK" button. The displayed value in F11 should be 0.078425.

Since this p value is less than the significance level of .10, we would reject the Null Hypothesis and conclude that there is evidence that the averages of all salespersons sent to the two courses and those sent to no course are not equal.

▼ Analyzing Simulated Samples

We can use Excel's Random Number Generation Tool to simulate new samples for the chart and ANOVA table. In order to meet the assumptions of analysis of variance, these random numbers will be drawn from a normal distribution.

- Open the "Tools" menu. Select "Data Analysis...," and choose "Random Number Generation" from the dialog window.

- On the Random Number Generation dialog window, enter "3" in the "Number of Variables" field (to overwrite the three columns of data in A1:D8) and "5" in the "Number of Random Numbers" field (for the five rows of data to be overwritten). Select "Normal" in the "Distribution" list and enter "2000" and "300" in the "Mean" and "Standard Deviation" fields, respectively. Click the "Output Range" radio button and enter the cell address for the upper left-hand corner of the existing data table (B2). Click the "OK" button. Click the "OK" button in the window warning you that data will be overwritten.

- Examine the new p value and look at the chart.

What we have done is simulate drawing three samples from a population with mean 2000 and standard deviation 300. The sample means and standard deviations will, of course, differ due to chance, but all samples were drawn from populations with the same means The correct result of an analysis of variance of these samples would be to fail to reject the Null Hypothesis (that the three samples are drawn from populations with the same mean). A large p value is what would be expected.

It is easy to draw an additional set of samples from the same population because the Analysis Tool will retain the values you previously entered. Try drawing additional samples from this population.

- Open the "Tools" menu and click "Data Analysis." Three dialog windows will appear in sequence; simply press the Enter key as soon as each appears, and a new sample will be drawn. (You must un-select the chart—click off the chart on the worksheet—before drawing additional samples.) Do this a dozen times or so, and look for a relationship between the p value and the chart. If you get a p value greater than .80 or less than .10, print its chart. Remember that to print just the chart, click it before choosing "Print Preview." In the page header, put your name and the p value.

Even though ANOVA should always produce large p values when the samples are all drawn from the same population, if you choose enough samples you will occasionally see ANOVAs with small p values—caused by random differences in samples. These small values would cause you to reject the Null Hypothesis. Since the samples are all drawn from the same population, it would be incorrect to reject the Null Hypothesis—an example of Type I error.

Let's next examine how ANOVA handles data when the samples are drawn from populations that don't have equal means. It is not quite as convenient in Excel to generate repeated sets of samples in this case, but we will make it as easy as possible by continuing to draw the first two samples from the same population and drawing only the third sample from a population with a different mean.

- Recall the Random Number Generation dialog window. Change the value in the "Number of Variables" field from "3" to "2" and click "OK" until the values are generated. This will generate new values for the "Course A" and "Course B" samples but not the "No Course" sample.

- Again recall the Random Number Generation dialog window, this time to generate new values for the "No Course" sample from a population with a different mean.

- Change the value in the "Number of Variables" field from "2" to "1." Only one column of numbers will be written.

- Change the value in the "Mean" field from "2000" to "2100." This is the new population mean for this sample.

- Change the address in the "Output Range" field from "$B$2" to "$D$2" (or "D2"). This will place the numbers in the "No Course" sample. Click "OK" (twice) so they will be generated.

Examine the graph and the p value. It is likely that this result is not very different from those obtained when all three samples were drawn from the same population. The p value is probably above .10, too high to conclude from the samples that the population means differ (even though we know they do). Furthermore, it's quite likely that the "No Course" sample, drawn from the population with the highest mean, doesn't even have the highest sample mean. Let's look at a few more samples drawn from these different populations. The easiest way to do this is to simply rerun the Random Number Generation Tool with the last set of values and then rerun it with the changes needed for the other sample or samples.

- Recall the Random Number Generation Tool. Repeatedly click "OK" (or press the Enter key) until a new set of numbers is generated. Since the tool was last used for the "No Course" sample, that sample will be regenerated.

- Again recall the Random Number Generation Tool. Make the changes needed to have it draw new values for the two "Course" samples. Change "Number of Variables" to "2," "Mean" to "2000," and "Output Range" to "$B$2." Click "OK" until the new random numbers are generated. Examine the chart and ANOVA table again.

- Generate yet another set of samples by first recalling and re-running the Random Number Generation Tool without change. This will result in new numbers for the two "Course" samples. Again recall the tool and make the changes needed to generate the "No Course" sample ("Number of Variables"= 1, "Mean" = 2100, "Output Range" = $D$2). After the new values are generated, check the chart and ANOVA table.

- Repeat the process of generating the two sets of samples a few more times. Each time the Random Number Generation Tool must be run twice. The first time, run it unchanged from the previous time. The second time, change the three fields (Number of Variables, Mean, and Output Range) to generate the rest of the data.

You should see from this exercise that ANOVA cannot reliably detect a difference between population means when the difference is only 100 and population variances are 300. Failure to reject the Null Hypothesis in this case is an example of Type II error. Avoiding this error requires some combination of a larger difference in population means, a smaller variance, or larger samples.

- Regenerate the two sets of samples except change the value of "Mean" for the "No Course" sample from "2100" to "3000" (and leave the others at "2000). This time you should get a quite different result. The ANOVA *p* value should be quite small (less than .01), and the chart should clearly show the third sample as having a mean clearly greater than the other two. If you don't get this result, regenerate the two sets of samples a couple of more times.

- Regenerate the two sets of samples again. This time change the "Mean" of "No Course" back to "2100" (leaving the other two at "2000"). Change the "Standard Deviation" of *both* sets of samples from "300" to "30." Even though the difference in the means is again only 100, the reduced variance of the population makes it easy for ANOVA to detect the difference from the samples. The *p* value should be very small, and the chart should clearly show higher values for the "No Course" sample than for the other two samples.

▼ Using the One-Factor ANOVA Tool

Excel has an analysis tool that will automatically create an ANOVA table and will also display other statistics not shown on the ANOVA table we have created. Like all analysis tools, it must be rerun whenever there is a change in the data.

- Select "Data Analysis..." from the "Tools" menu on the Menu Bar.

- Choose "Anova: Single Factor," which is located at the top of the list. You will probably have to scroll the list of tools up to see it.

- Enter the cell addresses of the sample data in the "Input Range" field. The addresses should contain the sample labels in the first row, so the address you enter should be B1:D6.

- Click the square beside "Labels in First Row" so that a check mark appears.

- The "Alpha" value allows you to specify a significance level for a critical *F*, a statistic not present in the ANOVA table prepared earlier. Enter "0.1" in this field. This corresponds with the significance level given in the original problem.

- Click the radio button beside "Output Range" to choose it and enter the cell address A15 in the field to the right. This will place the tool's ANOVA table directly below the one already on the sheet.

- Click "OK." As soon as the output is written, and while it is still selected, open the "Format" menu on the Menu Bar, select "Column" and then select "AutoFit Selection." If part of the output is covered by the chart, click the chart once in the margin and move it out of the way by placing the mouse pointer on the chart and dragging it (with the left mouse button pressed) to the right.

The output consists of a summary table providing the sums, means and variances of the data in each sample and an ANOVA table. Except for minor formatting differences and the presence of a critical *F* value (which should be 2.80679302), the table produced by the Analysis Tool should be identical to the table prepared earlier above it. If the two tables are not the same on your worksheet, you have made an error, probably in the dialog window of the Analysis Tool. Recall that dialog window and pay special attention to the "Input Range" field. Does it have either B1:D6 or $B$1:$D$6? Is the "Labels" box checked?

▼ Two-Factor Analysis of Variance

Excel provides two analysis tools for two-factor analysis of variance (also called *two-way* analysis of variance). In addition to controlling for which population an observation came from, two-factor analysis controls for other factors that might affect the variable being analyzed. The difference between two-factor and one-factor analysis is similar to the difference between the paired samples and independent samples in Chapter 12. One of the two-factor analysis tools is termed "Without Replication," and the other is termed "With Replication." There are several other common terms used for these analyses that you may see. The two-factor analysis without replications is often called *two-way analysis without interaction* or *randomized block* design. The two-factor analysis with replication is also known as *two-way analysis with interaction* or *factorial* design. The Excel terminology will be used here.

▼ Two-Factor Analysis without Replication

Consider the following problem:

In recent years, a number of "ergonomic" computer keyboards have become available. A business office wants to determine if the keyboard design has any effect on the speed of typists. Five typists of varying ability are chosen at random. Each is given the opportunity to become familiar with each keyboard prior to taking a test with that keyboard, and each typist is tested with all three keyboards. The results of that test are shown below (the numbers represent words per minute typed).

		Keyboard	
Typist	A	B	C
1	51	57	72
2	109	112	117
3	47	43	51
4	98	98	107
5	70	69	77

Is there evidence (at the .01 level of significance) that average typing speed differs among the three keyboards?

One of the factors that strongly influences a typist's speed is that person's skill. Two-factor analysis of variance provides a technique that accounts for the fact that much of the difference in typing speed is owing to ability differences among the typists, not keyboard differences.

- The data for this problem are on Sheet3 (cells A1:D6) of the anova.xls workbook. Select that worksheet and change its name to "Blocked." (This name will be explained below.)

The data in the worksheet are arranged the same as the data in the table. This follows a convention in statistics in which the characteristic distinguishing the data in one column from that in another is the characteristic to be analyzed. The characteristic distinguishing one row from another is controlled by the researcher and is used to permit better identification of the difference to be analyzed. It is standard terminology to refer to the column differences as *treatment* and the row differences as *blocking* or *blocks*. Think of an agricultural experiment to determine the effectiveness of different fertilizers on plant growth. Plant growth is also affected by other conditions, such as amount of water, soil characteristics, and amount of sunshine. In order to test the fertilizer, numerous small sections of land (*blocks*), which have identical soil, water, and sun, would each get plants that received each of the test fertilizers (*treatments*).

- Open the "Tools" menu, select "Data Analysis…," and choose "Anova: Two-Factor Without Replication."

- In the "Input Range" field, enter the cell range that contains the data and the labels for both the rows and columns. Note that with this Analysis Tool "labels" means both row labels and column labels. You cannot simply have column labels as was done with the data for one-factor ANOVA.

- Click the box beside "Labels" to place a check mark in it indicating that the cell range includes row and column labels.

- Change the value in the "Alpha" field to "0.01." This will cause the output to have the correct critical *F* values. This is unnecessary if the *p* value is used for the decision on the Null Hypothesis.

- Click the radio button beside "Output Range" and enter the address "E1" in the field to the right. Click "OK." When the tool finishes writing the output, select the following menu sequence: "Format," "Column," and "AutoFit Selection."

The organization of the output is similar to that of the one-factor ANOVA. The summary table provides summary statistics for each column *and* each row in the data. The ANOVA table also has more entries than did the one-way ANOVA table, but the structure of the calculations within the table is very similar.

Separate sums of squares are calculated and provided for the rows and columns (many statistics texts would use the terms *blocks* and *treatments* to mean the same thing). The "Rows" sums of squares are calculated from the difference between each value and the average of the three values in that row. That difference is then squared, summed for all columns, and multiplied by the number of values in each row (the number of columns). The "Columns" sum of squares is computed exactly as the "Between Groups" sum of squares was in single-factor ANOVA. The difference between each number and the average of the numbers in the same column is determined, squared, summed for all rows, and then multiplied by the number of values in each column (number of rows).

The calculation of the error sum of squares is a bit different. For each number, the sum of the average of all numbers in the row plus all numbers in the column is computed. That sum is then subtracted from the grand average of all the data. The difference between the value of that number and this result is then determined, squared, and added for all the numbers in the data. The error sum of squares is analogous to the single-factor "Within Groups" sum of squares.

The total sum of squares is calculated the same as in single-factor ANOVA: the difference between each value and the grand average of all the data is calculated, squared, and summed for all the data. The total sum of squares is also the sum of the row, column, and error sums of squares.

The degrees of freedom of the rows sum of squares is the number of rows minus 1, which is 5 for this problem. Dividing the rows sum of squares by its degree of freedom gives the rows mean squares, which is a measure similar to a variance. Similarly the degrees of freedom of the columns sum of squares is the number of columns minus 1. Dividing the columns sum of squares by its degrees of freedom gives the columns mean square error, another variance-like measure. The degrees of freedom of the error sum of squares is the product of the rows sum of squares degrees of freedom and the columns sum of squares degrees of freedom. Dividing the error sum of squares by its degrees of freedom yields the mean square error.

Two F values are given in the printout, along with their p values and corresponding critical values. The significance level for the critical values is set by the number in the "Alpha" field of the Tool's dialog window. The values in the "Rows" row of the table is appropriate for the Null Hypothesis that the means of populations from which each row was drawn are all equal. The low p value (5.42004E-08 or 0.0000000542) provides a strong basis for rejecting that Null Hypothesis and concluding that there is a difference in the population row means. This result, however, does not address the problem that the analysis is designed to solve. The rows correspond to the different typists. Rejecting the Null Hypothesis means that there is a real difference in the average typing speed of different typists, something we knew before analyzing the data. The only value of the "Rows" test is to help identify a situation in which we have erroneously chosen a control factor that is not strongly related to the outcome measure (typing speed) in which we are interested. This problem clearly does not suffer from that error.

The more important result is found in the "Columns" row of the ANOVA table. The low p value in that row (a bit less than .00343) is a strong basis for rejecting the Null Hypothesis of no difference in the population means of the three keyboards. By rejecting that hypothesis, we have evidence (at the .01 level of significance) that the keyboard *does* make a difference in average typing speed.

▼ Two-Factor Analysis with Replication

Two-factor analysis of variance with replication is a technique for examining the relationship between two different characteristics believed to affect a particular outcome. It differs from the two-factor analysis without replication in the following ways:

1. Usually the investigator is interested in both factors, unlike the typical situation with two-factor analysis without replication, where one of the factors is used as control or "blocking."

2. There is more than one observation for each set of values of the factors.

3. In addition to the effect of each factor, the analysis also looks at "interactions," the possibly different effect associated with combinations of factors.

These issues will be clearer as we look at an example:

A perfume manufacturer has test marketed a new perfume in a number of cities. In addition to the scent of the perfume, experience has shown that sales depends heavily on packaging and on advertising strategy. Three different advertising strategies (termed "Sophisticated," "Athletic," and "Popular") and three different package designs were tested along with the new perfume. Each combination was tested in two different markets, and each test market program was six months long. At the completion of the program, the level of sales per thousand women in the market was collected. The results, arranged by advertising strategy and package design, are shown below.

Package Design	Advertising Strategy		
	Sophisticated	Athletic	Popular
1	2.80	2.04	1.58
	2.73	1.33	1.26
2	3.29	1.50	1.00
	2.68	1.40	1.82
3	2.54	3.15	1.92
	2.59	2.88	1.33

These data are also present on Sheet4 of the worksheet in anova.xls.

Based on these data, is there evidence of a difference in population means for different advertising strategies? Different package designs? Interactions between package designs and advertising strategy?

In this example, we would expect to find *interactions* if the effect of the package design depended on the advertising strategy. It is reasonable to expect interactions in this case. Suppose, for example, one of the package designs was somehow more "sophisticated" than the others. It would make sense for this design to have a different (more positive) impact if the perfume were advertised with the "Sophisticated" strategy than if it were advertised with the "Athletic" strategy.

The fact that each "cell" (that is, each combination of a specific advertising strategy and package design) has more than one observation enables us to calculate a mean of those observations and use them to form an additional sum of squares. This will result in *four* sums of squares: one for the rows, one for the columns, one for the interactions, and an error sum of squares. These sums of squares are handled in an ANOVA table in a manner very similar to the previous ANOVA tables.

In two-factor analysis of variance with replication (unlike two-factor analysis without replication), there is no conceptual difference between the columns and the rows. The factor represented by the rows and that represented by the columns are both to be analyzed. The situation is thus different from the previous approach, where the column factor was the only one to be analyzed while the row factor was designed by the researcher to account for things already known to affect the outcome to be analyzed.

Excel's analysis tool does impose one requirement on the structure of the data: each value of the column factor must occupy a single column on the spreadsheet. Since there are multiple observations per cell, each value of the row factor must occupy *more than one* row. The data in the table on page 329 are organized this way, as are the data in the worksheet.

- Switch to Sheet4 of the anova.xls worksheet. Rename that worksheet "Interactions."

- Open the "Tools" menu, select "Data Analysis...," and choose "Anova: Two-Factor With Replication."

- In the "Input Range" field, enter the address for the cell range containing the data table including the labels in row 1 and column A.

Note that in this tool, unlike the two other ANOVA tools, labels *must* be present for *both* the columns and rows, and their addresses *must* be included in the "Input Range" field. There is no "Labels" check box because labels are required.

- The "Rows per Sample" field should indicate how many observations are in each cell. Since Excel requires them to be in different rows, this is equivalent to the number of rows for each value of the row factor. For this problem, the number is "2." Enter that value in the field.

- Make the entries required to have the tool place the output on the same worksheet beginning in cell E1. Click "OK." Once the output is written, use the Format menu to adjust the column widths.

The table of summary statistics is now quite long, although the same basic descriptive statistics given in the previous ANOVA tools are given here as well. For this output the statistics are arranged in a matrix, allowing you to determine the values for each cell (each combination of a particular row factor value and column factor value). A good check to be sure the dialog window was filled correctly is to verify that Excel reads two values for each cell and that the labels given in this output include all the row and column labels in the original data. The rightmost column and bottom row are labeled "Total." These give the summary statistics for all of the observations for each value of the column factor and row factor, respectively.

The ANOVA table is quite similar to all the other ANOVA tables except for the presence of the "Interaction" row. Excel uses the term "Sample" to denote what had been termed "Rows" in the two-factor analysis without replication. "Rows" would have been clearer here since the statistic in that row accounts for differences in the row factor. The calculations of the sums of squares and degrees of freedom are similar to those of the other ANOVAs, and the mean squares (MS), a variance-like measure, is determined by dividing each sum of squares by its degrees of freedom. The three F values were calculated by dividing each of the mean square values in that row by the mean square error. The answers to the problem are given best by the three p values.

The p value of slightly over .0761 for the rows ("Sample") factor indicates that we (just) fail to reject the Null Hypothesis (at the .05 level of significance) that there is no difference in the population means for the different package designs. The p value of a bit over .00037 for the column factor provides a strong basis for rejecting the Null Hypothesis of no difference in the population means of the different advertising strategies. In other words, advertising strategy clearly affects sales, while it appears that package design may not. The p value for interactions of slightly over .022 is especially interesting. This low value would lead to rejecting the Null Hypothesis of no difference in the population means of the different interactions. This suggests that while we were unable to conclude that packaging had any overall effect on mean sales, it appears that it does have an effect with certain advertising strategies. It would thus be a mistake to conclude that packaging is not important. A result like this clearly calls for additional research to determine with more precision how the interaction between packaging and advertising strategy works.

▼ Exercises

1. Use one-factor analysis of variance to analyze the data on the effect of keyboards on typing speed in the "Blocked Worksheet." Produce a printout that shows the results of both the one-factor and two-factor without replication analyses. Which technique is preferable? Why?

2. The results of the perfume data indicated the presence of significant interaction effects between advertising strategy and package design. For which advertising strategy are these effects important? Answer that question by using separate one-factor analysis of variance on the data for each advertising strategy to test for differences in the population means of different package designs. Produce a printout showing your results for each strategy. When is package design important?

3. Property taxation requires that appraisers periodically determine the market value of all the houses in a jurisdiction. Ideally this determination is completely objective, and every appraiser would come up with the same value. In practice this is impossible. The tax division of a county government wants to determine if there is evidence of a difference in the averages of appraised values among four different appraisers. In order to determine this, each appraiser is asked to determine the value of four houses. The same four houses are appraised by each appraiser with the following results.

House	Appraiser			
	Mike	Sally	Tom	Jane
1	$101,900	$101,944	$100,967	$100,175
2	$72,744	$76,893	$73,206	$74,820
3	$132,217	$136,232	$131,935	$132,889
4	$211,213	$213,941	$212,735	$213,796

Is there evidence (at the .05) level of significance of a difference in average appraised value among appraisers? Print the results of the appropriate analysis in Excel and explain why you chose that particular analysis rather than the others. Be sure to provide a yes or no answer to the question and your basis for that answer. (A copy of the data is in Sheet6 of the workbook in anova.xls.)

4. A grocery chain wants to determine if background music affects the average daily sales of stores. A sample of similarly sized stores was chosen and each was randomly assigned to four different groups: no background music, classical, hard rock, and soft rock. The results (in $10,000) are shown below. (These data are also on Sheet7 of the workbook in anova.xls.)

None	Classical	Hard	Soft
13	16	13	13
9	19	14	12
10	11	16	15
17	9	4	9
10	11	15	15

Based on this result, is there evidence at the .05 level of significance that music choice would affect average sales for all stores? Print the Excel analysis and explain how you determined your answer. Be sure and give a yes or no answer to the question and your basis for that answer.

Chapter 14

▼

Simple Linear Regression

Regression analysis gives us a way to investigate the relationship among a group of variables. *Simple* regression analyzes the relationship between two variables. *Multiple* regression removes this restriction and permits the analysis of the relationship among any number of variables. Although the mathematics of multiple regression is a reasonably straightforward extension of simple regression, the increased flexibility makes it a much more versatile and complex analysis tool than simple regression. By studying simple regression before multiple regression, we postpone some of the complexities of regression analysis and focus on the essentials. Another reason to study simple regression first is that the restriction to two dimensions (two variables) makes it easy to represent regression analysis graphically.

When a researcher uses simple linear regression to analyze a set of data, she must already accept certain assumptions. If these assumptions cannot be accepted, some technique other than simple regression will be required to analyze the data. In many (but not all) cases, multiple regression may offer a good technique for analyzing such data.

Data appropriate for simple linear regression consist of observations that each have two different measures. For examples, we might have a sample of houses and, for each house, a measure of that house's size and its selling price. Perhaps we have a sample of families, and for each family we have annual income and annual expenditures on clothing. A classic problem in regression analysis involved data containing the height of individuals and the average height of each individual's parents (the measure of height was adjusted for gender differences).

Simple regression allows us to investigate the relationship between the two measures and answer such questions as "What sales price could be predicted for a house with 965 square feet?" or "Do taller parents tend to have taller children?" or "Of every additional $1 increase in income, how much on average goes to additional expenditures on clothes?" Implicit in these questions is the notion of *causality*. The size of a house determines, or causes, the level of the sales price, and not vice versa. Similarly, tall parents are responsible for tall children. The height of the child doesn't determine the height of the parents. A family's income determines how much that family spends on clothes; the amount it spends on clothes doesn't determine its income. Note that regression is of no use in determining the direction of causality; that determination must be made before regression analysis is used.

In a causal relationship between two factors, one factor causes changes in the other factor, not vice versa. The causing factor (house size, height of parents, and family income in the [previous examples) is termed the *independent variable*. The idea here is that whatever determines the level of that measure is outside, or independent, of the relationship being analyzed between the two measures. Other names for this measure include *exogenous variable* and *x variable*.

The factor experiencing the effect of a change in the independent variable in the relationship (such as house selling price, height of children, and expenditure on clothes) is termed the *dependent variable*. Its value depends on the value of the independent variable. Other names for this measure include *endogenous variable* and *y variable*.

▼ Linear Relationships

When a set of data is analyzed by simple linear regression, the result is an equation that traditionally contains a *y* on the left-hand side of the equal sign and an *x* on the right-hand side. When a value is substituted in the equation for the symbol *x*, the equation provides the computation of a *predicted* value for *y*. The equation is called *linear* because it gives a relationship between the *y* and *x* variables that, when plotted, results in a straight line. Any equation for a line can be written in the following form:

$$y = b_0 + b_1 x$$

Both "b_0" and "b_1" would be numbers in a specific equation; when their values are determined, the equation is determined. Simple linear regression determines the values of "b_0" and "b_1" that "best" fit the data according to a specific criteria. When a linear equation is written in the form shown above, "b_0" is sometimes called the *y intercept* and "b_1" is called the *slope*. Let's use Excel to explore these meanings.

- Open the Excel workbook in the file simpreg.xls. Go to the first worksheet, which is titled "b0 & b1."

- In cell B17, enter the number "1." This will be an intercept value.

- In cell B18, enter the number "2." This will be a slope value.

- Select cell B2. This cell will contain a y value to go with the x value of −3. Each cell below it will contain the y value to go with the x value beside it.

- Enter the Excel formula in cell B2 that will take the value in cell B17 (which is "b_0"), and add to it the value in cell B18 ("b_1") times the value in cell A2 ("x"). Make the references to cells B17 and B18 *absolute* and the reference to A2 *relative*.

This formula is the Excel version of the equation of a line given above. With the values for "b_0" (1) and "b_1" (2) given above, the form of the equation is $y = 1 + 2x$. If −3 is substituted for x, the value of y is −5. This value should be displayed in B2.

- Copy the formula in B2 to B3 through B15. If error values are displayed in any of the cells, select B5 and double check it. Be sure the references to B17 and B18 are *absolute* and A5 is *relative*. If the value in A5, 0, is substituted for x in the equation $y = 1 + 2x$, the result is 1. This is the value that should be displayed in B5. Similarly, the value in B15 should be 21.

- Select the region A1:B15. Click the Chart Wizard Button.

- When the Step 1 dialog window of the Chart Wizard opens, select "XY (Scatter)" from the "Standard" types. Select the subtype shown in the bottom row on the right, which will connect the points with lines without data markers. Click the "Next>" button twice.

- In the Step 3 dialog window, select "Titles." Make the chart title "Slope and Intercept," the Value (X) axis title "X," and the Value (Y) axis title "Y." Select "Legend" and make the legend no longer visible. Click "Finish." Make the chart as large as you can so that you can view it and the data in columns A and B without scrolling.

If the data for an Excel chart change, Excel will normally rescale the axes so that all of the new data will fit. We will change the values of the slope and intercept to see how the line changes. In this case, a rescaling of an axis will make it more difficult to see exactly how the line changes. To avoid this, we can "fix" the vertical axis so that Excel will not change it.

- Place the mouse pointer on one of the the numbers along the horizontal (x) axis and click the (left) mouse button to select the axis. Either click the right mouse button and select "Format Axis…" or open the Format menu on the Menu Bar and and click "Selected Axis…."

- Click the "Scale" folder tab at the top of the window. On the left side of the window is a series of fields under the title "Value (X) Axis Scale." Change the value in the field to the right of "Maximum:" to "10." Notice that this removes the check mark to the left of "Maximum." That check mark indicated that Excel was to determine the value automatically. By entering a value, you have told Excel to always use the value entered rather than to determine that value from the data. The dialog window should look like the picture below. Click the "OK" button.

- Click a number on the vertical (y) axis to select that axis. Open the format axis dialog window, click "Scale," and remove the two check marks to the left of "Minimum:" and "Maximum" by clicking them. This will prevent Excel from changing the y axis when the data change.

Changing the value of the intercept (in B17) and the slope (B18) will make the line change. Observe how these changes work in the steps below so that you can think of a line you see in terms of its intercept and slope. Notice also the relationship between the x and y values in columns A and B.

- Change the value of the intercept to 5. Observe where it crosses the vertical axis. Change it to 10, 15, and then 20.

- Change the intercept back to 1. Make the slope larger and note the effect it has on the line. Try values of 5, 10, 15, 20, and 22. After each change, look at the x and y values in columns A and B.

- Make the slope 0. Look at the relationship between the values of x and y in the table. Change the intercept to 12 and reexamine the table.

- Keep the intercept at 12. Make the slope increasingly negative. Try values of −2, −5, −10, −50. Study the relationship between x and y in the table after each change.

When a line has a positive slope, increasing x values are associated with increasing y values. When a line has a negative slope, increasing x values are associated with decreasing y values. A positive slope indicates a *positive* or *direct* relationship between x and y. A negative slope indicates a *negative* or *inverse* relationship between x and y.

What happens to the relationship between the values in columns A and B when the slope is 0? A horizontal line has a special significance because it represents *no relationship* between the two variables. Changes in the value of the x variable in column A have no effect at all on the y variable in column B, and knowing x doesn't affect our best guess of y. The basis of some of the goodness of fit tests for a regression line involves comparing the relationship implied by the line that "best" fits the data with a horizontal line—equivalent to comparing the "best" relationship to no relationship at all.

▼ The Simple Linear Regression Model

When we use simple linear regression to analyze a data sample, we are making certain assumptions about those data. We assume, for example, that a linear relationship exists between two measures or variables in the population, which can be represented by the following equation:

$$Y = \beta_0 + \beta_1 X + \varepsilon$$

Compare this equation to the equation on page 335. The equation here shows a relationship in a population; that is why capital Y and X are used here rather than lowercase y and x. It is also why Greek letters β_0 and β_1 (*beta*) are used rather than b_0 and b_1. The meanings of β_0 and β_1 here are the same as b_0 and b_1 in that earlier equation. β_0 is the y axis intercept and β_1 is the slope of the line. Both of the β's are fixed numbers—population parameters. Like other population parameters (such as μ), we generally do not know their value and seek to estimate them by analyzing a sample of data drawn from the population.

The most important difference between the equation above and the one on page 335 is the "ε" (the Greek letter *epsilon*). Unlike the β's, ε is a random number. Its presence means that the relationship cannot be perfectly represented by a straight line. Even if we knew β_0 and β_1, we still couldn't perfectly predict Y. There is a difference between the actual value of Y and what the value would be if the relationship were perfectly linear. That difference is ε, and its value differs randomly for each observation. ε is usually regarded as representing the effect of a large number of individually insignificant and independent factors which affect the value of Y *other than* X. Regression analysis requires certain assumptions about the distribution of ε: It is normal with a mean of zero and a constant variance. The values of ε are assumed independent of one another.

▼ Fitting a Line to Sample Data

The values of β_0 and β_1 are estimated by selecting a sample of data and then finding the line that best "fits" the data according to a specific criterion: minimizing the sum of squared errors. This estimation line is represented by the following function:

$$\hat{y} = b_0 + b_1 x$$

The $\hat{y}$ is termed the "predicted" value of y given by the linear equation and is often called "y hat." Recall that each observation in the population has a value for ε associated with it, and these values cause the population values not to have a precise linear relationship. When a sample is chosen, the sample values will not lie precisely on a straight line. As a result, there will generally be a difference for each observation between the value of $\hat{y}$ and the value of y. This will be clearer if we consider a specific example.

A firm that manufactures a particular type of hardware fastener wants to determine the relationship between monthly operating costs and monthly output for its manufacturing plants. Each plant submits a report each month that includes this information, and from these reports the firm has selected a sample showing output (in thousands of pounds) and operating cost (in thousands of dollars). Based on this information, what is the relationship?

The data for this problem can be found on the "Line Fit" worksheet of the workbook in simpreg.xls. We will use the procedures above to try to manually fit a line to the output and cost data and see the relationship between the visual fit between the line and data and the sum of squared errors.

• Switch to the "Line Fit" worksheet.

The worksheet already contains observations with x and y values in columns A and B, respectively. Column C (labeled "y hat") will contain a second set of y values derived from a line whose intercept and slope will be entered in C16 and C17 using the same procedure as was used on the previous worksheet.

- Enter the value "2" in cell C16 and "1.5" in cell C17. We will see how well this line fits the data and then make changes to improve the fit.

- Enter formulas in cells C2:C15 that calculate the y value associated with the corresponding x value in column A for a line whose intercept and slope are given in C16 and C17. These formulas will be very similar to the ones you entered in column B on the "b0 & b1" worksheet. Be sure to multiply the value in C17 (b_1) by x (column A) and not y. Also be sure the addresses for b_0 and b_1 in the equation are *absolute*. When the correct formulas are entered, cell C2 will display the value 3.575, and cell C15 will display 6.29. These values are called the *predicted y values*.

The goal of fitting a line to the data is to come up with the values for the slope and intercept that result in values in column C that are "closest" to those in column B (predicted values close to actual values). For regression, "close" is defined in terms of the sum of squared errors.

- Enter the formulas in cells D2:D15 that will, for each row, calculate the value in column B minus the value in column C. It is these differences that are to be collectively minimized. Cell D2 should display −2.06, and cell D15 should display 3.61. These values are often called the *errors* or *residuals*, and fitting a line involves a way of collectively minimizing them.

- Use the AutoSum button to enter the formula in cell D16 that will calculate the sum of the numbers in D2:D15. The displayed value should be 99.4750. This is the *sum of the errors*. The sum is positive, like most of the individual errors. On average, the actual values exceed the predicted values.

- Enter formulas in cells E2:E15 that will calculate the square of the corresponding value in column D. E2 should display 4.2230, and E15 should display 13.0321. These are the *squared errors*.

- Enter the formula in E16 that will calculate the sum of the values in E2:E15. This is the *sum of squared errors*. The value displayed in E16 should be 1004.1859.

- Enter the label "SSE" (for sum of squared errors) in cell E17. This is a commonly used abbreviation in statistics.

As stated above, regression fits a line to the data by determining the value of the intercept and slope that minimizes the sum of squared errors (in E16). You may wonder why the sum of errors (in D16) isn't minimized instead. To examine this and the relationship between fit and sum of squared errors, we will plot the data and the line given by the value of the slope and intercept in C16 and C17.

- Select the region A1:C15.

- Click the Chart Wizard button. Choose "XY (Scatter)" from the "Standard" types

- Choose the subtype at the top that shows symbols at the data points but no connecting lines. Click "Next>."

- Examine the small preview plot in the Step 2 window. You should see two sets of data plotted; the symbols used to show the points should have different shapes and different colors. Look at the legend on the preview plot and identify which points correspond to "y hat." They should appear to lie along a straight line. We will convert the representation of those points to a line, and you need to remember which they are because we will remove the legend in the final chart to give the plot area more room.

- Click "Next>." In the Step 3 window, remove the chart's legend. Click "Finish."

- Move the chart so that the top of the chart is in row 18. Scroll your worksheet so that row 16 is the top row visible. Make the chart larger, but be sure the entire chart and rows 16 and 17 are all visible without scrolling the worksheet

- Place the mouse pointer over one of the "y hat" points and single click. Many (or all) of the points should change color ("light up"). Be sure you have the points that lie along a line.

- Open the Format menu on the Menu Bar and click "Selected Data Series…" (or click the right mouse button and select "Format Data Series…." The Format Data Series dialog window will appear.

- Click the "Patterns" folder tab at the top of the dialog window. In the area titled "Line," click "Custom." In the area titled "Marker," click "None." Click the "OK" button.

- Place the mouse pointer on a part of your worksheet off the chart and click once to de-select the "y hat" points. The chart should show a line with no point symbols on the line.

Clearly the line does not "fit" the data points very well; it is too low. As we noted before, most of the errors are positive; the points lie above the line. We will adjust the line so that the fit improves and observe what happens to the sum of squared errors (in E16). What about the sum of errors?

- Enter the number "17.28357" for the intercept and "0" for the slope. What happens to the sum of errors (D16)? (It should be 0.) This horizontal line clearly doesn't fit the data very well. Jot down the value of the sum of squared errors (SSE).

- Enter the number "28.18786" for the intercept and "-2" for the slope. What is the sum of errors (D16) this time? (It should again be 0.)

What is going on here? It turns out that any line that goes through the point whose x value is $\bar{x}$ (5.452143 for these data) and whose y value is $\bar{y}$ (17.28357) will have a zero sum of errors. Both of the two lines you just examined went through that point. Lines containing this point may not fit the data well! Although the horizontal line was a poor fit, it was better than the second line. The SSE reflected this, increasing from 1027.219 to 2778.444.

- To see a line that fits the data much better, try an intercept value of "1.5" and a slope of "3.2." The SSE for this line is 113.6625, much smaller than was the case before.

- Look carefully at the line and the data points. Does the line look just a bit high and perhaps a bit too steep? Adjust the intercept and slope to improve the fit. Try to reduce the sum of squared errors as low as possible. You should easily be able to find a line whose SSE is less than 100. Can you find one whose SSE is less than 70? (yes) Less than 65? (good luck)

▼ Determining the Regression Line

Calculating the slope and the intercept of the line which minimizes the sum of squared errors is very straightforward and similar to the calculations done in ANOVA. The formulas for the regression coefficients (intercept and slope) are

$$b_1 = \frac{\sum (x_i - \bar{x})(y_i - \bar{y})}{\sum (x_i - \bar{x})^2}$$

$$b_0 = \bar{y} - b_1 \bar{x}$$

The numerator of the expression above for b_1 is often represented by the symbol SP_{xy} (for Sum of Products). The denominator, which you should recognize as the sum of squared deviations of x from its mean, is represented by SS_x.

Since SS_x *must* always be positive, the sign of the slope of the regression line is determined by the sign of SP_{xy}. When a set of data has a positive relationship, small values of x will generally be associated with small values of y. Since these small values will be below the mean, both $(x_i - \bar{x})$ and $(y_i - \bar{y})$ will be negative, and their product will be positive. Large values of x will generally be associated with large values of y. Both $(x_i - \bar{x})$ and $(y_i - \bar{y})$ will still be positive, and their product will also be positive. When these are added up, they result in a positive value for SP_{xy}. On the other hand, if there is a negative relationship between x and y, small values of x tend to be associated with large values of y. In this case $(x_i - \bar{x})$ will be negative but $(y_i - \bar{y})$ will be positive, causing their product to be negative. When x is large and y small, the two expressions switch signs, but their product is still negative. Summing up these negative values will make SP_{xy}, and b_1 also, negative.

These formulas require a lot of arithmetic, but they are easy to set up in Excel.

- Switch to the "Regression" worksheet, where you will find the same output and cost data and the labels for calculating the values of b_0 and b_1. Columns D, E, and F require $\hat{y}$, which will be calculated after the regression coefficients.

- Enter formulas in B17 and C17 that will calculate the average of the data values in their respective columns. B17 should display 5.45, and C17 should display 17.28. Note that these cells have an Excel format that limits their display to two decimal places. You can use the Increase Decimal button to display more precision, but regardless of display, Excel uses full precision in calculations.

- Using either Paste Link or a simple formula with an absolute address, set the cells in the range G2:G15 so that they will refer to cell B17 and will display the same value displayed in B17.

- In the region H2:H15, enter the formula that will calculate the difference between that row's value for x in column B and the mean of the x's in column G. H2 should display -4.40, and cell H15 should display -2.59. Use the AutoSum button to display in cell H16 the sum of the values in the column above. The sum should be zero.

- Enter formulas in each cell of region I2:I15 that will square the value in column H of that row. I2 should display 19.3789, and I15 should display 6.7192. Use cell I16 to calculate and display the sum of the values above. This sum should be 111.1582. This is SS_x. Enter the label "SSx" in cell I17.

- Enter formulas in rows 2 through 15 of columns J, K, and L that give y the same treatment x received in columns G, H, and I. Cell L2 should display 248.4902, and cell L15 should display 54.5171.

- Enter formulas in row 16 of columns K and L that will display the column sums. K16 should display zero, and L16 should display 1027.22. This is the value of $\sum (y_i - \bar{y})^2$, also called SST. It is not needed to determine the regression coefficients, but will be used later.

- Enter the label "SST" in cell L17.

- Enter formulas in the region M2:M15 that will calculate and display the product of each row's value of $(x_i - \bar{x})$ in column H and $(y_i - \bar{y})$ in column K. The displayed value of M2 should be a little over 69.39 and that of M15 should be just under 19.14. Use M16 to determine a sum of the values in column M. That sum should be approximately 326.648. This is SP_{xy}. Enter the label "SPxy" in cell M17.

Notice that most (all but one) of the values in column M are positive. Look at how these positive values are the result of the signs of the numbers in each row in columns H and K. Both x and y tend to be associated with values on the same side of the mean.

- Select cell B19, which is to contain the regression value for b_1. Enter a formula that will divide the value of SP_{xy} in the worksheet by the value of SS_x. Cell B19 will display the value of the regression line's slope, 2.938587.

Recall that the formula for the intercept is $b_0 = \bar{y} - b_1\bar{x}$. The value for b_1 is in B19, the value for $\bar{y}$ is in C17, and the value for $\bar{x}$ is in B17.

- Enter the formula in B18 to calculate b_0. The result should display as 1.261978.

With these results, we can now write the regression equation as

$$\hat{y} = 1.261978 + 2.938578x$$

The slope coefficient can be interpreted as estimating that a one-unit (that is, 1,000 pounds) increase in output results, on average, in a little less than a 2.94 unit (thousands of dollars) increase in monthly operating costs. This is equivalent to just under \$2.94 a pound. The equation can be used to predict the average monthly cost for any level of output. We will first use it to provide predicted values for the output levels in the data.

- Using the same approach used on the previous worksheet, enter formulas in cells D2:D15 that will provide a predicted y value ($\hat{y}$) for each x

value in the row, using the values for b_0 and b_1 given in cells B18 and B19. The value displayed in cell D2 should be 4.3475, while that in D15 should be 9.6663.

- Enter formulas in E2:E15 to calculate the difference between the actual y value in column C and the value for $\hat{y}$ in column D (the *errors* or *residuals*). E2 should display -2.827, and E15 should display 0.234. Sum the values of column E in E16. The sum should be zero.

- Enter formulas in F2:F15 to calculate the squared errors. The value in F2 should be 7.9947 and that in F15 should be 0.0546. Use F16 to calculate and display the sum of squared errors (SSE). The displayed value should be 67.3350. Enter the label "SSE" in F17.

Recall that the regression-determined intercept and slope result in the smallest possible value for SSE.

- Compare the SSE here with the value you got when you manually tried to find the slope and intercept that minimizes SSE (cell E16 on the "Line Fit" worksheet).

▼ Using Regression to Predict y Values

The process you used to develop a value for $\hat{y}$ for each of the x values in the data can also be used to provide predicted y values (that is, $\hat{y}$'s) for any x value, not just ones actually in the data.

- Enter the labels "x" and "y hat" in cells C20 and C21 of the "Regression" worksheet.

- Enter the number "5" in cell D20.

- Enter a formula in D21 that will use the value of b_1 in cell B19, the value of b_0 in cell B18, and the value of x in D20 to calculate the regression equation for the x value in D20. The displayed value for D21 will be 15.95491.

The regression analysis enables us to predict that a monthly output of 5,000 pounds would incur an operating cost of \$15,954.91. What would be the predicted operating cost for an output of 3,000 pounds?

- Enter the number "3" in cell D20. After you press the Enter key, the value 10.07774 should immediately be displayed in cell D21. The predicted cost of a monthly output of 3,000 pounds would be \$10,077.74.

Using regression to predict the y values in this way will yield the most accurate results when the x value is close to the average value of the x's used to determine the regression coefficients (5.45 in this case). Special caution must be used in predicting a y value for an x value outside the range of x values used to determine the regression coefficients (1.05 to 9.98 in this case).

▼ Goodness of Fit—Descriptive Approach

For any set of data, regression analysis will always find the line that fits the data best in the sense of minimizing the sum of squared errors. Even if there is no relationship at all between the two measures, regression will provide the intercept and slope that best fits that "relationship." In this case the "best" fit will not be a "good" fit. As a result, whenever we do regression analysis we need to have, in addition to the estimated parameters (intercept and slope) that define the regression line, an indication of whether the fit between the line and data is "good." We will explore how that is done.

- Switch to the "Data" worksheet. You will find two columns of numbers under the heading "Bad Fit." Select the cells containing the numbers (A3:B16), click the Copy button, switch to the "Line Fit" worksheet, select cell A2, and click the Paste button. The previous data will be overwritten with the "Bad Fit" data.

Changing the data in the "Line Fit" worksheet will also change the data in columns B and C of the "Regression" worksheet. There is a "Paste Link" connection between those "Regression" worksheet cells and the ones in the "Line Fit" worksheet.

- Scroll the screen in the "Line Fit" worksheet so that row 16 is at the top and examine the chart. There is no line that will fit these data closely.

- Switch to the "Regression" worksheet. Copy the value for the mean of the y values ($\bar{y}$) into the clipboard by selecting cell C17 and clicking the Copy button.

Remember that cell C17 contains a formula for calculating the average of the y values in column C. If we use the Paste button to paste the clipboard, that formula would be copied to the cell we pasted to. We want to paste not the formula but the *current value* of the formula. It is this value (sometimes rounded) that is displayed in the cell.

- Switch back to the "Line Fit" worksheet and select cell C16 (the intercept of the line drawn on the chart). Open the "Edit" menu on the Menu Bar (or click the right mouse button) and select "Paste Special...." When the "Paste Special" dialog window appears, click "Values" under "Paste" on the left side of the window so the radio button beside it is chosen (as shown below).

- Click the "OK" button in the dialog window. The value for $\bar{y}$ (about 17.35074) will appear in cell C16.

- Enter the value "0" in cell C17 (the slope of the line). Scroll your worksheet and look at the values of $\hat{y}$ in C2:C15. They should all be equal to $\bar{y}$.

- Scroll your worksheet down so that cell A16 is in the upper left corner. Your screen should show the chart with a horizontal line.

Remember that a horizontal line represents no relationship between the x value and the y value. The horizontal line that goes through $\bar{y}$ has a lower sum of squared errors than any other horizontal line.

- Copy the value of $\bar{y}$ in cell C16 to cell F16 (use the Copy and Paste buttons). Also copy the *value* of SSE cell E16 to cell G16 (use the Copy button and "Paste Special"). Enter the label "horizontal SSE" in G17. As you make changes to the intercept and slope, compare the changing SSE in cell E16 to the SSE from the horizontal line through $\bar{y}$ in G16.

- Make small changes to the value in C16. You should see the horizontal line shift up and down depending on whether the changes increase or decrease the value in C16. Notice that any change in C16 alone will increase the value of the sum of squared errors in cell E16 (as compared to the original value in G16).

- Copy the value for $\bar{y}$ in cell F16 back to cell C16.

When you went through the process earlier in this chapter of manually fitting a line to the original set of data, you also started with a horizontal line through $\bar{y}$. With those data, it was not difficult to find a value of the slope and intercept that would reduce the sum of squared errors. For the current set of data, it will not be so easy (although it can be done).

- Adjust the values of b_0 and b_1 (in cells C16 and C17) to reduce the value of SSE in E16 below the horizontal line SSE in G16.

Not only is it more difficult to find values for b_0 and b_1 that reduce SSE, but the amount of reduction is less for this data set than it was for the original data set. By using the regression coefficients, we can determine the minimum value for SSE.

- Switch to the "Regression" worksheet. Copy the regression values for b_0 and b_1 (in cells B18 and B19) to the clipboard by using the Copy button. Switch back to the "Line Fit" worksheet. Select cell C16. Paste the *values* in the clipboard by using "Paste Special."

Despite the fact that it doesn't fit these data very well, the regression intercept and slope are identical to the regression intercept and slope of the previous data. We can't tell from the regression coefficients alone whether the fit is good or not.

Compare the values in E16 (SSE with regression line) and G16 (SSE with horizontal line). They are clearly much closer in value to each other than were the corresponding SSE's for the original data (which were 67.33504 for the regression SSE and 1027.22 for the horizontal line SSE). When a regression line fits a set of data well, its SSE is much lower than the SSE of a horizontal line through $\bar{y}$. If *no* line fits a data set very well, the regression SSE will be only a little smaller than the horizontal line SSE.

- Compare the value of the horizontal line SSE in cell G16 of the "Line Fit" worksheet with the value we earlier labeled "SST" in cell L16 on the "Regression" worksheet.

SST was calculated by summing the squared differences between $\bar{y}$ and each y. It is equivalent to the SSE derived from a horizontal line through $\bar{y}$ (if $b_1 = 0$ then SSE = SST). You should also recognize it as the numerator of the expression defining the variance of y. SST and SSE may also remind you of the sums of squared differences that constitute the building blocks of ANOVA. As with ANOVA, a simple relationship exists among the various sums of squares, one of which has not yet been introduced.

- Replace the "horizontal SSE" label currently in cell G17 on the "Line Fit" worksheet with the label "SST."

- Change the contents of cell G16 (either by entering a simple formula or using Paste Link) so the value displayed in that cell will always be the calculated value of SST in cell L16 of the "Regression" worksheet. This will not change the currently displayed value of G16, but the value will now change when the data in columns A and B are changed.

SST measures the "Total" sum of squared differences, or variation, in a set of data. After a regression line is fit to the data, SSE measures the variation that the regression line cannot explain ("Error"). If the line fits the data well, SSE will be substantially less than SST, as we just saw. If no line fits the data well, SSE and SST will be close in value. The difference between SSE and SST is termed SSR, the sum of squares due to "Regression." It can be directly calculated as $\sum (\hat{y}_i - \overline{y})^2$ (this is left for an exercise) or from the relationship $SSR = SST - SSE$.

- On the "Line Fit" worksheet, enter the formula in cell F16 (replacing the current contents) to display the value of SSR by subtracting the SSE in cell E16 from the SST in cell G16. The displayed value is 426.24615. Enter the label "SSR" in cell F17.

As we have seen, the greater the difference between SSE and SST, the better the regression line fits the data. Since SSR is the difference between SSE and SST, an equivalent formulation would be to say that the closer SSR is to SST, the better the regression line fits the data. A common measure of goodness of fit is the r^2 (or coefficient of determination) statistic, which calculates SSR as a proportion of SST:

$$r^2 = \frac{SSR}{SST} = \frac{SST - SSE}{SST}$$

An interpretation of r^2 is that it measures the proportion of the total variation in y which is explained by the variation in x. It must have a value between 0 and 1.

- Enter the formula in cell D16 (replacing the current contents) to calculate the value of r^2. The displayed value for this data is 0.0916. Enter the label "r squared" in cell D17.

For the "bad fit" data, slightly over 9% of the variation in the y values is explained by variation in the x values. Let's compare the value of r^2 for these data with that from the original data we used.

- Select the "Data" worksheet. Copy the contents of the original data in D3:E16 to the clipboard. Return to the "Line Fit" worksheet and paste those data in A2:B15.

Notice that the value of r^2 is now over 0.93! For these data, over 93% of the variation in the values of y is explained by the variation in the values of x. Note that normally when the data changes like this, the values of the coefficients in C16 and C17 need to be changed to the regression coefficients. In this case, however, the two sets of data we have examined happen to have the same regression coefficients. Hence, we need not copy new values for the slope and intercept from the "Regression" worksheet.

▼ Goodness of Fit—Inferential Approach

The r^2 statistic is descriptive—it tells us how well the regression line fits the particular sample on which it has been estimated. A different, although related, approach to goodness of fit is the inferential approach that looks at the issue from a different perspective. Recall that regression analysis assumes that the sample data on which a regression line is estimated have been selected from a population. In that population the X and Y variables have a relationship that can be expressed by the formula $Y = \beta_0 + \beta_1 X + \varepsilon$. When a regression line is estimated, the resulting regression equation is $\hat{y} = b_0 + b_1 x$. We can regard b_0 and b_1 as *estimates* of β_0 and β_1, respectively. Just as $\bar{x}$ is an estimate of μ, b_1 is an estimate of β_1. Both $\bar{x}$ and b_1 (and b_0, for that matter) are random numbers (*statistics*) whose values will vary from sample to sample and which will never precisely equal their corresponding fixed parameters (μ, β_1, and β_0).

If there is no relationship in the population between y and x, the value of β_1 is zero. In such a case, the value of b_1, determined by regression from a sample will, in all probability, be nonzero just by chance. The inferential approach treats the issue of goodness of fit in a hypothesis testing or confidence interval framework. Two different sets of calculations can be used in regression to implement the inferential approach. For simple linear regression they always yield identical results, but in multiple regression they have different interpretations and different results.

SSE, as we have seen, is similar to the numerator of a variance formula. If SSE is divided by its degrees of freedom, the result is termed MSE (mean square error), or residual variance, and is represented by the symbol s_ε^2.

$$s_\varepsilon^2 = \text{MSE} = \frac{\text{SSE}}{df}$$

where *df* is degrees of freedom of SSE.

MSE measures the variance of the y values around the regression line in the same way that an ordinary variance is measured around the mean of the *y*'s. It is analogous to a sample variance; the corresponding population variance for which it is an estimate is the variance of the residual values ε in the population equation.

- Select the "Regression" worksheet. Enter the label "MSE" in cell F18. Cell G18 will be used for the formula to calculate and display the value of MSE.

For simple linear regression the value for the degrees of freedom of SSE is $n - 2$, where n is the number of observations used in the regression analysis.

- Enter the formula in cell G18 to calculate and display the value of MSE. The displayed value should be slightly over 5.611.

You may recognize this step as similar to those used in analysis of variance. One of the inferential approaches to goodness of fit is an ANOVA approach. At this point we will consider the other approach.

As noted above, b_1 is a random number. It therefore has a distribution (whose mean is β_1) and a standard deviation. As a statistic, its standard deviation is termed a *standard error* just as the standard deviation of $\bar{x}$ is called a standard error. Once we determine the standard error of b_1, we can construct a confidence interval on β_1 and perform hypothesis tests on β_1. These will provide techniques for investigating whether or not there is a relationship between *y* and *x* in the *population* from which the sample was drawn.

The standard error of b_1 is easily calculated from MSE and SS_x (the sum of squared deviations of *x* from its mean—already calculated in cell I16) by the following formula:

$$s_{b_1} = \sqrt{\frac{\text{MSE}}{\text{SS}_x}}$$

Notice that if the regression line fits the data well, SSE and thus MSE would be small, as would s_{b_1}. A smaller standard error will also occur if there is a high variation in the *x* values.

- Enter the label "standard error b1" in cell A20 (and adjust the column width). In cell B20 enter an Excel formula that will calculate s_{b_1} as shown in the equation above by referring to the cells on this spreadsheet where MSE and SS_x are calculated. The cell should display the value 0.224677.

The statistic b_1 follows the *t* distribution with $n - 2$ degrees of freedom, much as the statistic $\bar{x}$ follows the *t* distribution with $n - 1$ degrees of freedom. We can use this to examine inferential goodness of fit by asking whether this sample provides evidence that the population slope, β_1, differs from 0. This can be done by testing the Null Hypothesis $H_0: \beta_1 = 0$ against the Alternate Hypothesis $H_A: \beta_1 \neq 0$. A sample t (or t statistic) for this hypothesis can be calculated with a formula very similar to that which is used to test a hypothesis test on μ:

$$t = \frac{b_1 - \beta_1}{s_{b_1}}$$

Since the Null Hypothesis is that $\beta_0 = 0$, this expression reduces to the value of b_1 divided by its standard error. The smaller the standard error, the larger the t value.

- Enter the label "t" in cell A21. In cell B21 enter the Excel formula that will calculate the sample t value for the Null Hypothesis given above. The value displayed in B21 should be 13.07915.

The final step in the worksheet is to determine the p value for this sample t. This will involve using the TDIST function. Remember that TDIST requires that the t value you give it must be positive, and we have previously embedded the use of the ABS function to ensure a positive value. When TDIST was used for problems involving inferences on a population mean, the degrees of freedom was always $n - 1$. For this problem it is $n - 2$. Given the Null Hypothesis above, a two-tail test is appropriate.

- Enter the label "p value" in cell A22. Enter a formula in cell B22 that will calculate the two-tail p value associated with the sample t in B21 for $n - 2$ degrees of freedom. The displayed value should be 1.84226E-08 (or 0.0000000184—a very small value).

The small p value tells us that it is highly unlikely that we could have gotten by chance a sample with a regression value for b_1 that differed from zero as much as this one did if the sample were actually chosen from a population in which β_1 was zero. For any of the usual significance levels, we would reject the Null Hypothesis and conclude that $\beta_1 \neq 0$. There *is* evidence (strong evidence) of a relationship in the population between X and Y. Another way of saying this is to say that the regression, or the regression coefficient, is *significant*.

Finding that a regression coefficient is significant is the inferential equivalent of a good fit. The value for s_{b_1} could also be used to develop confidence intervals on the value of β_1. This could be done using almost the identical procedure used for confidence intervals on μ. The confidence interval would be $b_1 \pm t s_{b_1}$, where the t value would have $n - 2$ degrees of freedom and would have a value determined by the level of confidence. A small standard error will result in a narrow confidence interval, and a *significant* coefficient's confidence interval will not include zero.

What kind of result would we get in the case where the regression line does not fit the data well?

- Switch to the "Data" worksheet. Copy the "Bad Fit" data to the clipboard. Switch to the "Line Fit" worksheet and paste the data in the region A2:B15. Switch to the "Regression" worksheet.

Although the regression coefficients are the same in this case, the standard error of b_1 is much higher. This has decreased the value of the sample t and resulted in a p value of a bit more than .29. With such a high p value, we would *fail to reject* the Null Hypothesis that $\beta_1 = 0$. This means we don't have very good evidence that there is a relationship in the population between Y and X. We would characterize the regression coefficient (or the regression) as *insignificant*, because the estimated slope is not significantly different from zero.

▼ Excel's Built-In Regression Capabilities

Excel has a number of features that will allow you to easily do a regression analysis on a set of data. These include an Analysis Tool, several built-in functions (which can be accessed through the Function Wizard), and a feature of the Chart Wizard. Although these capabilities duplicate each other, they have somewhat different advantages and disadvantages.

The Analysis Tool produces an output that is much easier to read than the functions. The functions have the advantage of being dynamic in the sense that they update their displayed value whenever a change in the worksheet affects the input data. The Analysis Tool, by contrast, must be rerun whenever the data change. Nevertheless, the tool is usually preferable for doing regression analysis. For this reason, the functions (INTERCEPT, SLOPE, TREND, FORECAST, and LINEST) will not be discussed in this chapter, although information on them can be found in Appendix D.

- Switch to the "Data" worksheet and copy the "Bad Fit" data (including the labels in row 2) to the clipboard. Switch to the "Sheet5" worksheet and paste the data beginning in cell A1.

- Change the name of the "Sheet5" worksheet to "Bad Fit."

- Using the Chart Wizard, prepare a scatter plot of the data (the same type as on the "Line Fit" worksheet) with the upper left corner in cell C1. Make the chart reasonably wide, but do not let it go below row

15. Check your chart against the one on the "Line Fit" worksheet. Except for the lack of a regression line, they should both clearly be charts of the same data.

- Place the mouse pointer over one of the data points and click once. Most or all of the data points should change color ("light up"), indicating that they have been selected. Open the "Chart" menu on the Menu Bar and select "Add Trendline…" (or, with the mouse pointer on a data point, click the right mouse button and select "Add Trendline….") In either case, the Trendline dialog window will open.

- Select the "Type" folder tab at the top. Click the picture above "Linear," which shows a straight line fitting a set of data points.

- Select the "Options" folder tab. The section labeled "Forecast" enables you to extend the line to left or right of the data points. Click the box beside "Display Equation on Chart" and the box beside "Display R-squared Value on Chart" so that each box has an "x" in it. Click the "OK" button.

As you may see, sometimes Excel does not place the equation and r^2 value in the best place on the graph.

- Place the mouse pointer over the equation and click once. A border will surround the equation and r^2 value. When the mouse pointer is inside the boundary, it has the insertion point shape. Outside the boundary it is a white arrow.

- Place the mouse pointer so that the tip of the arrow is on the border. Press and hold the (left) mouse button and drag the outline containing the equation and r^2 value to the upper left corner of the chart where there are no data points. Click the mouse pointer once off the graph to remove the border.

Excel's presentation of the regression line on a plot is nonstandard in that y is used instead of $\hat{y}$, and b_0 is put after, instead of before, b_1.

Compare the chart on this worksheet with that on the "Line Fit" worksheet. This is certainly an easier way of putting a regression line on a scatter plot! What happens if you change the data?

- Select cell B15 (which now contains 35.24). Enter the value "0" in the cell. Observe what happens to the chart when you press the Enter key. Click the Undo (↰) and Redo (↱) buttons to switch back and forth between the original and new values of B15.

Did the regression line change? Look at the equation and r^2 value written on the chart. Did they change? The answer to both questions should be "Yes."

The fact that changing a single observation caused such a drastic change in the regression line is further evidence of the lack of a good fit with these data. This is a demonstration of the result of the test we performed on the Null Hypothesis that the value of β_1 is 0 and that the nonzero value of b_1 could very well be due to chance.

- Return the value of B15 to 35.24.

▼ Using the Regression Tool for Simple Linear Regression

The regression tool can be used for either simple or multiple regression. Its use is very similar to that of the other analysis tools.

- Open the "Tools" menu and choose "Data Analysis...." From the Data Analysis dialog window, choose "Regression."

- Enter the cell ranges for the x and y data in the appropriate fields. As with other Analysis Tools, it is a good idea to have a label in the first row and to include the address of the label in the cell ranges entered in these fields.

- Click the small box beside "Labels" so that Excel will know the first row contains labels rather than data.

- As part of its output, Excel provides confidence intervals on the population β's. Excel always provides the 95% confidence interval for each β, and, unless you indicate otherwise, provides it twice. Let's instead ask Excel to provide us also with a 90% confidence interval by first clicking the box beside "Confidence Level" so an x appears and then changing the "95" in the field to the right to "90."

- Under "Output Options" select "Output Range." Enter the address "A17" in the field to the right.

There are a number of optional outputs that can be selected from the Regression dialog window. In the section titled "Residuals," you can choose four different optional outputs:

1. **Residuals**—If this is selected, Excel will produce a table showing, for each observation, the value of predicted values ($\hat{y}$), and the value of the *residual* (or error), which is $y - \hat{y}$.

2. **Standardized Residuals**—This choice will cause Excel to produce, in addition to the table of residuals just described, a column showing standardized residuals. Residuals are standardized by dividing them by the error standard deviation (also called the standard error of the estimate), which is calculated as $\sqrt{MSE}$. Choosing to have Excel output standardized residuals always results in the output of predicted values and nonstandardized residuals regardless of whether or not you also select Residuals.

3. **Residual Plots**—Selecting this will cause Excel to produce a scatter plot with the value of each observation's residual (or error) plotted on the vertical axis and the observation's value for the x variable plotted on the horizontal axis. Choosing this also always results in getting the output described in 1 above.

4. **Line Fit Plots**—If this choice is selected, Excel will produce a scatter plot showing both the actual data points and the predicted data points lying on the regression line. For simple (but not multiple) regression, the plot is very similar to the one already drawn on the worksheet by the Chart Wizard, except that the predicted values are shown as points rather than as a line that can, of course, be changed afterwards.

In order to see all of these outputs, check all of the boxes in the "Residuals" section.

The last output choice is for "Normal Probability Plots." A normal probability plot is a chart prepared in such a way that data values are plotted against their quartile values on the standard normal distribution. In such a plot, data that are normally distributed will appear to lie approximately along a line. Excel produces a plot of the y variable, but it is not a properly done normal probability plot. Do not choose it.

- Once these choices have been made, click the "OK" button on the dialog window.

- When the Regression Tool has finished writing the output, the column widths will need to be adjusted. While the cell region containing the output is still selected, open the "Format" menu, choose "Column," and then click "AutoFit Selection."

- Click on any worksheet cell to remove the selection highlighting.

The output of the Regression Tool is so large that you may only be able to see a small part on your screen at one time. To get a better view of your worksheet, use Excel's ability to "zoom."

- Click the downward pointing arrow on the right side of the Zoom Control on the Standard Toolbar 100% ▾ . A list of zoom factors will open. Try 75%. If your screen still cannot display columns A through L, change the zoom factor to 50%.

One of the effects of adjusting the column widths for the regression output is that the chart at the top of the worksheet has been made excessively wide.

- Adjust the width of the chart to a size more appropriate for its height. Select it by clicking it once with the mouse. Edit "handles" will appear at each corner and in the center of each side. Place the mouse pointer on the handle that is in the center of the right side. Press and hold the mouse button and drag the handle to the left until the chart's width is correct. Then release the mouse button.

- Notice that the Regression Tool has placed one of the charts it has produced on top of the other one. Single click the chart on top and move it so that it is to the right of the scatter plot you produced earlier. Move both charts to the left to keep the information on the worksheet in as compact an area as possible.

- Because of the size of the space used on this worksheet, you may find it easier to follow the discussion below from a printout. If you choose to do this, first click a worksheet cell to ensure that a chart is not selected. Next click the Print Preview button ◱ . When the screen previewing the output appears, click the "Setup…" button at the top. In the Page Setup dialog window, first click the "Page" folder tab. Under "Orientation" select "Landscape." Under "Scaling" select "Fit to 1 page(s) wide by 1 tall." Select the "Sheet" folder tab. Under "Print" select "Row and Column Headings." This will permit you to determine cell addresses on the printout. Click "OK." After you return to the Print Preview screen, have Excel print the worksheet.

Let's take a tour of the output. First the charts.

1. **"x Line Fit Plot,"** as mentioned above, is similar to the scatter plot you produced earlier with the Chart Wizard. The "x" in the title refers to the label for the x variable (the label in cell A1). A different label would result in a different title. Notice that the Analysis Tool labels both axes in the chart and provides a title and a legend. One result is that the area actually devoted to the plot is small. This can, of course, be changed by editing the chart. The regression line (called "Predicted y" in the legend) is depicted as points rather than as a line. This, too, could be changed by activating the chart, selecting the data

points, and then formatting the data series exactly as was done with the scatter plot produced by the Chart Wizard.

2. **"x Residual Plot"** shows the residuals (or errors) plotted against the value of the x variable. Like the line fit plot, the residual plot can be useful in finding "outliers," data points that are much further from the regression line than other points. It is often worthwhile to reexamine those data points. Perhaps the large value of their error (residual) might be caused by a data collection or recording error. Or perhaps an overlooked factor is responsible for the large residual. A residual plot can also be used to provide some evidence on the issue of whether the assumption that the population ε has constant variance is correct.

Next are the items under "Summary Output."

3. **Multiple R** is the square root of the r^2. When given the sign of the x coefficient b_1, this value is often termed the coefficient of correlation and is an alternate measure of the strength of the relationship between the x and y variables.

4. **R Square** is, of course, r^2. There is a convention, followed by many statisticians, to use a lowercase r for simple regression and an uppercase R for multiple regression. Check to be sure the value here agrees with the values you determined on the "Line Fit" worksheet for the same data.

5. **Adjusted R Square** is meaningful only in a multiple regression context where, as a measure of fit, it takes the number of independent variables into account. The unadjusted R^2 always increases when a new independent variable is added, even if there is no real relationship between it and the dependent variable. Adjusted R^2 is useful only to compare models with the same dependent variable; it has no meaning by itself.

6. **Standard Error** is the square root of MSE. It also is called the standard error of the regression or the standard error of the estimate and is a measure of goodness of fit, which is also used in calculating other statistics associated with regression. As mentioned above, it is used in calculating standardized residuals.

7. **Observations** is, of course, the number of observations in the data used for estimating the regression equation.

The next section is the analysis of variance section. The table is organized exactly like the ANOVA tables seen in Chapter 13. The first column (df) gives degrees of freedom, the second column (SS) gives sum of squared deviations. The third column (MS—for Mean Square) divides the sum of squared deviations by the degrees of freedom. The fourth column has the F statistic and the last column (labeled "Significance F") gives the p value for that F statistic.

The row labeled "Regression" is calculated from differences between predicted y values for each observation and the mean of the y values $(\hat{y} - \bar{y})$. The entry under the SS column is SSR. Compare this with the value you found on the "Line Fit" worksheet to be sure they are the same.

The row labeled "Residual" would, perhaps, better be labeled "Error." It is the differences between predicted y values and actual y values for each observation $(y - \hat{y})$. The value under SS is SSE, and the value under MS is MSE. Check these against the values on the "Regression" worksheet.

The row labeled "Total" is calculated from the differences between each y value and the mean of the y values $(y - \bar{y})$. The number under SS is SST. Check it against the values on the "Regression" worksheet.

The next section provides inferences about the population coefficients $(\beta_0$ and $\beta_1)$. The first row is for β_0 (labeled intercept), and the second row is for β_1 (whose label comes from the label used in the data—"x" in this case). For most purposes for which regression is used, β_1 is of greater interest than β_0 and therefore the inferences on β_1 are more important than those on β_0.

The first column gives the values for the regression coefficients, b_0 and b_1. Verify these values with the ones on the "Regression" worksheet. The second column gives the standard errors for the coefficients. You have calculated the standard error of b_1 on the "Regression" worksheet; check that this worksheet shows the same value. The Regression Tool also calculates and shows the standard error for b_0. The third column gives the value of sample t's for the Null Hypotheses $H_0: \beta_0 = 0$ (in the first row) and $H_0: \beta_1 = 0$ (in the second row). The fourth column gives the p values (two-tail) for the respective sample t's. Compare the t and p values on the second row with those showing on the "Regression" worksheet. The remaining four columns give 95% and 90% confidence intervals for the values of β_0 and β_1.

The last part of the output provides, for each observation, the predicted y value $(\hat{y})$, the residual $(y - \hat{y})$, and the standardized residual. The actual y values are not given in the table, but it would be a simple matter to copy them to an adjacent column.

It is clear from the regression output that there is little evidence of a relationship between x and y for these data. The most compelling evidence of this is the lack of significance of b_1 as shown by its high p value. We noted this previously on the "Regression" worksheet. The output of the Regression Tool includes some additional calculations.

- Compare the p value for the F statistic in the ANOVA table (cell F28) with the p value for the t statistic for β_1 (cell E34). Enter a formula in cell E29 that will display the square of the t value in cell D34. Compare this with the F value in E28.

For simple linear regression, the regression analysis of variance always provides information identical to that provided by the test on the hypothesis $H_0: \beta_1 = 0$. Either can be used as an inferential test of the existence of a relationship in the population between the x and y variables. The confidence intervals on β_1 include zero (as well as both positive and negative values), another way of presenting the lack of significance in this regression. The tests on β_0 also indicate that it is not significantly different from 0, although a test on β_0 does not give us information about the relationship between the two variables.

▼ Exercises

1. Select the "Regression" worksheet. Add two columns to calculate SSR. The first column would determine, for each observation, $\hat{y} - \overline{y}$. The second column would square each of those values. The cell just below this second column would sum all of the values. Confirm that you get the same answer here as you have on the "Line Fit" worksheet. Add to the "Regression" worksheet a calculation of r^2, using the value of SSR calculated here, and verify that it is the same as that on the "Line Fit" worksheet.

2. Rename the "Sheet6" worksheet "Good Fit." Copy the "Original" data from the "Data" worksheet to this sheet, but rename the x variable "output" and the y variable "cost." Use the Regression Tool to do a regression analysis of these data. Also prepare a scatter plot of these data. On the same worksheet, use the regression coefficients produced by the tool to give an estimate of the cost associated with these levels of output (in thousands): 3.8, 5.7, 6.3. Print the worksheet showing the output of the Regression Tool, the scatter plot, the original data, and the predicted costs for the three output. Be sure your name is printed in the page header.

3. The "State Revenue" worksheet in simpreg.xls contains 1992 data on median household income and per capita state government revenue. Produce a scatter plot with a superimposed regression line. Use regression analysis to examine the effect of household income on

state government revenue. Is there a significant (.01 level of significance) relationship between these two? Based on the regression, by how much, on average, does per capita state revenue change for each $1 increase in median household income? Are any of the states "outliers"? If so, can you explain why? Remove that state and reestimate the regression. Does this change your answer to the question of how much, on average, per capita revenue changes for each $1 increase in median household income? If so, what is the new answer? Print the worksheet showing the scatter plot and both regressions. Put your name in the page header. (Data is from U.S. Bureau of the Census, *Statistical Abstract of the United States: 1994* (114th edition.) Washington, DC, 1994, pp. 395, 468.)

4. Is there a relationship between a state's median household income and its violent crime rate (incidents of murder, rape, robbery, and assault per 100,000 population)? The "Crime" worksheet provides 1992 data on state median household income and violent crime rate. Produce a scatter plot of these data with a regression line. Use the Regression Tool to analyze the relationship. What proportion of the variation in state crime rates is explained by variation in household income? Is the relationship significant (at the .10 level of significance)? Explain. Print the worksheet showing the scatter plot and regression. Put your name in the page header. (Data is from U.S. Bureau of the Census, *Statistical Abstract of the United States: 1994* (114th edition.) Washington, DC, 1994, pp. 199, 468.)

5. Is there a relationship between a state's household income and its death rate (deaths by all causes per 1,000 population)? The "Death Rate" worksheet in simpreg.xls provides 1992 data by state for median household income and death rates. Produce a scatter plot with regression line and regression analysis of these data. Does higher income lead to higher or lower death rates? Is the relationship significant at the .05 level of significance? What proportion of the variation of death rates is explainable by variation in household income? Print the worksheet showing the scatter plot and regression output. Put your name in the header.

Chapter 15

Multiple Regression

Multiple regression analysis is a straightforward extension of simple regression analysis which allows more than one independent variable. This extension, however, makes multiple regression analysis an incredibly versatile tool that can be used in an enormous variety of statistical problems. A reasonably complete treatment of multiple regression would require a book at least as long as this one already is. This chapter will deal with some of the issues and techniques that frequently arise with multiple regression analysis. Multiple regression analysis provides the analyst with such a variety of techniques that the primary problem is to decide exactly what form the regression equation (or regression *model*) will take, including which independent variables will be used. This typically comes after investigating different possibilities, a process known as *model building*.

Although the basic principles are straightforward, their application to any actual set of data often requires a judgment that comes with experience. There is a skill, almost an art, to regression analysis. One of the reasons for this is that for a given set of data, different objectives will likely lead to different regression equations. Regression analysis is often used for prediction, for example, and an equation developed for predictive purposes may well be different from an analytical model developed to better understand the relationship among the variables in a set of data.

For some types of analysis where multiple regression is used, Excel is probably not the best software. Although Excel provides the basic regression output, many specialized statistical packages also provide additional output. Excel, for example, does not provide an easy method to determine confidence intervals on predicted values, it lacks some of the diagnostic statistics useful for evaluating the analysis of time series data, and it does not easily permit certain types of hypothesis tests on population coefficients. On the other hand, Excel's matrix handling capability does make it possible to construct these tests and even to create macros for them. No attempt will be made here, however, to cover these more advanced topics in this chapter.

▼ Multiple Independent Variables

Let's consider a simple case involving two independent variables. From this we will be able to see how to interpret the output of a regression involving any number of independent variables.

A music CD chain is trying to determine the effectiveness of television and radio advertising. It has collected data from stores in the chain on monthly record sales and on monthly advertising expenditures for both television and radio advertising. Based on these data, is there evidence of a relationship between expenditures on each type of advertising and sales? Which form of advertising appears to be more cost-effective?

Probably the chain would want to include other information, including market size, market type, average family income, and average age in a model explaining record sales. We're keeping it simple here.

- Open the Excel workbook in multireg.xls and switch to the "CDs" worksheet.

- Summon the dialog window for the Regression Tool by first opening the "Tools" menu on the Menu Bar and then selecting "Data Analysis...."

The dependent (or *y*) variable is in the column labeled "Sales," which gives monthly sales in thousands of dollars. The two independent variables have the labels "Radio" and "TV," which give monthly advertising expenditures on those two media.

- In the "Input Y Range" field enter the range address A1:A21, which has the level of sales with the label.

- In the "Input X Range" field enter the range address B1:C21. Notice that this range includes two columns containing both of the independent variables. It is a restriction of the Regression Tool that independent variables have to be in adjacent columns.

- Click the square indicating that the address ranges include labels. Direct the tool to construct 90% confidence intervals on the population coefficients. Choose "Output Range" and have the output written beginning in cell D1.

- Click "OK." Once the output is written, and while the cell range containing it is still selected, adjust the column widths by opening the "Format" menu (on the Menu Bar), selecting "Column" then "AutoFit Selection."

You may find it easier to follow the discussion below if you print the output. If you do print the page, first choose "Print Preview" on the "File" menu and click the "Setup" button on the preview page. Click the "Page" folder tab, choose "Landscape" orientation and "Fit to 1 page." Click the "Sheet" folder tab and select "Row and Column Headings." You will then be able to find cell addresses on your printout. Select "Header/Footer" and put your name and any other useful information in the header before you print.

For this regression, since there are two independent variables, the regression equation can be written as

$$\hat{y} = b_0 + b_1 x_1 + b_2 x_2$$

In the regression output on your worksheet, b_0 is labeled "Intercept," b_1 is labeled "Radio," and b_2 is labeled "TV."

The estimated coefficient for b_1 is 15.7151. This indicates that each additional \$1 spent on radio advertising is expected to increase sales by just under \$15.72, assuming all other factors (such as TV advertising) are unchanged. This measure is often called a *partial effect*, because it measures the impact of a change in just one of the independent variables. The partial effect is frequently referred to as the change in the dependent variable that would result from a one-unit change in one of the independent variables. It could more precisely be defined as a rate of change, but this would have the same meaning in this context. The estimated coefficient (or partial effect) for b_2 is 12.7583, indicating that an additional dollar spent on TV advertising will increase sales by just over \$12.75 (holding radio advertising constant). Based on these estimates, radio advertising looks like a better deal, but there is more to this issue, so don't regard this conclusion as final.

The value for R^2 (cell E5) of a bit over 0.36 indicates that variation in radio and TV advertising account for just over 36% of the variation in sales. Nearly 64% of the variation in sales is accounted for by factors other than radio and TV advertising.

Excel makes it easy to determine the significance of a coefficient or of the overall regression by providing p values. An important step in determining p values is the determination of the statistic's degrees of freedom. Consider an estimated coefficient and the t statistic calculated from that coefficient. It is desirable for the degrees of freedom to be as large as possible. A value for a t statistic can be significantly different from zero if the degrees of freedom is large, and insignificant if the degrees of freedom is small. The degrees of freedom for an estimated coefficient's t statistic in multiple regression is $n - (k + 1)$, where n is the number of observations in the data and k is the number of independent variables. In practice the number of independent variables must be considerably fewer than the number of observations. For data with few observations, that can be a serious constraint. It is *especially* important when using regression for prediction that there not be too many independent variables.

The regression F statistic (cell H12) has a p value of approximately .021. This p value is for the the hypothesis test that *all* population coefficients of the independent variables are zero:

$$H_0: \beta_1 = 0 \ and \ \beta_2 = 0$$
$$H_A: either \ \beta_1 \neq 0 \ or \ \beta_2 \neq 0 \ or \ both$$

If the Null Hypothesis were true, it would indicate that there is no relationship between *any* of the independent variables and the dependent variable. The p value tells us that if the Null Hypothesis were true, the probability we could draw a sample whose estimated coefficients (b_0 and b_1) differed from zero by at least as much as the values in the regression output is about .02. This low probability provides good evidence for rejecting the Null Hypothesis and concluding that at least one of the population coefficients must be nonzero.

For simple linear regression, the p value for the F statistic always equaled the p value for the estimated coefficient of b_1's t statistic. The t statistics permit a test of whether an individual population coefficient is zero, while the F statistic can be used to test whether *all* population coefficients are zero. In simple regression these have the same meaning. In multiple regression they do not. The p value for the t statistic for spending on radio (b_1) is approximately .013 (cell H18). This is the probability that a sample with a value of b_1 as different from zero as this sample's value (approximately 15.715) could be drawn from a population where there was no relationship between spending on radio ads and sales of CDs. This p value applies to the test $H_0: \beta_1 = 0$ and $H_A: \beta_1 \neq 0$. We would reject the Null Hypothesis at a .05 level of significance but not at a .01 level of significance. This p value is low enough to conclude that there is good evidence of a relationship between monthly expenditures on radio advertising and sales of CDs.

The p value for spending on TV advertising is considerably higher, almost .18. Although the size of the estimated coefficient is nearly the same as that for spending on radio advertising, this high p value means we can have much less confidence about the value of the population coefficient on TV spending. If there were no relationship in the population between spending on TV advertising and sales, the probability of a sample having an estimated coefficient as different from zero as this one (12.758) is the p value (.18). At the 10% significance level we would fail to reject the Null Hypothesis that β_2 is zero. A common convention would label the coefficient on TV spending *not significant*, which is short for *not significantly different from zero*.

look at coefficients and p-values

The fact that the estimated coefficient for spending on radio advertising is larger and more significant than the estimated coefficient for spending on TV advertising points to the conclusion that the music store chain should shift advertising expenditures from TV to radio. Look, however, at the two sets of confidence intervals on the population coefficients for TV and radio advertising expenditures. Notice that the upper bound of the confidence interval on TV spending is higher than the upper bound of the confidence interval of radio spending. This is true for both the 95% confidence interval (cells J18 and J19, which show the upper bound for radio to be 27.63 vs 31.99 for TV) and the 90% confidence interval (cells L18 and L19). The fact that the estimated coefficient for TV advertising is not statistically significant does not mean that spending of TV advertising has been shown to be unimportant. As is the case in all hypothesis tests, failure to reject a Null Hypothesis of no relationship between TV advertising spending and sales is not equivalent to concluding that the Null Hypothesis is correct! You just can't rule it out.

One aspect of model building is the decision of which independent variables to include. As a general rule, variables that are statistically significant in a regression should be included. This does not mean, however, that variables that are not statistically significant should necessarily be excluded. A variable that *should* have a relationship with the dependent variable, in most cases, ought to be included in the regression even if its estimated coefficient is not statistically significant. In other words, the decision of what independent variables to include in a regression is never purely mechanical, particularly if the objective of regression analysis is truly analytical. It doesn't make sense that radio advertising would have a strong effect on sales while TV advertising has no effect at all. Although its significance is low, the TV advertising variable should be retained.

Sometimes the objective of regression analysis is purely predictive. In this case the question of whether or not to keep a particular independent variable can be somewhat more mechanical. The adjusted R^2 (located in cell E6) is helpful in this case. The ordinary R^2 (cell E5) discussed in the chapter on simple linear regression always increases when a new independent variable is added whether or not that variable improves the model's predictive power. The adjusted R^2 will increase only if the presence of the new independent variable improves the model's predictive power. Would elimination of the TV advertising variable improve the regression's predictive power? As a rule of thumb, if the t statistic associated with an independent variable has an absolute value less than 1.0, dropping that variable will increase adjusted R^2. In this regression the t statistic for TV advertising is just under 1.40. Eliminating this independent variable would reduce the adjusted R^2. For predictive purposes, TV advertising should be kept in the model. Although the estimated coefficient is *not* very significant, it is significant enough to contribute to the model's predictive power.

▼ Nonlinear Relationships

Sometimes a relationship exists among two or more variables that cannot be represented as a straight line. In such a case a linear regression can give results that are absolutely misleading. In a case where data on more than one independent variable have been collected, nonlinearities can be present with some, but not all, of the data. For this example we will consider a case where there is only a single independent variable. This simplification will enable us to examine the relationship graphically.

A manufacturer of a precision bearings assembly produced at a number of different identical plants wants to determine the relationship between monthly output and short-run average cost. A sample of 50 monthly reports giving output and short-run average cost from several plants was collected. Based on these data, is there a relationship between level of output and average cost? (The data for this problem can be found in multireg.xls on the "Bearings" worksheet.)

An obvious first step would be to use simple linear regression.

- Select the "Bearings" worksheet. Use the Regression Analysis Tool to perform a regression analysis using monthly "Output" as the x variable and average "Cost" as the y variable. If the dialog window opens with the fields already containing values, they are left over from the last regression and must be changed. Have Excel place the output beginning in cell D1.

- In the "Residuals" section of the dialog window, select "Residual Plots."

- Click "OK." Use the Format–Column–AutoFit Selection menu sequence to adjust the column widths for the regression output. If you have done the regression correctly, the value for r^2 (in cell E5) will be 5.19084E-06. The number of observations (in cell E8) will be 50.

- Change the value in the "Zoom Control" on the Standard Toolbar to 50%. Locate the residual plot (which Excel will place to the right of the regression output), and move it so that it is below the portion of the output giving the estimated coefficients and their statistics, and to the right of the residual output. Click a cell right below the chart and change the "Zoom Control" back to 100%.

- Excel tends to make residual plots too short. Make the plot taller by selecting it (so that there are "handles" in each corner and in the middle of each side). If you accidentally "activate" it (so that is surrounded by the activation boundary), click the mouse pointer on a location on the worksheet away from the chart. Place the mouse pointer on the handle in the center of the bottom side. The pointer will change to this shape: ↕. Press and hold the (left) button and drag the handle down until the shape of the chart is more like a square.

It may be useful to print the worksheet. If you choose to do this, first unselect the chart by clicking the mouse pointer on a spot on the worksheet off the chart. This worksheet will print best if you first select "Print Preview" from the File Menu. Click the "Setup" button at the top of the preview screen. Select the "Page" folder tab. Select "Portrait" orientation and scale to fit one page. Click the "Sheet" folder tab and select "Row and Column Headings" in the "Print" section. Click "OK" then "Print."

It appears from this output that there is no evidence of a relationship between output and average cost. The R^2 is extremely low. Also, the slope (estimated coefficient for "Output" in E18) is -8.81558E-05, a number which is very close to zero. Even more telling, the p value for the coefficient (H18) is over .98, suggesting that this result is very consistent with a population coefficient of zero—no relationship. This conclusion would, however, be *wrong*.

Economic theory tells us that the relationship between output and short-run average cost should be U-shaped, not linear. Starting with a very low level of output, average cost should decline as the production machinery and other fixed capital become more fully used. If output continues to increase, average cost would again increase since, in the short-run, the machinery cannot be increased and would become overloaded. A U shape is a curve, not a straight line. If this is the case, it is possible that no straight line can do a good job of approximating even a very strong relationship.

▼ Curved Relationships and Residuals Plots

If the relationship between a particular independent variable and the dependent variable were in the form of a simple curve, this would create a

U-shaped (or inverted U-shaped) pattern in the residuals. Consider the charts below.

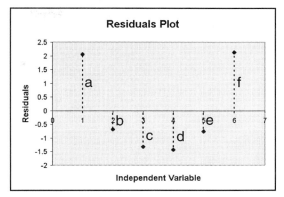

The left chart shows a scatter plot of data with only a single independent variable. The simple linear regression line is superimposed, and vertical lines are drawn between each point and the regression line. Notice that the relationship between the independent and dependent variable in that chart would be better represented by a curve than by a straight line.

The right chart shows the residuals plot for the same data. Each data point is identified by a letter with the same point in the two charts identified by the same letter. The length of the dotted line between each point and the horizontal axis measures the value of that point's residual.

Consider point *a* in the left chart. It lies above the regression line. The length of the dotted line between it and the regression line is the "error" or residual associated with that value. That length represents the same value as the length of the dotted line on the right between point *a* and the horizontal axis. Points *b*, *c*, *d*, and *e* all lie below the regression line in the chart on the left. Their residuals are negative. Exactly the same pattern is seen on the chart on the right. The point of this is that the curved relationship evident in the chart on the left is also (even more) evident in the residuals chart on the right.

If the curved relationship is apparent in the scatter plot, you may wonder why we bother to also consider a residuals plot. A residuals plot has a fundamental and important advantage when there is more than one independent variable—the usual situation in multiple regression. It is not really possible to do a meaningful scatter plot in this case. Although a scatter plot of the dependent variable against a single independent variable could be done, it would not be useful because it does not account for the values of the other independent variables. If the predicted values from a multiple regression equation were plotted on such a chart, they would not even appear to lie on a straight line. Residuals plots avoid many of these problems and are an often effective means of detecting a curvilinear (or nonlinear) relationship between the dependent variable and one of the independent variables. When Excel is asked to provide residuals plots, it produces one plot for each independent variable in the model.

Let's consider the residuals plot for the precision bearings average cost problem. That plot should be present on your Excel output. Click the mouse pointer once on the chart and use the "handles" to make the chart bigger and taller. Your chart should look like the one below.

This chart does not show as clear a curved relationship as did the previous chart. Look at it carefully. The data points in the center of the chart are more likely to lie below than above the horizontal axis, while those to the left and right appear more likely to lie above the axis. This is enough of an indication to warrant exploring a curved relationship between output and short-run average cost.

▼ Polynomial Regression

One common technique for estimating a curved regression is with a quadratic regression, which is an example of a polynomial regression. If there is a single independent variable, a quadratic equation would have the following form:

$$\hat{y} = b_0 + b_1 x_1 + b_2 x_1^2$$

This equation is quadratic because it has a squared term. Excel treats it as a separate variable. It's just another x_2 to Excel; the Regression Tool doesn't know where it came from. What changes is your *interpretation* of the results.

Although there is only one independent variable, a quadratic equation can have other independent variables as well as either linear terms (not squared), quadratic terms (squared), or both. The bearings problem only has a single independent variable (output), so we will estimate the equation shown on the previous page.

▼ Estimating a Quadratic Regression

The basic method for estimating a quadratic equation will be to create a new column of data in which the values in each cell are the square of the values in the "Output" column. A regression will then be run in which these data will be treated like a separate independent variable.

- Switch to the "Bearings (2)" worksheet. This worksheet is identical to the original "Bearings" worksheet.

- Select any cell in column B.

- Open the "Insert" menu on the Menu Bar and select "Columns." A new column B will open between the two columns of data. The "Cost" data will move to column C. Column B will be used to put the new output squared independent variable. It has to be beside the "Output" column because Excel requires independent variables to be adjacent.

- Enter the label "Output Sq" in cell B1.

- Enter formulas in the cells in column B so that each cell will display the value that is the square of the value in the same row of column A. You will have to adjust the width of column B to see these values. Cell B2 should display 2122849, cell B3 should display 2452356, cell B4 should display 881721, etc.

- Open the Regression Tool's dialog window. The entries for the input fields will have to be changed if they have the previous problem's values. Enter the address range of the "Cost" data in the field for the *y* variable and the address range for the columns with both the "Output" and "Output Sq" data for the *x* variable. Include the cells containing the labels, indicate in the dialog window that labels are included, direct the output to cell D1, and ask for residuals plots.

- Click "OK." When the tool has finished writing the output, use the Format—Column—AutoFit Selection menu sequence to adjust the column widths containing the output.

- Use the Zoom Control to change the Zoom factor to 50%. Locate the residuals plots. Since this regression has two independent variables, Excel produces two plots. Notice that Excel stacks them so that it is impossible to see the one on the bottom without moving the one on top.

- Select the top residuals plot and move it directly below the plot below it. Click on the worksheet just below and to the right of the bottom plot, change the Zoom factor back to 100%, and compare the two residuals plots.

One of the residuals plots shows the residuals values plotted against output. The other shows the same residuals values plotted against output squared. Compare them carefully. Although the two plots are not identical, the pattern of residuals is the same. The plots are not exactly identical because the horizontal scaling is slightly different for the squared term, but you can recognize the common pattern. Since the two plots provide the same information, there is no reason to keep them both.

- Switch the zoom factor back to 50%. Delete the residuals plot for "Output Sq" by selecting it and then pressing the Delete key. Move the residuals plot for "Output" below the regression output (the same place used for the regression on the first "Bearings" worksheet). Increase the height of the residuals plot as you did with the previous worksheet.

You may again decide to print this worksheet to better follow the discussion below. Use the same procedure described for the previous regression given on page 368. Adjust the width of column B if needed to see the data values.

While the simple linear regression showed no evidence of a relationship between *output* and average cost, the quadratic regression provides strong evidence of such a relationship. The r^2 (in cell E5) has increased to a value slightly over .20. The F test has a p value (cell I12) of .0052, versus .98 for the simple linear regression. This is sufficient to reject the Null Hypothesis of no relationship between the independent and dependent variables at all typical levels of significance.

Perhaps most striking in the quadratic regression is the significance of both *output* and *output squared*. The p values for the t tests of the significance of each variable are approximately .0015 and .0013 (cells H18 and H19), respectively. In the simple linear regression where output was the only independent variable, the estimated coefficient was insignificant. As well as having a significant coefficient itself, *output squared* causes the coefficient of *output* to become significant as well.

The estimated coefficients are in cells E18 and E19, and give the following regression equation:

$$\hat{y} = 90.24 - 0.0863x + 0.0000305x^2$$

The coefficient on *output squared* may appear to be very close to zero, but this must be evaluated in relation to the size of the numbers it is likely to be multiplied by. Look at the values of *output squared* in column B. In many cases, these numbers are in the millions. When such large numbers are multiplied by the coefficient shown above, the product will have a value between 10 and 100, a range that is reasonably large, given the *y* values.

▼ Partial Effects in Polynomial Regressions

When each independent variable in a multiple regression equation is included only as a linear term, the coefficient for that variable is also a measure of its partial effect. For polynomial regressions, the measure of the partial effect is not as simple. In estimating the regression considered here, Excel treats *output* and *output squared* as if they were separate independent variables. In determining partial effects, however, they cannot be regarded as separate. There is no way of changing *output* without also changing *output squared*. The estimated partial effect must be determined by taking the derivative of the dependent variable with respect to the independent variable. For a quadratic regression of the form $\hat{y} = b_0 + b_1x + b_2x^2$, the partial effect is not b_1 but $b_1 + 2b_2x$. For this regression discussed here, the partial effect of output on average cost is $-.0863 + .0000611x$. The effect of a change in output on average cost *depends on what the total level of output is*. For small levels of output, increases in output will decrease average cost because the negative term will dominate. As output gets larger, this negative effect will diminish. Eventually the partial effect's term with the *x* will dominate and increases in output will increase average cost. The partial effect of output on cost measures marginal cost. According to economic theory, marginal cost initially declines, reaches a minimum, and then increases. This is exactly the kind of behavior implied by the estimated regression equation.

▼ When Should Polynomial Regression Be Used?

Determining the set of independent variables for a particular dependent variable is much easier than knowing whether the relationship is likely to be linear or curved. As a general rule, it is best to keep a regression model as simple as possible. In some cases, such as the example given here of the relationship between output and average cost, there is good reason to expect a curved relationship and even to have some idea of the general shape of the curve. Other techniques exist within multiple regression analysis for estimating more complex curved relationships. One technique, for example, is to use higher-order polynomials. This could be done by including a cubed term, or perhaps a term raised to the fourth power among the independent variables. This should be avoided in most cases. Although it is appropriate to examine the residuals from a linear regression for evidence of a curved relationship, it is best to avoid higher-order polynomials (and other techniques) unless you have good theoretical reasons to expect the relationship to have some specific shape that can only be represented by a polynomial of order greater than two.

▼ Dummy Variables and Categorical Data

The data used in the regressions we have looked at so far have been continuous. Such measures as output and household income can take on different values, and we expect changes in the values of these variables to have a consistent effect on the value of the dependent variable. Categorical data are different. These data place observations into a particular category, and there may be no obvious ranking to these categories. A fast food chain, for example, may wish to develop a model predicting sales at individual restaurants. One of the important factors affecting sales may be differences in behavior among people living in different regions and different countries. The country or the region where a fast-food restaurant is located may have a big effect on its sales. A variable giving this information is categorical—very different from the continuous variables we have considered so far with regression.

We have considered categorical data in connection with another statistical technique—analysis of variance. We looked at the effect of keyboard design on typing speed (page 326), for example, and the effects of package design and advertising strategy on perfume sales (page 329). Keyboard design, package design, and advertising strategy are all examples of categorical variables, and analysis of variance is designed exclusively to analyze the effect such variables have on a continuous measure (such as typing speed or perfume sales). The dummy variable technique enables multiple regression analysis also to handle categorical independent variables. With this technique, multiple regression analysis can handle any problem that could be analyzed with ANOVA (and will provide the same results). Unlike ANOVA, multiple regression analysis can handle problems involving a mixture of categorical and continuous variables.

A dummy variable is one that has only two possible values—0 or 1. When a dummy variable is used to indicate a single characteristic, observations that possess the characteristics will have the dummy variable made equal to "1," while observations without the characteristic will have it equal to "0." Let's consider the following example:

A university is interested in comparing the performance in the first business statistics class of students who use computers to learn business statistics with those who do not use computers. Data were collected from a sample of statistics students who took courses that either used or did not use computers. Average course grade and GPA were also collected. Is there evidence that using computers increased average course grades, controlling for GPA?

To determine whether there is evidence that students using computers receive higher grades, we would test H_0: $\mu_{computer} \le \mu_{no\ computer}$ vs. H_A: $\mu_{computer} > \mu_{no\ computer}$, holding constant the effect of GPA. This is a one-tail test.

- Select the "Computers" worksheet.

The data in this worksheet will be used to estimate a regression model in which a student's average statistics course grade is analyzed as a function of GPA and of whether or not the student used computers to learn statistics. GPA is included because it is expected to have a major impact on the statistics grade, and it may be related to whether or not the student took a course which used computers. Although the column labeled "Use Computers?" has the information for a dummy variable, it cannot be used as is because it does not have just the values 0 and 1. We will need to create a dummy variable from the values in this column. For any observation with the answer "Yes," the dummy variable will have the value "1." When the answer is "No, " the dummy variable will equal "0." Note that the yes/no information is logically exactly the same as 1/0.

The Regression Tool requires that all the independent variables be adjacent. We will thus first move the current data on computer use out of column C and create a dummy variable in that column.

- Select region C2:C21 and move the data from column C to column D so that each value stays in the same row. Column C will be used to create the dummy variable, which must be adjacent to the other independent variables.

- Enter the label "Computer Dummy" in cell C1.

- Select cell C2. Since the observation represented by this row is of a student who did use computers, we want this cell to contain the value "1." Use the Function Wizard button to select the IF function (in the "Logical" category). In the "logical_test" field, enter an expression that will be true if the value of cell D2 equals "Yes" (you must include the double quotes). You should see the word "TRUE" in the region to the right of the "logical_test" field where Excel shows the parameter's value.

- When the expression is true, have C2 equal "1," and when it is false have C2 equal "0" (without the quotes). After you click the "Finish" button, cell C2 should display the value "1."

- Copy the contents of cell C2 to cells C3 through cell C21. Check that those adjacent to a "No" in column D (like cell C6) display "0" while those adjacent to a "Yes" display "1."

You now have a completed dummy variable in column C. When running a regression, the data in column C (and *not* column D) will be used as an independent variable.

- Using the Regression Analysis Tool, regress Course Average in column A (*y* variable) against GPA and Computer Dummy in columns B and C (*x* variables). Be sure not to include column D. Have Excel place the output on the same worksheet beginning in cell E2. Residual plots will not be needed.

The estimated coefficients and significance statistics are shown below.

	E	F	G	H	I
17		Coefficients	Standard Error	t Stat	P-value
18	Intercept	35.98582354	3.33531463	10.789334	5.0277E-09
19	GPA	14.34949132	1.097573966	13.0738262	2.683E-10
20	Computer Dummy	5.86737271	2.031507889	2.88818603	0.01021505

These coefficients provide the following estimated equation:

$$\hat{y} = 35.99 + 14.35x_1 + 5.87x_2$$

where x_1 is GPA and x_2 is the "use computers" dummy variable.

The coefficients suggest that a one-point increase in GPA results in an average increase in the course grade of 14.35, holding constant computer use. Observations on those who use computers will have the value "1" for x_2, while those who do not will have the value "0." Those with the value "1" are going to have a predicted grade ($\hat{y}$), which is 5.87 higher than those with the value "0" *and the same GPA*. This coefficient (5.87) is a measure of the value of using computers *controlling for the independent effect of GPA*.

Had we simply regressed average grade against the computer dummy without including GPA, we might also have found that those students using computers scored higher grades. In that case, however, *we would not have been sure that this wasn't because better students (with higher GPAs) were more likely to take courses that used computers than were weaker students*. If this were the case, the apparent higher grades of those using computers might not have been because of the computer use. It might have been simply that better students (who would have gotten higher grades anyway) happened to be the ones using computers. By including GPA as an independent variable, we have specifically eliminated this possible interpretation. Our results indicate that *regardless of GPA*, students using computers did better than those who did not, a result which is inconsistent with the Null Hypothesis.

This result is equivalent to saying that there is one equation relating GPA and average statistics grade for those who use computers and another equation for those who do not. This situation is shown on the graph at the top of the next page. The dashed line shows the estimated relationship between GPA and average statistics grade for those using computers, while the lower solid line shows the estimated relationship for those not using computers. The vertical distance between the two lines is the estimated value of using computers, the coefficient on the dummy variable, 5.87.

In this equation only one coefficient for GPA is estimated; it applies to both those who do and those who do not use computers. Thus the two lines are parallel, and their common slope is the estimated coefficient on GPA, 14.35. The dummy variable has an effect like a change in the constant term (y intercept or b_0). For those not using computers, the constant term is the constant term from the printout, approximately 35.99, but for those using computers it is that *plus* the coefficient on the dummy variable, or approximately 41.85.

Is the difference statistically significant? The Null Hypothesis we are testing is H_0: $\mu_{computer} \leq \mu_{no\ computer}$. When using dummy variables, think of the equivalent H_0: $(\mu_{computer} - \mu_{no\ computer}) \leq 0$. The estimated coefficient on the dummy variable is an estimate of a β that measures the difference between the average grades of those using and not using computers: in

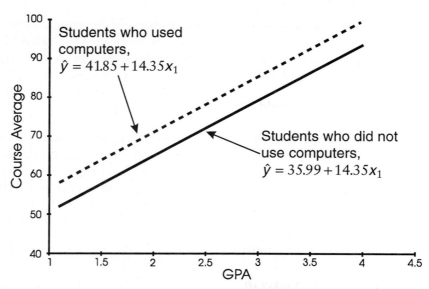

other words $\mu_{computer} - \mu_{no\ computer}$. So the Null Hypothesis could also be written as $H_0: \beta_{computer\ dummy} \le 0$. The estimated coefficient is 5.87, clearly not consistent with H_0. The reported p value is .0102. This, however, is a two-tail p value. To convert it to a one-tail p value, it must be divided by two, giving .0051. This low p value is highly significant, leading us to reject the Null Hypothesis and conclude that there is evidence that those using computers received higher average grades, controlling for the effect of GPA.

▼ Multilevel Categorical Data

Categorical data often have only two levels or values, such as the measure in the example above of whether or not a student used a computer. Any variable giving the answer to a yes/no question has two values. A single dummy variable will, in these cases, enable us to estimate the effects of the categorical variable. Much categorical data, however, have more than two levels or values. Location is one common such variable. An observation in a data set might include a variable indicating the state in which a respondent is located. If observations come from more than two states, the location variable can have more than two values and is referred to as *multilevel*.

A multilevel categorical variable is represented in multiple regression analysis by a *set* of dummy variables. Each dummy variable measures the presence or absence of a *single value* of the multilevel categorical variable. The total number of dummy variables equals the number of different values (or levels) of the categorical variable *minus one*. If, for example, a location variable could have nine different values (referring, for example, to nine different states), there would be *eight* dummy variables, each of which would have the value of one or zero for each of eight different locations. If an observation came from the ninth location, for which there is no dummy variable, the value of all eight dummy variables would be zero. When creating a set of dummy variables for a multilevel categorical variable, one of the values will not have a dummy variable; that value is said to be *omitted*. The reason for this, as well as the issue of which value to omit, will be considered in the example below.

As with most American municipalities, the primary revenue for the town of Elder Hollow comes from the property tax. To administer the tax, the value of each piece of property is estimated by a tax assessor. The town's Board of Equalization has the task of ensuring that all taxpayers are treated equally. A complaint from several residents of the Chester Court development asserts that residences in that neighborhood are assessed at a higher level than houses of the same value in the town's other neighborhoods, Armsley Hills and Blawndale. A higher assessment would cause tax bills in Chester Court to be higher than those of identically valued houses in other neighborhoods. In order to test the assertion, you have selected a random sample of residential properties from each neighborhood that have recently sold. The sales price and the assessed value, together with the property's neighborhood, have been collected. Based on these data, is there evidence that properties in Chester Court are overassessed compared to properties in the other two neighborhoods?

The Null Hypotheses for this problem would be $H_0: \mu_C \leq \mu_B$ and $H_0: \mu_C \leq \mu_A$, while the Alternate Hypotheses would be $H_A: \mu_C > \mu_B$ and $H_A: \mu_C > \mu_A$. These require one-tail tests, which means that we will have to modify the two-tail test provided by Excel.

Ideally, each property's tax assessment would exactly equal the sales price, but this ideal can never be achieved in practice. Equity is achieved if there is no consistent difference among neighborhoods of the relationship between sales price and assessed value.

- Select the "Assessment" worksheet. The data for this problem are located there. We will estimate a regression with assessed value as the dependent variable and sales price and neighborhood dummies as independent variables.

There are three values for the "neighborhood" variable. Two dummy variables must be created. Since we are interested in a comparison between Chester Court and the other neighborhoods, Chester Court will be the omitted value. One dummy variable will therefore indicate if an observation is in Armsley Hills and the other will indicate if it is in Blawndale.

- Select the neighborhood data in column C and move it to column E, keeping each value in the same row. The now-empty columns C and D will be used for the dummy variables.

- Enter the label "A Dummy" in cell C1. The Armsley Hills dummy will be placed in column C.

- Select cell C2. Use the Function Wizard to enter values for the arguments of the IF function to test whether the contents of cell E2 equals "Armsley Hills." If it does, have the IF function set the value of C2 to 1. If it does not, have the IF function set the value of C2 to 0. C2 should display the value 1. If C2 displays the #NAME? error, you may have forgotten to put quotation marks around "Armsley Hills" in the IF function's "logical_test" argument field.

- Enter the label "B Dummy" in cell D1. Select cell D2 and use the IF function to set the value of D2 to 1 if E2 equals "Blawndale" and 0 otherwise.

- Copy the formulas in cells C1 and D1 down the column of cells to row 31. Carefully check the values of the two dummy variables. Rows 2 through 10 should have "1" in column C and "0" in column D. Rows 11 through 20 should have "0" in column C and "1" in column D. Rows 21 through 31 should have "0" in both column C and column D.

The next step is to use the Regression Tool on these data. Note that the set of dependent variables will include the dummy variables in columns C and D, but not the original neighborhood information in column E.

- Open the Regression Tool dialog window by selecting "Regression" from the "Analysis Tools."

- Enter the cell region address for "Assessed Value" (including label) in the field for the Y range and the cell region address for "Sales Price" and the two dummy variables (including labels) in the field for X range.

- Click the box to indicate to Excel that your data regions include labels and indicate that you want the output to start in cell F2. Residual plots are not needed. Click "OK."

- Once the regression output is complete, adjust the column widths of the region containing the output. Be sure to save the worksheet. Compare your output with the one shown at the top of the next page to be sure you have done this correctly.

We will refer to this regression as "Model 1" in the following discussion.

Model 1 indicates that, in any neighborhood, for each $1 increase in the market (sales) price, the average assessed value increases by slightly more

	F	G	H	I	J	K
2	SUMMARY OUTPUT					
3						
4	*Regression Statistics*					
5	Multiple R	0.99130939				
6	R Square	0.9826943				
7	Adjusted R Square	0.98069749				
8	Standard Error	3180.03693				
9	Observations	30				
10						
11	ANOVA					
12		*df*	*SS*	*MS*	*F*	*Significance F*
13	Regression	3	14930247205	4976749068	492.131787	5.18302E-23
14	Residual	26	262928506.7	10112634.9		
15	Total	29	15193175711			
16						
17		*Coefficients*	*Standard Error*	*t Stat*	*P-value*	*Lower 95%*
18	Intercept	-2133.13776	4324.756946	-0.49323876	0.62598436	-11022.8088
19	Sales Price	0.94447434	0.034134647	27.669082	8.1515E-21	0.874309522
20	A Dummy	2279.49229	2026.167539	1.12502656	0.2708567	-1885.35746
21	B Dummy	-1305.06578	1431.303948	-0.91180198	0.37025011	-4247.155104

than 94¢. The estimated coefficient is highly significant. The p value is slightly more than 8.15×10^{-21}, an extremely small value. The entire regression is highly significant, as indicated by the p value for the F test (5.18×10^{-23}). The R^2 is over 0.98.

The coefficients of primary interest in this problem are those on the dummy variables. Each coefficient represents a shift in the value of the constant (or y intercept) for observations in that dummy variables group *compared to the omitted group.* For example, the coefficient for the B Dummy is about -1305. This indicates that observations for which the value of the B Dummy is 1 (residences in Blawndale) have an assessed value about $1,305 less than otherwise identical observations in the omitted group (Chester Court). If we were to calculate, for example, the predicted assessed value for a residence in Chester County that sold for $100,000, the value of both the A Dummy and the B Dummy would be 0. The predicted assessed value would therefore be

$$\hat{y} = -2,133 + (0.9445 \times 100,000) = \$92,317$$

Since a $100,000 residence in Blawndale would have the value "1" for the B Dummy, its estimated value would be

$$\hat{y} = -2,133 + (0.9445 \times 100,000) + (1 \times (-1,305))$$
$$= 92,317 - 1,305 = \$91,012$$

This result appears consistent with the complaint of the residents in Chester Court. The lower assessed value for residences in Blawndale would result in lower average taxes on identically valued houses. The estimated coefficient, however, is not significant since its p value is over .185. (The p value shown on the output is slightly over .37, but this is a two-tail p value and must be divided by two to be converted to a one-tail p value.) Although this sample indicates that residences in Chester Court are overassessed compared to those in Blawndale, this result might well be due to chance. Thus, despite the estimated coefficient, this regression *does not* support the contention of the residents of Chester Court.

The contention of Chester Court residents that their houses are overvalued is also contradicted by the positive coefficient on the A Dummy. This dummy indicates that residences in Armsley Hills are assessed even more than identically valued residences in Chester Court, by an average of about $2,279. This estimated coefficient, however, is also not significant since its p value is about .135 (one tail). The final conclusion is that this regression does not provide good evidence that Chester Court residences are assessed any differently from residences in the other neighborhoods. This, of course, does not mean that we have evidence that residences in all neighborhoods are assessed identically. A stronger conclusion *might* result from a regression on a larger sample.

The regression provides (weak) evidence that residences in Blawndale have lower assessments while residences in Armsley Hills have higher assessments than identical houses in Chester Court. Suppose we wanted a direct comparison between Armsley Hills and Blawndale? Such a comparison would most easily be made by creating and including a dummy variable ("C Dummy") for Chester Court and omitting either the A Dummy or the B Dummy. Let's consider a regression with the A Dummy omitted and refer to it as "Model 2." It turns out that a simple pattern exists between the estimated coefficients of Model 1 and Model 2, or any pair of regressions estimated on the same data that differ only in which dummy variable in the set is omitted. All independent variables other than the set of dummy variables (only Sales Price in this case) are the same. The intercept of Model 2 will be the sum of the intercept of Model 1 and the coefficient in Model 1 of the omitted dummy variable in Model 2. The estimated coefficients for the dummy variables in Model 2 will be their Model 1 value minus the estimated coefficient in Model 1 of the dummy variable omitted in Model 2. This pattern for the regressions discussed here is summarized in the table at the top of the next page.

Although the values of the coefficients for Model 2 are easy to determine from Model 1, their significance is not as easily determined. For this reason, if we want to test whether or not there is evidence that residences in Armsley Hills are assessed more than identically valued residences in

Coefficient	Model 1	Model 2
Intercept	–2,133	–2,133 + 2,279 = 146
Sales Price	0.9445	0.9445 (unchanged)
A Dummy	2,279	2,279 – 2,279 = 0
B Dummy	–1,305	–1,305 – 2,279 = –3,584
C Dummy	0 (omitted)	0 – 2,279 = –2,279

Blawndale, the Model 2 regression should be estimated. This is left as an exercise.

▼ Multicollinearity

Although we refer to the explanatory variables in multiple regression analysis as *independent,* it is very rare for them to be independent of each other in the statistical sense. In other words, independent variables tend to be correlated with each other. One of the reasons for this correlation is that two or more independent variables may contain similar information.

Consider the following problem:

A lawn service company is interested in predicting the average annual amount households in a neighborhood will spend on lawn and garden care. A sample of neighborhoods is chosen, and the average amount spent is collected, along with average lot size, average household income, and average value of home. Use multiple regression to estimate the determinants of average neighborhood expenditures on lawn and garden care.

• Select the "Lawn Care" worksheet in the workbook in multireg.xls.

The primary problem with these data is that household income and home value may be highly correlated. Those with valuable homes tend to have high incomes, and vice-versa. Both variables are measures of economic well-being, which most directly affects the willingness to spend money for lawn and garden care. We would expect, however, the two factors to have positive, but somewhat different, effects. Multiple regression, however, may have difficulty distinguishing between those effects. This is the problem of multicollinearity.

• Use the Regression Analysis Tool on the Lawn Care data. Lawn Care Expenditure in column A should be the y variable, and the three variables in columns B, C, and D should be x variables. Use labels. Have Excel place the output beginning in cell E2. Residual plots are not needed. When the Regression Tool has finished, adjust the column widths where the output was placed. The estimated coefficients and measures of significance are shown below.

	E	F	G	H	I
17		Coefficients	Standard Error	t Stat	P-value
18	Intercept	-9.73670975	18.10704706	-0.53773041	0.593355346
19	Lot Size	21.21401018	3.076925279	6.894548374	1.31177E-08
20	Avg HH Income	0.000680953	0.001286404	0.529346471	0.599110592
21	Avg Home Value	-0.00018334	0.00060725	-0.30191837	0.76407513

Although lot size has the expected highly significant positive relationship with lawn care expenditures, the results for the other two independent variables are puzzling. The *p* values of approximately .60 and .76 indicate that neither variable is significantly different from zero. Average house value has a negative estimated coefficient, suggesting that as house values go up, lawn care expenditures go down. This certainly runs counter to intuition. The problem here is multicollinearity arising from the strong relationship between average household income and average house value.

When two independent variables are highly correlated, including both variables in the regression will raise the problem of multicollinearity. In multiple regression analysis, measures of the significance of a single independent variable (including the variable's standard error, *t* statistic, and associated *p* value) should be thought of as measures evaluating that variable's contribution to a model containing all other independent variables. Suppose that we have a model estimating the demand for lawn and garden service in which home value is included as an independent variable. How much *additional* explanatory power will be added by also including family income? Not much, since home value already has the information about economic well-being. As a result, the estimated coefficient on family income will be insignificant. What about the coefficient on home value? In a model that already contains family income, the additional explanatory power of home value will be small. It, too, will be insignificant. Although economic well-being is unquestionably an important determinant of the demand for lawn and garden service, including two highly correlated measures may well result in both of them being insignificant! What if one of them is removed?

- Recall the Regression Tool. Change the *x* variables to include only lot size and average household income. Put the output in the range beginning with cell E23.

The coefficients should now be as shown in the picture at the top of the next page.

	E	F	G	H	I
38		Coefficients	Standard Error	t Stat	P-value
39	Intercept	-14.1358829	10.64538406	-1.32788848	0.190628119
40	Lot Size	21.18292929	3.045324741	6.9558852	9.53499E-09
41	Avg HH Income	0.000293061	6.43727E-05	4.552558973	3.75003E-05

Although the estimated coefficient for average household income has declined from about 0.0007 to about 0.0003, the coefficient is now highly significant, with a p value of 3.75×10^{-5}.

Let's try excluding household income and including average home value.

- Swap columns C and D. One way of doing this is to first select column C by clicking the column heading. Then select "Columns" from the "Insert" menu on the Menu Bar (or click the right mouse button while the pointer is on the column and select "Insert" from the pop-up menu). This will open a new column C and shift the worksheet contents of the previous C and above one column to the right. Move the contents of column E (Average Home Value) to the empty column C. Delete the now empty column E by clicking on the column heading and then selecting "Delete" from the "Edit" menu on the Menu Bar (or from the pop-up menu, which appears when you click the right mouse button).

- Use the Regression Tool to run a new regression. The fields in the tool's dialog window will be the same as for the previous regression (x variables in columns B and C) except for "Output Range," which should be set to cell E43.

The estimated coefficients and their significance measures for this model are shown in the picture below.

	E	F	G	H	I
58		Coefficients	Standard Error	t Stat	P-value
59	Intercept	-17.2155571	11.23778421	-1.53193519	0.132242437
60	Lot Size	21.15324399	3.051147558	6.932881347	1.03329E-08
61	Avg Home Value	0.000137695	3.04495E-05	4.522072066	4.14586E-05

Rather than being negative and insignificant as in the first regression, the estimated coefficient for average home value is positive and highly significant.

The multicollinearity between average household income and average home value caused both variables to have insignificant estimated coefficients when both were included as independent variables. Yet when either variable was included as an independent variable without the other, it was highly significant. There is clearly a relationship between economic well-being and expenditures on lawn and garden care (which both variables measure), but it is impossible to get a good estimate on the unique effect of each variable.

One question that multicollinear data poses is exactly which variables should be included in the set of independent variables. Of the three models presented here, which is correct? There is, unfortunately, no clear answer. If the object of the regression analysis is simply prediction, then the model with the highest value for the adjusted R^2 is probably the best. If the object is to understand the relationship among the variables, then the model with both independent variables may be best. The coefficients of variables that suffer from multicollinearity are unbiased, although they have large standard errors.

There are techniques that can be used to verify multicollinearity, but they are beyond the scope of this book. Excel has a Correlation Analysis Tool that could be helpful in finding pairs of potential independent variables that are highly correlated. One method sometimes used involves regressing independent variables on each other. As a general rule, multicollinearity should be suspected whenever including or excluding an independent variable has large effects on the significance of the estimated coefficients of one or more other variables. In the example given here, the collinear relationship existed among only two variables. It is possible, however, for a multicollinear relationship to involve more than two variables. Detecting the exact nature of the multicollinearity can be difficult in that case.

Even when severe multicollinearity is not a problem, real independent variables are never statistically independent. There always is some degree of correlation. We call it "multicollinearity" only when the problem is severe, but it always affects regression analysis. Much of the challenge of determining exactly which set of independent variables to use in regression analysis occurs because the decision to include or exclude one variable very frequently changes the sign and significance of other variables. We will encounter this problem again when we look at model building.

▼ Heteroscedasticity and Autocorrelation

One of the assumptions of ordinary least squares regression is that the population error terms are random, independent, and have constant variance. If the assumption of constant variance of the error term is violated, the data are said be heteroscedastic (or heteroskedastic). If the assumption of independence is violated, the data are said to be autocorrelated. Sometimes these problems can be handled by adding additional variables to a model or by altering the functional form of the estimated relationship. These problems can also be dealt with by using the technique called generalized least squares, a technique beyond the scope of this book, which uses information from the residuals to estimate the relationship between the independent and dependent variables.

The most common type of heteroscedasticity arises when the variance of the error term increases (or decreases) as the value of an independent variable increases. The most common type of autocorrelation occurs when the error term has a pattern associated with the observation over time.

Heteroscedasticity occurs most often with cross-sectional data, which are data collected from different observation units at the same point in time. It is likely to occur, for example, if the observations are very different in size. This might be the case if our unit of observation were the firm, and the data mixes small businesses with giant corporations. Heteroscedasticity can also occur in time series data (data collected from the same unit of observation at different points in time). Heteroscedasticity with such data is sometimes seen as an increase or decrease in the error term over time.

Heteroscedasticity can be detected by examining the estimated residuals $(y - \hat{y})$ to see if their variance seems to vary with the value of an independent variable, the observation number, or some other measure. Although there are formal tests that can be performed on the estimated residuals, they are not calculated by Excel's Regression Analysis Tool. Hetereoscedasticity can often, however, be detected by examining residual plots, which the Regression Tool can prepare.

Consider the following problem.

It has long been known that there is an important relationship between economic development and energy consumption. To investigate this relationship, international data on per capita energy consumption (in kilograms of coal equivalent) and per capita gross national product (in dollars) were collected for 1990 (Data is from U.S. Bureau of the Census, Statistical Abstract of the United States: 1994, *CD-ROM version, Washington, DC, 1994, tables 1366 and 1393). Use these data to estimate the effect of per capita GNP on per capita energy consumption.*

- Switch to the "Energy" worksheet. Call up the Regression Tool dialog window.

- In the "Y Range" field, enter the range address of the per capita energy consumption in column B, and in the "X Range" field enter the range address of the per capita GNP in column C. Have the output placed in the range beginning with cell D2.

- In the section of the dialog window labeled "Residuals," select "Residual Plots" by clicking it so that an "x" appears in the small box to the left of the words. This will cause Excel to produce a chart showing the value of residuals plotted against each of the independent variables. Since there is only one independent variable in this case, there will be only one plot.

- Click the "OK" button. Adjust the column widths.

The chart showing a plot of residuals against the independent variable (Per Capita GNP) will be located on the worksheet to the right of the regression output.

- Click the residuals plot once so that sizing "handles" appear in the four corners and the middle of each side.

- Use the sizing handles to make the chart larger.

The chart should look similar to the one below.

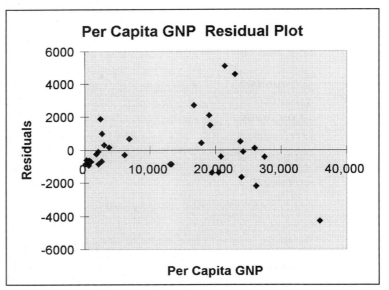

Heteroscedasticity is indicated by the change in the *vertical spread* in the residual values associated with different values of per capita GNP. For those observations with low values of per capita GNP (less than about $5,000), the points are relatively close together. As per capita GNP increases to about $25,000, the points become more separated. Although heteroscedasticity is fairly evident in this residuals plot, it is easy to mistakenly find heteroscedasticity when there are big variations in the number of observations associated with different values of an independent variable. Spread in the residuals would not be apparent for some value of an independent variable if there were few observations in the sample close to that value. In this case, by contrast, there are roughly the same number of observations with low per capita GNP as with high per capita GNP (up to a bit over $25,000). The relative lack of spread for the residuals for observations with low per capita GNP is *not* an artifact of few observations with low per capita GNP.

If you noticed that these residuals also suggest a nonlinearity, good for you! Note how the residuals at both the low and high ends of the horizontal axis tend to fall below the axis, while most of the residuals in the middle are above the axis. This model should include a squared term for per capita GNP. Would that correct the heteroscedasticity? This issue is left as an exercise.

Autocorrelation is similar to heteroscedasticity in that it is caused by a pattern in the residuals. In the case of autocorrelation, the pattern is not in the spread of the residuals but in their lack of randomness, their tendency to form a pattern. The most typical autocorrelation occurs in time series data and is caused by the fact that the effect of a change in an independent variable (which may or may not be included in the model) on a dependent variable can occur over several time periods. Consider the following problem:

The number of oil wells drilled in the United States is known to be affected by the price of oil. Higher prices should lead to more wells drilled. An oil industry trade group wants to determine that relationship more precisely. Data on the number of wells drilled in the United States each year since 1930 were collected, along with the average price of a barrel (bbl) of oil that year. Based on these data, what is the relationship? (These data are from Twentieth Century Petroleum Statistics, *Dallas Texas: Degolyer and McNaughton, 1992, pp. 34, 98.)*

The data are on the "Oil" worksheet in the workbook in multireg.xls. In determining a response to price, it is usually necessary to correct a price series to account for inflation. That worksheet also contains the value of the Producer Price Index based on 1982 prices. This index will be used to adjust the price data for inflation.

- Switch to the "Oil" worksheet. Insert a blank column in front of the current column C by first selecting a cell in column C and then either selecting "Column" from the "Insert" menu on the Menu Bar or pressing the right mouse button and selecting "Insert" from the pop-up menu. The new column C will be used for the inflation-adjusted price of oil.

- Enter the label "Real Price per bbl" in cell C1.

- Enter a formula in cell C2 that will take the nominal (in 1930 dollars) price of oil in cell D2, multiply it by 100, and divide it by the price index in cell E2. Use relative addresses. The value displayed in cell C2 should be a little over 7.9865.

- Copy the formula in C2 to cells C3:C63. The value displayed in cell C63 should be slightly less than 14.1631.

- Use the Regression Tool to estimate a regression equation in which Total Wells Drilled is the y variable and Real Price per bbl is the x variable. Use labels. Request residuals plots. Have the output placed in the region beginning in cell F2.

- After the Regression Tool has completed, adjust the column widths of the region containing the output to fit the cell contents.

The regression output appears to confirm the relationship between price and number of wells drilled. The coefficient on the real price of oil is positive and has a p value of 2.55×10^{-15}, an indication of very high significance. Analysis of the residuals, however, will reveal a problem.

- Scroll your worksheet so that H25 is in the upper left corner of your screen. That cell should contain the label "*Residuals*" and is the last column of a table giving predicted y values and residuals for each observation in the data.

- Select the entire column of residuals (H25:H87). Click the Chart Wizard button.

- Choose a scatter plot in which only the points are plotted with no connection lines. Your plot should be similar to the one at the top of the next page.

These residuals show a clear up-and-down wavelike pattern. Positive residuals tend to be adjacent to positive residuals. There is a strong indication of autocorrelation. It may be possible to correct for this by respecifying the model to include additional independent variables. These might include "lagged" values from earlier time periods. A technique other than ordinary least squares regression may also be needed.

▼ Model Building

The process of model building involves a search for the best way to specify a relationship between a dependent variable and a set of independent variables. A dependent variable is first regressed against an initial set of independent variables based upon a theoretical expectation of the relationship. The results of that regression are used to modify the set of independent variables or even the dependent variable. A second regres-

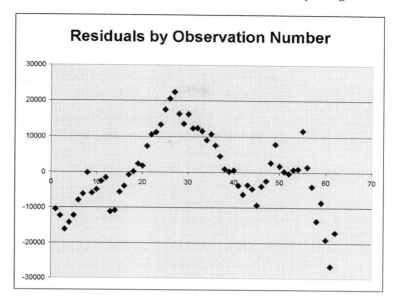

Residuals by Observation Number

sion is estimated, and the results of that regression are used to make further modifications. Since each change in the set of independent variables may change the estimated coefficients and significances of the other independent variables, only a few modifications should be made after each regression. This iterative process continues until the analyst is satisfied that the regression best captures the relationship among the variables. Each step may involve creating new variables, as we did in the oil drilling example to create a measure of the price of oil adjusted for inflation. Dummy variables may have to be created and decisions made about which levels to omit. Squared values of independent variables may be added to correct for nonlinearities. Independent variables may have to be checked for multicollinearity and a decision made of whether to include only some or all such variables. Variables that do not contribute to the model in a logical or statistical sense need to be omitted.

Different analysts approaching the same set of data are not likely to end up with identical regression models. If there are strong relationships among the variables, they should be apparent in differently constructed models. Becoming proficient with multiple regression analysis takes practice. It is not possible to provide a set of step-by-step rules that will inevitably lead to the "best" regression models. Nevertheless, here are some tentative considerations that a beginner might find useful in the process of model building.

1. Start with the strongest possible regression equation by thinking in advance what types of relationships you expect to find. Is the set of independent variables reasonably complete? If not, can you fill the gaps by gathering additional data? Try to determine in advance what

signs you expect for the estimated coefficients. Unexpected signs are "sign-posts" for areas that need further investigation. Try to determine which variables you expect might have multicollinearity. Don't, however, infer multicollinearity whenever the results look a little "funny" unless you have solid evidence of multicollinearity.

2. Keep in mind that the number of independent variables you can have is constrained by the number of observations. If you have only a few observations, you may not be able to have as many independent variables as you might want. This can be a particular problem if you want to use categorical variables with multiple values since this may require the construction of many dummy variables, only a few of which can be included.

3. Have Excel produce residuals plots. Examine the residuals plots for nonlinearities and heteroscedasticity. For time series data, look for autocorrelation by constructing a plot of the table of residuals Excel produces by observation number. Add squared values of independent variables where nonlinearities are expected.

4. Test for multicollinearity by dropping individual variables and observing whether this increases the significance of other variables that you suspect might be measuring the same or similar factors. Then put the omitted variable back in the regression and drop one of the other variables you suspect of being in a multicollinear relationship. If you confirm multicollinearity, decide exactly which variables to keep. Remember that this decision depends partly on the objectives of the regression analysis.

5. Follow a multiple-step approach. Try to deal with only one problem in each step. Expect to estimate several regressions before you come up with a final model.

▼ A Comprehensive Example

The following problem, although still simpler than most real-world regression problems, will illustrate the step-by-step approach to model building.

A bank wants to determine the factors affecting withdrawals from automatic teller machines (ATMs) located in residential neighborhoods. A sample of daily withdrawals from such machines has been collected, together with information thought to affect total withdrawals. This information includes the median value of homes in the neighborhood, the median family income in the neighborhood, the average checking balance of customers living in the neighborhood, the distance to the next nearest ATM, and whether or not the withdrawals occurred on a weekend. Use these data to determine the factors affecting daily withdrawals from this class of ATMs.

What signs would you expect the coefficients for these independent variables to have on total daily withdrawals? Income, home value, and checking account balance should have positive coefficients but may have problems with multicollinearity. Distance to the next ATM should also have a positive sign since the further the distance, the more likely customers are to use the one in their neighborhood. Weekend days might be expected to have higher withdrawals because more recreational spending and more shopping occurs on weekends, and bank offices are closed so customers cannot cash checks there.

- Switch to the "ATM" worksheet in the workbook in multireg.xls. Notice that the data on whether or not withdrawals occurred on a weekend is not in the form of a dummy variable that can be used in regression analysis.

- Construct a dummy variable whose value is "1" for weekend withdrawals and "0" for withdrawals on other days.

- Estimate a regression in which total withdrawals is the y variable, and median home value, median income, average checking balance, distance to next ATM, and the weekend dummy are the x variables. Direct the output to a new worksheet with the name "Run 1." Have Excel produce residual plots.

The estimated coefficients from this regression are shown below. Notice that distance to next ATM has a negative sign, contrary to what is expected. The other coefficients have the correct sign, but median income and median home value are not significant. Possible multicollinearity?

- Examine the residuals plots. You will note that Excel stacks them on

	A	B	C	D	E
16		Coefficients	Standard Error	t Stat	P-value
17	Intercept	69.5270148	10.11810532	6.87154488	1.764E-08
18	Median Home Value	0.0040221	0.100237489	0.04012567	0.96817446
19	Median Income	0.10454382	0.096207905	1.08664482	0.28311107
20	Average Checking Balance	0.04815931	0.006801364	7.08083043	8.704E-09
21	Distance to Next ATM	-12.0761525	1.400071802	-8.62538087	5.1959E-11
22	Weekend Dummy	35.1633275	4.631482775	7.59223971	1.5643E-09

top of each other. They will have to be separated. This may be most easily done by first zooming to 50%. Once the plots are separated, make each a bit taller. Do any show signs of nonlinearities or heteroscedasticity? Pay particular attention to the plot of residuals on distance. This clearly shows evidence of a nonlinearity. None of the plots show evidence of heteroscedasticity.

- Return to the ATM worksheet. Create a new variable that equals distance squared. Run a new regression with all the independent variables previously used plus distance squared. Put the output on a new worksheet titled "Run 2." The estimated coefficients are shown below.

	A	B	C	D	E
16		Coefficients	Standard Error	t Stat	P-value
17	Intercept	34.92043427	10.28778334	3.394359419	0.001488765
18	Median Home Value	0.018993715	0.078872682	0.240814879	0.810843134
19	Median Income	0.17476765	0.076802314	2.275551884	0.02791444
20	Average Checking Balance	0.046812573	0.005354302	8.742983604	4.31707E-11
21	Distance to Next ATM	7.362837349	3.825243965	1.92480203	0.060886353
22	Distance Squared	-2.49249045	0.469723674	-5.30629088	3.69169E-06
23	Weekend Dummy	32.39924027	3.679050953	8.806412492	3.52793E-11

Notice that the coefficient on distance is positive while that on distance squared is negative. If the next closest ATM is very close and is moved away, initially withdrawals from this ATM will go up. If the nearest ATM is very far away, withdrawals go down. This result seems surprising. Perhaps a very distant ATM means that the residents of the neighborhood are less likely to be ATM users at all. The coefficient of distance squared is highly significant; the coefficient of distance has a p value of .06. It would thus be judged significant at the .10 level of significance but not at a level of significance of .05 or below. The theoretical basis for keeping it in the model is strong, however.

The signs of the coefficients on income, home value, and checking account balance are still positive. The coefficient on income, however, has become significant. The reasons for this are not clear.

- Examine the residual plots. You should see no evidence of heteroscedasticity or additional nonlinearities.

- Return to the ATM worksheet. Move the column of data for median income from column C to a location to the right of the other independent variables. This will allow you to estimate a regression without this variable and be able to replace it in a future regression. Estimate a new regression with all variables used in the previous model except median income. Have the output placed on a new worksheet titled "Run 3." There should be five independent variables (including the intercept). The estimated coefficients are at the top of the next page.

The primary reason for dropping median income was to see if there were multicollinearity with median home value. If there were multicollinearity, the significance of the estimated coefficient for median home value should be higher. Is it? The p value for that coefficient on this regression

	A	B	C	D	E
16		Coefficients	Standard Error	t Stat	P-value
17	Intercept	36.7402938	10.73258284	3.4232481	0.00134886
18	Median Home Value	0.01380361	0.082498035	0.16732053	0.8678845
19	Average Checking Balance	0.05307057	0.004807246	11.0397042	2.8981E-14
20	Distance to Next ATM	7.05192016	4.000189594	1.76289648	0.08486258
21	Distance Squared	-2.30830796	0.484167834	-4.7675781	2.0692E-05
22	Weekend Dummy	34.8764492	3.677374393	9.48406266	3.3351E-12

is about .87. This suggests that the low level of significance for median home value is *not* the result of multicollinearity with median income. Instead, median home value seems not to be a factor determining ATM withdrawals.

- Return to the ATM worksheet. Replace the median income variable and remove the median home value variable. Estimate a new regression with the same set of independent variables as the previous regression except use median income and don't use median home value. Place the output on a worksheet titled "Run 4." The coefficients and significance statistics for this analysis are shown below.

	A	B	C	D	E
16		Coefficients	Standard Error	t Stat	P-value
17	Intercept	36.2108506	8.687539719	4.16813641	0.00014152
18	Median Income	0.17423281	0.075943952	2.29422898	0.0266079
19	Average Checking Balance	0.04775548	0.003612767	13.218532	6.3411E-17
20	Distance to Next ATM	7.3671604	3.784032896	1.94690707	0.05794687
21	Distance Squared	-2.48844397	0.464370838	-5.35874299	2.9249E-06
22	Weekend Dummy	32.1871907	3.533675725	9.10869962	1.0963E-11

An examination of the residuals plots reveals no evidence of nonlinearities or of heteroscedasticity. No irrelevant variables are in the set of independent variables. This, then, is the final model.

▼ Exercises

1. Refer to the problem on page 379. Is there evidence (at the 0.05 level of significance) that homes in Armsley Hills are assessed at a significantly higher rate than homes in Blawndale that sell for the same price? Use the "Assessment (2)" worksheet, which is a copy of the one used earlier. Verify that the coefficients in your analysis agree with those in the table on page 381. Print your regression with the title "Assessment - Model 2" and your name at the top of the page.

2. In the problem on page 387, we found evidence both of nonlinearity and heteroscedasticity between per capital GNP and per capita energy consumption. Correct the model to account for the nonlinear-

ity. Use the "Energy (2)" worksheet. Does this correction eliminate the heteroscedasticity? Print out the basis for your conclusion and explain your reasoning.

3. An electric utility is interested in determining whether or not it can develop a model that would be useful in predicting the electricity consumption of a residential user during the month of November. A sample of houses was selected. For each house, total electricity usage (in KWH) was measured. In addition, the size of the house (in square feet), whether or not the house meets the utility's requirement for energy efficiency, the family income of the residents, and the type of heating fuel used was also collected. The data are available in the "Electricity" worksheet. Use these data to develop a model that can be used to predict electricity usage for November.

4. As part of the staff of an electronics industry consortium, you have been asked to investigate the issues surrounding the manufacturing costs of integrated circuits. You have chosen a commonly used memory circuit that is currently manufactured at a large number of "foundries," as chip manufacturing plants like to style themselves. One issue of concern is whether foundries in the Pacific Rim countries have a cost advantage over those in this country.

Use the data in the "IC's" worksheet to investigate this issue. These data include the following:

a) The average manufacturing cost of a lot of 1,000 chips.

b) The foundry's daily output in millions of chips.

c) The location of the foundry (PAC=Pacific Rim, SA=South America).

d) The thickness of the silicon "wafer" used by the foundry for manufacturing the chip (millimeters).

e) Whether or not the firm is vertically integrated; that is, does the firm also make products that use the chip? For example, a firm that manufactured computers as well as manufacturing the memory chip would be vertically integrated.

f) The amount of silicon used per chip (micrograms).

Appendix A

Obtaining the Data Diskette

In order to make full use of this book, you must have and use the data diskette that can be easily obtained from the Internet. The first step is to download the program file *LrnBStat.EXE*. Execute this program once it has been downloaded, and it will write all of the data diskette files to your blank diskette (or other location).

To obtain the file from the Prentice Hall web site:

- Point your web browser to www.prenhall.com/neufeld. You will find links to *Learning Business Statistics with Microsoft Excel 97* (this book) and *Learning Business Statistics with Microsoft Excel* (the previous edition).

- Click on the link for this book (Excel 97). Scroll to the bottom of the next page and click "Software Download." You will see a list of files. The file *readme.txt* contains a brief description of the other files.

- Click on *LrnBStat.EXE*. Your web browser may ask you if and where you want to save the file. Save it to the C:\Windows\Desktop folder. Close or minimize your web browser and all other applications so you can see your desktop. The icon for the downloaded file will appear on your desktop.

- Place a blank diskette in your machine's A drive and double click the icon for *LrnBStat.EXE* on your desktop. A dialog window will open. Click the "Unzip" button, and all files will be written to your diskette (unless you specify another location). Once this has been done, click the "Close" button.

You can also obtain the diskette from the author's web site (www.uncg.edu/bus_stat). That web site will also contain an updated errata list. It is strongly recommended that you obtain that list.

Appendix B

Setting Up the Analysis Tools

Excel regards the Analysis Tools as *add-ins* and does not make them accessible until you take certain steps. If "Analysis Tools…" is not one of the choices on the "Tools" menu on the Menu Bar, there are two possible explanations:

1. The Analysis Tools have been installed but have not been added to the Tools menu. (This is the most likely case.)

2. The Analysis Tools have not been installed. After installation, they will have to be added to the Tools menu in a separate step.

A standard installation of Excel will usually install the Analysis Tools onto the machine's hard disk, but will not add them to the Tools menu. It makes sense to start by assuming they have been installed and try adding them to the Tools menu. It will soon be apparent if they have not been installed.

Adding the Analysis Tools to the Tools Menu

Open the Tools menu. Click "Add-Ins" as shown in the picture to the left.

A dialog window will open (shown on the next page). This window shows all of Excel's installed add-ins. Those with check marks beside them will appear in Excel's menus. Two add-ins are needed to use all of Excel's statistical capabilities, "Analysis ToolPak" and "Analysis ToolPak - VBA." They will be the first two choices at the top of the list. Click the box beside these choices, and check marks will appear in the boxes. Click the "OK" button. The next time you open the "Tools" menu, "Data Analysis" will be a choice. It will remain on the menu in future sessions unless it is explicitly removed.

If "Analysis ToolPak" and "Analysis ToolPak - VBA" do *not* appear on the menu, they will have to be installed on the machine using the following instructions. If your installation is on a network, this installation will probably have to be done by someone responsible for the network.

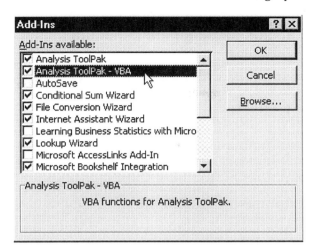

Installing the Analysis Tools

Excel can be installed as part of a number of different Office packages or by itself. It also can be installed from CD ROM or from diskettes. The instructions below specifically describe adding the Data Analysis Tools to an installation of Excel as a part of Office 97 supplied on CD ROM.

- Exit from Excel and all other Windows software.

- Place the original installation CD ROM in your computer's CD reader. Windows 95 often will start an installation program on a CD ROM automatically. Since Office or Excel has already been installed, the installation program will not start automatically; instead a window showing the files on the CD ROM will open.

Setup.exe

- Locate and double click the Office (or Excel) Setup icon (shown to the left) and double click it.

- Click the Add/Remove button on the first dialog window (the first picture on the next page).

- Highlight "Microsoft Excel" on the list in the next window (the second picture on the next page). Be sure a check mark appears to the left. Click the "Change Option" button to the right of the list.

- Highlight "Add-ins" on the list in the next window (third picture on the next page). Be sure that there is also a check to the left. Click the "Change Option" button.

- On the final list (shown on page 401) click "Analysis ToolPak" so a check appears to the left. Notice the phrase "Components to Add:" on the lower right portion of the window. Verify that this is followed by the number "1." Click the "OK" button.

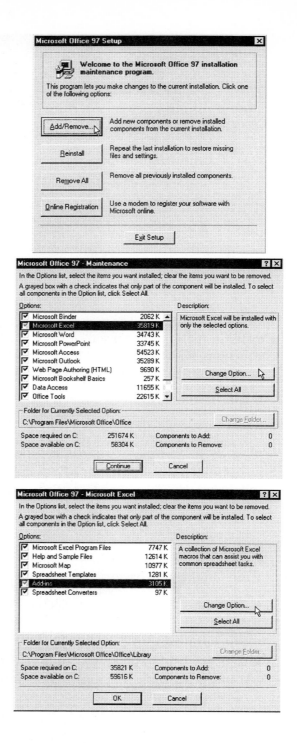

- The previous dialog window will appear again. Check that it also has "1" after "Components to Add." Click "OK" and the second dialog window will reappear. Be sure it also thinks you want to add a component and click "Continue."

This process will install the Analysis Tools on your computer's hard disk but will not add them to the menu. After Setup has completed, start Excel and follow the procedures given at the beginning of this appendix to add Analysis Tools to the Tools menu.

Appendix C

Installing the Learning Business Statistics Add-In

Several of the chapters require using tools that are provided by the *Learning Business Statistics* Excel add-in. This add-in is contained in the file named LearnBusStats.xla located on the data diskette. This appendix explains the procedure to install that add-in.

- Copy LearnBusStats.xla to your hard disk.

It can be copied to any location on your hard disk, but you should not attempt to run it from a diskette. A good place to copy it is the folder containing the add-ins that you already have on your system. If you have installed Microsoft Office, those add-ins were probably installed in:

C:\Program Files\Microsoft Office\OFFICE\LIBRARY.

If you want to find the exact location on your machine, use the Find tool (click the Start button) and search for *.xla. This will show you the locations of all the Excel add-ins on your machine. If you are using a shared networked machine in a computer lab, you may need to have a lab administrator copy the file.

- Start Excel. Open the Tools menu on the Menu Bar. Click "Add-Ins." A dialog window will open showing a menu of add-ins. This menu will not, however, include the Learning Business Statistics add-in.

- Click the "Browse..." button. In the dialog windows that follow, show Excel where you have copied the LearnBusStats.xla file. Once you have located the file, double click its name in the dialog window, or click it once to highlight it and then click the "OK" button.

The menu of add-ins will return with the Learning Business Statistics add-in included and selected. The add-in will be loaded every time you start Excel. If you want to stop it from being loaded, retrieve this menu and click on the name so that the check mark beside the add-in name is cleared.

Appendix D

Statistical Functions and Analysis Tools

This appendix provides brief information about each of the statistical functions and Analysis Tools. The goal here is to provide information that is not duplicative of that in the on-line help. In some cases, errors or possible errors have been discovered in some of the functions and tools, and these are noted. These errors may have been corrected in your versions of Excel. Examples of a few of the functions can be found in the workbook statfunc.xls.

Statistical Functions

Each of the functions in the "Statistical" category is discussed below. The argument names are the ones used in the Function Wizard. The discussion usually refers to the values of the arguments as cell or range addresses. Actual values, of course, can also be used as arguments. Note that some arguments are required; their names appear in the Function Wizard in bold type. Some arguments are optional. Some optional arguments appear in the Function Wizard dialog windows only if they might be needed. The AVERAGE function, for example, can accept multiple range addresses. Only two appear initially; if both are used, a third will appear.

AVEDEV—Calculates the Mean Absolute Deviation, sometimes used as an alternative to the standard deviation of the values in the cells within the range addresses given in the arguments "Number1," "Number2," etc. The mean of the values is calculated, the difference between each argument and the mean (the deviation) is calculated, the absolute value of each deviation is determined, and the mean of these absolute values is returned by the function. See the example in the workbook in statfunc.xls.

AVERAGE—Calculates the arithmetic mean or average of the values in the cells within the range addresses given in the arguments "Number1," "Number2," etc. AVERAGE ignores logical values, while AVERAGEA includes them, counting *false* as 0 and *true* as 1.

BETADIST—The cumulative probability distribution for the beta distribution, also called the standard beta. The range of values for the random numbers are between 0 and 1. The function returns the probability of a random variable whose distribution is the beta distribution with parameters given by the arguments "Alpha" and "Beta" having a value less than the value given by the value of the "x" argument. The beta distribution can be generalized to a variety of shapes including U-shaped, bell-shaped, symmetric, and skewed. When both "Alpha" and "Beta" are set to 1, the distribution becomes a continuous uniform distribution. This distribution is not used often in business statistics.

BETAINV—Inverse of the cumulative beta distribution. The function returns the value of the beta distribution such that the probability of a random variable whose distribution is the beta distribution with parameters given by the arguments "Alpha" and "Beta" is given by the argument "probability." To generate random values from the beta distribution, enter "rand()" (without quotes) in the "probability" argument.

BINOMDIST—Provides either the probability or the cumulative probability associated with the value of a binomial random variable given by the argument "Number_s" (number of successes). The "Trials" argument is set equal to the number of trials, and the "Probability_s" argument is set to the probability of success on each trial. The "Cumulative" argument should be set equal either to "true" or "false" (no quotation marks). "True" causes BINOMDIST to return the cumulative probability of obtaining the exact or fewer number of successes given by "number_s." "False" causes BINOMDIST to return the probability of obtaining exactly the number of successes given by "Number_s." The use of BINOMDIST and the binomial distribution is covered in Chapter 4.

CHIDIST—chi square distribution. The function returns the probability that a χ^2 random variable will have a value greater than the value given by the "X" argument. The degrees of freedom of the χ^2 distribution is given by the "Deg_freedom" argument. Examples of the use of this function are given in Chapter 11.

CHIINV—The inverse chi square distribution. The function returns the value of a χ^2 random variable such that the probability of another random value exceeding the returned value is given by the "Probability" argument. The degrees of freedom is given by the "Deg_freedom" argument. Examples of the use of this function are given in Chapter 11. To generate random numbers from the chi square distribution, use "rand()" (without quotes) for the "Probability" argument.

CHITEST—Implements the chi square test for independence which also is used to test for differences in the proportion of successes between different populations. The function determines the p value for the Null Hypothesis that all populations have the same proportions. The "actual_range" argument is the cell range address of a contingency table of values. The "expected_range" argument is the cell range address of a contingency table of expected values assuming the proportions are the same for all populations. This last contingency table must usually be calculated. See the statfunc.xls workbook for an example.

CONFIDENCE—Returns half the sampling error (half the width of the confidence interval) for a population mean. The arguments are "alpha" (one minus the confidence level), "standard_dev" (the standard deviation of the population), and "size" (the sample size). CONFIDENCE uses the normal distribution rather than the t distribution in calculating the sampling error because the standard error is assumed to be the *population* standard error. This limits the usefulness of this function to the rare case when the population standard deviation is known. If the sample standard deviation is used and the sample is large, CONFIDENCE will return a value that is approximately correct.

CORREL—Calculates the correlation coefficient (also called the Pearson product moment correlation coefficient) for two arrays of data. The range addresses of the arrays are provided in the two arguments "array1" and "array2." These arrays need to have the same number of cells and the same number of cells that display numeric values. This function is identical to the PEARSON function.

COUNT—Counts the number of cells in one or more ranges that display numeric values (including dates and text that can be converted into numbers). Cells which are blank or that display nonnumeric text or error values are not counted. Range or cell addresses are provided in the "value1" and optional "value2"... arguments.

COUNTA—Counts the number of cells in one or more ranges that are not empty, including cells that appear empty (e.g. contain blanks) but are not empty. Range or cell addresses are provided in the "value1" and optional "value2"... arguments.

COUNTBLANK—Counts the number of cells in a range that are blank or empty.

COUNTIF—Counts the number of cells in a range whose values meet a specified logical criteria. COUNTIF is used in a number of chapters beginning with chapter 3.

COVAR—Calculates the *population* covariance of two arrays of data. This can be converted to a *sample* covariance by multiplying by $\frac{n}{n-1}$. The range addresses of the two arrays are given in the "array1" and "array2" arguments, which must have the same number of cells and the same number of cells displaying numeric values.

CRITBINOM—This function is related to the cumulative binomial distribution that provides the probability of a given number of successes (or fewer) for a given number of trials and a given probability of success on each trial. CRITBINOM returns the number of successes given the cumulative binomial probability ("alpha"), the number of trials ("trials"), and the probability of success on a single trial ("probability_s"). If the value given for "alpha" is not exactly equal to a binomial cumulative probability, the smallest number of success for which the cumulative binomial probability exceeds "alpha" is returned.

DEVSQ—Calculates the sum of squared deviations from the mean for the values in one or more ranges. This is most useful as an input to other calculations. The sample standard deviation, for example, is the sum of squared deviations divided by $n - 1$. The sum of squared deviations of the y variable in a regression is also called the total sum of squares, or SST. The range addresses are provided in the "number1" and optional "number2"... arguments.

EXPONDIST—The exponential distribution. EXPONDIST determines the probability for the cumulative distribution function if "cumulative" is true or the value of the probability density function (which is *not* a probability) if "cumulative" is false. This continuous distribution is related to the discrete Poisson distribution. The Poisson distribution can be thought of as modeling the number of occurrences during a fixed time period. The exponential distribution can be thought of as modeling the period of time between occurrences. The "lambda" argument is the reciprocal of the mean time between occurrences ($\frac{1}{\mu}$). The argument "x" is the value of the time for which a cumulative probability is desired. Suppose the average time required to complete registration at a public university is 3 hours. The probability that registration could be completed in 2.5 hours or less could be determined by EXPONDIST with "x" equal to 2.5, "lambda" equal to $\frac{1}{3}$, and "cumulative" equal to "true."

FDIST—Returns the probability that a random variable drawn from the *F* distribution will have a value *greater* than the value given by the "x" argument. The *F* distribution has two degrees of freedom. The numerator degrees of freedom is given in the argument "Deg_freedom1" and the denominator degrees of freedom is given in "Deg_freedom2."

FINV—The inverse *F* distribution returns the value of a random variable drawn from the *F* distribution such that the probability of a *greater* value equals the "Probability" argument. The two degrees of freedom are given as in the FDIST function. To generate a random number from the *F* distribution, enter "rand()" (without quotes) for the "Probability" argument.

FISHER—Calculates Fisher's *z* transformation. This is very seldom encountered in business statistics. It is primarily used in hypotheses tests on the correlation coefficient between two sets of data when the Null Hypothesis is that the coefficient has a value other than 0. Suppose the correlation coefficient between two sets of data is *r* and we wish to test the Null Hypothesis that the correlation coefficient equals ρ_0. The test statistic would be: $z = \dfrac{\phi(r) - \phi(\rho_0)}{1/\sqrt{n-3}}$ where $\phi(r)$ and $\phi(\rho_0)$ are the Fisher transformation of the calculated and hypothesized correlation coefficients.

FISHERINV—Calculates the inverse of the Fisher transformation.

FORECAST—This function returns a predicted *y* value for a single *x* value whose address is given in the "X" argument. The prediction is based on a simple regression calculated on a set of *y* values whose range address is given in the "Known_y's" argument and a set of *x* values whose range address is given in the "Known_x's" argument. This function is similar to TREND except that TREND can return an array of multiple predicted *y* values.

FREQUENCY—Provides a count of the number of values in a range of cells that fall within several specified numeric ranges. The output of this function is a vertical array of values. The address of the cell range containing the values to be counted is given in the "Data_array" argument. The numeric ranges are defined by a set of "bin" values, each of which is an upper bound of a numeric range (which includes the upper bound if positive but excludes it if negative). The number of values in the output array equals the number of bins. Like all functions that output arrays in Excel, entering the function is tricky. First, select the range of cells into which the output array is to be written (as many cells as "bin" values). Click the Function Wizard button, enter the argument values, and click the "OK" button. At this point, only a single value will be displayed in the output range. Click the mouse pointer in the Formula Bar as if you were going to edit the formula. Hold down the Shift and Ctrl keys and, while holding them down, press the Enter key. Values will appear in all of the cells of the output array. An example of the use of the FREQUENCY function is given in the workbook in the file statfunc.xls.

FTEST—This tool calculates and returns the *p* value from an *F* test on the Null Hypothesis that two arrays have the same variance. The arguments of the function, "Array1" and "Array2," are the addresses of the two arrays of values whose variances are tested. The dialog window (and help) asserts that the probability returned by FTEST is one-tail. It is two-tail.

GAMMADIST—Returns a cumulative probability if "Cumulative" is equal to "true" or the value of the density (which is not a probability) if it is equal to "false." The value of the variable drawn from the gamma distribution to be evaluated is given by the "X" argument. The distribution has two parameters given by the "Alpha" and "Beta" arguments. The gamma distribution is right-skewed. Small values for alpha result in greater skew. Both the exponential and chi square distributions are special cases of the gamma distribution. The sample variance, s^2, follows the gamma distribution in which $\alpha = \dfrac{n-1}{2}$ and $\beta = \dfrac{2\sigma^2}{n-1}$. The distribution can thus be used for hypothesis tests and confidence intervals on population variances and standard deviations. It has become traditional, however, to calculate the chi square statistic and use the chi square distribution for these problems, doubtless because of the difficulty of constructing a table for the gamma distribution.

GAMMAINV—Inverse of the cumulative gamma distribution. GAMMAINV returns the value of a random variable drawn from the gamma distribution whose cumulative probability is given by the "Probability" argument. The parameters of the gamma distribution are given by the "Alpha" and "Beta" arguments. To generate a random number from the gamma distribution, enter "rand()" without quotes in the "Probability" argument field.

GAMMALN—Returns the natural logarithm of the gamma function (*not* the gamma distribution).

GEOMEAN—Returns the geometric mean, a descriptive measure of location favored in certain circumstances over the arithmetic mean when the data consist of ratios, percentages, rates of change, or rates of return.

GROWTH—Calculates predicted values for an exponential growth model. An exponential growth model has the form $\hat{y} = b_0 b_1^{x_1} \ldots b_n^{x_n}$, and is used when data are increasing at an increasing rate, such as biological population growth. The GROWTH function returns an array of any length. Simple versions of this model are sometimes used to predict growth against time; in this case there would be only a single x variable measuring time. To see the display of an output array containing more than one value, first select a region of cells for the output array. Click the Function Wizard button, select the GROWTH function, and enter the values in the argument fields. Click the "OK" button. Only a single value will be displayed in the selected region. Click the mouse pointer in the Formula Bar as if you were going to edit the formula. Press and hold both the Shift and Ctrl keys and, while holding those keys, press and release the Enter key. All of the cells in the selected region will now display values. The TREND function performs a similar role for the linear model.

HARMEAN—A measure of central tendency rarely used with business data.

HYPERGEOMDIST—Returns the hypergeometric probability of drawing the number of successes given by the argument "Sample_s" from a sample of size "Number_sample" if the sample is drawn without replacement from a population whose size is given by the argument "Number_population" in which there are "Population_s" total successes. For example, if you wanted to determine the probability of selecting three aces in five cards from a poker deck, the value of "Sample_s" would be 3, the value of "Number_sample" would be 5, the value of "Population_s" would be 4, and the value of "Number_population" would be 52. Note that the probability returned by this function is *not* cumulative, which reduces its usefulness for problems involving large ranges of number of successes.

INTERCEPT—Calculates a simple regression on a set of y and x values and returns the value of the intercept (b_0). Note that this (and more) is also available in the LINEST function, which is capable of multiple regression.

KURT—Returns the measure of kurtosis of a set of data. Kurtosis is a descriptive statistic that adds information about a set of numbers not captured by mean, variance, or skewness. Data with relatively high kurtosis tend to be more "peaked" than data with low kurtosis. The measure is infrequently used but does have application in the analysis of investment returns.

LARGE—Returns the largest ("k" equals 1), second largest ("k" equals 2), to the smallest ("k" equals n) value in a range of cells containing n numbers.

LINEST—Performs a multiple (or simple) regression analysis on a set of data and returns an array containing the estimated coefficients and (optionally) a number of statistics including r^2, standard errors, SSR, and SSE. An example of the use of this function can be found in the workbook in statfunc.xls. The output of the function is an array. To use the function, select a region of cells in which the number of columns equals the number of independent variables plus one (for the intercept), and the number of rows is 5. If only coefficients are desired, set the "stats" argument to zero and select only one row in the output range. After the region is selected, click the Function Wizard button, select LINEST, and enter the appropriate values in the argument fields. Click the "OK" button. Only one value will appear in the selected region. With the region still selected, click the mouse pointer in the Formula Bar as if you were going to edit the formula. Press and hold the Shift and Ctrl keys. While holding those keys, press and release the Enter key. All the cells in the selected region will now display values. If you have more than a single independent variable, some of the cells will display the #N/A error code. This is normal.

LOGEST—Returns estimated coefficients and statistics for an exponential growth model. The output of this function is an array identical to that produced by LINEST except that instead of estimating a linear model it estimates an exponential growth model of the form $\hat{y} = b_0 b_1^{x_1} \ldots b_n^{x_n}$. This is the same model estimated by the GROWTH function. GROWTH returns predicted values while LOGEST returns estimated coefficients and statistics. The statistics (standard errors, r^2, etc., the same as LINEST) must be interpreted with caution. The exponential growth model is estimated by using linear regression in which the dependent variable is the natural log of the y variable in the exponential growth model. This linear regression results in estimated coefficients. The b's in the exponential growth model are the antilogs (Excel's EXP function) of the linear regression's estimated coefficients. The statistics reported by LOGEST come from the linear regression. Thus we cannot, for example, calculate a t statistic on an estimated coefficient by dividing an estimated coefficient reported by LOGEST by its standard error reported by LOGEST. That standard error was calculated from the linear regression's coefficient, the log of the value reported by LOGEST.

LOGINV—The inverse of the lognormal distribution. See LOG-NORMDIST for more on this distribution. To generate a random number drawn from the lognormal distribution, enter "rand()" (without quotes) in the argument field for "Probability."

LOGNORMDIST—Returns the probability that a lognormally distributed variable will have a value less than the "X" argument. If x is a variable that is lognormally distributed, then $\ln(x)$ will be normally distributed. The error terms of exponential growth models are typically assumed to be lognormal. Lognormal variables are nonnegative and right-skewed. The extent of skew depends on the size of the variance compared to the mean. A large variance and small mean causes a greater skew. The lognormal distribution is sometimes used to model variables that are known to be skewed and nonnegative, such as family income.

MAX—Returns the largest number in one or more cell ranges. MAX ignores logical values while MAXA includes them counting *false* as 0 and *true* as 1.

MEDIAN—Returns the median value of a set of numbers in one or more cell ranges.

MIN—Returns the smallest value in one or more cell ranges.

MODE—Returns the modal (most frequently occurring) value in one or more ranges. If there is no modal value (e.g., each value occurs once), the function displays the #N/A error code.

NEGBINOMDIST—Returns the probability that a random variable from the negative binomial distribution will equal the "Number_f" argument. The probability is not cumulative. This distribution is useful for problems in which you want to know the probability of obtaining "Number_f" failures before you obtain "Number_s" successes, given that the probability of success in each trial is "Probability_s" argument.

NORMDIST—Returns the cumulative probability (or density) of a random variable drawn from the normal distribution with mean given by the "Mean" argument and standard deviation given by the "Standard_dev" argument having a value less than the "X" argument. If the "Cumulative" argument is "true," the function returns the cumulative probability. If it is "false," density—not a probability—is returned. There is little or no practical use for density values.

NORMINV—Returns the value of a normally distributed random variable for which the probability of a smaller random variable equals the value of the "Probability" argument. The values of the "Mean" and

"Standard_dev" arguments set the parameters of the normal distribution. To generate a normally distributed random variable, enter "rand()" (without quotes) in the "probability" argument field.

NORMSDIST—Returns the probability of a standard normal (mean equal to zero, standard deviation equal to one) having a value less than the "Z" argument.

NORMSINV—Returns the value of a standard normal random variable such that the probability of another standard normal random variable having a smaller value equals the "Probability" argument. To generate a standard normal random variable, enter "rand()" (no quotes) in the "probability" argument field.

PEARSON—This function is identical to the CORREL function.

PERCENTILE—Determines a given percentile value in a set of numbers whose range address is given in the "Array" argument. Two aspects of this function are unusual. The percentile value is given in the "K" argument and must be a number between 0 and 1 inclusive, rather than an integer between 1 and 99, which is more common. Excel's method for determining the percentile value differs from that most widely used in business statistics. Let p represent a percentile value expressed as an integer between 1 and 99 and assume the data have been ordered from smallest to largest. The value of the pth percentile is usually defined as the $\frac{p(n+1)}{100}$ th value. Excel instead selects the $\frac{pn+(100-p)}{100}$ th value. These two methods give the same value for the 50th percentile, but differ for all other percentiles. If the formula does not yield an integer, Excel interpolates.

PERCENTRANK—The inverse of the PERCENTILE function. When given a range address in the "Array" argument and a value in the "X" argument, PERCENTRANK returns the percentile score of that value in the array. See the discussion under PERCENTILE for the method Excel used to determine percentiles.

PERMUT—Calculates the permutations of "Number_chosen" objects drawn from "Number" objects. Permutations differ from combinations in that order matters for permutations. Excel also has a combinations function, COMBIN, with the same arguments as PERMUT, in the Math & Trig functions.

POISSON—Returns the probability or cumulative probability of drawing the value "X" from the discrete Poisson distribution in which the mean is given by the argument "Mean." If the "Cumulative" argument is "true," POISSON will return the probability of drawing a value less than or equal to "X." If "Cumulative" is "false," the probability of drawing a value exactly equal to "X" is returned.

PROB—Returns the probability of a discrete random variable equalling a specific value or falling within a given interval. The probability distribution is given in the "X_range" and "Prob_range" arguments. If the probability of a variable falling within an interval are desired, the boundaries are given in the "Lower_limit" and "Upper_limit" arguments. Those boundaries are included in the interval. If the "Upper_limit" argument is omitted, PROP returns the probability of a random variable's value being equal to the value given in the "Lower_limit" argument.

QUARTILE—Returns either the minimum, maximum, or one of the three quartile values of a set of data. The range address of the data is provided in the "Array" argument, and the value to be returned is provided by the "Quart" argument. If "Quart" is set to 0 or 4, QUARTILE returns the minimum or maximum values in the data, respectively. If "Quart" is set to 1, 2, or 3, QUARTILE returns the corresponding quartile value. As in the case of PERCENTILE, Excel uses a nonstandard definition for quartiles. Assume the data are sorted from the smallest to largest value. The first quartile is usually defined as the $\frac{n+1}{4}$th value. Excel instead uses the $\frac{n+3}{4}$th value. Similarly, the third quartile is usually defined as the $\frac{3(n+1)}{4}$th value. Excel uses the $\frac{3n+1}{4}$th value. Excel's definition of the second quartile (the median) is the same as that usually used.

RANK—Returns the position an individual number would have in a list of values if the list were ordered. The individual number's cell address or value is given in the "Number" argument and the address of the range of cells is given in the "Ref" argument. If the "Order" argument is "true," the position is given as if the list were ordered from smallest to largest. If "Order" is "false" or omitted, the position is given as if the list were ordered from largest to smallest. The #N/A error code is displayed if the number is not in the list.

RSQ—Returns the r^2 value of a simple regression of the set of values whose range address is given in the "Known_y's" argument against the set of values whose range address is given in the "Known_x's" argument. This information (along with other regression-derived information) is also provided by the LINEST function, which is also capable of multiple regression.

SKEW—Calculates and returns the coefficient of skewness of a set of numbers in one or more cell ranges.

SLOPE—Returns the slope (b_1) value from a simple regression of the set of values whose range address is given in the "Known_y's" argument against the set of values whose range address is given in the "Known_x's" argument. This information (along with other regression derived information) is also provided by the LINEST function, which is also capable of multiple regression.

SMALL—Returns the smallest ("K" equals 1), second smallest ("K" equals 2), to the largest ("K" equals n) value in a range of cells containing n numbers.

STANDARDIZE—Takes the value given by the "X" argument, subtracts the value given by the "Mean" argument, divides the difference by the value given by the "Standard_dev" argument, and returns the result.

STDEV—Returns the *sample* standard deviation (divides by $n - 1$) of the values in one or more cell ranges. STDEV ignores logical values while STDEVA includes them, counting *false* as 0 and *true* as 1.

STDEVP—Returns the *population* standard deviation (divides by N) of the values in one or more cell ranges. STDEVPA includes logical values much like STDEVA.

STEYX—Returns the standard error of the regression for a simple regression of the set of values whose range address is given in the "Known_y's" argument regressed against the set of values whose range address is given in the "Known_x's" argument. This information (along with other regression derived information) is also provided by the LINEST function, which is also capable of multiple regression.

TDIST—If the "Tails" argument is 1, returns the probability that a random variable drawn from the t distribution with degrees of freedom given by the "Deg_freedom" argument will exceed the value of the "X" argument. If the "Tails" argument is 2, the probability is doubled. An unfortunate characteristic of TDIST is that a negative value for the "X" argument results in an error code. For this reason, it is wise to embed the absolute value function, ABS, in the "X" argument field whenever the t value to be evaluated is calculated on a worksheet. The TDIST and TINV functions were discussed and used starting on page 180.

TINV—The inverse of the t distribution. TINV interprets the value of the "Probability" argument as the equally divided area of both tails.

The positive *t* value (upper tail boundary) drawn from a distribution with degrees of freedom equal to the "Deg_freedom" argument is returned. If the *t* value corresponding to a one-tail probability is desired, the "Probability" argument of TINV should be twice the one-tail probability. The TDIST and TINV functions were discussed and used starting on page 180.

TREND—Estimates a simple or multiple regression of the dependent variables whose range address is given by the "Known_y's" argument on the independent variables whose range address is given by the "Known_x's" argument. The regression is then used to provide estimated *y* values for another set of *x* values whose range addresses are given by the "New_x's" argument. The output of TREND is an array consisting of the predicted values. The number of values in this array equals the number of observations for which there are new *x* values. To see the display of an output array containing more than one value, first select a region of cells for the output array. Click the Function Wizard button, select the TREND function, and enter the values in the argument fields. Click the "OK" button. Only a single value will be displayed in the selected region. Click the mouse pointer in the Formula Bar as if you were going to edit the formula. Press and hold both the Shift and Ctrl keys and, while holding those keys, press and release the Enter key. All of the cells in the selected region will now display values. The GROWTH function performs a similar role for the exponential growth model.

TRIMMEAN—Estimates the mean of a set of data after eliminating a proportion of the extreme (highest and lowest) values set by the "Percent" argument. Despite its name, the value used in the "Percent" argument should be a proportion (between 0 and 1).

TTEST—Calculates a *t* test on the Null Hypothesis that two populations have the same mean. The range address of the sample from the first population is given in the "Array1" argument and that from the second population is given in the "Array2" argument. The "Tails" argument can have the value 1 or 2 and determines whether the test will be one-tail or two-tail. The "Type" argument determines which test will be used. If "Type" equals 1, the samples are assumed to be paired samples. If "Type" equals 2, the two samples are assumed to have been drawn from populations with equal variance. If "Type" equals 3, the two samples are assumed to have been drawn from populations with unequal variance. The function returns the *p* value from this test.

VAR—Estimates the variance of a *sample* of numbers in one or more ranges. VAR ignores logical values, while VARA counts them with 0 for *false* and 1 for *true*.

VARP—Estimates the variance of a *population* of numbers in one or more ranges. VARP ignores logical values while VARPA counts them, much as does VARA.

WEIBULL—Returns the probability of a random variable drawn from the Weibull distribution with parameters given by the "Alpha" and "Beta" arguments having a value less than that given by the "X" argument (if the "Cumulative" argument is "true"). The Weibull distribution is not often used in business statistics. It is typically used for the distribution of time intervals such as time before failure of a mechanical component.

ZTEST—The purpose of this function is not obvious. If the value of the "X" argument is interpreted as a hypothesized population mean (Null Hypothesis H_0: $\mu \leq x$), and the numbers whose range address is given in the "Array" argument are interpreted as a sample drawn from that population, the function returns the *p* value for the test. An optional argument, "Sigma" permits you to give the function the population standard deviation. Only if that argument is given would it be appropriate to use the normal distribution to calculate the *p* value, as this function does. Without the population standard deviation, the *t* distribution, not the *z* distribution, is appropriate. The on-line help description of ZTEST as a two-tail *p* value that can be used to "assess the likelihood that a particular observation is drawn from a particular population" is inaccurate.

Data Analysis Tools

The Data Analysis Tools are accessed through the Tools menu on the Menu Bar. Appendix A provides instructions for adding "Data Analysis" to the Tools menu if it is not present.

The Data Analysis Tools often duplicate procedures provided by the statistical functions. There are important differences between the tools and the functions, however. The output of a single tool generally provides more information than that of a single function. The output of most tools is formatted and labeled. The functions provide no formatting. The values written by most of the tools are numbers, not functions. An important consequence of this is that a change in the input data analyzed by a tool will not change the already written output of a tool. The tool would have to be explicitly run on the new data. The displayed value of a cell containing a function, by contrast, automatically reflects any changes in its arguments. Functions can be used directly in Excel formulas; tools cannot.

The use of most of the Analysis Tools is covered in one or more chapters of this book. The discussion below will primarily cover those tools *not* otherwise discussed in this book. The objective again is to provide useful information not available through Excel's on-line help.

Anova: Single-Factor—The use of this tool is covered in Chapter 13.

Anova:Two-Factor with Replication—The use of this tool is covered in Chapter 13.

Anova: Two-Factor Without Replication—The use of this tool is covered in Chapter 13.

Correlation—Calculates the correlation (or Pearson moment correlation coefficient) between all pairs of any number of variables. The PEARSON and CORREL functions, by contrast, do the calculation for only a single pair of variables. The output of the tool is a semirectangular array in which each variable has a column and a row. If the input data have labels, the rows and columns of the output will also be labeled. The entries give the correlation coefficient for the pair of variables in whose row and column the entry lies.

Covariance—Calculates the covariance between all pairs of any number of variables. The difference between the Covariance Tool and the COVAR function is like the difference between the Correlation Tool and the CORREL function. Like the COVAR function, the Covariance Tool provides *population* covariances rather than *sample* covariances.

Descriptive Statistics—The use of this tool is covered in Chapter 2 starting on page 65. Each of the outputs produced by this tool can be produced by a single function except the range and the "confidence." The latter is the sampling error and, if subtracted and added to the sample mean, provides a confidence interval on the population mean. If "Summary Statistics" is not selected in the dialog window, the "confidence" value is the only number the tool outputs.

Exponential Smoothing—Excel uses exponential smoothing as a form of forecasting. The formula used is $P_{t+1} = \omega A_t + (1-\omega)P_t$, where P_{t+1} is the predicted value in time $t+1$ and A_t and P_t are the actual and predicted values for time t, respectively. The predicted value for time 2 is set to the actual value for time 1. The "damping factor," ω, must be between 0 and 1. If "Standard Errors" are requested, Excel provides for each observation (beginning with number 4) the square root of the mean square error of the three previous observations. Unlike most tools, the output of this tool is formulas, not numbers. If the input values change, so will the output of the tool.

F-Test Two-Sample for Variances—The use of this tool is discussed in Chapter 12 starting on page 305. It has two problems. First, the p value and critical F it computes are one-tail when the proper test for the equality of two population variances is usually two tail. This can be corrected for the p value by simply doubling it. Note that the FTEST function returns the correct two-tail p value for the same data (although it calls it one tail). To convert the critical F in the tools output two two-tail, the value for alpha entered in the tool's dialog window should be half the desired two-tail value.

Fourier Analysis—Fourier analysis is a technique that represents a set of data as a sum of periodic (trigonometric) functions. Widely used for certain engineering problems, the technique is seldom used in business statistics, although it does have some application in sophisticated analysis of time series data.

Histogram—The use of this tool is discussed in Chapter 2 starting on page 63.

Moving Average—This is a forecasting (or smoothing) technique in which the predicted value is the average of a specified (by the "Interval" field of the dialog window) number of previous values. Excel in fact includes the current period's value in that average. Thus the values provided by Excel must be interpreted as predictions for the *next* period rather than the current period. The standard error, if requested, calculates, for each value, the square root of the mean square error of previous predictions. The number of predictions used for that calculation is the same as the number of data values used in the calculation of the moving average. Unlike most tools, the output of this tool is formulas, not numbers. The output will thus automatically change if the input data change.

Random Number Generation—This tool has been used extensively in this book to explore statistical concepts. Its use to generate discrete random numbers appears in Chapter 3 (page 89) and in Chapter 4 (page 104). It was used to generate uniform random numbers in Chapter 6 (page 175). Its use to generate normally distributed random variables appears in Chapter 7 (page 211), at many locations in Chapter 8, and in Chapter 13 (page 321). The tool will also generate random numbers from other distributions as well as nonrandom sequences ("Patterned"). It is possible to generate random numbers from any of Excel's inverse probability functions by using RAND() as the "probability" argument. This approach, however, would result in cell values that changed every time the worksheet is recalculated, which may well be undesirable. The functions can be converted to numbers by, for example, selecting their cells, clicking the Copy button, selecting "Paste Special" from the Edit menu, and selecting "Values" to be pasted. The Random Number Generation Tool avoids this problem since its output is numbers.

Rank and Percentile—One or more variables are sorted from highest to lowest, and the rank and percentile of each value are shown. Rank is the position of each value within the sorted order with the largest value assigned rank 1. Excel's method of determining the percentile of each value is based on the same nonstandard method of determining percentiles discussed in the description of the PERCENTILE function.

Regression—The use of this tool is covered in Chapters 14 and 15. Variables for this tool must be arrayed in columns (not rows). All independent variables must be in adjacent columns. The "Normal Probability Plots" option does not work correctly and should not be used.

Sampling—Draws a sample from a population. The sample can be random, in which case it is drawn with replacement, or periodic. A periodic sample simply chooses elements from the population that are a fixed number of positions (determined by "period") apart.

t-Test: Paired Two-Sample for Means—The use of this tool is covered in Chapter 12.

t-Test: Two-Sample Assuming Equal Variances—The use of this tool is covered in Chapter 12.

t-Test: Two-Sample Assuming Unequal Variances—The use of this tool is covered in Chapter 12.

z-Test: Two Sample for Means—This performs a z test on the equality of two population means when the population variances are known, but the population means are unknown. This is an unlikely situation to occur in real data, but is often discussed for pedagogic reasons by statistics texts.

Appendix E

Answers to Selected Exercises

Chapter 2

2. In ascending order of per capita GDP: Turkey, Greece, Portugal, Ireland, Spain,..., Luxembourg, Switzerland, United States

Range	Frequency	
$ 0-$ 4,000	1	
$ 4,001-$ 8,000	1	
$ 8,001-$12,000	2	
$12,001-$16,000	4	
$16,001-$20,000	13	
$20,001-$24,000	3	The data are left-skewed.

Descriptive Statistics: mean $=16,014.75$, standard deviation $=4,441.326$, etc. Left skew is indicated by fact that median (16,900) exceeds mean, and coefficient of skewness (-1.230130) is negative.

3. There is an abrupt change in the mean bolt length beginning at sample number 65 (while variance appears to remain constant). This sudden upward shift suggests an assignable cause such as equipment problems.

Chapter 3

2. As n increases, the proportion of stock providing each level of profit should become closer to the probability given in the distribution. For all portfolios, $E(x)=8.00$ and $VAR(x)=4,086$. As n increases, there should also be a tendency for the portfolio mean and variances to converge on these values although the same kind of deviation is possible here as in the table printed for Problem 1.

3. For soda, the expected value and standard deviation are 46 and 7.3485, respectively. For ice cream they are 44 and 17.1464, respectively. Since soda has a higher expected value, the vendor is likely to make more money with soda. Since it has a lower standard deviation, it is less risky. The vendor should sell soda.

Chapter 4

1. a) 0.5832, b) 0.023711, c) .00002656, d) =0.4168

2. a) 75, b) 7.9844, c) 0.0499, d) since the number of cars requiring repair must be an integer, $P(60 \leq x \leq 90) = 0.9481$

Chapter 5

1. $z = 1.2816$, $x = 75 + (1.2816)(10) = 87.8155$

2. $P(x < 16) = P(z < -2.2222) = 0.0131$

3. (25.7264, 30.2736)

4. $P(x > 55) = P(z > -1.4583) = 0.9276$

5. The use of the correction for continuity substantially improves the normal approximation for the binomial.

Chapter 6

1. $P(\bar{x} \leq 1.99) = P(t \leq -1.49071) = 0.0762$

2. (1.9852, 2.0548)

3. $P(\bar{x} \leq 50.2) = P(t \leq -2.75862) = 0.0055$

4. $P(\bar{x} \geq 2.05) = P(z \geq 1.581139) = 0.0569$

5. $z = -1.64485$, $\bar{x} = 1.9632$

Chapter 7

1. (6.893, 8.149)

2. $n=52$

3. Sample size is inversely proportional to the square of sampling error. As sampling error increases, required sample size decreases exponentially (that is, at a decreasing rate). Another way of looking at this is that as sampling error *decreases*, sample size must be increased at an *increasing* rate. It becomes very difficult to continue reducing the sampling error.

6. $48.97194 < \mu < 51.15766$, $n=48$

7. $13.07286 < \mu < 16.92714$ (or $13 < \mu < 17$), $n=38$

8. 99%-0.703417, 95%-0.51461, 90%-0.42514. $n=33$

9. $1.847568 < \mu < 2.752432$, $n=154$

10. $991.2779 < \mu < 999.3888$, $n=54$

Chapter 8

1. $P(x = 0) = 0.7318$, $P(x = 1) = 0.2286$, $P(x = 2) = 0.0357$, $P(x \geq 3) = 0.0040$

2. $\bar{x} = 15.5927255$ results in $p = .0100000$. $z = -2.575830106$. p value less than .01 would result from problems asking for sample means less than 15.5927255 or greater than 16.4072745.

3. The z value is ± 2.57583. The other critical value is 16.40728.

5. For Population II, the probability of Type II error is .00539. For Population III, the probability of Type II error is .745553.

Chapter 9

1. $H_0: \mu = 1$, $H_A: \mu \neq 1$. Reject the Null. The p value is 0.000407. Yes, there is evidence the machine is not working properly.

2. $H_0: \mu \geq 50$, $H_A: \mu < 50$. Reject the Null. The p value is 0.001116. Yes, there is evidence that average stopping distance is less than 50 feet.

3. $H_0: \mu \geq 120$, $H_A: \mu < 120$. Fail to reject the Null. $\bar{x} = 122.1778$, which is consistent with the Null Hypothesis. No, there is not evidence that the average amount of time spent by all customers in line is less than 120 seconds.

4. $H_0: \mu \geq 68$, $H_A: \mu < 68$. Reject the Null. The p value is .02657. Yes, there is evidence that the average height of all students is less than 68 inches.

5. $H_0: \mu = 6.10$, $H_A: \mu \neq 6.10$. Fail to reject the Null. The p value is 0.110354. No, there is not evidence that the average pH of all bottles differs from 6.10.

6. $H_0: \mu \leq 68$, $H_A: \mu > 68$. Fail to reject the Null. $\bar{x} = 62.9$, which is consistent with the Null Hypothesis. No, there is no evidence that the average height of all students is more than 68 inches.

7. $H_0: \mu = 68$, $H_A: \mu \neq 68$. Fail to reject the Null. The p value is .053139. No, there is no evidence that the average height of all students differs from 68 inches.

Chapter 10

1. 9604

2. $0.286333 < \pi < 0.430334$

3. $0.422863 < \pi < 0.478182$; 4,227

4. Weekday: $0.730958 < \pi < 0.815708$; Weekend: $0.780399 < \pi < 0.861219$. Although the sample proportion of shoppers who accepted free samples was higher on the weekend, there is considerable overlap in the confidence intervals. This does not provide good evidence of a difference between the proportion of the two groups of shoppers who accept free samples.

5. $0.107093 < \pi < 0.228907$; 371

6. $0.783282 < \pi < 0.883385$

7. $H_0: \pi \leq 0.20$, $H_A: \pi > 0.20$. $p_s = {}^{33}\!/_{200} = 0.165$. The sample is consistent with the Null Hypothesis; therefore the Null is not rejected. No, there is not evidence that the ad campaign was successful.

8. If $\pi = 0.4$, $n = 4{,}098$. If $\pi = 0.5$, $n = 4{,}269$. If $\pi = 0.6$, $n = 4{,}098$. If $\pi = 0.7$, $n = 3{,}586$. By using $\pi = .5$, the largest sample size is chosen. This assures that the sample will be large enough to achieve the desired sampling error regardless of the true value of π.

9. $H_0: \pi \geq .50$, $H_A: \pi < .50$. Approximate $p = .07865$. Precise $p = .089482$. No, there is not evidence that the claim is invalid.

10. $(.088287, .245047)$

11. $H_0: \pi \leq .005$, $H_A: \pi > .005$. Approximate $p = .170786$. Precise $p = 0.242155$. No, the firm should not stop the line and inspect its equipment.

12. $H_0: \pi = .29$, $H_A: \pi \neq .29$. Approximate $p = 0.029801$. Precise $p = .033265$. Yes, there is evidence that the proportion has changed from the value found 20 years ago.

13. $H_0: \pi \leq .20$, $H_A: \pi > .20$. Approximate $p = .055806$. Precise $p = .069031$. No, there is not evidence that the ad campaign was successful

Chapter 11

1. $2.067297 < \sigma < 3.683171$

2. $7.72548 < \sigma^2 < 33.22543$

3. 99%: $0.771618 < \sigma < 1.832073$, 95%: $0.836204 < \sigma < 1.605985$, 90%: $0.872968 < \sigma < 1.506848$

4. $0.189247 < \sigma^2 < 1.333141$

5. $55.2089731 < \sigma^2 < 134.684607$

6. $H_0: \sigma \leq 1.1$, $H_A: \sigma > 1.1$. p value $= 1.64 \times 10^{-7}$. Reject the Null Hypothesis. Yes, there is evidence that the machine is not meeting specification with respect to variation.

7. $H_0: \sigma^2 \leq 25$, $H_A: \sigma^2 > 25$. $s^2 = 17.5263$, consistent with the Null Hypothesis. Fail to reject the Null Hypothesis. No, there is not evidence that the machine is about to break down.

8. $H_0: \sigma \geq 12$, $H_A: \sigma < 12$. Since $s = 15.26228$, the sample is consistent with the Null Hypothesis. Fail to reject the Null Hypothesis. No, the evidence does not support the new supplier's claim.

Chapter 12

1. Using independent samples, we would not have found evidence of a difference even though the difference in the sample means was the same as in the paired sample approach. The independent sample approach would require a greater difference in the sample means before we could conclude that there was a difference in the population means. Remember that failing to conclude that there is a difference does not mean that we conclude that there is not a difference. We are left unsure. The paired sample approach is more sensitive because it can lead us to a clear conclusion with a smaller difference in sample means.

2. $H_0: \mu_A = \mu_B$, $H_A: \mu_A \neq \mu_B$. Independent samples. For these data, the procedures assuming equal and unequal population variances yield the same two-tail p value, .3283. Fail to Reject the Null Hypothesis. No, there is not evidence of a difference in average productivity.

3. $H_0: \mu_{Std} \geq \mu_{Int}$, $H_A: \mu_{Std} < \mu_{Int}$. Paired samples approach. $\bar{x}_{Std} = 6.836$ $\bar{x}_{Int} = 6.76$. The sample data are consistent with the Null Hypothesis. No, there is not evidence that intensive maintenance increases mileage.

4. $H_0: \mu_{Prgm} \leq \mu_{Ctrl}$, $H_A: \mu_{Prgm} > \mu_{Ctrl}$ Independent samples approach. $\bar{x}_{Prgm} = 576.69$ $\bar{x}_{Ctrl} = 670.20$ The sample data are consistent with the Null Hypothesis. No, there is not evidence that program attendance would increase average sales.

Chapter 13

1. Using one factor analysis, the p value is .8276. This would lead to a failure to reject the Null Hypothesis, and there was not evidence of a difference of keyboards on typing speeds. The two-factor approach is preferable because it is more sensitive and showed a difference where the one-factor approach could not.

2. The p values for each strategy are Sophisticated, .3729; Athletic, .0285; Popular, .8610. Package design is only clearly important with the Athletic strategy.

3. Use two-factor ANOVA without replication because it controls for other factors affecting house value. The p value for the Null Hypothesis that the population average of all appraisers is the same is .0285. Reject the Null. There is evidence of a difference in the average appraisals of different appraisers.

4. One-factor analysis. The p value for the Null Hypothesis that all stores have the same average is .9444. Fail to reject the Null Hypothesis. There is no evidence of a difference in the population average sales for the different types of music.

Chapter 14

2. If $x = 3.8$, $\hat{y} = 12.4286067$. If $x = 5.7$, $\hat{y} = 18.011921$. If $x = 6.3$, $\hat{y} = 19.775073$.

3. Regression with all states: $\hat{y} = -313.47 + 0.0940x$. By this equation, state revenue increases about 9.4¢ for each dollar increase in median household income. One outlier, Alaska, probably because of the effect of oil revenue. Regression with Alaska omitted: $\hat{y} = 0.1624 + 0.0409x$. This regression suggests an effect half as great: each dollar increase in median income increases state revenue about 4.1¢. Both regressions are significant.

4. Regression equation: $\hat{y} = 617.43 - 0.001793x$. Only 0.1009% of the variation in state violent crime rates is explained by variation in median household income. The relationship is not significant ($p = .82$).

5. Regression equation: $\hat{y} = 13.25 - 0.0001556x$. Higher state household incomes appear to lead to lower death rates. About 38% of the variation in death rates can be explained by variations in household income. The relationship is highly significant.

Chapter 15

1. The Null Hypothesis in this case would be $\mu_A \leq \mu_B$, and the Alternate Hypothesis would be $\mu_A > \mu_B$. With Armsley Hills as the omitted dummy variable, the p value for the Blawndale dummy is .060213144. This is, however, a *two-tail* p value. Since the test requires a *one-tail* test, the appropriate p value is half the reported value, or .0301. Since this is less than the significance level, the Null Hypothesis would be rejected. Yes, there is evidence that homes in Armsley Hills are assessed at a higher rate than homes in Blawndale.

2. With per capita GNP squared added as an independent variable, the regression equation is $\hat{y} = 89.6060 + 0.5024 \times x_{GNP} - 0.000009952 \times x_{GNP}^2$. An examination of residuals plotted against GNP still shows that for low values of per capita GNP the vertical spread is small, while for larger values (between 20,000 and 30,000) the vertical spread is large. There is thus still evidence of heteroscedasticity.

3. Since the objective here is *prediction*, the value of the adjusted R^2 is key. Since adjusted R^2 is sensitive to the number of independent variables, it is important to eliminate independent variables that do not add sufficient explanatory power. Two dummy variables are required to account for all fuel types, but the real importance lies in whether or not electricity is used as a fuel, and this can be done in a single dummy equal to "1" if electricity is used for heat and "0" otherwise (or vice versa, of course). The resulting equation is:
$$\hat{y} = 136.23 - 42.69 d_{Enrgy\ Eff} + 62.12 d_{Elec\ Heat} + 0.083 x_{House\ Size} \\ + 0.0023 x_{Fam\ Income}$$
Dummy variables are represented by d, and continuous independent variables by x. The adjusted R^2 for this is 0.5954.

4. The relationship between output and average cost is clearly nonlinear and should be handled by adding an output squared term. There is multicollinearity between the amount of silicon and the thickness of the wafer. Omitting either of these causes the coefficient on the other to become significant. Foundaries which use less silicon, or thinner wafers, have significantly lower costs. The "integrated" dummy has low significance. It's inclusion is optional. It certainly would not be wrong to drop it from the model. Several models can conclusively demonstrate that foundries in the United States have a significant cost advantage over Pacific Rim foundries. They also appear to have an advantage over South American foundries, although the significance is not as high. The following regression equation has an R^2 of almost 0.99:
$$\hat{y} = 480.48 - 9.72 x_{Output} + .0987 x_{Output}^2 + 57.62 d_{PAC} + 54.30 d_{SA} \\ + 9.25 x_{Thickness} + 3.75 d_{Integ} - 5.64 x_{Silicon}$$

Appendix F

Storing a Large File on a Diskette

In some of the chapters, including 6 and 8, the Excel workbook you create will be too large to fit on a diskette. If you are using a machine in a computer lab, you may not be able to leave files on the machine's hard disk or on a network after you finish your session with the computer. This appendix explains a method that will enable you to shrink the Excel workbook so that it can fit on a diskette and later re-expand the workbook so that you can write it temporarily to a hard disk or network disk in a later computer session.

File Compression

File compression is often used to speed the downloading of files by modem. Because of its importance, a number of programs are available to compress files. Typically these programs will not only compress files; they also have the capability of storing any number of compressed files in a single file (usually called an *archive*). This is done to allow the downloading of a group of related files in a single step. The data diskette for this book is an example of an archive file although it is *self-extracting*, which means it does not require a separate program to restore the stored and compressed files. We don't need the archiving capability, but it is a part of the compression programs we will be using.

The method we will use will involve converting a file containing a large workbook to a *Zip* file. A Zip file can contain one or more compressed files. There are a number of programs available that are capable of creating Zip files and of restoring the files in a Zip file to their original form. Included on the data diskette are two programs, zip.exe and unzip.exe, which can perform these operations. These programs are DOS programs, rather than Windows programs, but they can be freely distributed. More information about these programs can be found in the file *readzip.txt*, located on the data diskette. This appendix contains instructions for using these programs to compress and restore large datasets.

The most popular program for manipulating Zip files in Windows 95 is WinZip. WinZip cannot be freely distributed and is not included on the data diskette. You can, however, download an evaluation copy from http://www.winzip.com, and it may already be installed on your network or machine. Although it is not included, it is widely available and instructions for its use are also included.

Compressing a Workbook—First Things First

Before you can compress a workbook, two things are necessary. First, you need to know what folder the workbook file is located in. If you did not specify a folder when you first saved the workbook (using Save As... on the File menu), it probably is located in the folder "My Documents" on the C:\ drive. In order to locate the file, do the following:

- Click the "Start" button, then click "Find." Select "Files or Folders." The Find: All Files dialog window will open.

- In the "Named" field enter the file name you are looking for (such as "chap6.xls"). If you know which disk the file is on, enter it in the "Look in:" field. If you are not sure, start with C:. Click "Find Now."

All files with that name on the searched drive will be listed with the location given under the heading "In Folder." It is likely the column will not be wide enough to fully show the folder name. If so, place the mouse pointer in the header row between "In Folder" and "Size," click the (left) button and move the pointer to the right, exactly as if you were increasing the width of an Excel column. Write down the folder containing the file.

Second, the file containing the workbook must not be open—in other words, you have to get it out of Excel. Do this either by clicking "Close" on the File menu or by closing Excel completely.

Using Zip.exe to Compress a File

The instructions below will describe how to create a compressed version on a blank diskette of *chap6.xls* in the "My Documents" folder using the zip.exe program included on the data diskette.

- Click the "Start" button and select "Programs" on the menu that opens. Click the "MSDOS Prompt" icon: 📁. A DOS window will open.

- Place the data diskette (which contains the file zip.exe) in the A drive.

- Enter the following commands in the DOS window. The symbol ↵ shows where you should press the Enter key. Please note that where quotation marks are shown in the commands, they should be entered as they are shown.

c:\ ↵
cd "\My Documents" ↵
copy a:\zip.exe ↵

- After the diskette drive light goes out, remove the data diskette and insert a new diskette, preferably a blank, formatted diskette and enter

zip a:\chap6 chap6.xls ↵
del zip.exe ↵
dir a: ↵

The "a:\chap6" on the first command above gives the name of the *compressed* file that will be created on your diskette. The extenstion ".zip" will be automatically added. The "dir" command will cause the DOS window to show a list of files on the diskette. Be sure that "chap6.zip" is on that list.

- Enter the command:

exit ↵

The DOS window will close.

Using WinZip to Compress a File

- Place a diskette (preferably blank and formatted) in drive A.

- Click the WinZip icon: ▨. if it is on the desktop. If not, click "Start" then "Programs." Look for a WinZip folder and click it. The WinZip icon will be in that folder.

- If you are using the evaluation version of WinZip, a window will open explaining the conditions of use for that version. To proceed you must click the "I Agree" button. If you are using a registered version, this window will not appear

- WinZip has two interfaces "Wizard" and "Classic." You want the "Classic" interface. If the window before you has the title "Welcome to the WinZip Wizard," click the "Winzip Classic" button in the lower left corner of the window.

- Click the "New" button. A window titled "New Archive" will open allowing you to specify the location of the compressed file. Click the

downward pointing arrow to the right of the "Create In:" field and select "3½ Floppy (A:)," In the "File name:" field you are to provide the
name of the *compressed* file to be created on your diskette. Give it the
same name as the workbook to be compressed, without the ".xls." If
you are compressing chap6.xls, simply enter "chap6." Click "OK."
The "Add" dialog window will open.

- Use the "Add" dialog window to navigate to the folder containing the
file to be compressed (chap6.xls) or enter the full name preceeded by
the location in the "File name:" field (*e.g.* c:\My Docu-
ments\chap6.xls). Click the "Add" button. The main WinZip window
will show that the workbook has been added to the archive on the diskette and will show both its original and compressed sizes.

Restoring a Workbook

In the following discussion, it is assumed that you have the compressed
version of the workbook (chap6.zip) on a diskette and that you want to
restore it to a machine's hard disk in the "My Documents" folder on
drive C.

- To restore a workbook using the DOS unzip.exe program on the data
diskette, place the data diskette in drive A and open a DOS window by
clicking the "MSDOS Prompt" icon.

- Enter the following DOS commands in the window (be sure to enter
the quotation marks as shown):

c:\ ↵
cd "\my documents" ↵
copy a:\unzip.exe ↵

Remove the data diskette and replace it with the diskette containing
the compressed workbook. Enter the command unzip a:\chap6 ↵.
A copy of the original file, chap6.xls, will be written. Close the DOS
window.

- To restore a workbook using WinZip, insert the diskette containing
the compressed workbook in drive A: and start WinZip with the "Classic" interface.

- Click the "Open" button. The Open Archive dialog window will open.
Select "3½ Floppy (A:)" for the "Look In:" field. The filename
chap6.ZIP should appear in the window with a WinZip icon. Click
that name and "chap6.ZIP" will appear in the "File name:" field. Click

the "Open" button. The main WinZip window will appear and the original workbook name (chap6.xls) should appear with an Excel icon.

- Click the "Extract" button. The Extract dialog window will open. Use the "Folders/Drives" field to navigate to the location you want the restored file placed or simply enter it in the "Extract to:" field (c:\my documents). After the file has been extracted, close WinZip.

General Index